ADVANCE PRAISE FOR *COMING OF AGE THE* RITE *WAY*

"'How are the children?' the Masai ask in their daily greetings, knowing that the integrity and promise of community is not realized unless youth and their aspiration for an authentic life are embraced by the adult world. In this important and compelling book, David Blumenkrantz skillfully illuminates our current state of fragmented community, where adolescents are a tribe apart. He then brilliantly and gracefully shows us a way home to a very old idea and practice of the human village, where children and adults belong to one another, and where the question can be rightfully answered that the children are well."

—Len Fleischer, EdD, Professor of Education,
Keene State College; Licensed Clinical Psychologist

"This groundbreaking book provides profound and practical community strategies for promoting the positive development of youth. It is a must-read for educators, human service providers, and policymakers who aspire to improve community institutions that successfully raise knowledgeable, responsible, caring, contributing youth on their way to happier, more fulfilling lives."

—Roger P. Weissberg, PhD, University/LAS Distinguished
Professor of Psychology and Education, University of Illinois at Chicago;
Chief Knowledge Officer, Collaborative for Academic, Social,
and Emotional Learning (CASEL)

"David Blumenkrantz's life's work expressed in this seminal book gives us the philosophy, the foundation, and the tools we need to support our children and young people at a time when they are experiencing so much neglect. We should have inherited this road map from our ancestors, but I am so grateful that David has reinvented it and given it to us as a gift for ours and future generations."

—Mark Weiss, PhD, Education Director, Operation Respect;
former New York City schools principal

"*Coming of Age the* Rite *Way* will prove to be a significant bridge between scholarship and practice for the fields of education, social work, and youth development. Dr. Blumenkrantz weaves exquisite initiatory tales based on his 50 years of experience in community organizing and youth development. The book sets forth tested navigational aids to guide communities in the creation of unique place-based rites of passage for their young people."

—Bethe Hagens, PhD, Faculty, School of Public Policy
and Administration, Walden University

"*Coming of Age the* Rite *Way* is a thought-provoking and a healing manual that addresses some of the fundamental ills of the world today: In presenting rite of passage and community development as inseparable, the book reveals the profound wisdom that highlights how focusing in our youth is focusing in our communities. This book comes at the right time as a gift to parents and communities everywhere concerned about the future of their youth and longing for tools to fertilize their imagination. This book is a generous contribution to modern consciousness challenged by the decay of human creativity and imagination."

—Malidoma Patrice Somé, PhD, West African Elder, teacher,
and author of *Ritual: Power, Healing and Community*
and *Of Water and the Spirit: Ritual, Magic and Initiation
in the Life of an African Shaman*

"David Blumenkrantz continues to show how much we all still have to learn about rites of passage. Rite of passage 'specialists' struggle to connect a youth's community with their children's initiatory experience so they can affirm their transformation and acknowledge their emerging adulthood. Blumenkrantz solved this decades ago by developing a supportive community before attempting any rite of passage approaches. This should be required reading for anyone interested in helping youth transition to adulthood and strengthening the village to raise their children, especially within the story of rites of passage."

—Bret Stephenson, MA, author of *From Boys to Men: Spiritual Rites of Passage in an Indulgent Age* and owner, The Adolescent Mind— Archetypal Adolescent Services, Programs and Training

"David Blumenkrantz offers a compelling—and sometimes provocative—vision of rites of passage as a powerful yet neglected responsibility, resource, and focus for community and youth development. He weaves together his practical experience working in communities with stories and insights from many divergent sources to offer an integrative vision of rites of passage that transmit values, ethics, skills, and commitments from generation to generation. In the process, he shows how intentional rites of passage transform adolescence from what too often has become a time of alienation and rolenessness into a meaningful journey into both individual thriving and community strength."

—Eugene C. Roehlkepartain, PhD, Vice President, Research and Development, Search Institute, Minneapolis, Minnesota

"Blumenkrantz is an activist. His community organizing through the Rite of Passage Experience© (ROPE®) process, put into action in the 70s, has included over 200,000 American youngsters and their parents. Had Blumenkrantz been a Brit, he would without a doubt have been 'Sir David' or even 'Lord' Blumenkrantz by now. I cited his work in 2008, which helped to influence rites of passage in the UK. I wrote: 'One day it is hoped this fascinating and pioneering work will be readily available in bookshops all over the world.' That day is now. A must-read for educators and youth workers alike who want a new story and practical steps to change the future for our children, ourselves, and our planet."

—Geoffrey Ben-Nathan, author of *I'm Adult! Aren't I?: The Case for a Formal Rite of Passage*

"David Blumenkrantz has done it again. His previous book, *Fulfilling the Promise of Children's Services*, provided readers with a wide-ranging exploration of the myriad factors that either make or break prevention efforts targeting children, families, and communities. In this new book, Dr. Blumenkrantz creates another comprehensive examination of human services work, this time focusing attention on concepts and activities related to rites of passage. This is a tour de force, a book that contains encyclopedic coverage of concepts and activities related to the various ways in which societies provide their youth with pathways toward adulthood."

—Stephen M. Gavazzi, PhD, Dean, Ohio State University, Mansfield

"I've witnessed the transformation of many children into young adulthood via rites and rituals. In *Coming of Age the Rite Way*, we learn adolescent becoming, moral and otherwise, finds fuller expression in the reciprocal reconstitution and growth of communal elders responsible for receiving their youth beyond their passage. A master storyteller, Dr. Blumenkrantz weaves narrative and theory into a magnificent study and celebration of initiation and rites of passage."

—Rabbi Craig Marantz, Congregation Kol Haverim; Chaplain, Connecticut State Legislature

"In beautiful and often lyrical language, this book is a gift to all facing the challenge of preparing young people for the rewards of safe passage toward a fruitful life as adults. It is a welcome contrast to the often arcane and distancing language of social science that only other scholars might understand and embrace. All who believe in the rich potential of cherished youth will find gems here to aid them in the serious task of preparing children for bravely facing their next serious step in the life cycle. This is a must-read by anyone – especially parents, teachers, and counselors."

—Lee Ann Hoff, PhD, author of *People in Crisis: Interdisciplinary and Diversity Perspectives, 7th Edition*, and related titles on crisis and violence issues

"'Is it about *raising test scores* or *raising children?*' asks Blumenkrantz. Our coming of age stories focus on problems: school shootings, drugs and alcohol, and testing. Children hate these boring stories, and they just scare adults. You have to pay people to work with stories that bad. But, *Coming of Age the Rite Way*, is a story that grabs children. Through it they get to answer their favorite question, 'How do we grow up?' We know this story, we've just forgotten it. Weaving scholarship, practice, and his deep experience of traditional wisdom, Blumenkrantz spins nothing less than the origin story for tomorrow's communities."

—Richard Owen Geer, PhD, community practitioner, Founder, Community Performance International; co-author of *Story Bridge: From Alienation to Community Action*

"*Coming of Age the* Rite *Way* is a timely publication and its attractiveness is far-reaching. This book is strongly needed and is a welcomed addition to the literature. I applaud David Blumenkrantz for his keen attention to detail and creativity. Clearly a must-read for anyone who has the noble responsibility of providing guidance and direction to today's youth. Blumenkrantz has done a masterful job in presenting stories as well as factual data that will help synthesize our understanding of Rites of Passage and its curative value. I am pleased we now have a vivid and comprehensive body of work in one volume that will advance how to help youth move from one stage of life to the next."

—Keith A. Alford, PhD, School of Social Work, Syracuse University

"To read this book is to experience an awakening. It provides tools and understanding to take action in changing this story—through restoring and innovating the rites of passage that our youth and communities so urgently need. Drawing upon research from diverse fields of study, as well as upon the author's own life work, *Coming of Age the* Rite *Way* contributes vital new thinking to youth and community development. It also inspires us to imagine new possibilities in emergent design for co-creating the narratives and rites that are needed to change our trajectory and reorient our planet toward balance, responsibility, and well-being. A must-read for parents, teachers, and all those working for social change."

—Joanna Cea & Jess Rimington, Visiting Scholars, Stanford University Global Projects Center

"For three summers in the late 1960's and early '70s, during my early teenage years, David Blumenkrantz was my counselor at Camp Wamsutta in Charlton, Massachusetts. It is only in retrospect that I realize that through my experiences as a camper under his guidance and mentorship, I actually *lived* the Rite Of Passage Experience© ROPE® program he would later create to assist youth through the coming-of-age process. There are many who lament that there are no 'user's guides' or manuals for helping kids to navigate the turbulent waters of adolescence. Ah, but they have not read this book!"

—Kenneth F. Heideman, MS, Meteorologist, Director of Publications, American Meteorological Society; Past President, Board of Directors, Council of Science Editors

Coming of Age
the *Rite* Way

*Youth and Community Development
through Rites of Passage*

DAVID G. BLUMENKRANTZ

OXFORD
UNIVERSITY PRESS

OXFORD
UNIVERSITY PRESS

Oxford University Press is a department of the University of Oxford. It furthers
the University's objective of excellence in research, scholarship, and education
by publishing worldwide. Oxford is a registered trade mark of Oxford University
Press in the UK and certain other countries.

Published in the United States of America by Oxford University Press
198 Madison Avenue, New York, NY 10016, United States of America.

Library of Congress Cataloging-in-Publication Data
Names: Blumenkrantz, David G., 1952- author.
Title: Coming of age the RITE way : youth and community development
through rites of passage / David Blumenkrantz.
Description: New York : Oxford University Press, 2016. |
Includes bibliographical references and index.
Identifiers: LCCN 2015040578 | ISBN 9780190297336 (paperback)
Subjects: LCSH: Youth development. | Rites and ceremonies. |
BISAC: SOCIAL SCIENCE / Social Work. | PSYCHOLOGY / Social Psychology.
Classification: LCC HQ796 .B558 2016 | DDC 305.235/5—dc23
LC record available at http://lccn.loc.gov/2015040578

1 3 5 7 9 8 6 4 2
Printed by Webcom, Canada

For Louann

CONTENTS

1. Let Me Tell You A Story: Introduction 1

2. "Whaddaya Read? Whaddaya Know?": An Invitation to Share Stories 16

3. The First Story: My Creation Myth 25

4. The Trinity of Inquiry: Rites of Passage and Our Quest
   for Community 48

5. The Meaning of Community: Symbols of Initiation—Reciprocity 59

6. On Rites of Passage: Symbols of Initiation 78

7. Ritual Form: Design Elements 89

8. Which Write, Wright, Rite Is Right? Knowing Your Rites
   from Your Rights 94

9. It Is a Long Journey to a Ritual 119

10. Something Happened: Stories to Dream By 139

11. Making Something Happen: Community Institutions as Places
    of Initiation and Rites of Passage 169

12. End Notes: Reflections of a Public Artist: A Call to Inquiry
    and Action 217

Gratitude 239
References 245
Index 257

Coming of Age the *Rite* Way

1

Let Me Tell You A Story

Introduction

The sound of a story is the dominant sound of our lives.
—Reynolds Price

To be a person is to have a story to tell.
—Isak Dinesen

Mommy. Tell me about my day.

This was Michael's nightly invitation to begin his bedtime ritual. His mother, Louann, would weave an exquisite tale, recapturing in glorious detail the events of his day. Each night the events of Michael's day relived themselves through a story and made his day real. The story fueled his imagination, propelling him through the doors of wakefulness and into the world of dreams. The story made his life real. Telling it made him real. Story time was special. Listening to stories of the past cemented a bond between a boy and his mother and helped a new life unfold into the future.

Let me tell you a story.

This is the way it has been since the beginning of our history. It is the oldest invitation in the human experience (Taylor 1996). "Story is what enabled us to imagine what might happen in the future, and so prepare for it—a feat no other species can lay claim to" (Cron 2012, 1). Passed on from mouth to ear, from generation to generation, it told us where we had been and helped us set a course for our future. I am who I am because of the stories that I live and tell. You are who you are in this same way. We are the collected works of the human experience, because we have been touched by other people's stories. We are a library of life.

A Collection of Stories

In his book *Change the Story, Change the Future* (2015), David Korten writes, "When we get our story wrong, we get our future wrong" (1). If children are indeed our future, then the stories about how we educate and help them come of age are the most important stories we need to get right. When we get that story wrong our future will certainly be wrong. Our present reality is the future produced by yesterday's story of how we educated and helped our children come of age.

What are the stories we tell about raising our children? Collected through research and chronicled in the media, there is abundant evidence on whether we have gotten the "story right" about our children's education, development, and welfare. Getting the story wrong not only now but also in the past has given us the world we have today. Examples of this are environmental degradation and decline, volatile world financial markets, civil unrest, and social injustice around the world. In America, our story includes continued escalating political and social incivility with flashpoints erupting over police and civilian relations, especially those in urban communities and with the African American population. All indications lead to the fact that we have gotten the story wrong for a very long time.

Data collected on our children's development and well-being reflect their voices. But does the data really tell the whole story? Data can give us statistics that measure the incidence of child abuse, high school graduation rates, teenage pregnancy, substance abuse, mental illness, delinquency, incidence of violence, and suspensions and expulsions from schools, as discussed in recent commentary on the school-to-prison pipeline (Kim, Losen, and Hewit 2010, Mora and Christianakis 2012). But can data really let us "hear" the voices of our children? Are the mountains of statistics able to articulate the feelings of our children deprived of loving attention and craving a sense of belonging and connection to others, their community, and nature? Is the data guiding us in ways that strengthen our children's sense of self and give them hope that they will find meaning and purpose in the world and lives that are fulfilling?

The voices of children of color (Madhubuti and Madhubuti 1994, Freire 1998, Potts 2003), Native Americans (Senese 1991), and others not in the majority scream loudly about widespread disparity in opportunities, supports, education, and economic conditions, which leads to a paucity of hope about achieving "success" and having a positive future (Alford 2007). An article headlined "Rising Toll of Mental Illness" in the *Hartford Courant* reported on a substantial rise in teenage hospitalizations due to mental and behavioral health problems. "We seem to be dealing with a 'more highly stressed population,' with 'more serious suicide attempts,' among people not receiving regular mental health care" (3), said Dr. Harold Schwartz, psychiatrist-in-chief at the Institute of Living.

In the early nineties, the Search Institute (Benson 1997) began to study a set of qualities that foster desirable outcomes in youth, leading them to become caring, responsible, and productive adults. They identified forty qualities they called "developmental assets" (Scales and Leffert 1999). Among these developmental assets were perceiving that the "community values youth," living in a "caring neighborhood," and attending schools that have a "caring climate." Although the Search Institute is reluctant to aggregate and publish the data, there is a striking trend in these areas. Roughly 17 percent of youth surveyed perceive that their "community values youth." No more than 40 percent of youth perceive that they live in a "caring neighborhood" or attend schools with a "caring climate" (Ryan 1998, Goldstein 2015), 83 percent of youth surveyed believe that their community does not value them. Almost as high are the numbers of youth who perceive they do not live in a "caring neighborhood" and do not attend schools that have a "caring climate."

The reluctance of the Search Institute to focus extensively on data accumulated from their survey "Developmental Assets Profile" (Search Institute 2005) on over six hundred thousand youths' perceptions speaks to an important issue. While data may reflect the "voices of our children," they are not *their* voices. Quantitative data have become such a big part of the conversation on the meaning of particular aspects of life, like how our children are doing, that our children's actual feelings, their real yearnings and deep sense of need, are increasingly obscured in such conversation. While helpful in many cases, data-driven decision-making (DDDM) sometimes takes the whole child out of formulating programs. A Rand report (Marsh, Pane, and Hamilton 2006) points out that DDDM will not guarantee good decision-making and that a variety of different data is needed to provide a broader picture of a "whole child." The report recommended spending more time creatively imagining innovations to meet needs rather than analyzing data. Taking action is far more challenging and frequently gets lost in the justification that more analysis is needed. In sports, this is called "paralysis by analysis."

News of the Day

During the famed interview portrayed in the book and video *The Power of Myth* (1988), Bill Moyers asked the renowned mythologist Joseph Campbell what happens when there are no rites of passage. Campbell replied, "We get the *news of the day*. Youngsters not knowing how to act in a civilized manner, you have these raiding gangs, and so forth—that is *self-rendered initiation*" (82). If the news of the day comprises real-life stories of coming of age the wrong way, what can we learn? Let us take a look at actual headlines.

"Family Suing Bus Company in FAMU Hazing Death"

Robert Champion died in November 2011, after he was beaten on a bus driving the Florida A&M band to a game. A report from CNN on January 10, 2012, states:

> Some band members have said Champion died after taking part in a rite of passage called "crossing Bus C. . . . students walk from the front of the bus to the back of the bus backward while the bus is full of other band members, and you get beaten until you get to the back." But "this was not a hate crime," Attorney for the family Chris Chestnut said. "This is a hazing crime. Florida A&M University has a 50-year history, a culture in this band, of hazing."

Is a "hazing crime" a deadly form of self-rendering initiation?

"Bullying Should Not Be a Teenage Rite of Passage"

A report from the Center for American Progress (Hunt 2011) and many others claim, "Bullying in schools is viewed by many Americans as a rite of passage for all young adults, but for many gay and transgender teens it is a serious problem that increases their chance of dropping out of school, becoming homeless, using drugs, or attempting suicide."

"Bullying Is Not a Rite of Passage"

In a special report to CNN (October 14, 2011), Julie Hertzog writes, "Tragic stories of young people committing suicide after being tormented by bullies have been widely publicized. So you'd imagine that most people would know how seriously bullying hurts people. Unfortunately, this is not always true. Schools must be united in the cause and abandon the myth that bullying is a rite of passage."

Thus far responses to bullying do not address youth's basic need for initiation. Youth are yearning for a pathway to adulthood that helps them understand the values and behaviors expected from their culture and community. Schools and communities need to unite around a positive approach to create proper initiation rather than focusing on abandoning the myth that bullying is a rite of passage. Rites of passage are the ancient story, the myth, that our children need to help them transition to adulthood and to feel included in their schools and community.

> What could happen if schools and communities united in the cause to adopt the myth that youth and communities need a rite of passage experience?

"Teens and Drugs: Rite of Passage or Recipe for Addiction?"

A *Time* magazine article from June 29, 2011, leads with the line, "Teen drug use shouldn't be looked at as a rite of passage but as a public health problem, say experts, and one that has reached 'epidemic' levels." Experimentation and adolescence go hand in hand. Exploring altered states of consciousness is one of the historical hallmarks of the human species, especially following the onset of puberty (Weil & Rosen 1993).

> What if teens considered drug and alcohol use another attempt at self-rendered initiation—a rite of passage? What would a rite of passage epidemic look like that promoted positive health outcomes for teenagers and strengthened a sense of community?

"Rethinking Rites of Passage: Substance Abuse on America's Campuses"

The Commission on Substance Abuse at Colleges and Universities (Malloy 1994) reports that drinking is seen as a rite of passage on college campuses. Bullying, hazing, gangs, and drug use are also referred to as rites of passage. The commission's report states, "What was once regarded as a harmless 'rite of passage' has in the 1990s reached epidemic proportions."

What if we put our creative energies into providing a positive rite of passage experience rather than constantly trying to prevent all these health-compromising and dangerous behaviors presently labeled "rites of passage"?

"Risking Rites of Passage: When Teens Control the Transition to Adulthood"

This online article (Knott 2010) cites a mother "wondering what Trish will do if she is pressured to go through teen 'rites of passage' in order to belong." It continues:

> But lacking the formal rites of passage that in traditional cultures have marked the transition from adolescence to adulthood, teens are inventing their own rites of passage. Many of these can be risky, and sometimes even life threatening. They involve sex, drugs, alcohol and driving, sometimes in dangerous combinations. In rural communities, sometimes successful hunting—"killing your first deer"—counts as initiation, which can add guns to the mix. Gangs in larger cities have rituals that may involve fighting, breaking the law, or other transgressions against society. Even in Trish's seemingly safe small town, teens may dare each other to try "adult" behaviors to prove that they are no longer just children or immature adolescents. (Knott 2010)

Trish and all adolescents grow up within their culture and school and community climates, which convey certain values that guide behaviors and expectations of what it means to be an adult. What rites of passage activities can be "remembered and redesigned" where youth can access their cultural resources within a climate of caring to test their mettle, to prove they are no longer children or immature adolescents but moving along a clear pathway to adulthood?

"High School as a Rite of Passage for Social and Intellectual Development"

This paper by Vivienne Collinson and Lynn Hoffman (1998) addresses the "artificial" separation of intellectual achievement and social development that leads to "American high school classes continuing to be unsuccessful and boring to students." Their extensive research suggests that "a way to respond to their (students) needs and their disenchantment with academic classes would be to design academic rites of passage that capitalize on their desire to become adults."

If there is one predominant theme in the story captured in the Collinson and Hoffman's paper, it is that good students are not born but are guided to learn how to learn and demonstrate the proper attitudes and skills that support becoming a life-long learner and good student (Blumenkrantz 2009). Initiation actively addresses the needs of students to feel like they can be included in a community of scholars and be able to learn well and achieve in anything that they set their minds to learn.

A central function of initiation is to reignite in teenagers their natural curiosity and respond to their desire to seek answers to the great mysteries of life that are beginning to unfold.

What would a rite of passage look like if it focused on the Initiation of Scholars?[1]

"English Riots: A Rite of Passage for the UK Economy?"

The *Huffington Post Politics—United Kingdom* cites the retired psychiatrist, author, and past district councillor Richard Lawson in an August 18, 2011, post. He attributes the absence of initiation as one leading cause for the disenchanted and alienated youth rioting in Britain. Lawson notes that the widespread practice of initiation, through which a child enters the process of becoming an adult, is absent. Through initiation Lawson sees youth as "rewarded with a place in the community." Instead, in the absence of initiation, he sees British youth without a sense of connection or inclusion in a community forged by a rite of passage, "standing on the corner of a sink estate[2] with no home, no hope no opportunity."

"The absence of rites of passage leads to a serious breakdown in the process of maturing as a person," declares the *Encyclopedia of World Problems and Human Potential* (1986). In most societies, child development and the problems of teenagers have taken center stage as a public health issue of worldwide concern. Since child and adolescent development are among the major domains of social life, it follows that educators and health and social service providers are in pivotal positions to examine and reinvent youth development approaches that are guided by rites of passage practices so pervasive throughout human history.

Rites of Confusion

There are almost 150,000 Google search results for "drug and alcohol use as a rite of passage." This pales by comparison with searches for "bullying, hazing, suicide, and rites of passage," which result in almost one million responses. "Gang and rites of passage" produced another 1.1 million results. While the diversity of definitions and the range of stories about rites of passage dilute its real meaning and significance, a theme is emerging. In the absence of initiation into a community—be it the adult community; communities of faith, culture, nature, or school; work; sports teams; or any subset of contemporary society—health-compromising, dangerous, antisocial, "self-rendered initiations" are likely to occur. This is the news of the day. And, this is not only about youth but also about uninitiated adults. Rites of passage are

---

[1] See the Rite Of Passage Experience©, ROPE®—Initiation of Scholars at www.rope.org

[2] A sink estate is government-sponsored high-density housing characterized by high levels of economic and social deprivation. Such "estates" are not always high-crime areas, although there is a strong correlation between crime rates and sink estates in large urban areas.

intentionally designed to transmit community and cultural values while strengthening the bonds of community.

The absence of rites of passage and the growing incidence of health-compromising "self-rendered initiation" also impact a sense of community, which Robert Putnam (2000) documents in his book *Bowling Alone: The Collapse and Revival of American Community*. "For the first two-thirds of the twentieth century a powerful tide bore Americans into ever deeper engagement in the life of their community, but a few decades ago—silently, without warning—that tide reversed and we were overtaken by a treacherous rip current. Without at first noticing, we have been pulled apart from one another and from our communities over the last third of the century" (27).

Initiation of children into the adult world sets forth values and expectations for their behavior that increases social ties and civic engagement. A central purpose of initiation, as discussed in what follows, is not only to guide and assist the transformation of an individual but also to strengthen the individual's sense of responsibility to participate in the essential tasks of a community for the highest good. Putnam points out that the term "social capital," used to describe social ties that positively impact people's lives, has come in and out of favor for over a hundred years.

His historical accounts of the first use of "social capital" are enlightening and relevant to this conversation. The term was first used not by a "cloistered theoretician, but by a practical reformer of the Progressive Era—L. J. Hanifan, state supervisor of rural schools in West Virginia" (19). Hanifan wrote in 1916 about the importance of community involvement in successful schools. "Social capital," according to Hanifan, meant "tangible substances [that] count foremost in the daily lives of people: namely good will, fellowship, sympathy, and social intercourse among the individuals and families who make up a social unit" (130). Hanifan felt that the individual was quite helpless socially and unable to satisfy his or her own needs for affiliation unless and until the structure of community was in place and continually strengthened. He writes, "The community as a whole will benefit by the cooperation of all its parts, while the individual will find in his associations the advantages of the help, the sympathy, and the fellowship of his neighbors" (130).

Rites of passage might be considered our shared sacred story. Evidence of their existence has been calculated to reach back between thirty and seventy thousand years (Campbell and Moyers 1988; Cohen 1991; Vogt 2006). The story has taken on forms and meanings that would be unimaginable to van Gennep (1908) over a hundred years ago when he first coined the term and set forth its chief characteristics and three-part structure. It continues to surface more and more in our language, making news that even included this front-page headline in the *New York Times*: "War—Bush's Presidential Rite of Passage" (Apple 1989).

What if we have gotten our story wrong, as Korten suggests, and are continually getting the story about our children wrong, too? It is important not only to recognize what is wrong with the story but also to understand that only when we change the story and engage our children in the story's unfolding will we really be able to change and transform the future. Yes, it is important to understand that our present economic story has contributed to global financial instability (Korten 2015). We did not quite get the story right about our relationship with nature and our environment, either (Wildcat 2009; Henley & Peavy 2015; Carlson 1962). Also, we did not get the full story about "small is beautiful" and people and nature should matter along with sustainable development when engaged in commerce and considering economics (Schumacher 1973). Even when you do get the story right, as in the case of Galileo Galilei, who was the first to observe and put forth that the sun and not the earth was the center of our solar system, you could be ignored and, in his case, persecuted and arrested. He and many others throughout history have pointed out in almost every other area of life that we did not get the story quite right and hence the unfolding story we live out in our daily lives is bringing us closer to peril and putting our world on the precipice of a "Great Turning" (Reason and Newman 2013). Schumacher understood this, however elsewhere, people did not pay attention to the whole story.

Education: The Most Important Story to Get Right

The title of Part II in Schumacher's classic book *Small Is Beautiful: Economics as if People Mattered* (1972) says it all: "The Greatest Resource—Education." He argues that the central reason we find ourselves in our economic and environmental mess is the absence of education that transmitted values to children that enabled them to form right relationships with the natural world. They were taught about *natural resources* rather than *natural relations* and were not brought back into their essential deeply connected relationship with nature. Schumacher writes that we got our education story wrong (84).

What does Schumacher say is wrong with education? In a word, *ethics*. "Education produced hundreds of narrowly focused silos to contain and distinguish the different disciplines of science and technology. They reduce the primary focus to producing 'know-how,' without 'knowing how' to use the end result of science and technology for the highest good—to benefit of all human kind and nature" (Schumacher 1972, 86).

Schumacher calls for "a revolution in education, whose task would be, first and foremost, the transmission of ideas of value, of what to do with our lives. There is no doubt also the need to transmit know-how but this must take second place, for it is obviously somewhat foolhardy to put great powers into the hands of people without making sure that they have a reasonable idea of what to do with them" (Schumacher 1972, 86).

More than anything, youth need values and ethics in education that inform and guide how they live and that make their lives understandable and meaningful. The low priority we place on values and ethics in education has led to the "permanent crisis." Children are not able to come of age knowing how to live in ways that serve the highest good. Nor do they know how to use the power of technology and science they have learned in a way that works for everyone and is respectful of our relationship with nature and our sacred Earth.

"The problems of education are merely reflections of the deepest problems of our age. . . . Education which fails to clarify our central convictions is merely training or indulgence. For it is our central convictions that are in disorder, and, as long as the present anti-metaphysical temper persists, the disorder will grow worse. Education, far from ranking as man's greatest resource, will then be an agent of destruction, in accordance with the principle *corruptio optimi pessima*" (Schumacher 1972, 107), roughly translated: *The corruption of what is best is the worst tragedy.*

> *Real education should educate us out of self into something far finer—into selflessness which links us with all humanity.*
> —Viscountess Nancy Astor, American-born
> British politician (1879–1964)

Getting the Story Rite

Stories are powerful and dangerous and can indeed change the world. "A Christmas Carol" has been "credited (or blamed) for elevating the holiday to the stratospheric level of attention it now receives; prior to the book's publication, Christmas was treated as a relatively minor celebration on a par with Memorial Day or Veterans Day" (Kottler 2015, p. 32).

It is not only about getting the story right—*rite*—but also who the central audience should be for "The Story" and how "The Story" is told that really matters. In almost all cases where we got the story wrong (Korten 2015), we failed to get it right because we failed to recognize that any "new story" destined to truly change the future must be cowritten and told with and for our children.

Stories move people at an emotional level. People are not moved by data dumps, PowerPoint slides, or Excel spreadsheets packed with numbers (Gottschall 2012). "Once upon a time …" moves people. "Let me tell you a story…" brings people closer together, yearning to connect a piece of the story with their own lives in ways that deepen their own sense of self by extracting some assemblance of meaning for their lives.

Peter Guber, in his book *Tell to Win* (2012), reminds us of the dangerous story of the Trojan horse. The ancient Greeks after years of bloody battles that did not amount to anything, failing to win by strength, figured out how to win by outsmarting the Trojans with a clever story. They left Troy and sailed away, leaving an enormous wooden horse as an offering to the Gods. Impressed with the magnificent horse, the Trojans brought it inside their walls. As the story goes, the horse was full of Greek warriors, who emerged in the night to take over the Trojan city.

"The story is actually just a delivery system for the teller's agenda. A story is a trick for sneaking a message into the fortified citadel of the human mind" (Gottshcall 2012). When you come right down to it we have central "stories" in the form of theories that inform policies (another form of story) that result in programs, which are the manifestation of the theoretical story in action. All of these stories—theories, policies, programs—are "delivery systems for the teller's agenda." They are based on the teller's worldview. Current perceptions or worldviews in contemporary public education may not always be aligned with all students' central values or culture. We only have to reflect on Native American boarding schools during the late nineteenth and early twentieth century to know how in America's education policies the "story" was the "delivery system for the teller's [government] agenda" (Senese 1991). Recent reflections (Madhubuti & Madhubuti 1994; Freire 1998; Potts 2003) depict schools as "major socializing mechanisms that help maintain existing hierarchical relationship of power and privilege" (Bowles & Gintes 1976, Shujaa 1995). There is no such thing as a neutral educational process. Education either functions as an instrument that is used to enculturate the young into the logic of the present system, or it is the means of dealing critically and creatively with reality to discover how to participate in the transformation of the world (Freire and Macedo 1987, cited in Potts 2003, 174).

Theories are stories informed by empirical evidence. We have hundreds of stories about what helps children grow up well and different stories about how they learn. Dr. Spock was one of the pioneers in story-telling for children's development, and at one time his book *The Common Sense Book of Baby and Child Care* (1946) was the best-selling book on the planet apart from the Bible. We all crave a story. And, if it is the definitive story about how to live, lose weight, increase our strength, improve our marriage, find our inner children, or any one of the tens of thousands of self-help storybooks, then we have found "our story." We are each seeking a story that helps us understand an aspect of life and ways to integrate all the complexities of life in ways that give us meaning and make us happy. Yes, we look to stories for our happiness. Find the right story, like "better living through chemistry," and we will find happiness.

Children, especially at the time of puberty and adolescence—coming of age—seek a story that they can relate to and live into and that unfolds as their emerging adulthood.

> What are the stories our children hear and live by today? Do they compel our children to engage in critical inquiry about who they are, where they have come from, and who they will become, especially in ways that can help them live meaningful, productive lives that serve the highest good?

The French artist Paul Gauguin depicted the central theme of the story they are seeking. They are embedded in three fundamental questions, which are the title of his famous work, *D'où Venons Nous/Que Sommes Nous/Où Allons Nous?*—Where Do We come From?/What Are We?/Where Are We Going? Gauguin was a seminary student and learned these questions as part of the catechism that was taught to be lodged in the minds of the young schoolboys. It would lead them toward proper spiritual reflection on the nature of life. The three fundamental questions in the catechism were: "Where does humanity come from?" "Where is it going to?" "How does humanity proceed?" (Gayford 2006, Stuckey 2001).

Questions and Conversations Change the World

I hope this collection of stories brings to life a topic that has been important to me for over six decades and is of growing relevance to many around the world. Its purpose is to stimulate further inquiry and expand the conversation about an emerging field that I call *youth and community development through rites of passage*. Several related questions are relevant to this inquiry: How do we help our children grow up well? And, what do rites of passage have to do with this in a diverse, multicultural society? I respond to these questions with stories that have two interrelated themes: rites of passage and the psychological sense of community.

What are rites of passage? Why are they important and what is their purpose? What are the consequences of their absence? Is there a place for contemporary rites of passage in the lives of our children, their families, and communities? How can contemporary rites of passage help youth successfully cross the threshold from childhood to adult? What could they look like in contemporary western society?

> If it takes a whole village to raise a child, as the ancient proverb says, what are the consequences of not having villages anymore? Villages, where mutual interests and agreed-on values connect people and cooperative living fulfills each individual's needs and aspirations in ways that contribute to the life, vitality, and survival of their community. Villages, where people feel a deep connection to each other and share their lives and stories.

What is a psychological sense of community? And, what is the relationship between a psychological sense of community, ritual in general, and rites of passage specifically?

Can a society have a psychological sense of community without community rituals like rites of passage? And can rites of passage exist in a society without a sense of community? I have said for decades, "It takes a whole child to raise a village." What does this have to do with youth and community development through rites of passage?

The answers to these questions are addressed throughout the book and are intended to build a case for the answer to the central question: What would we be doing now if institutions that mattered in the lives of our children were considered to be places of initiation and rites of passage? This question is addressed in the last two chapters, which provide specific examples of strategies and guidelines for putting design principles into practices. These are the questions that I have struggled with, not only as an educator, youth worker, psychologist, and human service professional but also as a husband, a father, and a human being.

Whenever the rabbi of Sasov saw anyone's suffering, either of spirit or of body, he shared it so earnestly that the other's suffering became his own.

Once someone expressed his astonishment at this capacity to share in another's troubles.

"What do you mean 'share'?" said the rabbi. "It is my own sorrow; how can I help but suffer it?"

—Martin Buber, 1947

Imagine There Are No Funerals

Imagine for a moment that we have no collective understanding of the human experience of loss. In fact, we do not even have funerals. It is difficult to imagine. How would one try and convey to a reader the experience of losing a loved one? In the absence of a funeral, which is a rite of passage in the life cycle, what would we do when someone dies? We would have to make up something every time. Explaining it would be a problem not only for the writer but also for the reader. It is the same with initiation and rites of passage.

Another way for you, the reader, to come to terms with the material in this book is to reflect on a time in your life when you had direct experience with an ordeal and how inadequate language was to convey the experience. I am not here to judge the validity of anyone else's experience. I am not saying, "Here's my story. It's the truth!" I am saying, "Here is my experience—my story." What part of my story tugs at a thread in your story? Following this thread can illuminate for you the experience associated with the process of rites of passage and its importance to building community cohesion.

This book explores an emerging field of youth and community development through rites of passage and presents an organizing framework for an interdisciplinary approach to education, youth development, and community development. It offers opportunities for the fields of social work, education, youth development, and allied fields to integrate their particular areas of concentration within a unifying story of rites of passage. By examining the relationship between rites of passage and the psychological sense of community, I attempt to identify and define the central issues within each concept and illustrate their relationship. I do this not only through references in the literature but also through stories about life. I provide illustrations of the phenomenology, the actual experiences of the relationship between rites of passage and the psychological sense of community, to build a case for their integral relationship and importance to youth development, our future, and the future of the sacred earth and all our relations. I wanted to build the case for rites of passage as a unifying story among related disciplines and areas of practice. I realize this is a lofty, perhaps unrealistic goal. But, in order to accomplish it one has to not only understand it intellectually but also experience it at the level of one's heart. Stories are told and heard through the heart.

"If at first, the idea is not absurd, then there is no hope for it."
—Albert Einstein

Lay of the Land

This is not your typical academic book devoid of the author's personal story. While I am reluctant to cross this boundary between the personal and professional, the entire landscape of initiation is about thresholds and crossing boundaries. I recognize sharing personal stories lies outside of standard scholarship, but as written previously, stories and not data or statistics can convey the essence and true meaning of complex human phenomena. This is especially true with initiation, rites of passage, and a psychological sense of community. Initiation, crossing thresholds, is about taking risks, breaking out of old and traditional ways of thinking; and doing that leads to breakthroughs.

The book is organized to bring the reader back and forth between stories and more traditional scholarship citing related literature. Just as with the ritual form, which ebbs and flows within a container that at the onset may appear chaotic but serves to engage participants in deeper and deeper levels of meaning. The contents of the stories are used as case studies or narrative methodology to bring what has been found in the literature to life.

Chapters 1 and 2 offer background related to rites and *wrongs* of passage and set forth questions that will be explored throughout the book. Chapter 3 provides a narrative case study of a vision quest, which is one traditional practice during initiation and part of the larger rite of passage experience. Then we move into a brief history and theory of rites of passage and a psychological sense of community. It is designed to provide navigational aids to explore both the territory where these two constructs merge and the emergence of reciprocity.

Chapter 4 introduces the concept of reciprocity and its relevance in rites of passage, which in western society have typically focused on individual transformation. An ongoing debate in evolutionary biology recognizes the tension between the roles of the individual and the community in the survival of human beings. This chapter lays the foundation for exploring the relationship between rites of passage and the psychological sense of community. It introduces the concepts and their relationship by focusing on how an individual's initiation strengthens the bonds between citizens, thus increasing social capital and a community's capacity for adaptation, which serves survival. I describe and explain the central elements that constitute the interface of the individual and community experiences of rites of passage. I call this youth and community development through rites of passage.

Chapter 5, "The Meaning of Community: Symbols of Initiation—Reciprocity" explores the concept of reciprocity through examples contained in the vision quest narrative in chapter 3. It explores the notion of a psychological sense of community, expanding definitions of community to include nature, ancestors, and Spirit in an "initiatory constellation," which is central to adolescent identity formation. A working model for understanding and using the central elements in a psychological sense of community are introduced for guiding youth and community development through rites of passage design strategies. The chapter proposes three core questions to help frame our exploration into the intersection of rites of passage and community: What are youth being initiated into, by whom, and for what purpose? The answer to these key questions can guide the design of more viable and potent village-oriented rites of passage.

Chapter 6, "On Rites of Passage; Symbols of Initiation," returns to an analysis of the vision quest through the lens of rites of passage. It offers a rationale for, and provides examples that strengthen, the argument that individuals can not be transformed without a context and connection with their community and/or culture. If it takes a whole village to raise a child, then it could be suggested that it takes a whole community to recognize an adult. The rite of passage phase of "incorporation" is discussed in relationship to the essential need of youth to be initiated within and by their own community and culture.

Chapter 7, "Ritual Form: Design Elements," presents a generic five-part structure for ritual that includes similar elements evident across different cultures and contexts within the ritual process. These elements integrate specific design symbols and principles that can be adapted into contemporary strategies for rites of passage experiences. The five-part structure provides guideposts for our analysis of the vision quest in chapter 3 and exemplified in the ritual designed by Malidoma Patrice Somé in the following chapter.

Chapter 8, "Which Write, Wright, Rite Is Right? Knowing Your Rites from Your Rights," explores the history of ritual and its relationship to myth. It introduces eight general properties of myth and discusses these properties in relationship to theories in science. The chapter describes rites of passage as a contemporary story that has the properties of myth and provides more potent and effective design strategies to link together and improve contemporary education and youth development practices.

Chapter 9, "It's a Long Journey to a Ritual," provides another case study as an example of the general principles and structure of myth, ritual, and rites of passage. Famed educator and ritual-maker Malidoma Patrice Somé, PhD, who grew up among the Dagara in Dano, Burkina Faso, West Africa, fashioned the ritual, based on his tribe's funeral customs. It highlights the relationship between ritual, the individual, and the community. The general principles of myth described in chapter 7 are illustrated in the narrative as are the tripartite structure of rites of passage—separation, liminality, and incorporation.

Chapter 10 is called "Something Happened. Stories to Dream By" contains one of the largest collections of ethnographies that explore the intricacies of human relations among 340 different cultures from around the world. This chapter reviews the Human Relations Area File on "puberty and initiation rites" and identifies common elements in initiation rites that appear central to many diverse cultures. The common elements are synthesized and inform the formation of the twenty design principles for youth and community development through rites of passage.

It makes a compelling case that "something happens" around the time of puberty. And, what happens is essential for the individual, the family, and the community in specific ways that ensure adaptation for the survival of their culture and community.

Chapter 11, "Making Something Happen: Community Institutions as Places for Initiation and Rites of Passage," incorporates material from all the previous chapters and provides specific design strategies for helping institutions that matter in the lives of children become places of initiation and rites of passage. It integrates multiple systems and disciplines into the practice field of youth and community development through rites of passage. Strategies are framed in response to the three core questions introduced earlier: Initiation into what? By whom? And for what purpose? The chapter examines critical issues that demonstrate the essential purpose of rites of passage and how they support individual transformation and strengthen a sense of community. Issues explored include the "collision of transitions" (midlife and adolescence), the separation of children from biological parents and/or guardians, defining and engaging elders and mentors, program replication, innovation transfer, and emergent design. It reports on how the language of rites of passage is used to reframe therapy as another "ordeal" and part of an ongoing process of initiation where youth and their parents are "co-researchers" in the process of initiation. A model for large-order systems change is provided through the story of a government grant program that adopted a new paradigm of innovation transfer and illustrates emergent design in practice. The "Story" of rites of passage was used to organize and mobilize ten communities and engaged almost seven thousand people in integrated design strategies that promoted positive youth development.

Chapter 12, "End Notes—Reflections of a Public Artist: Call to Inquiry and Action," expands on what we would be doing if institutions that mattered in the lives of children were considered places of initiation and rites of passage. It brings together almost fifty years of work in community organizing, education, social work, and youth development into a new story of youth and community development through rites of passage. Community organizing, intervention, therapy, education, and youth development are linked together through the common language of rites of passage. Powered by the synergy of myth and science, values that inform and guide expectations for behavior are transmitted to the next generation. The chapter provides public policy and design recommendations that can transform and integrate the practice of education, social work, and youth development in ways that improve the conditions for raising our children and strengthening communities.

Continue Learning On Line

Additional resources for putting youth and community development through rites of passage into action along with information about the 4th edition of the Rite Of Passage Experience© ROPE® Guide for Promoting Youth & Community Maturation & Health can be accessed at www.communityritesofpassage.org.

2

"Whaddaya Read? Whaddaya Know?"

An Invitation to Share Stories

"We are lonesome animals. We spend all our life trying to be less lonesome. One of our ancient methods is to tell a story begging the listener to say – and to feel – "Yes, that's the way it is, or at least that's the way I feel it. You're not as alone as you thought."

—John Steinbeck

The greeting among the rugged Jewish fathers in the New York neighborhood where I grew up was "Whaddaya read? Whaddaya know?" This was an invitation to share stories. It was our ritual greeting—a prompt to tell a story. People who have never known each other can come together in solidarity through a shared story and focus on resolving problems and confronting common predicaments. Just think of the national story that emerged after the events of September 11, 2001: our nation endured a powerful emotional experience that ignited a shared story and fueled collective action. I am not judging the accuracy of the story nor the actions taken in response. Rather, I am saying that after we experienced an event a story emerged to help us understand what happened, and from this understanding actions were undertaken. Stories stimulate and inform actions.

Stories, myths, and legends passed down from generation to generation convey values and ethics that serve survival. Everyone has a story that informs their view of the world and guides their lives into meaningful actions. I have my story, and you have your story. An essential inquiry at this time is to explore a more unifying story that can help us understand what it means to be a human being and how we want to live together. Just as with Gauguin's three fundamental questions posed and meditated on as a catechism, we need to collectively help our children explore these questions: "Where does humanity come from?" "Where is it going to?" "How does humanity proceed?" In this way our children will come to know where they come from, who they are, and where they are going. Enacting rites of passage as a community story will enable us to cocreate our collective story.

We are at a time of dramatic change. The stories that emerge to narrate and help us understand these times are shaping our lives and guiding how we act. They inform who we are as human beings, and the news of the day tells us how we are doing living together in our shared home called Earth.

Over the course of my lifetime, and especially in my professional career, I have seen a multitude of stories about children and youth that have shaped our lives and driven national thinking about youth development that compelled actions through programs. In the 1950s the story revolved around the spread of gangs and juvenile delinquency. *West Side Story*—it even has "story" in the title!—was the common story that emerged in theatrical form at the end of the fifties. During the sixties, the Age of Aquarius, hippies and alternative lifestyles—exemplified in the Broadway musical *Hair*—witnessed the emergence of a story about the dangers of drugs and teenage pregnancy that resulted in the slogans and programs of the seventies and eighties. *Just Say No!* was the national policy for preventing teenage drug abuse but also could have served just as well to prevent teen pregnancy.

The horrific tragedies of school shootings and violence in our communities have generated their own set of stories. If we believe that violence is caused primarily by the availability of guns then this story will direct our actions to focus on gun control. If the incidence of school shooting is seen as a mental health story then we will focus on mental health services. When we see the world through a mechanistic story of cause and effect our actions will be limited and linear, leading us to focus on a single solution, like *Just Say No*. How has that been working out? In a living system—where all things are related—a single solution is inadequate.

Stories seem to emerge in ways that strike fear into the populace, justifying the need for actions that result in funding for government, education, and social services programs that marshal forces and declare war on the mayhem of the moment. Stories that generate fear foster passive consumerism and purchasing solutions, typically offered by "professionals" and "experts." After a hundred or more years of this kind of story, it is time for another way to look at the world and for a different story to emerge.

Golf in the Community

When I began to play golf I was taught from the very beginning that the last thing you want to do when faced with a hazard or obstacle that lies between you and the hole is to think, "I don't want to hit it in the water." Thinking about the water makes it more likely that you will hit the ball in the water. You are supposed to think of the flight of the ball and envision its path flying straight down the fairway to a specific target. At least that is the lesson they taught to a beginner. And it worked!

Thinking about all the problems we are trying to prevent our children from getting into is like keeping our kids from falling into the hazard. We have been focusing on each particular problem—gangs, delinquency, teen pregnancy, substance abuse, violence, and so forth—as a hazard. It has become the dominant story-making method, and thus our concern has been to prevent kids from getting into hazards. Over the years we have been focusing on all the hazards our children might fall into, yet they are still falling into them at a rate we should not be proud of. We can do better by changing the story. Rather than focusing on hazards, we should envision a path for our children that will enable them to successfully land on the fairways of their community with strong identities in balance and harmony and connected to nature. What is the story that can help us envision a flight for our children that will launch them to soar?

What Is the Story?

What do you think the story is behind the proverb "It takes a whole village to raise a child"? What was the whole village doing to raise a child?

There are two notions that you have probably heard of but may never have linked together in the way I propose. The first is that African proverb, "It takes a whole village to raise a child." The second idea is rites of passage. I propose that rites of passage were probably what a whole village was doing to raise a child and collectively raise their children. Rites of passage were their shared story.

What do we mean by "rites of passage"? For many, the concept of rites of passage may have been influenced by media headlines like those in the previous chapter. Rites of passage could be associated with mysterious, secret acts undertaken by drunken college students, gangs, secret societies, or other groups to welcome or "initiate" a member. These rites are focused on the individual and are related to their perceptions of being included or excluded from a group.

But there is another side to the story. Before rites of passage were ever construed as initiation of individuals, they were, in fact, community-organizing processes that villages engaged in for the purpose of community survival. After all, community survival is contingent on children knowing and committing themselves to the values and practices that have allowed their village to exist across multiple generations. So when we say it takes a whole village to raise a child, I invite you to consider that it means it is the essential responsibility of the village to educate the young in the community lore that will allow successful continuity into the future.

That is why we say, "It takes a whole child to raise a village":

- Collectively raising children strengthens community connections and social capital.
- Planning for our children focuses attention on future generations and the long-term consequences of our values and actions.

Raising children in ways that ensure the survival of our species for generations into the future is our most important work. We knew this eons ago and therefore did not simply leave it in the hands of individual parents and hope for the best. Instructing children through a rite of passage uses significant rituals that reinforce the shared values and beliefs of a community. This strengthens the community's resiliency and ability to adapt and renew its commitment to life-affirming values and behaviors.

At the beginning of the story lies a question: What would we be doing now if institutions that mattered in the lives of our children were considered to be places of initiation and rites of passage?

Indeed, rites of passage are the story of community survival. Rites of passage are the next best story that already was. But this is a story we as a society seem to be forgetting. For over forty-five years I have explored and put into practice this story of rites of passage as a community-organizing process that acknowledges and exploits the reciprocity between the individual and community. I have called this ecological process "youth and community development through rites of passage." This story includes guiding principles for organizing groups in ways that strengthen their commitment to collaborate in order to mutually solve problems and raise their children. It is a unifying story, built on a vision of hope rather than fear, that can emerge from the creative imagination of a community and offer a bridge between western science and traditional wisdom.

This book is about the challenges facing parents, educators, social workers, schools, communities, and human service professionals working to help children come of age within a community. It proposes practical strategies for supporting new designs that link youth and community development as if all institutions that mattered in the lives of our children were already places of initiation and rites of passage.

It does this by exploring the historical evidence in literature, oral traditions, and case studies that connect rites of passage with a psychological sense of community. Historically, rites of passage were not only a process for supporting individual transformation and transition but also an organizing framework for connecting citizens with each other, strengthening their resiliency, adaptability, and capacity to collaboratively raise their children and solve problems to ensure the survival of our species.

Historical accounts of rites of passage are reviewed in light of the literature on concepts related to a psychological sense of community. A distinguishing feature of this book is the synthesis of over five decades of practice using rites of passage to strengthen and link community organizing, interventions, therapy, health promotion, and youth development practices. Key elements that characterize the essential aspect of rites of passage have been identified and linked with key ingredients in a psychological sense of community. This synergy has resulted in a series of guiding principles that have informed practice in a wide variety of fields concerned with and working in education and the development of healthy children, their families, and their communities.

This book lays a foundation for a new field of youth and community development through rites of passage. It provides a blueprint for actions that have already been applied and validated through thousands of people in dozens of communities that integrate multiple disciplines with contemporary rites of passage into the way we educate and engage in youth development. It addresses how the needs of children and the needs of their community can be met through one of our oldest traditions, going back forty thousand years—initiation and rites of passage.

Stories from forty-five years of experience in education, youth work, public policy, and community organizing bring to life the reciprocal relationship between rites of passage and the individual, their community, and everything within their environment. It brings the reader through the author's own process of discovery from decades of study and practice with hundreds of communities and thousands of youth and adults. The story has two interconnected strands that are woven into a practical blueprint for helping to bring rites of passage into contemporary form in ways that can regenerate healthy communities, strengthening their ability to adapt and help children cross the threshold into adulthood.

The first strand is the story of initiation and rites of passage. Rites of passage are reciprocal. The individual is no more important than the community, which is no more important than the individual. Communities become stronger, more resilient, and more adaptable when they raise children who are committed to values, ethics, and attitudes that result in civility and civic engagement for the good of the greater community and their environment.

The second strand is the story of a psychological sense of community. Rituals and rites of passage have never occurred in a vacuum or separate from the context of culture, community, and one's relationships with nature, ancestors, and what some call "the great mystery." They happen with and for both the individual and community in a reciprocal relationship that serves to meet the needs of the individual and more importantly the survival of the community—human beings.

This book is for anyone concerned about the answer to the question "And, how are the children?" Policymakers in education and youth development along with those entering professional fields associated with human development, education, and community development will find the material accessible and applicable to many different settings. Over the past several decades, information on rites of passage has emerged. Curricula and programs on rites of passage are growing around the world. More and more people are using the phrase "youth and community development through rites of passage," or something similar. Practitioners in the field of rites of passage are coming to recognize the importance of the community. This book responds to the conspicuous absence of designs and practices that intentionally exploit the relationship between rites of passage as a community-organizing process and individual transitions within a setting such as community and the natural world.

Settings that currently offer programming oriented toward rites of passage are ripe to become repurposed as places where youth and adults from the same community can come together in *re-creation* and *re-treat* to learn together about initiation and youth and community development through rites of passage. They could become gathering places for "core groups" of community elders and older youth to share in common initiatory experiences and conversations that could unveil the seeds for rites of passage to be planted back in their communities.

I invite scholars and practitioners in the fields of education, youth work, rites of passage, community psychology, social work, and allied disciplines to explore the historical evidence of rites of passage and examine what is in the "field" of inquiry related to initiation and rites of passage that already exists and can be brought together, in authentic and meaningful ways, that has heart and can be of service to children, community, and our sacred Earth, and the future of all our relations. This book is an invitation to a conversation.

Not Just an Academic Exercise

Rites of passage have been with us for a long time. Evidence of pollen discovered in burial caves in northern Iraq reveals that Neanderthal communities put flowers on the graves of their dead, suggesting some kind of organized event, perhaps the forbearer of today's funeral ritual. Whether with flowers or gravestones, we have been marking periods of transition in our human existence for at least thirty thousand years (Cohen 1991). To debate whether these rituals are genetically encoded, as some would suggest, is not what is important now. What is important to consider is that rituals have always helped with individual transformation and maintaining a sense of community, which serves the survival of our species. Exploration into rites of passage cannot only be an academic exercise but also must include experiences in which the self is fully immersed.

In his address at the seventeenth annual E. F. Schumacher Lectures, John Mohawk, Seneca Indian activist and philosopher, noted that the philosophers and academicians who put forth ideas and theories "stayed within a set of boundaries they defined for themselves. They belonged to a club, as it were. Each one was required to know what was said by the preceding one, and each one was required to build on that" (Mohawk 1997, 4). Building theories facing only one direction—science—gives only one view of the world. We puff our chest at the advances we have made in our understanding of the world and universe. But what can we really be expected to know with absolute certainty about things that have happened for over 13.5 billion years, especially when they are viewed through the lens of one discipline that is usually built on reductionist, concrete, sequential logic?

> Knowledge gained through experience or plants and animals is not an inferior substitute for proper scientific knowledge: it is the real thing. Direct experience is the only way to build up an understanding that is not only intellectual but intuitive and practical, involving the senses and the heart as well as the rational mind. (Sheldrake 1991, 213)

I could have handled the material on rites of passage and sense of community simply by doing a literature review. However, this would have required me to stay "within a set of boundaries they [disciplines] defined for themselves." While I did conduct an extensive literature review, I also engaged in experiences to deepen my understanding of ritual, initiation, and rites of passage. That is the only way I felt that I could serve the information with honor and integrity. Summarizing what has already been written might have been sufficient in some circles, but it would not have done justice to the materials I reviewed, nor would it have been respectful to those who have come before us and pioneered this path.

In this inquiry, I chose to move outside of traditional boundaries, honor and face all of the directions, and invite lessons to emerge from the Great Mystery. I recognize this orientation and language may be not only foreign to some but also confusing, even offensive or irritating. It is not within the parameters of traditional scholarship, which is divorced from personal experience. I am hoping to construct a bridge between the stories embodied in the scientific literature called "theories" with the stories of human beings living together in community, with nature and their ancestors embodied in culture and handed down through oral traditions. This bridge is designed to help our shared sacred story, recently named rites of passage, to cross over into fertile territory and become more authentic and potent in service to individuals and communities for their survival and the survival of all on our sacred shared home, Earth.

The next chapter is a story. Through the use of a case study method I narrate a vision quest experience. It makes available other ways of knowing that shed light on unexplored aspects of rites of passage. One is always part of the greater whole. An individual cannot be transformed or become an adult unless the community witnesses and validates it. I owe it not only to the reader but also to myself to fully enter the initiatory experience from a number of different perspectives, honoring and facing all of the directions.

The literature cited is intended to provide a theoretical structure for rites of passage, initiation, and the psychological sense of community to place the experiences within the context of formal disciplines of inquiry. Although reluctantly, I tell the story of my experiences and link them with principles and theories set forth in the literature not as a memoir or narcissistic exercise for self-gratification but to offer concrete illustrations that can inform and guide the application of rites of passage designs and practices for people in communities and other settings.

Practice Informs Scholarship Informs Practice . . .

Storytelling is one of the most potent tools available to the scholar-practitioner. Jenlink (2003) observed that the scholar-practitioner draws "from diverse conceptual, theoretical, philosophical, and methodological tools to create a bricolage of scholarly practice, shaping one's identity and at the same time working to enable 'Others' to develop identities" (5–6). I consider myself to be more in the realm of practitioner who has sought diverse experiences to inform a more holistic view of the complex phenomenon of the human condition. I am more a seeker than a scholar who happens to have wound up in relationship with academics and places where higher education might occur. I seek to bring together seemingly unrelated material from a diverse range of available resources. "Scholar-practitioners desire to gain an intimate awareness of their practice, with the objective being to better navigate the course that lies ahead." They are the "interpreter, creator, user, evaluator, and re-creator of theory" (Bloomer and James 2003, 249). The scholar-practitioner typically has a "perpetual curiosity, a focused commitment, and a willingness to risk challenges" (Heinrich 2001, 99). The central purpose of inquiry is to understand practice within the history of both the human experience and literature. Scholar-practitioners as "seekers" are not comfortable with taking someone else's word but have to get as close to experiencing a particular phenomenon of interest themselves.

Honoring My Ancestors and Elders

Now look, David. . . .

I began writing this book in 1994. But, the seeds were planted generations ago and nurtured into form by many experiences and countless mentors. As the African proverb says, "If I stand tall, I'm standing on the shoulders of those who have gone before." Chief among my mentors over the past three decades was Professor Seymour

Sarason. It was quite by accident and after years of encouragement from Seymour and his wife Esther that I decided to write this under the cover of a doctoral program. "You might as well get a degree out of writing a book," he used to say.

Seymour was a brilliant scholar and a longtime professor at Yale University (1945–1989). He was a proponent of educational reform and one of the cofounders of the field of community psychology. Not only was he a brilliant scholar in many fields but he was also adept at formulating questions that helped to focus an inquiry on the most important details. He had a gift for simplifying complicated concepts in ways that could lead to innovative designs in practice. He was adamant that in order for people to understand rites of passage I had to start off by giving them a narrative to describe the actual experience.

He continually made a compelling argument for how to engage people in this work and how to organize this book. With every conversation he brought passion, deep thinking, and a sense of humor and usually began our conversations by saying, "Now look, David . . . ." This was always done with love and respect. He would say with great frequency, "Now look, David. No one is going to understand what the hell you are talking about unless they have either been through their own rites of passage or you hit them over the head with it." By this he meant that I should start right out by sharing a very personal experience. "A rite of passage is a moving, stirring experience," he used to say. "It's not like taking an achievement test, and unless you understand this, you cannot understand the force of it in terms of community cohesion. We are not dealing with a phenomenon that lends itself well to written descriptions. For example, you can verbally explain a person's ordeal at a concentration camp, but anyone who experienced it knows how impoverished language is—however adequate it may be in other respects—for conveying the depths of the experience." I have been very reluctant to share the story you are about to read. But anyone who knows Seymour knows that he can be quite persuasive.

I first met Seymour in 1986 while a visiting midcareer fellow at what was then called the Bush Center for Child Development and Social Policy (now named after its founder and longtime director, Edward Zigler). I was in the human services profession, deep in the trenches of direct service, administering a youth and family agency called the Youth Service Bureau located within municipal government in a suburb of Hartford, Connecticut. I was also working on a topic that reflected a lifelong passion, rite of passage experiences for both youth and community development. Seymour encouraged me to complete a Ph.D. and agreed to serve on my dissertation committee. As many of his current or former doctoral students know, this meant a betrothal to a lifelong intellectual "marriage" with him. For almost 25 years, long before *Tuesdays with Morrie*, I had weekly meetings with Seymour, who listened to my stories from the firing line of youth work and education. He was enthralled by my explorations into other ways of knowing, traditional wisdom of indigenous peoples, and my long association and study with the Huichol people. His compassion and insight during these meetings, which always included food, was the legacy he left for me and countless others.

Seymour was enthusiastic about the conceptualization of an innovative "process" of youth development tied to community development. His book *The Creation of Settings and the Future Society* (1972) explored what happens and what can go wrong when "two or more people come together in new relationships over a sustained period of time in order to achieve certain goals." The creation of setting was a central element in how well people were able to achieve certain goals. The design of community-based rites of passage, among many things, is also about the creation of settings. He strongly believed in this work and thought that rituals in general and rites of passage specifically were our first attempts at a community psychology. They impacted the future of society, our species, and Earth, our shared community. We discussed one question at length—if it really took a "whole village to raise a child," what were the implications and challenges of raising the village for the child? "What Happens to a Community Intervention When the Community Doesn't Show Up? Restoring Rites of Passage as a Consideration for Contemporary Community Intervention" (Blumenkrantz and Wasserman 1998) was one of many articles inspired by our conversations.

One result of these conversations (and the unwavering support of my brother Steven) was the formation in 1990 of the Center for the Advancement of Youth, Family, and Community Services, now called the Center for Youth & Community, Inc. to advance the practical application of these ideas. Seymour was a founding board member. The primary focus of the Center has been a youth and community development process known as the Rite Of Passage Experience©, or ROPE®, which has now served as a model for over 200,000 youths and families in the United States and different countries around the world.

Although he was a highly prolific author on a wide range of important topics, to me, Seymour's greatest legacy was his ability to frame questions in ways that stretched people's imaginations. Whenever I reflect on both new and old ideas, I always hear Seymour's admonition, "Now David, you can't begin to understand the situation you describe unless you ask yourself and others a series of questions, such as, What *might be possible* if ...?"

I was with Seymour on January 12, 2010, his ninety-first birthday. He was too ill to go out to lunch as we usually did, and I visited him at the Whitney Center. Noticing how sick he was, I summoned an ambulance that took him to the hospital. I visited him daily. On Wednesday, January 27, I could see he was very ill and fading. I kept telling stories that made him laugh. He looked at me grinning widely, with his big blue eyes, and his last word to me was, "Marvelous." Seymour died on Thursday, January 28, 2010. It is in his honor, with great humility and gratitude that I follow his guidance and begin this book with the story that he wanted me to tell.

3

The First Story

My Creation Myth

Where there is no vision, the people cast off restraint
Proverbs 29:18

As they have since the dawn of the dream of the universe, stories can present opportunities for transformation. The search for our individual story is an important part of our personal evolution, which in turn serves the evolution and survival of the planet and our community. Without the story of where we have come from, reflecting our heritage, can we really know where we are and where we are going? Rites of passage allow us to encounter ourselves, to listen for our stories, and to know who we are—perhaps for the first time.

We hear our stories through the creation of an internal dialogue. This provides a commentary on our experiences in the universe. It is an essential skill for children to know how to hear their own stories. We know who we are—gain an identity—by knowing our own stories, which unfold to become our lives. There is no better place to begin this work than to share a story. I did not know initially that it was my story until I began to hear it and live it consciously.

In the beginning was the story. And the story contained the seeds for the unconscious form of the future of the universe. Each of us carries a story that unfolds as our life, just as the world was preceded by the story of its creation and unfolding. Connecting with our own essential life stories links us to our past and future, enabling complete balance with and engagement in the bliss of the present. Awakening to what those stories are is a challenge for us all.

Exodus 33:12–23 is one of my essential life stories. It was handed down to me by my ancestors *L'dor vador*—from generation to generation—as my *parashah*, the weekly Torah portion fate assigned to me for becoming a Bar Mitzvah. In the tradition of my ancestors I was responsible to learn, chant, and provide a commentary on its lessons during my Bar Mitzvah. This was the way of my ancestors. The story tells itself over and over again in the unfolding of my life.

[12]Moses said to the Lord, "See, You say to me, 'Lead this people forward,' but You have not made known to me whom You will send with me."

[17]And the Lord said to Moses, "I will also do this thing that you have asked; for you have truly gained My favor and I have singled you out by name."

[18]He said, "Oh, let me behold Your Presence!"

[19]And He answered, "I will make all My goodness pass before you, and I will proclaim before you the name Lord, and the grace that I grant and the compassion that I show.

[20]But," He said, "you cannot see My face, for man may not see Me and live."

[21]And the Lord said, "See, there is a place near Me. Station yourself on the rock

[22]and, as My presence passes by, I will put you in a cleft of the rock and shield you with My hand until I have passed by.

[23]Then I will take My hand away and you will see My back; but My face must not be seen."

—Exodus 33:12–23

We do not go on the vision quest because we want to; we go because we have to. In the Bible it says, "Where there is no vision, the people cast off restraint" (Proverbs 29:18); without vision the people will perish. And so each year, in the tradition of Huichol Indians, we carry the trilogy of the Shaman, Spirit, and ourselves and go forth into the wilderness. We die a little so that we may live fuller and better lives. The one million acres of the Cranberry Wilderness Preserve in Hillsboro, West Virginia, is the burial ground for our past and the birthing place of our future.

> *I think we never become really and genuinely our entire and honest selves until we are dead—and not then until we have been dead years and years.*
>
> *People ought to start dead, and they would be honest so much earlier.*
>
> —Mark Twain in *Eruption*

We go out into the wilderness to seek a vision for our lives, to infuse our souls with the connection between the physical world and the Spirit, to become human again. We cast off the trappings of the material world and become one with our natural selves—inseparable from Spirit and the universe. Within each of us is buried an indigenous heart, a heart knowledgeable of and connected to the natural world.

It is just before sunrise. A mist hangs onto the morning, shrouding the village[1] in a blanket of silent gray dawn. Clothed in ceremonial attire, we take our Huichol bags up to the ceremonial fire. Nervous chatter fills the air; the drum focuses our attention, and song lifts our hearts to the fire. The circle is complete; we are connected to each other, the universe, and the Gods through the fire.

A brightly colored tapestry surrounded by flowers is set out before the Shaman's chair. We place our prayer arrows on the altar of Mother Earth to be blessed. Our prayers hold the seeds for change, seared into the arrows with the force of our intentions, as the ancestors have done for thousands of years. Now we are connected to them and the Gods through our prayers. The *Mara Akame*—Shaman—consecrates the arrows, dedicating them for their journey to the Spirit world, helping to bring forth our prayers. Now it is up to the Gods.

We begin to shed our selves, leaving our past as we pray and make an offering to *Tate Wari*—the fire. The fire remains burning in the village and connects us with the energy of Spirit, the village, and the Shaman. We connect through the fire to all the fires of our ancestors and all the fires burning around the planet. These fires link us together with the first Shaman, Grandfather Fire, Tate Wari. This is the tradition. Those who do not go on the vision quest maintain a vigil at the fire. They support the journey. We are in the village with one heart during this sacred time.

The Shaman smudges us with *kopal*, giving *Kupuri*, life force and strength. I take in its sweet familiar fragrance, which immediately coaxes comforting images and sensations, preparing me to follow in the tradition of the ancestors. A new strength fills me; I am purified and prepared to meet my destiny in the hills of West Virginia.

---

[1] I use the term "village" to connote the setting of the group. It includes the encampment of tents on a hillside, the ceremonial fire circle, and meeting areas deep within the forest.

The separation begins. I solemnly lift the Huichol bag onto my shoulder. It contains my sacred object, prayer arrow, and *tiquatsi*, my medicine bundle. Everything to become one with and survive in the Spirit world. Nothing to support the life of my physical being. I leave uncertain if I will return, ready to cast my destiny to Spirit, ready to die in order to live more fully with a good heart. I avoid making eye contact with anyone or saying good-bye, fearful that my purified spirit will be diminished. I head out to the trail leading into one million acres of remote wilderness area of the Cranberry Wilderness Preserve. Nestled in the arboreal forest of West Virginia, 4,300 feet above sea level, the forest is lush with ground vegetation. A dense canopy of trees filters the sun. Flickers of light piercing the dawn, dancing in sparkles as if from a giant mirrored ball, momentarily illuminate and magnify, bringing into focus leaves, twigs, trees, small pools of water. Everything is enveloped in a muffled dreamlike cocoon.

I walk in a daydream, trying to leave my physical form behind and head out to find my sanctuary. My heart beats in rhythm with my footsteps, squishing and scrunching my way through the mud and branches. Sunday is just being born. I travel on in the mist toward the rest of my life. A million thoughts enter my mind with uncanny stealth, like a stalker approaching their victim. I think of my wife and family, my job, the hunger and thirst I will experience, the terror and joy of being with my *self* and *Spirit*. I carry my prayer arrow on this pilgrimage for my life. Each footstep is a prayer, for my life, for the lives of my brothers and sisters who are making the journey, and for a powerful vision quest.

We walk in silence. Twenty-five Spirits journey on the trail with one heart. Along the Pocahontas trail we set out to seek our sacred place in the forest. The songs sing in my head. I try to block out all of the other thoughts that trap me in my life. I know that I must find my place with my heart not my mind. It has been waiting for me. Calling me. All I have to do is listen. The trail meanders along the ridge of a mountain. Deer tracks clearly weave their way on and across the trail. A smile crosses my face and I am comforted by the Deer Spirit, *Kauyumari*, walking with me, singing the song of mother earth in my ear.

> *Tate Yurianaka, Tate Yurianaka*
> *Camu Ne Iyari, Camu Ne Iyari*
> *Tate Yurianaka*
>
> *Mother Earth I offer you my heart,*
> *here you have my heart.*

The mist is illuminated in a golden glow of sunshine. It is still early, dawn is just awakening, shrugging off the horizon. Time begins to melt, my mind is quiet, wrapped up in the dancing rays of light—transforming the forest into a world of enchantment.

I walk for what seems like a long time. The line of Spirit trekkers thins as the adventurers move off the trail in search of their own place. Crossing pools of standing water, down through a ravine, I then head up Nob Hill trail, veering sharply up a steep incline. The weight of my bag begins to break the rhythm of my stride. My conscious mind *thinks* and examines the situation. I am between the world of dreaming and reality. Sweat begins to drip into my eyes, the burning brings me back to a physical reality. The trail is cut into the side of a steep hill. To the left, the hill rises just as sharply as it falls off to the right. The trail ahead continues to climb. My mind shifts between thoughts of reality and fantasy:

There is no path pilgrim, the path is made by walking.

I'm a pilgrim. I keep walking.

Oh, no! I'm starting to sweat, losing water, that is not good. I don't want to dehydrate knowing that I'll have no water for some time. Where is my place? Which way should I go?

I am taken aback by the familiar whine of my growing despair. I think, *What am I doing out here? Why am I doing this?* Again, the whining of my inner voice catches me by surprise. I feel embarrassed.

I struggle to shed the sniveling inner narrative. I stop, taking the bandanna from around my neck, and wipe my brow. Perspiration pours down my face and drips onto my glasses. My breath is labored as I wipe my glasses, streaking the lens with my wet bandanna. I search the hillside, holding my glasses, shaking them to dry the fogged and streaked lenses.

I hold my prayer arrow to my heart and ask Spirit for direction. Glasses in hand, I look up the steep incline to my left. Thick ferns cover the ground met by a tightly knit tangle of thorny vines falling from the dense stand of trees. I sense that I am being called.

Replacing the smeared glasses on my face, I leave the trail, and begin to cut through the heavy underbrush. The tangle of vines catches my bag, knocking off my hat and yanking me back down the hill. Within minutes I am again perspiring and panting as I carefully weave my way up the steep hill. Crouched over, ducking under and between branches and vines, I sense my way up the side of the mountain. At times I am bent forward, almost walking on all fours, my hands grasping tree roots, pulling me up higher and higher off of the trail to the top. Through the mist and fog blurred by my streaked glasses I see something glistening in the distance. It is a stand of white birch, leaves shimmering in dancing light. I keep climbing, sensing a call, drawn by a new force, feeling the *gait of power* lift me, knowing that my place lies before me. My eyes focus on the ground, and seeking firm footing I begin to move with ease. I glance upward, sensing the top of the mountain. Suddenly, appearing out of nowhere, I see it. Taking off and wiping my glasses to clear my sight, I freeze in my tracks. A solid gray mass of stone rises out of the top of the mountain before me. At first it looks like the old foundation of a cottage. With racing heart I move quickly to the top.

My hand reaches out. I touch the face of a huge slate monolith that rises up out of the ground. A grin creases my lips. I reach out and grab hold of the cool, moist, glistening rock traversing around its steep sides, exploring the area I know is *my place*. The ground slopes steeply away from the sides of the huge stack of shale. Its thin plates, layered so beautifully, seem to respond to my touch. There is a warm, soft buzzing. I walk around the perimeter of the massive mound. Yes, I am certain this is *my place*. It knows me. I feel her welcome.

Preparation

I set my bag down in a large cleavage in the center of the shale mound. The ground is hard, but flat by comparison to the surrounding terrain that falls off sharply on all sides. Small shallow shelves appear in the hollow recesses of the walls. Cleaved out space like miniature caves. I place my prayer arrow into one of the small caves. It is a perfect lodging for my offering; I stand in the middle of the monolith. Looking down the steep slope, slowly turning to survey the place, I look out in all directions. The mist has cleared and the sun is dancing between the heavy canopy of leaves, kissing the earth around me. I am filled with renewed joy and strength. The subtle buzzing emerges and then vanishes. Yes, this is a good place, the place of my vision quest.

Foraging for wood, I begin the preparation of *my place*. My old Boy Scout training taught me to get twice as much wood as you think you'll ever need. It is Sunday morning. I'll be here until Thursday morning. How much wood could I possibly need? I think about this for a long moment. Then, I figure, *What else do I have to do today except make the arrangements for my place? It'll come to me when to stop gathering wood.* I smile, knowing that I really do need to stop *thinking*. Thinking, in the sense of the same old linear, logical Western pattern of confining rationalizations that structure and limit our perception of reality. The reality I seek to enter is unavailable at that level of awareness. This is the reality that will help me survive during the long fast.

I collect dead branches, limbs, and twigs, separating them into neat piles according to their size. The warmth of the day radiates over me. I survey the growing pile, pleased at its size and order. I sit down, listening to the songs of the birds and the earth, I pray for my life. I slip into a meditation for the ritual of preparing my place.

I tie the bandanna around my neck, carefully tucking it into my white embroidered linen shirt, and adjust the beaded Huichol necklace. It is right. We adorn ourselves for the Gods, making ourselves as beautiful as Spirits so we can take our place when we dance with them in the other world. We dress and live with intentions focused on presenting ourselves to the Gods, to remember our connections to the Universe.

I begin releasing my conscious mind, inviting Spirit to guide a sacred architecture to emerge and create my place. Sitting in the center of the small-room-sized space, I send out a beam of light through my coccyx, an umbilical cord to the center of Mother Earth. A warm sensation emerges. I slowly turn my gaze to pierce the veil, merging what is known and what is still to know. Shifting my gaze to the pile of wood, I send out a beam of light from my chest and from my third eye. I take the wood in as it takes me in with my gratitude for its gift and sacrifice. The wood is grateful to be helping Grandfather Fire live. It is reciprocity of respect for each other's state of being and survival. This is repeated with everything in the circle—the place. Tate Wari will come to live in a central fire pit. My tiquatsi lies on a small colored cloth with the rattle that the Huichols call *kersie*, "voice of Spirit," and *putsie*, the clay urn in which kopal, or incense, is offered.

I am becoming connected to the place. The place is me. I stand up very slowly, sensing greater attunement, which is at first startling. Starting in the East, I make an offering to Creator, placing a rock in that direction. Calling out my prayers, offering myself, my life, for a vision to bring to the village in the service of our survival. I am compelled to offer myself and focus with great intensity on my prayers. I move slowly, with deliberate intentions that have been repeated many times before on these journeys of the heart. I honor the Spirit in each direction, making an offering and asking for protection and a good vision, setting the perimeter of my world, my cosmic spaceship to the great beyond. In each direction I call out loudly to attract the attention of the Gods. They cannot turn away. I have come to give my life for them and the earth. Beseeching them to listen, I call out in the east to the Creator and in the Southeast to the Heart, making my prayers strong, my requests for protection purposeful and clear. I awaken the Gods and the Spirits of the place to tell them that I have come to be with them in a good way and receive their teaching, should I be so blessed.

In the South I place a crystal—calling out to the eagle—imploring the Great Spirit to soar upward toward the sun for greater visions. Each prayer is forceful as if my life depended on it, which it does. To the Southwest I invite in the underworld, the unconscious—opening the possibility of access to the mysteries of the Universe. I walk slowly to the West, a critical place in the circle, as I pray to Grandmother Ocean—*Tate Haramara*—the sacred waters, which I will need to drink from in spirit time to live.

I repeat a similar ritual, altering the prayers for connection with each direction. In the Northwest is consciousness, the place we live and are at in our logical western-oriented reality. The North is the portal to the Spirit of Mother Earth—I throw down a luminous cord between my legs to Mother Earth and send out another up through my head and outstretched arms to the sun and sky. Feeling the connection, holding space in the middle ground, becoming the mediator between earth and sky. Traveling around to the Northeast, I make an offering to heaven—the superconsciousness—I am deepening a sense of peace, calm, rising above the earth—looking down at my place. It is illuminated, shining with a golden ball of luminous cords turning in on each other and glowing in the center.

I am sitting in the center of the circle in front of the fire pit where I have already crafted a neat little box of kindling wood ready to invite Tate Wari to join me in a prayer to the ninth direction—the Great Mystery, the center of the Universe. I take a match out of its container. Striking it, I make a prayer and call out for Tate Wari to join me, placing the small flame at my fingertips into the box of kindling. Grandfather leaps up with joy.

Oh, Creator—Here I am. You can't look away. I am here to pray. I am your child. Help me on my vision quest.

I have made my relations with the directions and continue to prepare my place in the tradition of the ancestors. Grandfather Fire grows with enthusiasm as I carefully nourish him with wood and my prayers. I lay open my tiquatsi, a grass basket that carries my sacred objects, *muvieris* (feather wands), and fill my putsie with kopal. Selecting two pencil-sized twigs, I take several glowing embers out of the fire and put them in my putsie, followed by some kopal. The sweet smoke quickly erupts and talks to Tate Wari. Picking up the muvieris from the tiquatsi, softly stroking the feathers and fluff at the end of the exquisitely fashioned medicine wand, I hold the breath of life. I am no longer in the form of who I thought I was but am transformed to something extraordinary. The feathers are a map to the other world that I will enter through a passageway called the *Nierika*. I lay them back into the grass basket. Setting out a candle (the light for Mother Earth), chocolate (an offering of love), and some corn, I prepare to call out to the Gods and the four directions.

Oh ancient ones, I call out. Tate Wari—Grandfather Fire, I offer you this arrow. Take my prayers. Taqutsti Nakaway—Grandmother Growth, I offer you this sacred arrow. Take my prayers. Elder Brother Deer Spirit, Kauyumari, I offer you this prayer arrow. Take my prayers, Tate Yurianaka.

I pray with all of my heart, raising my prayer arrow up to the sky. We are the connection between earth and sky. Our prayers help show our reflections to the Gods. They connect us to the earth. We pray to reconnect with the earth as our mother so we know who we are and find our place in the world. I pray for my life, a good vision to bring back to the people, and guidance for my spirit.

There, it is done. I am here opening myself to the Gods in order to remember who I am and experience the love of Mother Earth. It is said that if you can feel the love of Mother Earth for just a moment, it will last an entire lifetime. What more can I ask?

I am completely absent from time. There are no clocks—there is no time. The trees block the sun, which makes it difficult to know for certain where the directions are and what time it is with any accuracy. The need for accuracy and certainty begins to fade as I lie down, feeling for the first time extremely exhausted. I look up at the swaying trees and the dancing light of the sun lurking between the leaves and flickering across my eyes. A cool breeze carries the smell of the forest and moves me ever farther along on my journey.

"I've come here. I've done my part, now show me something," I say mockingly out loud. Spirit likes a sense of humor. I smile, trying to be in the moment in my physical—not mental—form. Thoughts intrude on my attempts to clear my mind.

We spend too much time creating the world through our mind rather than living through our hearts in the physical world. I keep cautioning myself. I try to open my heart to Spirit world and let the old world die in my efforts to be reborn into the Nierika.

Light continues to dance among the trees. I stare up into a canopy of leaves and see images of the places where the light was a moment ago. Like the flash of a camera bulb fading in the shadow of the quaking leaves. New images form, and the trace of the last one evaporates into itself. I welcome small black unfamiliar forms that shimmer into my view. I drift off.

When there is silence there is God.

I have a dream. I can clearly visualize it. I am entering a cave, a black form carved into the side of a rock that seems to appear from nowhere. The entrance is dark, guarded by two enormous insects. They have long thin bodies and wings, helmets affixed to their heads with protruding antennae and big eyes, looking straight ahead. I have been at this place before. I remember the guardians that intimidated me before, making entry to the cave impossible. I summon courage and begin to think, *They're only gnats, what could they do?* I walk directly past them into the mouth of the cave.

Suddenly I notice I am holding a torch. It no longer feels like a dream. The torch illuminates a small area around me. I walk ahead and sense that I am going down. I don't know how I know this. I am there to find the treasure that is in the cave. The trail I am on becomes narrow and is surrounded by large boulders, stalagmites, and stalactites. I have to walk more deliberately and squeeze between the small cracks on the path in front of me. One crack in particular is quite small and low, forcing me to squeeze my body into it, holding the torch ahead of me as I follow it into the passageway. I enter a large chamber and for a moment my torch gets brighter, enabling me to see further into the cave. I am immediately stunned by what I see and stand there frozen in terror.

There are large paintings on the walls of deer, elephants, bison, and other forms that I can't decipher. The chamber is a half-dome, perhaps the size of a small arena. In the center of the dome's floor I think I detect some kind of fire pit. What strikes me with fear is that the path has become a narrow walkway that traverses around the sides of the chamber, gradually making its way to the floor that falls away into the distance. I stand frozen, unable to move, my heart is pounding. Or is that a drum? I begin to inch my way forward, slowly making sure that each step is carefully placed. I can see that my light is getting fainter and fainter with each step, and vaguely make out that there is indeed a fire pit in the center. As soon as I know this, my torch goes out. The blackest darkness envelopes me, and I feel suspended on the narrow path, now clinging to the wall of the chamber, with my back to the center of the large cavern. After some time of sidestepping slowly through the blackness, inch by inch along the catwalk, I see a small flicker of light over my shoulder at the bottom of the chamber, where I first detected the fire pit. I turn to face the flicker, my back pressed against the rock face of the cavern. Ever so slowly the flicker of light grows as I get closer and closer.

I feel a rock in my back and move away from it. I am startled by my sense of rolling over and have an immediate terror as I think I am about to fall off the path into the chamber below. I sit straight up. The light is so bright I have to shield my eyes. I realize I am on the ground at my vision quest site. I look at my prayer arrow blowing in the breeze. I have a sense that I am vibrating. I lay back down on the ground, bending my knees, crossing one leg over the other, uncertain where I was or what just happened. I am tired and still in a state of transcendent calm. The buzzing seems to return, but this time a bit different, more like the quick fluttering of wing. A small green hummingbird appears in front of me and lands on my knee. I freeze, uncertain whether I am dreaming or this is real . . . I hold still, moderating my breathing, hoping to prolong this experience. There's an exchange. We're looking into each other's eyes. I'm breathing regularly. The hummingbird seems happy and is unaffected as if my knee was the perfect perch.

In the distance I can faintly hear the sound of the drum from the circle at the village. The light from the sun is now dancing through the trees on the other side of me. It must be close to sunset. I build a fire for evening ceremony. The wood crackles with the light of Grandfather, who is coming to life. Lighting the fire preoccupies my mind, as the light of day begins to fade into the dusk of darkness and night. The crack between the worlds begins to split, and I open my tiquatsi, taking out my muvieris. I light kopal, offering it to the four directions, and invite Spirit to be with me while I pray. Gazing into the fire, thinking about the chamber, the path, the fire in the center, and the guardians of the cave, I grow uncomfortable in the silence and increasing darkness. Staring into the fire, shaking my kersie, the whirring sound brings me deeper into the fire. Tiquatsi in front of me alone on the mountain with Tate Wari, surrounded by the sounds of the forest and the blanket of blackness that is the nightgown of Mother Earth, I am reminded of what Jung said: "The most terrifying thing is to know yourself."

Night passes with an anticipated restlessness that comes from leaving the comforts of a good mattress, pillow, soft blankets, and sheets and bedding down on the hard earth. Moths circle around the fire, occasionally ending their life in the flame with a hissing and crackling sound that awakens me. I doze on and off throughout the night, unconcerned that I might be tired the next day. *So what*, I think. *I don't have to do anything but Be.*

A gray mist grows out of the darkness as the first light of the rising sun washes over the treetops, gently cleansing all as it falls to the floor of the forest. I am pleased that it is morning and that the night was good to me. With the completion of my first day, I make a mark on a rock. Some who have gone on vision quest before me are said to have gotten so lost in time that they either came back earlier or later than intended. Marking the rock every twenty-four hours is my only arrangement with time.

I resume the physical work of the vision quest, the human doings that connect us with the universe and nourish our pilgrimage toward becoming human beings. Once again, as I do at midday and dusk, I bring Tate Wari into the circle. This is the job of human beings, to *do* ceremony that maintains the balance between earth and sky. To play in harmony with the world so that our songs can maintain the natural rhythm of the earth, gently singing to every creature, hoping our vibrations can help us all dance and experience joy in our lives.

Grandfather fire wakes up well to a breakfast of dry kindling. He grows and becomes beautiful, comforting me with his presence. I welcome Him to my circle, and gaze into his face. Sitting on the earth I extend an umbilical cord from my coccyx down to the center of the earth and from my heart and eyes toward the fire, making a triangle. I breathe in the light of the fire with my heart and pass it on to the circles around the world.

The light connects me to the fire, the ancestors, and all the fires burning within the flower of the human heart as well as the hearths around the world. I make this connection to move outside myself and into the Nierika, the world of the Gods. At night we die a little death, and on the way back we dream. The dream can be our ally. It is brought into the light of Grandfather Fire.

I perform the ritual, handed down through the centuries over thousands of years, as our way of approaching the day, by remembering and honoring where we have been in the darkness of night. The dream connects me to a transcendent experience moving me closer to all things. The practice represents a daily conscious acknowledgment in the existence of Spirit and the potentiality of their world. It builds a strong pathway to the Spirit world and engages me in a relationship with the fire.

We look into the fire and **see** *the Deer and the face of Grandfather Fire. The fire is lifted up and can enable all possibilities to unfold as it enters the flower of our heart.*

I finish telling my dreams to the fire, bringing the light into my heart, cleansing myself with its warmth. Slowly standing, I make an offering to the fire. There it is, I have completed the circle connecting night and day, darkness with light, the sacred and profane; all of the opposites are brought into balance. I pray for my life on this day unfolding before me, the second day of my vision quest. I am calm and quiet, at peace. I sit, staring into the fire; all is right, the world can go on. The mist begins to dance all around me in the breaking light of day.

I continue to stare into the fire. Thoughts invade my mind as if protecting it from traveling to another place. Scene after scene dances before my eyes, connected by the chatter of my inner dialogue. I think about how I have started the day here, in relationship with the Gods, compared with the typical daily awakening of many adults. It provides a real awakening, a *wake-up call,* and a jolt into the day with God on your side. I think about how many people in Western culture need a jolt into the day and consume coffee to accomplish this. *What are our morning rituals that awaken us to the day?* I think. *Do they promote an I and thou relationship or do they reduce most things to an object, an it?* I drift off in thought, seeking to see the face of Grandfather Fire, trying to quiet my inner chatter, even though my philosophical musings are very entertaining.

I must allow the voice of the Spirit to enter into me and guide my vision.

It is a challenge to quiet my inner voice, so generous with its comments and notions about everything. That friendly companion who feeds me the world on an internal platter dressed with rationalizations, denial, intellectualization, and more. All in the service of shaping and molding an experience to comfortably fit on my plate, so I may feed on the world with a minimum of indigestion. Thoughtful and caring, this inner chatter unknowingly keeps me from moving into and through an experience. Through to another dimension, the dimension of real knowledge. Again, I think . . .

I must allow the voice of the Spirit to enter into me and guide my vision.

I focus my attention on the flicker of the flame. Dark spots appear, separated by a brown patch with white spots. The dark spots appear to look at me. I begin to move toward them. For a moment I feel an incredible calm and am filled with energy. I start to think, and the moment is gone. I shake my head at my foolish ineptitude. My inner chatter continues, uncontrollably, as if protecting me from leaving it behind. It is deafening. I explore why I am exploring everything, going further and further down an intellectual experience leading to nowhere.

Traditions require you to be in the experience directly. That is one of the essential elements of an oral tradition. You are not only told the stories of creation and the world of the Gods, you are brought into them through the Nierika, to relive them again and again, obtaining true knowledge. I keep thinking about how hard it is to stop thinking and analyzing everything. Sayings and famous quotes run through my mind on some continuous tape looping around over and over again. Feeling exasperated at my failed attempts to quiet my inner chatter, I am drawn to think about Thomas Kelting's remarks on experience in "The Nature of Nature":

> We say we have "explained" something when we have found and described
> the root phenomena from which it springs. But what has been gained? Have
> we not just deferred questioning to another domain?

Another domain, I think over and over, *Another domain*. I try to recapture the dream of the cavern. Looking into the fire, I try to remember my place on the path. I clearly see the dream again, but remember it only up to the part I finished. I go over it again and again but don't get any farther along the path. I want to see what is in the center by the fire pit. What is the treasure?

I begin to see a whitish-red incandescence in the fire. The incandescence blurs with the flame and turns a whitish blue. It grows in the flame, and I focus my attention on it. The blue incandescent blur becomes a textured fabric and then the suit I wore at my Bar Mitzvah. I am in the suit standing on the Bimah with the Rabbi and Cantor. My tallis is over my shoulders and I am reading from the Torah. I am reading in Hebrew and although I don't understand the words, they are familiar to me. I listen to my high-pitched voice then recognize the passage, Exodus 33:12–23. I grimace in pain, squinting my eyes as if afraid to see anymore. I grow tired of sitting and lean back on my bag, staring intently into the fire, transfixed by the scene of my past unfolding before me.

I see my face and notice with amusement the way my hair is parted on the side and how I am carrying the pride I feel moving through this liminal experience. The fire invades my consciousness, and I am fixed in my gaze. Images appear and then disappear. As my vision resumes, brilliant white sparkles turn first into teeth, then into the smile on my young face as I greet a line of people leaving the synagogue amid their congratulations. I begin to remember more and more this period in time, long ago, which I have not thought about in ages. Gazing into the fire jogs my memory, and thoughts of my thirteenth year resonate into my consciousness.

Here before the fire I allow these thoughts to enter my mind and remember preparing for my Bar Mitzvah. Years and years of study and practice leading up to this one moment, now suspended in time, as I was then suspended in place between a Jewish child and adult. I remembered Isodor Gruttman, principal of the Hebrew school, summoning my mother and father a week before the ceremony. It was not good, I knew this instinctively. Mr. Gruttman, a short man with large glasses and thinning hair spoke with an Eastern European accent, uttering words that leaped back at me thirty years latter with all of the power they had at that moment.

With a degree of seriousness fit for the disclosure of a terminal illness to a patient, he firmly stated to my parents, "David's not ready." I saw the shock on my mother's face. Her eyes opened wide, lips parted emitting an audible gasp as she reached out toward my father. "What do you mean he's not ready? We've booked the caterer and reception hall!" She exclaimed meekly, searching for an appropriate response. My father looked at me, shaking his head. My eyes dropped to the floor.

The emotion in the ordeal of that moment rushed over me, and though it was diluted by time, I still felt a ball of anxiety well up in my stomach. I lay back onto the earth and stared up at the canopy of trees. Floating in and out of a conscious/dream state my thoughts continued to drift to the events surrounding my Bar Mitzvah.

A sparkling light enters my vision. There is a reflection in the light. It is my reflection emanating from the silver pointer, the *yad* that I hold in my hand, which glides over the Hebrew letters on the parchment page of the Torah. My voice is strong, the congregation is silent, and their eyes are on me. I am their emissary, they have entrusted me with the honor of continuing the cycle begun many millennia before. I have been an ambassador for my ancestors. The reading ends, the congregation signals in unison, "Amen." It is done. With that single word, "Amen," they have affirmed my status as their emissary, fulfilling the community's responsibility to continue the heritage of Abraham, Isaac, and Jacob. Handed from them to me through my father and mother, and through their father and mother before them. L'dor Vador—from generation to generation—the traditions are passed down, the tribe survives.

I recalled, quite vividly, two other events that I had not thought about for years, replaying them in my mind like an old movie. The first recollection was the scene from the next Sabbath service during the holiday of Simchas Torah, which immediately followed my Bar Mitzvah. The holiday marks the end and the beginning of the circular Torah reading cycle. It is a joyous time of thanksgiving for the blessings of Torah and a time to mark an important ending and beginning.

During the service they call to the Bimah, the podium on which the service is conducted, the oldest and youngest adult members of the congregation. They called out a name and a small, frail, elderly gentleman was helped up onto the Bimah and given a Torah to hold. His face brimming with pride and excitement. Then the Rabbi looked out over the congregation and with delight said, "and, now we have the youngest adult member of the congregation who just became a Bar Mitzvah last Saturday, David Blumenkrantz." I was in shock. All eyes turned toward me as I rose and ascended to the Bimah. Receiving the Torah from the Rabbi, I recall the feelings of pride and fulfillment as I stood facing the congregation, holding the Torah, linking myself with my five-thousand-year-old ancestry. Accompanied by the Rabbi and Cantor, the elder and I paraded the Torah around the synagogue as the people rejoiced. For the first time I realize that *I am someone, an adult among adults*. I was carrying the Torah, the story, traditions, and laws of the Jewish people. They had come to me. For the first time I walked among the rejoicing congregation as an adult part of the minyan of my people. I felt as though they were rejoicing for me as they came forward, touching the Torah with their prayer books and tallis. They rejoiced in my becoming a Bar Mitzvah and they rejoiced as a community, with the satisfaction that the tribe of my ancestors, Abraham, Isaac, and Jacob, and all that is sacred and special in Judaism—will survive and continue.

This fleeting image leaves my mind, and I return to an awareness of my surroundings and the comfort of the earth on my back. A soft breeze is blowing, rustling the leaves, waving at me from their lofty perch. I think about my life, and scene after scene turns in my mind's eye, as if they are pages in a book. Most of the scenes skim across my mind, while others replay themselves in more spirited detail, all the while moving deeper and deeper into the earth, transcending my physical form. I let myself go and travel on the whisper of the images that float into my mind.

Again, a scene comes to me in animated detail. I am in a living room, once again dressed in my incandescent blue Bar Mitzvah suit. I immediately know the setting. It is Mrs. Goldbaum's house, two weeks after my Bar Mitzvah. The memory pours forth in one picture with a million words, echoing its description in my mind. Mrs. Goldbaum's husband, Harold, died, and the temple called my house, asking my mother to have me sit Shiva, the Jewish period of mourning requiring a minyan of ten adult members of the congregation.

I recalled my immediate refusal. "Why do I have to go? I didn't even know him," I declared. "Because it is your responsibility as an adult member of the congregation," my mother told me. "You don't have to know someone to be included in a minyan and sit Shiva," she firmly concluded. I knew that my fate was sealed.

There I was, as uncomfortable as any thirteen-year-old would be in a suit, receiving the steady stream of mourners who entered the house. All of them saying the exact same thing—how sorry they were that Harold died and what a wonderful man he had been. Thinking that I was a close relative, some alluded to how bad I must have felt. The only thing that I felt was guilt for having no remorse except to be sitting there on such a beautiful day. Now, with the wisdom of time, my reflections revealed the experience for what it was. Again, serving in the role of adult Jewish male I joined the mourners in the liminal space of transition, helping the bereaved incorporate the new world without their loved one. I was an adult, part of the minyan fulfilling my social responsibility as a member of the Jewish community.

That scene exited my mind as abruptly as it entered, leaving me wondering about these Jewish experiences and why they were entering this vision quest. I lay on the ground looking at the shale mounds cut around me. Exploring every detail of the rock face, counting the layers of shale, miscounting, and starting over again. Losing myself in thought and dozing on and off, counting the layers of shale, never getting the same number of layers twice. The day goes slowly by, unfettered by the invasion of time, places to be, and things to do. All I have to do is *Be*.

At some point, I imagine it is noon. Time just becomes something of the imagination. I light the fire, taking in the light and warmth as if nourishing myself on the only sustenance I need. I rattle and sing, closing my eyes and focusing on the whirring sound of the rattle and resonance of my own voice merging with the Spirit voice of the rattle. Soon they both become detached from me, and I am a mind, wandering in space without a physical form. I am not conscious of my physical connection to shaking the rattle. Kersie, the voice of Spirit, is in me but does not come from me shaking the rattle, like the cool mountain breezes blowing forest fragrances through my consciousness.

I am cautiously traversing a path carefully sweeping my feet sideways, the right slowly following the line of the left. I am back in the chamber, perched high on the wall overlooking the ground and the glow in the center. I creep forward, feeling my chest heave with each breath, which moves me slightly away from the safety of the wall at my back. I keep moving, and the light from the fire gets brighter, reflecting off the walls and the vaulted ceiling from which stalactites fall. Although fearful, I am drawn forward by the fire.

I am sitting by the fire and feel its warmth. Looking into the fire I hear, "What are you going to teach me," and am startled to perceive that I have said this. Without clothing, legs crossed, I am shaking a rattle. My eyes are closed, but I can see the flicker of the fire as if through a window shade. The flicker becomes a glow and then the outline of a bronze oval face. Long gray hair flows over the sides of the image, and I struggle to make out the details. Each time I struggle harder to make out the details of the face, the image returns to the glow of the fire. I keep my eyes closed and shake the rattle, trying to clear my mind, prying it open to the fire.

See with your heart, hear through the light of the fire. The words fill me with an immediate anxiety. *Stay with it,* I think. *Don't think. Don't be afraid.* I continue to focus my physical presence on shaking the rattle and fix my gaze on the fire, hoping my mind will follow. A picture forms in my mind in the shape of a question. *What is this place?*

This is the place of the first vision quest. I do not hear this as a typical auditory experience or a voice, rather I *see* it, I *smell* it, I *feel* it crawl under my skin, sensing it within every fiber of my soul. I become it. Words lose their potency and ability to describe the story. They seem to fall dead and lack the true luster of the soul of the song that the fire sings to my heart. I am not startled by the sudden knowledge. I am taken into it through the fire. I am the fire.

At the dawn of time the Gods were pure energy, transforming into matter at will. They lost their way and forgot who they were when they came into physical form. The fire was the first Shaman. Tate Wari sent them out on a vision quest to remember who they were.

To go out and find themselves.

To know how to live with form on the earth.

A long time ago the Gods lived without form. They were ignited with Kupuri, the life force. In the transformation the energy moved their Spirit, their soul, with such force that it shifted the force of their connection with the earth and tilted their memories of how to act and who they were. The vision quest helps them to remember. It opens them to the knowledge that they once had before the great shift.

For five days and five nights Tate Wari sang the songs from the creation, and the Gods would see their reflections from their hearts and these reflections would come back as part of their shields, the covering that they wore on their front and back. The shields were the dreams of the deer told to the Shaman. And Tate Wari saw his reflection in the fire. He looked into himself, and saw the circle of stones and the way it was to be for the Gods to be in physical forms. They go out on their vision quest so that they can remember the knowledge of who they are and how they are to live on the earth.

Just as the Gods had to find their way to live in physical form so does all of creation: the plants and animals; the winged and the creepy crawlers. But they are connected more and are not as apt to lose their way or forget who they are. A tree does not forget it is a tree because it is too busy being a tree. It does not have to do anything to be a tree. It just is. It is the same for the fish and fowl, plants and rocks. They are all in the loving act of being who they are.

It is not the same with human beings. They are busy doing in their humanness, which keeps them from being. It is easy for them to forget, just as it was for the Gods, who too were filled with Kupuri and had the capacity for transcendence. But with that power for transcendence comes the potential to move away from the essence of your being. To be lost in your own doings. As with the Gods, the vision quest connects you to the knowledge of the creation of your first being. It gives you a chance to be reborn into your true self. The self that knows its place on the earth.

Here you sit on the earth, in the cleft of the rock. Feel the love of your mother. See with your heart. You have brought so much to so many. There are many more who will walk with you. They are both your guides and mentors, just as you are their guide and mentor. You have received the song before, many times, but you did not hear it. Let yourself learn from your place in the cleft of the rock. The cleft of the rock . . .

I am drifting in and out of a dream state, lying on my back, gazing once again at the sky. I look up and notice an enormous spiderweb soaked with the morning dew, glistening in the streams of light that reflect off the dewdrops like tiny sparkling diamonds. My gaze is so fixed I can see only the web. It is the biggest web I have ever seen, and I study it, searching for the spider. The web speaks to me of the spider's patience. The sun comes to it. The dew comes to it. All things come to it. I see the spider's back and squint to look harder, trying to change my eyes into binoculars, struggling to see more.

As I gaze upward I am keenly aware of the connection between my back and the earth. I have a powerful physical sensation that I am very deep in the ground and then have an incredible feeling. My body becomes heavy and I can feel it unlike I have ever felt it before—it is indescribable. It simultaneously invades my mind and body, and I see for the first time that my vision quest place is a cleft in the rock. I am literally *in the cleft of the rock.* The shale is split, and I have taken up the center of my place in the cleft of the rock. I am overcome with emotion and start to sob, at once connecting with my past, present, and future in a heartbeat. I have an overwhelming feeling of joy, peace, and a great sense of understanding.

And a story enters my awareness . . .

He said, "Oh, let me behold Your Presence!" And He answered, "I will make all My goodness pass before you, and I will proclaim before you the name Lord, and the grace that I grant and the compassion that I show. But," He said, "You cannot see My face, for man may not see

Me and live." And the Lord said, "See, there is a place near Me. Station yourself on the rock and, as My presence passes by, I will put you in a cleft of the rock and shield you with My hand until I have passed by. Then I will take My hand away and you will see My back; but My face must not be seen."

I have an increased sense of comfort and connection, experiencing satisfaction that a lifetime of caring and blessings to be in relationship with communities, youth, and families was in service for the higher good. For youth and community in hopes of a future that works for all.

A wave of exhaustion washes over me. I lay back clutching my taquatsi to my chest and feel the flickering light through the trees kissing me. The light is fading, and I am called to do ceremony. Waiting for a moment, basking in this feeling of supreme bliss, I breath in deeply, more deeply it seems than I have ever breathed before. Once again I welcome Tate Wari into my circle and pray. The fire burns bright and I am transfixed—peering into the face of Grandfather Fire, seeking his wisdom and love. I drift in and out of sleep and dream as darkness envelopes me and all that is left are the sounds of the forest.

I wake the next day and feel rested in a gritty kind of way that comes with several days in the forest, absent water for drinking or washing. It is a familiar feeling that reminds me of my physical self, in need of transcending, now more than ever. Days and nights merge. There is no calendar, only consciousness of being in relationship with Spirit and Mother Earth. I prepare the morning ritual and welcome Grandfather into the circle. The rhythm of the forest has overtaken that of modernity. I make another check on the rock to mark another day. The checks have no meaning. Someone else is making the marks. The glittering sunrays through the tree canopy dance across my consciousness. Early-morning mist mingles with the beams of light cascading over the forest. I recline once again on the altar of Mother Earth in an aura of grace. I fall in and out of dream states, shifting my body to the contour of the ground. At times there is no separation—I am the ground. The familiar buzzing returns, and I see that the hummingbird has returned, flitting above my place. I lift my knees up and cross one leg over the other in the same way I had before, inviting my friend to alight. I am listening and waiting, but the hummingbird darts about, almost as if waiting for another moment to make connection. I divert my attention and focus on Kauyumari circling around me for protection, recalling the journeys we have taken on pilgrimages to *Wirikuta*, the place where the sun was born in Mexico. I drift in and out of remembering when I am awakened into a dream state. A hummingbird is hovering above me; the buzzing becomes coherent, and I enter another story:

Long ago in the Sierra Madre Mountains of Mexico, home of the Huichol Indians, there was a village. And the Huichol people of the village were terribly unhappy. The children cried all day and all night. For they had lost their connection to the spirit, the four directions, and their sense of place and purpose. They lost their spirituality. Life had become desolate and meaningless.

In the middle of the night two young children, brother and sister, heard the wind, Ecatewari, call out to them. "Come with me," the wind cried. As in a dream, the children followed the wind to the East and the mountain where the sun was born, Wiricuta. They walked on the wind to the mountain, where they remained for five days and five nights on a vision quest. They were seeking a vision for the path to the return of the spirituality of their village.

While their parents cried out in lament at their disappearance, over the course of the five days the children had visions. At the end of the fifth day, Ecatewari once again called out to the children to follow her and once again the children did as requested and rode the wind back to their village.

Their parents and the village were happy to see them, although still lamenting and sad. Once in the village they told the people about their vision. And, they said, "We have seen and we have heard of the way to help us connect with our four directions and the spirit. While we were on the mountain where the sun was born we learned how to make Ojos de Dios—God's Eye. We were instructed to teach the village," which they did.

And, they said, "we will make these Ojos de Dios that are the eye of our heart and the eye of the God's reflecting back to us. We will place an Ojos de Dios in each of the four directions around the fire—Tate Wari—the first Mara Akame, Shaman. We will set a chair made of wood to the East of our Grandfather Fire. Then, we will call to Tate Wari to come out of the fire and teach us.

"Ojos de Dios is like a mirror to connect the inside of us to the outside world. It helps us to be aware of the spirit, honor that it exists, see everything around us as sacred and embedded with spirit and to help bring all things within you so you are a part of it and it is a part of you. This helps to fill a person with the love of all things and a connection to all things. If you can feel the love of Mother Earth, Tate Yurianake, for just an instant it will be sufficient for a lifetime."

And, so, the children told the story. The people made Ojos de Dios, did ceremony, and their spirituality, the spirituality of their parents, and the whole village returned.

The rustling of the leaves shifts my attention. I am now sitting up, facing Grandfather Fire, and feel a warm breeze on my face. Tate Wari is alive with uncanny vigor, and I am staring into his face taking in his warmth wondering about the story. His warm embrace combined with the steady breeze seems to fill each cell in my body, but I am not certain with what. I am not in my conscious mind as the effect of several days without food and especially water is having its way with me. I am in the fire as it is in my cells.

It is all merging together. The vision quest was about a vision quest, the ancient traditions of initiation and rites of passage. As the wind picks up, the trees sway and the light flickers more rapidly around the forest. The flickering light is dancing more rigorously in the swaying trees responding to the nudging of the wind—Ecatewari is here. More and more my cells take it in.

There is another way of knowing penetrating deeply. In the vision quest, as in initiation and village-oriented rites of passage there is reciprocity between the children, the Elders, Spirit, and Universe. All are in relationship and teachers for each other, which serves survival. It is so clearly not about one child's experience of transformation. How limited. It is about the reciprocity, the agreement we have with the Universe to re-member—reconnect with our primal state of being human. In that way, the path of Spirit, is about Love, the most powerful force in the Universe.

The next several days continue on in their glory. I move between the asleep world of consciousness and the wakeful world of the unconscious, dreaming of the visions for my life and the lives within the circles of my community. I reenter the cavern of light that I have come to know as the place of my vision. The Spirits of the place continue to help me see and understand the ancestry of the vision quest. The spider, also, becomes my guide and along with the fire connects me to knowledge about the world and myself. The visions will live a lifetime, and take just as long to fully understand.

Time and space merge toward a unity with each moment. Night and day unite into the realm of the Spirit. A state of *Being* consumes me into a connection with all things. My breath becomes the breath of the wind, and the rains become the blood coursing through my veins. The ground envelops me like a skin. I am connected to the knowledge of the creation of my first being. Reborn into my true self. The self that knows its place on the earth. I come to remember and find my way through the deer into the fire, all the way to my heart.

My time on the mountain, *in the cleft of the rock,* comes to an end. The markings I have made on the rock, my calendar, signal it is time for my descent. I rise with the first light of my final morning. A heavy mist guards the forest against the first light of day. I pray for a safe return, that my visions will guide me forward on the path of life. I walk out of the cleft in the rock and into the mist of the morning. Weak, yet full of renewed energy with the knowledge of my self and place in the world, I am honored to have received the dream of my life, uncovering the story of my existence. An excitement builds as I cut my way down the hillside, unaware of the ordeal that lay ahead.

I begin the descent with joy in my heart, full of myself, which begins to bask in the self-satisfaction of the moment. An ego, whittled away by time and exposure to the natural world returns with uncanny treachery. I begin to gloat at my accomplishment, at how good I feel physically, and can hardly wait to share my experience back at the village. My steps are lively and pumped up with the expectations of my return to food, water, and the connections with the people of the village. There is an unexpected energy in my gait, which propels me toward the ravine at the base of the mountain. I am beginning to sweat, my breath becomes labored as the mist engulfs me and shrouds my bearings. As I come to the bottom of the mountain expecting to find the trail, thick underbrush grabs me. I strain to find my bearings obscured by the gray mist. The light is faint, coming through the canopy in shades of yellow, orange, and darker grays. My heart races and I am overcome with terror. I am lost. What began as a joyous return, full of a renewed knowledge of myself abruptly becomes the biggest ordeal of my life. The descent down the hillside was indeed the beginning of a descent into darkness.

A million thoughts rush through my mind. I am rudely returned to my physical form, with all its limitations of weakness, thirst, and hunger, and lumber heavily through the tangled underbrush, crashing loudly through vines, trampling ferns, and scampering over rocks, hoping the trail will magically appear. There is a bog right in front of me and I turn angrily around, retracing my steps. I quickly become exhausted and sit down, clearing the sweat from my brow and glasses. Fear and doubt begin to invade my mind, hoping to conquer my will and preoccupy my energy, consuming and shifting it toward anguish and pity. I battle to regain composure and to shift my focus away from considering the situation within a logical frame of mind, hoping to return to the Spirit realm. Thoughts about where the sun is and which way the water is heading in the small stream I crossed all confuse my attempt to gain a bearing. I walk aimlessly into the thickness of the forest.

Finally, almost out of hope, I stumble onto a trail, quickly turning toward the direction I had left the trail days before, and move immediately along the path. I am on a trail and feel consolation, yet growing discomfort. I walk on knowing, but not wanting to acknowledge, that this is not the same trail. I keep moving, wanting to escape from this fate. My legs become tired and burn with pain that I know is the result of the muscle being consumed as fuel for my life. I trek onward, dazed at the growing seriousness of the situation.

After a time the trail emerges from the forest at a road. I step out of the forest and onto the road, for the first time hearing the beat of the drum from the village. My heart sinks to a new depth, as I know that the camp is miles away and I am heading farther and farther from its safety and comfort. I turn back toward the forest and the trail, exhausted, sweating, and panting, knowing that I am miles from the circle and fire. I lie down and lament in self-pity and anguish. I cannot believe what has happened and begin to think that I will not make it back. I fight back thoughts of my death, as I begin to weep.

I put my tiquatsi on my chest and breathe slowly in and out, drawing in energy and strength, asking for direction and the courage to continue on. For the first time since I left the cleft in the rock I return to Spirit. I try to shed my physical form and the tricks and traps of my logical mind and go into the Nierika, searching for a path on which to return. I pray and feel renewed energy pour into me. I stand up and continue my journey.

Retracing my steps, I try to clear my mind and listen for the beat of the drum. Walking for what seems like a long time, I finally return to the place on the trail where I began. I continue on, each footstep a prayer lifting my focus out of my physical form and conscious mind, placing my fate in the hands of the Gods. The trail comes to a crossroads and I immediately panic. Again, I am cast into the abyss of my logical mind and begin looking for direction, wondering which way to go. I first head to the left, walking a hundred yards, and then turn and walk back to where the trails cross, and again become disoriented and bemoan my fate. I lie down feeling the excruciating pain in my legs and for the first time incredible thirst. Staring up at the canopy of trees still shrouded in the heavy morning mist, without thinking I reach for my tiquatsi and lay it on my chest. Slowly breathing in and out I look for the deer to guide me into the Nierika and find my path.

I lay on the ground and cannot move. My legs begin to cramp with pain and slowly the throbbing moves to other parts of my body. I am dying. I labor to look for the deer, calling out loud, "Kauyumari, where are you? I need your help. Please help me. Guide me to the village." I see my voice radiating from my lips, as I look down on my body prostrate on the ground. A blanket of blackness creeps into my vision as if the mist that hangs on the forest begins to darken around me. I struggle to see through the pinpoint of light that is before me. I hold my tiquatsi tighter and feel my body lift up. Once more looking down I see that I am perched on the antlers of a deer gliding along the trail. The moment passes quickly, and I find myself walking down the trail, which intersects with the path I had taken days earlier up Nob Hill. I immediately know my whereabouts. With this knowledge comes relief and energy. I walk on through the mist and begin to hear the beating of the drum calling me home.

I return to the circle in the village hours after sunrise and the beginning of my journey. I first make an offering to the fire and then shake the Shaman's hand in thanks. The community welcomes my return. They have kept a vigil around the fire, conducting ceremony three times a day for our safety. We wait together until all have returned from their vision quest. Although each of the Spirit Questers is literally dying of thirst, no one drinks, until everyone returns. Then, as in the tradition, we reconnect with the physical world, offer salt to the fire, water to the directions, and then ourselves. It is done. We all returned safe and alive with the rebirth of our souls.

After the morning ceremony we eat watermelon and potatoes with salt and then return to the fire to tell our stories. Each of us offers a tale with varying amounts of detail. Some offer emotional renderings of their journey complete with descriptions of extraordinary visions and experiences.

I listen in a state of melancholy. Each story told sends a vibration out into the Universe and connects to others in the vast place between time and space. A vibration sent out from one story resonates with another in a cosmic orchestra. I am reminded of so many gifts, images, dreams, visions, adventure, life and death. I am silent, uncertain what to say. What to share. Then it comes to me. "What if initiation is not for the children but for the survival of the people and the earth? The children are closest to spirit and able to hear the Universe, Mother Earth and the ancient ones tell stories that serve survival." I retold the story of the children, Ecatewari, and renewal of the people's spiritual connection. It was the vision quest of the children, the five days and five nights spent on the mountain, that enabled them to return and renew the village's connection with Tate Wari, the Shaman, and their spiritual path. Saving their village.

All is taken in, like the water that brought us back to life hours earlier. We are connected in the physical plane by the encounter shared, the stories told, the ritualization of the experience, wrapped collectively in our natural human identities. We bask in the security and comfort of our basic human fraternity of hunger, thirst, cold, exhaustion, and loneliness.

Stories are told around the fire. Experiences are shared. The Shaman offers esoteric interpretations—stories of the mysteries of the visions. We are encouraged to consider them during the unfolding of the rest of our lives.

> If you feel the love of Mother Earth for just one moment
> it can fill you with love for a lifetime.

The journey continues . . .

The disciples were absorbed in a discussion of Lao-Tzu's dictum:

Those who know, do not say:
those who say, do not know.

When the Master entered, they asked him what the words meant.
Said the Master, *Which of you knows the fragrance of a rose?*
All of them knew.
Then he said, Put it into words.
All of them were silent.

The Master gave his teaching in parables and stories, which his disciples listened to with pleasure and occasional frustration, for they longed for something deeper.

The Master was unmoved. To all their objections he would say, "You have yet to understand, my dears, that the shortest distance between a human being and Truth is a story."

Another time he said, "Do not despise the story. A lost gold coin is found by means of a penny candle: the deepest truth is found by means of a simple story" (de Mello 1988, 137)

4

The Trinity of Inquiry

Rites of Passage and Our Quest for Community

Through initiation our tribe survives.
—Navaho/Apache saying

The central purpose for sharing the vision quest story in the previous chapter was to bring the reader as close as possible to a rite of passage experience. As Professor Sarason advised me, "Hit them over the head with it." The vision quest case study is analyzed in subsequent chapters to extract and highlight certain distinguishing features that clarify what is meant by youth and community development through rites of passage and to illustrate the reciprocal relationships between initiation, rites of passage, and a psychological sense of community.

If you were taken aback, bewildered, confused, perhaps even angered by the story, it achieved another primary purpose. Eliciting this sort of emotional response might approach what a person engaged in the initiatory process of a vision quest would experience. Strong emotions. At times you wonder what you're doing in such an uncomfortable and unfamiliar place, coming face to face with your own death. Anger directed at your self and others bubbles to the surface and makes the waters of life murky, hiding the fear just under the surface. Fear might appear during times of deep reflection, which is one of the gifts from a vision quest. Confusion, "betwixt and between," and anger when in a liminal state will be explored in depth in coming chapters.

"Liminality is the mother of invention" (Turner 1969). It is a breeding ground. A place one cannot linger in for long. It stimulates real change. Opening my own personal narrative to the reader, which I have done with great reluctance, illustrates the way in which individuals might experience the depth and power of initiation. Initiation is not only for the benefit of the individual, solely as an aid to one's own transformation, but in reciprocity the story is shared for the benefit of the village. As Daniel Taylor writes, "Stories tell me not only who I am but also who you are, and what we are together. In fact, without you and your story I cannot know myself and my story. No one's story exists alone. Each is tangled up in countless others. Pull a thread in my story and feel the tremor half a world and two millennia away" (Taylor 1996, 6).

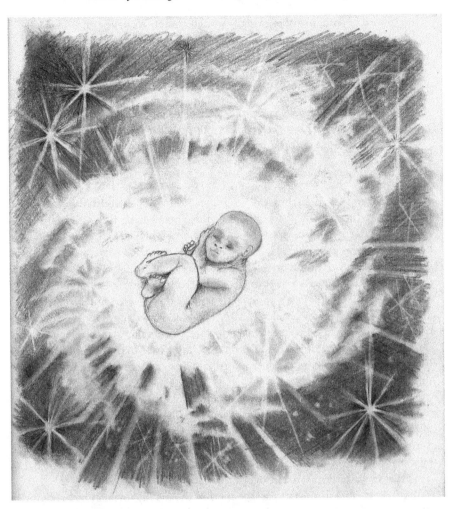

There's an old Yiddish story with roots in the teachings of Talmud that I first heard decades ago:

When in the womb everything that is known about the universe we know. At the time of birth we forget. God runs his finger under our nose, making an indentation to the top of our lips. This serves as a reminder of something we need to know. When the time is right, sometime around puberty, a window opens for us to remember that ancient knowledge. The window is only open for a short period of time. If we do not remember we are left with fear and an inner sense of yearning for that knowledge. Our fear stems from not knowing something that we needed to know in order to live life to its fullest. Many times this fear turns to anger that is directed outward or inward or both. In either case the wounds fester. We have a gnawing and uncomfortable feeling that something is missing. Perhaps at another time in life, usually just before death, the window opens again. But, then it is too late to use that knowledge in the service of life for one's self, the community, and nature.

> *If the fires that innately burn inside youths are not intentionally and lovingly added to the hearth of community, they will burn down the structures of culture, just to feel the warmth.*
>
> —Michael Meade, 1993

It struck me then that this was a significant story about initiation and youth development. The time of puberty is right for remembering this essential knowledge. Years later I told this story to an evolutionary biologist friend of mine. He looked at me quizzically and said, "Well of course. Haven't you heard of *ontogeny recapitulates phylogeny*?" He went on to explain, "As an embryo of an advanced organism grows, like humans, it will pass through stages that resemble the adult phase of less advanced organisms. There is a point during gestation when the human embryo has gills and resembles a tadpole" (Gould 1977). We can't know the tadpole's experience in the womb or what it knows. While reluctant to enter into anthropomorphism, could it be possible that it has tadpole thoughts going back to the beginning of time? Perhaps at the point where the sperm fertilizes an egg there is actually a big bang! Amazing . . . .

Exploring the transition of children to adulthood through rites of passage presents challenges. It is a highly personal experience. The initiate feels deep and powerful emotions that lay beyond generalized description. It is also a complex group or community experience that strengthens the bonds between people—*the village*—in ways that help them to reconnect to values, attitudes, skills, and behaviors and to each other in ways that serve survival.

The full measure of rites of passage rests in the mostly unexamined reciprocity between the individual, the community, and other forces, which I call the "initiatory constellation." In chapter 10, I explore the Human Relationship Area File at Yale University, which contains ethnographies, the stories about particular aspects of diverse cultures around the world. File number 881 is called "Puberty and Initiation." It contains descriptions of events surrounding puberty for both boys and girls that appear to be related to "initiation." As the title of chapter 10 states, "Something Happened," and we don't quite know what it is. We may never fully know it within the western framework that guided the observer/recorders contributing to the file's contents. What "happens" lies beyond a more traditional mechanistic analysis in which there are events that have causes and outcomes. Rather, it is a dynamic interplay between many forces. The *initiatory constellation* includes the individual's ancestors, Spirit, and immediate environment of people, place, and culture. The traditional academic might find this unreasonable, unintelligible, or unscientific. So be it. Those who have a foundation in other ways of knowing—nonwestern wisdom—will understand and see the full measure of rites of passage (Deloria 1973, 2006; Kingsley 1997; Moore 1997; McGaa 1990). They would acknowledge western science's orientation and gifts as well as its limited ability to use different ways of knowing. They would see why science is challenged to fully understand and appreciate the broader, subtle dynamics of the initiatory process and rites of passage. These dynamics lay beyond the boundaries within which many previous explorations have occurred.

This is not to discount the value and contributions of contemporary western science but to invite consideration into what might be possible when western science is in reciprocity with traditional wisdom. Taken together, with respect and in balance, new advances can be achieved to increase our understanding of how we can help our children to grow up well. It is similar to respecting and balancing two seemingly competing ideas in the long-standing debate among evolutionary biologists.

One idea holds that the single most important entity in the human species is the individual. The other idea is that the community is the single most important entity of our species. Each side presents reasonable arguments, which inform and guide important decisions that impact all of our lives. For example, if one believes that the individual is the most important unit in our species then our educational system would be designed to focus on individual development and achievement, which it does. Within the individual all things are possible. If, on the other hand, community is the most important unit in our species our educational system would be oriented to building individual capacity to collaborate and function well within a group, where all things are possible (Wilson 2013).

"Kasserian Ingera?"

This is the greeting exchanged between members of the famed Masai tribe of East Africa. It means, "And, how are the children?" This reflects a consciousness of connection. How others are doing, especially children, is directly related to how an individual is doing. It points to the difference between a cultural consciousness where the community is the most important and one where the individual is the most important. Members of an individual-oriented culture greet each other by saying "How are you doing?" as if the individual is the only one that matters and in relationship with no one except themselves.

Discovering this phrase years ago was a great gift from another culture's wisdom. With the same respect accorded to my own ancestral wisdom and culture, I've been blessed to know the wisdom of other cultures and have integrated them in balance with knowledge from western science. "Kasserian Ingera" not only conveys a consciousness of connection but also manifests in daily practice every culture's deep value placed in the care of their children and the understanding that their children's welfare is directly connected to the welfare and future of their culture and community. What would our lives be like if we greeted each person by asking not "How are you doing?" but "And, how are the children?"

The central focus of this book addresses how the needs of the individual, especially children, and the needs of the community can be met through one of our oldest traditions—rituals in general and initiation and rites of passage specifically. They have

helped to bridge the divide between the needs of the individual and those of community. Evidence of the existence of ritual in general goes back 70,000 years (Vogt 2006),
and initiation and rites of passage 30,000 years (Cohen 1991), both in service to the
health and survival of the individual and community. Initiation and rites of passage
along with a psychological sense of community are complex concepts by themselves.
Integrating them in ways that respect the culture and framework of both traditional
wisdom and contemporary science through language understood and accepted by
both and that exposes the reciprocity proposed in youth and community development through rites of passage is a challenge. Especially when the goal is to inform and
guide contemporary practice.

Challenges abound. There is the challenge of how to orient the reader to the
full depth and breadth of this topic without compromising important definitions
or glossing over necessary shifts in paradigms. Challenges also exist in honoring
what has come before in the literature and the history of our collective ancestors
that truly reflects the potency of rites of passage. Different perspectives have been
included to manage these challenges. By weaving stories of western science (theory)
with traditional wisdom (history and narratives) informed by personal experiences,
I describe and explain the central elements that constitute the interface of the individual and community experience of rites of passage. I call this youth and community development through rites of passage.

Its definition unfolds through the integration of twenty elements that serve as
design principles in the architectural structure for youth and community development through rites of passage. The first three elements are called the "Trinity of
Inquiry." They are designed to guide conversations when questions arise in any given
situation where change might yield better conditions. The first element is "What's
the Story?" It is an invitation to explore questions that matter, such as "What's the
story with what we are doing to raise and educate our children? And, what have rites
of passage had to do with it?" The second element is "Values and Ethics": "What are
the values and ethics underlying the story? What do we think is important to teach
our children and what are the values and ethics we want them to know to guide
their behaviors? How do our policies and methods of education and childrearing
align with these values and ethics? What are the present behaviors, attitudes, and
conditions of our children that indicate our policies and methods are achieving our
dreams and desires for our children?" The last in the Trinity is "Paradigm Shift."
Given our present situation and the values and ethics related to it—revealed in the
answers to these two questions—we inquire, "Are we satisfied with the present conditions, and how we are doing with educating and raising our children? What do we
want and need to do? Change?"

The Story Has a Name

Historically, anthropologists and later sociologists have laid claim to the study of
rites of passage. They organized their observations into theories in an attempt to
understand and explain the practice and ascribe meaning for both the individual

and community. There is considerable literature that examines and explains rites of passage. It has typically focused on the process as an individual experience.

> *Theory helps us bear our ignorance of facts.*
> —George Santayana, 1896

Arnold van Gennep (1908) first used the term in his seminal work *Les Rites de Passage* almost a century ago (later translated by Vizedom and Caffee). Since then, exploration and speculation have been undertaken about the practice and place of rites of passage in both ancient and contemporary culture and community. Although there may be debate about the generalization of the tripartite structure (separation, liminality, incorporation) of rites of passage that van Gennep proposed, there does appear to be general acceptance of their historical importance. Eliade (1958); Turner (1969); Foster (1980); Lincoln (1981); Mahdi (1987); Campbell and Moyers (1988); Blumenkrantz (1992); Gavazzi and Blumenkrantz (1993); Mead (1993); Somé (1993); Arnett (2004); Alford, McKenry, and Gavazzi (2001); and Plotkin (2008) are just a few of the many who have made contributions in this area.

Each of the authors cited above developed their own personal, theoretical, and cultural lens through which they viewed and classified their observations and thinking. Victor Turner classified and labeled the three-part structure "separation, marginalization, and aggregation." Bruce Lincoln focused on female initiation, classifying its structure as "enclosure, metamorphosis, and emersion." Plotkin's eight-stage model focused attention on transformation across the life cycle that engaged the individual more fully within nature and his/her culture. Whatever the classification and language that named, narrated, and explained the common phenomenon, which occurred during significant times in an individual's life, they all agree that something very important was happening, or needed to happen. More and more people are noting that the absence of rites of passage for today's youth, families, and communities has extraordinary consequences. Perhaps no one has said it better than Joseph Campbell in his dialogue with Bill Moyers, captured in the book and PBS special, *The Power of Myth* (1988):

MOYERS: What happens when a society no longer embraces a powerful mythology?

CAMPBELL: What we've got on our hands. If you want to find out what it means to have a society without any rituals, read *The New York Times*.

MOYERS: And you'd find?

CAMPBELL: The news of the day, including destructive and violent acts by young people who don't know how to behave in a civilized society.

MOYERS: Society has provided them no rituals by which they become members of the tribe, of the community. All children need to be twice born, to learn to function rationally in the present world, leaving childhood behind. . . .

CAMPBELL: That's exactly it. That's the significance of the puberty rites.

MOYERS: Where do the kids growing up in the city . . . where do these kids get their myths today?

CAMPBELL: They make them up themselves. This is why we have graffiti all over the city. These kids have their own gangs and their own initiations and their own morality, and they're doing the best they can. But they're dangerous because their own laws are not those of the city. They have not been initiated into our society.

Transitions are challenging. Passages between childhood and adulthood are fraught with danger. Wendell Berry addressed this dramatically when he wrote:

> My friend . . . jumped off the Golden Gate Bridge two months ago. . . . She was try-
> ing to get from one phase of her life to another and couldn't make it. . . .
>
> The letter had already asked, "How does a human pass through youth to maturity
> without breaking down?" And it had answered, "help from tradition, through cer-
> emonies and rituals, rites of passage at the most difficult stages"
>
> —Wendell Berry, 1977

National Awakening

The fall of 1991 was a watershed period for rites of passage. During the past hundred years or so, they were discussed and practiced in relative obscurity by small groups of academicians and youth workers. *Life* magazine devoted its entire October 1991 issue to a new book, *The Circle of Life: Rituals from the Human Family Album* (Cohen 1991). In the opening editorial Ms. Bonniwell, the publisher, wrote that this book "chronicled an immense subject—global rites of passage." Ms. Bonniwell closed her remarks by writing, "We are proud to be part of this extraordinary project, and hope it well seize your imagination as well" (Bonniwell 1991).

It is not certain whether the project seized the imagination of the populace. It did offer an accessible vehicle to expand the dialogue and document the practice and importance of rites of passage across the life cycle and throughout the world. It did serve to move the conversation out of academia, bringing together a growing group of rites of passage practitioners, and make accessible to wider audiences informa-tion on rites of passage. It helped to inform, guide, and expand the conversation by documenting the similarity in form and purpose of rites of passage among diverse practices across the life cycle for individuals and their villages around the world. More than anything, the magazine's extensive coverage of rites of passage helped to bring out of the sacred and into the domain of the secular world the utility of ritual and its ability to nourish and fortify the lives of individuals and strengthen the psy-chological sense of community. Through exquisite photographs, *Life* magazine told the story about the prominence of rites of passage in diverse cultures around the globe during times of life-cycle transitions, especially coming of age and the transi-tion from childhood to adulthood.

Reciprocity

Rites of passage are reciprocal. The individual is no more important than the community, which is no more important than the individual. Rituals and rites of passage have never occurred in a vacuum, separate from the context of nature, ancestors, spirit, or the culture(s) of a community. They happen with and for the individual, the community, and all of their relations, both present and past, seen and unseen, that appear to meet the needs of the individual and, more importantly, the survival of the community—and hence our species. This reciprocity is expanded in what I call the "initiatory constellation," which includes the individual, family, community, ancestors, spirit, nature, and the Universe. This is further addressed in chapter 10.

The majority of recent attention to rites of passage has focused on the individual. This has given rise to many programs (Youth Passageways 2015) that purport to offer a rite of passage. Many are typically for youth and follow on the heels of the "men's movement"; many others are geared to middle-aged men. In these programs the individual is the central player. Rites of passage are done to and for them in ways to affect some individual transformation and assist with a transition. It has been referred to as group therapy within a medium of rites of passage (Rites of Passage Wilderness 2015). Three questions help to consider the orientation of designs and programs called rites of passage: Initiation into what? For what purpose? By whom? These are addressed in detail in subsequent chapters.

Evolutionary biologists claim that a species will not maintain any practice unless it serves to increase the survival of that species. This is the case for rites of passage, with evidence of their existence, discussed previously, spanning 30,000 years. It is for this reason that the orientation of our work for over forty years—and the focus of this book—views another central reason for the rite of passage: its ability to strengthen the village and the community in ways that increase their resiliency and adaptability to ensure their survival. Hence, the survival of our species.

The Psychological Sense of Community

A psychological sense of community is the second focus of this book. What is it? What is the impact of its absence or presence? And in what way can rites of passage impact the psychological sense of community and future of society? Victor Turner (1969) may have said it best when he wrote, "*communitas* emerges where social structure is not" (126). The liminal period of the initiation rite, that period Turner calls "betwixt and between," thrusts a group of initiates together in the absence of secular distinctions of class and rank. It strengthens the bonds between the initiates, the youth who will come of age and collectively inherit the reins of authority of their community. Ritual also serves as the "principal ingredient of its [the community's] operating dynamics" (Somé 1993, 70). Somé is very clear on this and says, "a community that doesn't have ritual can not exist" (71).

This book carves out and highlights specific materials and experiences that focus on the relationship between rites of passage and a psychological sense of community. Rites of passage traditionally exist during major transition points in life (i.e., birth, initiation to adulthood, marriage, and death). Our emphasis here will be on rites of initiation—the transition of children to adulthood. It is the absence of these rites that has received increased attention and is considered by many to be a contributing factor in the difficulties that youth are having in making a successful transition from childhood to adulthood (Blumenkrantz 1992, 1996; Blumenkrantz and Goldstein 2014; Campbell and Moyers 1988; Cohen 1991; Eliade 1958; Foster 1980; Lincoln 1981; Mahdi 1987; Mead 1993; Somé 1993; Turner 1969). But what if the absence of a sense of community is another contributing factor to the challenges facing adolescent development? How might this shift our approach to education and youth development? The absence of viable contemporary community rites of passage coupled with the growing deterioration of the social covenant of community has placed the future of society in a precarious position.

There can be no greater demonstration of a commitment to this sense of community than accepting responsibility for collectively rearing the next generations of children. If nothing else, community is and has always been for the children. It is no accident that since the dawn of time we have organized ourselves into tribes and villages. It was purposeful and deliberate and, as with all biological organisms, designed for survival. In our case that meant hunting, gathering, building shelters, and protecting against predators. Survival centers on providing the optimum environment for the birth and nurturing of a species' offspring. The tribe and village were for rearing children as much as for the group's safety. The absence or inadequacy of a sense of community is a contributing factor to many of our problems of living. This is not a new problem, but one whose growing severity is deteriorating the fabric of humanity, which is woven with our mutual connectedness.

> There can be no keener revelation of a society's soul than the way in which it treats its children.
>
> —Nelson Mandela

Why Rites of Passage Now?

Many would agree that we are confronted with increasing social, political, and economic crises. "The news of the day," as Joseph Campbell points out, confirms this. The increased difficulty young people are having moving into healthy and positive adult roles, repeated closings of the federal government, the exponential increase in the national debt, the decline in living standard and rate of unemployment, insult to and decimation of the natural world, climate change, increasing human-made and natural disasters, fragmentation and disconnection of people from each other, and incivility in the places where we work, play, and are educated are all indicators and testament to the scope and intensity of the problems we face. Some may claim that present conditions are no worse than they have ever been. However, most will not disagree that something different has to be done. The way we are currently preceding, especially in terms of how we are raising our children, is failing to result in a reasonable quality of living and personal satisfaction for many people. A new paradigm must emerge.

The growing discontent with the status quo is the breeding ground for conflict and gives rise to the prospect of a new paradigm and the conflict that will undoubtedly result. As Thomas Kuhn (1962) pointed out, when the old models and points of reference contained in paradigms don't seem to hold true or work to achieve a desired result, the ensuing conflict will produce a "revolution" and the birth of another paradigm, or way of perceiving the world. However, before this can happen there must be agreement that the old paradigm is ineffectual and that a crisis is at hand. As a society are we really ready to do this? Old beliefs and habits are very hard to break.

The goal of this book is not to convince the reader that a crisis exists, but to make a compelling case for rites of passage as a way to promote a psychological sense of community and contribute to the future of society. It is directed toward remembering the roots of a sense of community and replanting them in a new paradigm for youth and community development through rites of passage that is sensitive to the complex and interrelated challenges of modern western society. Yes, most of these problems are interrelated, yet we still marshal resources to declare war on only one problem at a time. A new paradigm must emerge that sees all things as related in a global community, which includes all of nature. One broad possibility for the regeneration of a sense of community is explored in the human tradition of ritual in general and those of initiation and rites of passage in particular.

Powerful personal beliefs and competing ideologies about the nature of humans will undoubtedly impact the potential of this new paradigm to emerge and mature. For example, people who are oriented to a believe in "rugged individualism" will be quick to cast aside the notion that a psychological sense of community is an important factor in the promotion of an increased quality of life and, in fact, our survival. Second, "ritual" and "initiation" are emotionally charged words that cast a person back to thoughts of religion or cults. Perhaps for some they will even evoke inclusion or exclusion from certain groups. Third, others will shudder at the prospect of change and cling to what they have, fearful at what they might have to give up to make for a more just and equitable world.

> *There's always room for a story that can transport people to another place.*
> —J. K. Rowling

As stated in the Introduction, the use of stories is an integral part of this work. Stories have always been the carriers of essential messages. They deepen our understanding and give meaning to our lives. Stories tell us who we are, inform our imagination as to who we might become, and can bind us together in a common narrative. Direct descriptions of an event are limited by comparison to a metaphor or allegory. Hebb (1974), the former president of the American Psychological Association, puts it this way:

> It is to the literary world, not to psychological science, that you go to learn how to live with people, how to make love, how not to make enemies, to

find out what grief does to people, or the stoicism that is possible in the endurance of pain, or how if you're lucky you may die with dignity; to see how corrosive the effects of jealousy can be, or how power corrupts or does not corrupt. For such knowledge and understanding of the human species, don't look in my *Textbook of Psychology* (or anyone else's), try *Lear* and *Othello* and *Hamlet*. (74)

Remembering a Story Will Be Sufficient

When the founder of Hasidic Judaism, the great Rabbi Israel Shem Tov, saw misfortune threatening the Jews, it was his custom to go into a certain part of the forest to meditate. There he would light a fire, say a special prayer, and the miracle would be accomplished and the misfortune averted.

Later, when his disciple, the celebrated Maggid of Mezritch, had occasion, for the same reason, to intercede with heaven, he would go to the same place in the forest and say, "Master of the Universe, listen! I do not know how to light the fire, but I am still able to say the prayer," and again the miracle would be accomplished.

Still later, Rabbi Moshe-leib of Sasov, in order to save his people once more, would go into the forest and say, "I do not know how to light the fire. I do not know the prayer, but I know the place and this must be sufficient." It was sufficient, and the miracle was accomplished.

Then it fell to Rabbi Israel of Rizhin to overcome misfortune. Sitting in his armchair, his head in his hands, he spoke to God, "I am unable to light the fire, and I do not know the prayer, and I cannot even find the place in the forest. All I can do is to tell the story, and this must be sufficient."

And it was sufficient.

For God made man because he loves stories.

This old story, retold through a Jewish lens, reflects the heart of a growing awakening throughout the country of the importance of rituals of initiation. One has only to glance at a newspaper or listen to the countless media reports to know that we are in a time of great peril and face imminent danger. We are in a time of misfortune threatening our children, the most vulnerable among us. They are killing themselves and each other at an alarming rate (Sullivan et al. 2015; Robers et al. 2014; Finkerhor and Ormrod 2001). They are confused and despondent about the complexities of the world and whether they will have a suitable place in it. They do not have a clear and safe path, set out by society, for them to travel on their journey to adulthood. They are not taken to a special place to meditate or to be taught the prayers or how to properly light the fire. We are losing many young people to gangs, violence, drugs, and despair. This is the initiation the young have taken for themselves. These children are our future. They will carry our legacy. We must remember the story of rites of passage. Hopefully it will be sufficient. And a miracle will happen.

5

The Meaning of Community

Symbols of Initiation—Reciprocity

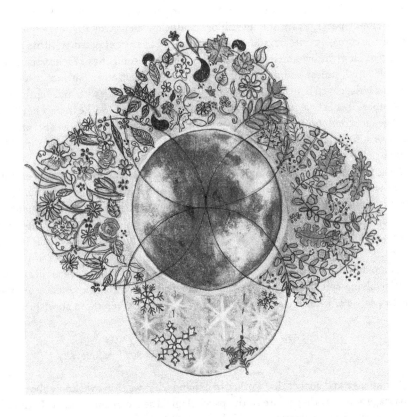

We say we have "explained" something when we have found and described the root phenomena from which it springs. But what has been gained? Have we not just deferred questioning to another domain?
—Thomas Kelting

Let us return to "The First Story–My Creation Myth." You may be struck not so much by the details of the story, but the fact that I chose to include the story at all. It was an attempt to bring the reader as close as possible to the essence of what a rite of passage is and its relationship to the psychological sense of community. The vision quest is one traditional form of a rite of passage. Its unfolding within the Huichol tradition provides a story that could lend itself to analysis and inform the emergence of village-oriented rites of passage. I heard it said once that one of the greatest gifts a story has to give is a lesson from a life you don't have to live. This may, however, not be the case with a rite of passage, which, as I have said, is very difficult to comprehend unless one has actually been through the experience. While I honored Professor Sarason by including the story up front, "hitting you over the head," as he would say, with a rite-of-passage tale, it may still be insufficient to convey the real experience. One of the core elements in guiding the emergence of rites of passage within a community or for an individual is that: "You can only bring someone as far as you've been yourself." And, unless and until you have traveled the initiatory pathway, especially within a village, you may be unable to fully understand the breadth and depth of the experience. This is true for the individual, and even more so for the impact of rites of passage on a community. As Seymour said, "If you have never been in a concentration camp, or suffered from extreme hunger or thirst, even a great literary giant would be challenged to adequately convey its real meaning."

I was reluctant to tell this very personal story to those outside my family or unfamiliar with the Huichol tradition, let alone write about it for public scrutiny. To say that Professor Sarason urged me to share the story would be an understatement. He could be very persuasive. Without the story of a vision quest as a frame of reference, he said, people unfamiliar with rites of passage would have no idea what it is. That was sufficiently compelling to me. At the most fundamental level, rites of passage are not an intellectual or academic exercise. Above all else they are powerful encounters, involving self and nature, that provide a transformative experience on one's way to a sense of wholeness and a connection with the universe and all within it.

> *But how could you live and have no story to tell?*
> —Fyodor Dostoyevsky

A challenge and goal of this work is to expand what we think we know about rites of passage and how they relate to the psychological sense of community. Both have been described in academia through books and literature. Opening a doorway to "other ways of knowing" through experiences synthesized with academic materials might help to inform more adequate and appropriate designs for youth and community development through rites of passage. That is the overarching goal.

I invite the reader to suspend disbelief and consider the story for the lessons it holds. That was the intent of telling it in the first place. Sharing the story of my vision quest is deeply personal, and I do not open it for public examination without great consideration. In the tradition of a vision quest and rites of passage parts of the experience are kept personal, while others are shared as "gifts" for the benefit and survival of the community. Out of all the vision quest and other rite of passage experiences I could have offered, this one was chosen for several reasons. First, it occurred in an established community where members had mutual responsibilities and commitments and depended on each other for survival. Second, the experience was full of symbols of initiation: the images of my Bar Mitzvah, living in the cleft of the rock, and the story of initiation rites told in the cave all conspired to compel me to tell it. The vision quest is a gift. I pass the story of it on because that is what I am supposed to do. Telling this story is nothing less than an attempt to help our tribe and the planet to survive. Answers are not always found at the end of a search, but often during the search itself.

Our brains are uniquely designed to be receptacles for stories. Evolution has given us speech and refined our capacity for articulating stories as ways to narrate the world to track changes that occur in our environment and community as well as to pass along information in ways that serve survival (Wilson and Wilson 2007; Kottler 2015). "Stories tell me not only who I am but also who you are, and what we are together" (Taylor 1996, 6). I am resigned to hope that Daniel Taylor's insight will be sufficient for the reader to enter into this story with an open mind and heart. Perhaps some thread in my story may help you remember your own story and in that way we may come to know each other together and imagine what might be possible. Kottler (2015, 49) writes, "stories can literally transport you into the mind of protagonists just as though it were your own direct experience."

In telling the story I was not thinking through a particular lens of analysis. It flowed out of me, as I was able to recall the experience. In this way what happened was narrated as close as possible to the actual experience, unmitigated by intentionally structuring it in a way that would facilitate any subsequent analysis.

This story can be viewed from a number of perspectives. At the time it was first written, several decades ago, I narrowed the scope of analysis to focus on rites of passage and the psychological sense of community. In seeking to make this as useful as possible for guiding village-oriented rites-of-passage design strategies, I have amplified certain sections that revealed elements found to be consistent in all initiation and rites of passage. This gives the reader additional information that led to the emergence of twenty guiding principles in a framework for youth and community development through rites of passage.

Exploring aspects of both rites of passage and a psychological sense of community is impacted by a number of factors. There are considerable variations in the definitions, which are a function of history and of the context of a particular community and culture. It might seem at first glance that rites of passage should be easier to define than a psychological sense of community. After all, they have a longer history of study and the initial theoretical propositions were generated from ethnographer's descriptions of behavior within different groups and cultures. This early work set forth certain agreed-on characteristics (separation, liminality, reincorporation) contained in the consistent patterns of human behavior expressed and observed in the structure of events subsequently labeled "rites of passage." Theory was informed by observation of cultural practices that appeared to be evident throughout the world. In one sense, rites of passage found us; we did not find them.

The concept of a "psychological sense of community" became a cornerstone for the newly established discipline of community psychology in the mid-1960s (Lott and Lott 1965; Kelly 1966) born following a conference at Swampscott, Massachusetts (Rickel 1987). Certain components, with distinct characteristics, emerged that informed and drove investigations to describe, quantify, and explain a particular phenomenon of human relationships that contributed to a growing body of literature, (McMillan and Chavis 1986; Sarason 1974). Although we may have always had a quest for community and varying degrees of success in defining it, there is still considerable debate about exactly what is meant by the term "psychological sense of community." There have been greater attempts to scientifically measure a psychological sense of community than there have been to scientifically measure rites of passage (Fisher, et al 2002). As a result, the terminology of psychological sense of community lends itself to observation and measurement, which is not as easy to do for rites of passage. Confusion on the meaning and definition of rites of passage is exacerbated when one considers all the different forms that they have taken in programs called rites of passage. Again, both experiences fall into the category of description similar to thirst and hunger. You know it when you experience it, but describing it is another story. Suffice it to say that we are once again on unstable ground when exploring either of these concepts if we simply try to make declarative statements about them.

Conducting this analysis is awkward at best. Considering these human phenomena within a logical, linear, and scientific framework may lead one further away from real understanding. Using only the scientific orientation to understand and explain a human phenomenon may distort its reality and narrow one's thinking. These experiences are best understood at the level of the heart. Those of a scientific bent who read this may have trouble recognizing the value of this orientation. Others, who have been fortunate enough to experience these lessons through the heart, will find familiarity here. But this raises the question, Where does a psychological sense of community reside, in the mind or heart? The same question can be asked for rites of passage. Do the transformations that accompany rites of passage reside in the mind or heart? The heart is not the place of conscious, linear, logical, or rational thought. It is anchored in intuition, emotions, joy, sorrow, and the remarkable depth of human feelings. Some say the longest journey one may take is from the mind to the heart.

A Place Called Community

Let us start at the place of community. How can you really explore the phenomenology of ritual and its relationship to community unless you intentionally immerse yourself in an actual experience? This question prompted me to seek out and explore an ongoing community that engaged in rituals anchored in authentic ancestral practices. Sometime in the mid-1980s I wanted to explore this in more depth whether there were similarities in the ritual form among different cultures. I was very familiar with the traditions of my ancestors and wanted to see if there were practices that might be universal, perhaps more precisely considered as patterns, symbols, core elements, or principles contained in the literature and validated by my experience in life. At that time there was an uptick in interest in Native American traditions, and many were doing "spiritual shopping," going to different day and weekend workshops and retreats. I did that a few times. But it was like window-shopping, and I knew I needed to commit to something deeper. In 1990 I attended a workshop on Huichol Shamanism led by Brant Secunda at the Rowe Conference Center in Massachusetts.

Secunda completed a 12-year apprenticeship in Mexico with the late Don José Matsuwa, to become a Shaman, healer, and ceremonial leader in the indigenous Huichol tradition. Living in the Sierra Madre Mountains, the Huichol are considered to be one of the last tribes in North America to have preserved their pre-Columbian traditions (Dance of the Deer Center for Shamanic Studies 2012). They are called *Virarica*, the Healing People.

The weekend workshop included members in an ongoing group that met with Brant at least four times a year to deepen their understanding and practice in Huichol Shamanism. After experiencing the workshop, where I met many of the members of the ongoing group, Brant invited me to attend the next group meeting. This began a nine-year relationship with Brant and the ongoing "East Coast" group. Members were committed to ceremonies commemorating the change in the seasons and the lessons that emerged during pilgrimages to many places of power, including the Huichol village in the Sierra Madre Mountains in the traditions of Virarica.

There are specific ceremonies for the four seasons, which are intended to bring balance and harmony to each individual, the community, and all of life. This is what intrigued me about the practice of Huichol Shamanism. Individuals were in ceremony for the community and all of nature and the Universe. *Ceremony and sacred practices connected us and were in service to community and nature. We were a part of nature and the community, not apart from it. Of course there were benefits for the individual, but that was not the central focus. The practices and ceremonies engaged in by individuals were intentionally directed to effect change and improve the health of their community and wider world. This was familiar to me and similar to the tradition of Tikkun Olam—repairing the world— a major tenet of Judaism, which I practice.*[1]

Entering a Psychological Sense of Community: A First Step

As you read further, think of your own story related to feeling included or excluded from something. Think of situations you may have had that might have been or approached rite of passage experiences. While I make some reference to the content and narrative in "My First Story" and relate it to the concepts we are discussing, I also leave it to the reader to think about the concepts of a psychological sense of community and rites of passage and how they relate to your story.

---

[1] Italics are used to represent Huichol-oriented language and/or lessons recorded in my personal journal. The lessons emerged either directly from Brant or taught by and through direct experiences in Nature.

If a central function of rites of passage is to impact and strengthen a sense of community, then what do we mean by "community"? In community psychology the term is used in two main ways. The first concept of community focuses on territory and geography. This includes neighborhoods, towns, and cities, places where localized groups of people interact to become a system in which they are dependent on one another and their environment. The second concept of community is "relational," which is concerned with the "quality of character of human relationship, without reference to location" (Gusfield 1975, xvi). Within a rites of passage framework, both geography and relationships are important. Geography and relationships include everything in nature, the environment, and the Universe. These two considerations are not mutually exclusive. Rather, a psychological sense of community considers the quality of all of the relationships we can have, including relationships with nature. Its strength is related to factors that either increase or decrease the sense that people in a community perceive that they are connected to other people and all things. We'll address this further in a moment.

First, we must begin at the beginning with Seymour Sarason's early definition of a psychological sense of community, which put in motion subsequent discussions and research. ". . . a psychological sense of community: the sense that one belongs in and is meaningfully a part of a larger collectivity; the sense that although there may be conflict between the needs of the individual and the collectivity, or among different groups in the collectivity, these conflicts must be resolved in a way that does not destroy the psychological sense of community; the sense that there is a network of and structure to relationships that strengthens rather than dilutes feelings of belonging," (Sarason 1974, p. 41)

One way to begin our exploration into the intersection of rites of passage and community is to consider three questions: What are youth being initiated into, by whom, and for what purpose? The answers to these key questions can guide the design of more viable and potent village-oriented rites of passage.

A sense of community is a feeling that members have of belonging, a feeling that members matter to one another and to the group, and a shared faith that members' needs will be met through their commitment to be together (McMillan 1976, Nowell and Boyd 2010, Talò, Mannarini, and Rochira 2014). McMillan and Chavis (1986) underscore four distinct components in their definition of a psychological sense of community: *membership, influence, integration,* and *fulfillment of needs and shared emotional experience or connection.* It is through a rite of passage that an individual becomes a member of a group. Transmitting values and knowledge that inform individuals about their responsibility and rights as members of a group is essential. In this chapter we explore how each of these four components relates to rites of passage.

The first component, membership, is considered to be the feeling of belonging or of sharing a sense of personal relatedness. It has five attributes: boundaries, emotional safety, a sense of belonging and identification, personal investment, and a common symbol system. These attributes work together and contribute to a sense of who is part of the community and who is not. That is one central purpose of a rite of passage—to distinguish who is and who is not a member of the culture and community. It is about inclusion and exclusion (Fisher and Sonn, 2007).

Initiation into What?

In this analysis and indeed with all rites of passage, we need to thoroughly examine the question "Initiation into what?" One of the limitations of a community psychology, particularly in western orientations, is the exclusion of nature as a central part in the conception of community. Western orientations perceive nature as resources—*natural* resources—to be used without any consideration that all of nature is a sentient being that has influence on us as we have influence on it. The traditional nonwestern orientations of indigenous peoples emphasize the idea of *natural relationships* between humans and the environment. This is a considerable shift in paradigm in terms of how one views the world.

The elders within First Nations' people and other indigenous cultures speak of the need for our collective maturation into actions that manifest this consciousness. Oren Lyons, Faithkeeper of the Turtle clan of the Onondaga Nations, is among many traditional wisdom keepers who compel us to look toward the wisdom and traditions within our natural relationships to guide us into a healthier future, for individuals, their communities, and all who live on Mother Earth.

In the Huichol tradition, as with many indigenous people, life revolves around nature, the passing of the seasons and of night into day and day into night, in ways that affirm and honor their natural relationships. Ceremonies are intended to bring balance and harmony to each person, the community, and all of life. They are intended for people to come together and focus on the spirit world—to reenter that world, and reconnect with essential knowledge:

> *If you feel the love of Mother Earth,*
> *even for just an instant,*
> *it will be sufficient for your whole life.*

One of the central tasks of traditional initiation was to thrust the child out of the preoccupation with self along with the trappings of the human ego. A focus on one's own self, heightened in childhood, lessens the sense of self in relationship to a community and one's sense of connection with the environment. This orientation to community includes the natural relationships with all the animals, minerals, and plants. All are sentient beings that are in a reciprocal relationship with individuals and their community. It is the initiation back into one's primal relationships with the natural world, those things we used to know and yearn to reconnect with again, that links everyone in a common membership with all life. The central purpose of Huichol Shamanism and initiation is to bring individuals into direct experience with their natural relationships in ways that serve to heal themselves, their family, community, and the environment. Hence the name Virarica, which means "the healing people."

Through initiation we can rediscover and reconnect with our natural relationship in ways that can transcend culture and lead toward our mutual survival. This is not to minimize the importance and influence of individual and village culture, but to regard all cultures as deeply connected through their natural relationships.

It is these relationships that offer common boundaries—that lie in the natural world—from which one receives emotional safety and a sense of belonging and identification. Access to these relationships is achieved through ceremony and the common symbols that unfold in the rituals that compel a personal investment from all who participate.

We go out into the wilderness to seek a vision for our lives. To let the connection with the physical world and Spirits infuse with our soul. To become human again. We cast off the trappings of technology and the material world and become one with our natural selves— inseparable from Spirit and the universe. Within each of us is buried an indigenous heart. A heart knowledgeable of and connected to the natural world.

We begin to shed our selves, leaving our past as we pray and make an offering to the fire. The fire remains burning in the village and connects us with the energy of Spirit, the village, and the Shaman. We connect through the fire to all the fires of our ancestors and all the fires burning around the planet. These fires link us together with the first Shaman, Grandfather Fire, Tate Wari. This is the tradition. Those who do not go on the vision quest maintain a vigil at the fire. They support the journey. We are in the village with one heart during this sacred time.

The light connects me to the fire, the ancestors, and all the fires burning within the flower of the human heart as well as the hearths around the world. I make this connection to move outside myself and into the Nierika, the portal to the world of the Gods. At night we die a little death and on the way back we dream. The dream can be our ally. It is brought into the light of Grandfather Fire.

Initiation and rites of passage can take many forms and serve a wide range of purposes. There are formal initiations into religious, cultural, and civic groups; fraternal organizations; and other groups. Anyone who has been a member of a sports team knows the kind of initiation that goes on. Or, in less formal or structured ways initiations can occur in more subtle ways within any group. An example of this has been discussed in relationship to school bullying and the hierarchy that develops in peer groups, especially those of adolescents. In almost all cases an individual undergoes initiation for the purpose of ensuring that the values, skills, and behaviors expected of its members, which maintain the group's vibrancy and existence are understood and passed on to the new members. The purpose is both to help transform the individual to function and be accepted within the group and to ensure the survival of the group. Both were essential for the ongoing adaptability and survival of the community and the health and well-being of its members.

Initiation by Whom and for What Purpose?

The second component of the psychological sense of community, influence, is a sense of mattering, of making a difference to a group and of the group mattering to its members. It is about ongoing relationships that are reciprocal. Individuals matter to each other and relationships are dependent on people helping to meet each other's needs while not compromising the higher-order needs of the community. When this is considered in connection with the first question, "What is the purpose of initiation?," we can get a sense of the importance of initiation and rite of passage experiences that occur within and for a community. It is illustrated in the relationship between those who go out on the vision quest and those who remain behind.

People who remain in the village and those who seek a vision are all connected through common symbols and ritual practices in support of a common purpose. There is transcendence and a sense of mattering that is not only present in the physical plane of the individual but also in the spiritual dimension where all things are related. We do not go out on a vision quest alone, exclusively, as some kind of personal transformative experience, as individual psychotherapy might be, but as a whole-village approach to health and unifying our lives in common pursuit of strength, healing, and love. What might this mean for contemporary rites of passage? In what way do the initiate's family and community become reconnected, as a village, in support of their own survival through their children's initiation?

Influence is directly connected to the third component, integration and fulfillment of needs, the feeling that members' needs will be met by the resources received through their membership in the group. Ceremonies engage the community together, with one heart, to perform rituals that serve all members of the group individually and collectively as well as all of their natural relationships. Rites of passage connect the individual, the group, and the natural world; there is an explicit understanding of connection and interdependence that is manifested in individuals' attunement to one another and the environment.

Integration and fulfillment of needs correspond to the rewards that an individual receives from their membership in the group. This is linked to an individual's perception of their status as a member in the group as perceived by the "outside world" (like being a member of a civic or cultural organization or a fancy country club for some people). Another dimension of this element is related to competence. While McMillan and Chavis view this to be unidirectional, that is, a person seeks others who are competent; Glynn (1981) suggests that there is a strong relationship between a sense of community and the ability to function competently in the community. Community presents the context in which members can perform a wide variety of roles for the maintenance of the community and find a way to demonstrate their own competency.

This is especially relevant for youth, who yearn to come of age within a community that can provide opportunities for them to demonstrate competencies that are in service to their own sense of self as well as the health of their community. These competencies are manifested in the environments of home/family and school, with their peers, and in community, nature, and the Universe. Competencies in each of these environments are demonstrated and affirmed by their family, peers, and members of their culture and community (Catalano and Hawkins 1996; Lerner 2005). The "story" of a rite of passage integrates service to the community and others as an essential value, manifesting compassion, altruism, and caring that is purposefully expressed in community service. This is a clear expectation throughout the community and a behavioral characteristic of someone moving into mature adulthood. It is part of the bigger picture of moving toward maturation and adulthood energizing and empowering it to be more than programs expressed as "National Citizen Service" or "youth volunteerism" that are expanding across the landscape. The story of rites of passage and their program designs serve an integrative function that focuses on a community's capacity to fit people in, or what Rappaport (1977) calls the person–environment fit. People will be more apt to fit into a group that offers a reciprocity of relationships, that is, people can help to meet each others' needs while they meet their own needs as well. While there are a host of possible needs that individuals may aspire to satisfy, common values offer a link to the types of activities in which a community engages (Muchinsky and Monahan 1987; Kristof-Brown, Zimmerman, and Johnson 2005).

A community psychology does not consider the "environment" to include the natural world. What might be possible if the "environment fit" included the natural relationships that could be in reciprocity for meeting the needs of an individual and the natural world? It means that youth who come of age deeply connected and in relationship with nature would more adequately meet their needs and the needs of all their relations in the natural world. This would contribute to the health of the individual and the planet.

> "The consequences of not intentionally reconnecting children with nature, especially when they are coming of age, are contributing to our sense of separation from nature and foster the environmental conditions that exist today. Children who spend less time outdoors and more indoors plugged into electronics have a higher incidence of depression and 'nature-deficit disorder' and the treatments of children for internet addiction are skyrocketing." (Louv 2005)

We eat after the morning ceremony, and then return to the fire to tell our vision quest stories. Tales are told with varying amounts of detail. Some offer versions imbued with emotion describing extraordinary visions and experiences. All is taken in, like the water that brought us back to life hours earlier. And, like the life-sustaining water, we search within each tale for a thread of meaning that connects us to our own story and nourishes our lives and the life of the community. We are connected in the physical plane by the encounters shared and the stories told. The ritualization of the experience wraps us collectively in our natural human identities. We bask in the security and comfort of our basic human fraternity of hunger, thirst, cold, exhaustion, and loneliness.

> Here is this vast, savage, howling mother of ours, Nature, lying all around, with such beauty, and such affection for her children, as the leopard: and yet we are so early weaned from her breast to society, to that culture which is exclusively an interaction of man on man
> —Henry David Thoreau (1862/1906)

The fourth component of a psychological sense of community is shared emotional connection. It includes the commitment and belief that members have shared and will share history, common places, and time together with similar experiences.

One might consider this component of a psychological sense of community to be of particular relevance. On the surface it does not depend on a territorial and geographical notion of community (i.e., neighborhood, town, city). It is mostly concerned with the relational aspects (i.e., the quality of character of human relationship) without reference to location. However, when we focus on each of these components of a psychological sense of community, one cannot help but see that an ongoing relationship—created by living in close proximity—does matter.

Consider the conception of shared emotional experience. We see that it relies on the commitment and belief that members have shared and will share history, common places, and time together with similar experiences. Individuals might be able to share a common emotional experience that lasts a short period of time, but they would be hard-pressed to continue a sense of influence and reinforcement that breeds integration and fulfillment of needs, when they do not live in the same place and have an ongoing relationship. How could an individual be able to feel that the resources received through membership in a group would meet their needs if the group were not continually present? What are the unintended consequences of initiating children outside of the culture and context of their family, community and the natural environment in which they live?

This question is especially important for children who are coming of age and seek meaning and purpose that contributes to a strong sense of who they are—their identity. Their identity is tied to their sense of influence and the reinforcement that they receive on a continual basis from the people they live with, the people who were their guides and initiators. Some would contend, especially those oriented in traditional wisdom, that the only way one can achieve a strong identity is through an affiliation with and connection to the environment—the place in which one lives. In fact, the noted native scholar Daniel Wildcat points out, "fewer and fewer people have tangible lifeway relationships to the places in which they live" (Wildcat 2009, 32). Place is such a central element in traditional wisdom that the concept of "indigenous" refers to "peoples or nations who take their tribal identities as members of the human species from the landscape and seascapes that gave them their unique tribal cultures" (32). In effect one cannot define a sense of community as one that is purely relational. That is an academic exercise and another illustration of the mechanistic "silo view" of the world. A fish cannot be a fish if it is not in and connected to water. We are the same way in relationship to the "pond" or "ocean" where we reside.

From one perspective, it could be argued that because members of the Huichol group did not live in in the same place they could not be considered a community. However, another perspective would assert that the primary purpose of the Huichol community is to learn how to connect with nature and the spirit world, which is always present wherever one physically resides. Each person can continue to strengthen their relationship with spirit and nature through rituals in the place they live. Nature, as a sentient being, is brought within each of us during ceremony and the rituals, as those with Grandfather Fire strengthen connections between individuals at a distance and with nature and our sacred earth. In this way they are actually continuing the community through their shared practices even though they are in different locations. It is the rituals, customs, and culture that bind a people as much as the place in which they live. I can practice Judaism alone, or in my synagogue with others. In both of these instances I am always connected to the worldwide Jewish community, especially in my daily practice of Tikkun Olam—repairing the world. Regardless of the perspectives and judgment on whether the Huichol group is a community, the central purpose for bringing this into the conversation was to illustrate the relationship between rituals, initiation, rites of passage and sense of community.

Durkheim (1964) observed that modern society develops community around interests and skills more than around locality. This can be in places of employment, university and school settings, and now even in cyberspace and virtual communities. The debate on whether community can be exclusive to "interests" and not include "place" will continue. A person's perception should remain in the definition and related to relationships that can provide them with a sense of community. One would be hard-pressed to convince a devoted user of the Internet's "chat rooms," "bulletin boards," and now Facebook that they have not found a significant degree of fulfillment and sense of community in cyberspace, especially if they found a mate and married through their connection in a virtual community like Match.com (Haase et al. 2002; Forster 2004). Shared interests, learning lessons, and developing skills to further their relationship with spirit and nature connect members of the Huichol community.

In an effort to expand our understanding of community and have more information to guide the development of village-oriented rites of passage let us explore several other definitions of community. Keep in mind that this is not only an academic exercise. Rather, it is offered to help inform and guide those who are helping rites of passage to emerge in a community. It is also provided to convey the importance of place for rites of passage. And, when that place is in the community in which the youth and adults live and is secured within nature the full strength of rites of passage can be realized.

A number of researchers define community primarily based on spatial and geographic relationships. Ahlbrant and Cunningham (1979) viewed a sense of community as intimately related to one's satisfaction and commitment to a neighborhood. They use the term "social fabric" to capture the "strengths of interpersonal relationships" as measured through different types of neighborhood interactions. The degree to which youth deepen their relationship with adults in the community directly impacts their ability to successfully transition into adulthood. The theory of positive youth development put into practice encourages strong adult–youth relationships (Lerner, Brittian, and Fay, 2007). This is achieved when the community provides opportunities for youth to become meaningfully involved in their community and receive recognition and rewards for demonstrating the new skills they have learned. Village-oriented rites of passage establish the pathway for youth to take toward these meaningful opportunities and the adult relationships that naturally ensue. It also recognizes that rites of passage are not singular events. Rather, they occur over a long period of time and within a number of different environments, such as one's home and family and schools, and within a peer group, the community, and nature. And different values inform expectations for behaviors that are manifested in competencies.

> A community's celebration of the acquisition of competencies in the different environments in which youth live, over time, is part of a village-oriented rite of passage. It addresses the three central questions raised earlier: What are youth being initiated into? By whom? and For what purpose? Youth are being initiated into the values, culture, and context of their community, which includes nature, spirit, and their ancestors. By whom? They are initiated by elders from the community, who will be there to continually support and affirm their ongoing journey to maturity. And, the purpose is to effect a transformation in the individual in ways that enable them to transcend their own self-interests and move into a place of empathy, compassion, and service to that which is greater than them. The purpose is to also increase the resiliency of a community, enabling it to adapt to a changing world and ensure its survival.

Tropman (1969) employed five factors to assess the "critical dimension of community structure." They include informal interaction (with neighbors), safety (having a good place to live), pro-urbanism (privacy, anonymity), neighboring preferences (preference for frequent interaction with neighbors), and localism (opinions and a desire to participate in neighborhood affairs).

Glynn's (1981) strongest predictors of an actual sense of community were (1) expected length of community residency, (2) satisfaction with the community, and (3) the number of neighbors one could identify by first name. There is a strong relationship between sense of community and the ability to function competently in the community. This factor is essential to contemporary rites of passage in so far as youth learn prosocial skills, achieve a sense of mastery in different environments, and are provided with opportunities, within the community, to demonstrate these masteries, make a contribution in the community, and be recognized and affirmed for these contributions as demonstration of their movement toward maturity and adulthood. This is aligned with the social development model of youth development (Hawkins and Weis 1985) and lends strength to the ability of youth and community development through rites of passage to serve as a unifying theory with multiple design opportunities that can be put into practice as a compelling story that strengthens a community's capacity to promote optimal youth and human development.

Any sufficiently advanced technology is indistinguishable from magic.
—Arthur C. Clarke

Riger, LeBailly, and Gordon (1981) suggest four types of community involvement: feelings of bondedness, extent of residential roots, use of local facilities, and degree of social interaction with neighbors.

There are elements in each of the above perspectives that can inform the creation of a "whole system" village-oriented rite of passage:

- Feelings of bondedness/connection/sense of membership, as a mature adult within family, community, spirit, ancestors/culture, and nature.
- Degree of social interactions with neighbors and others where there is mutual influence
- Use of local facilities and resources
- Sense of safety, privacy, and anonymity
- Ability to function competently in the community—(social development model, i.e. within and between several environments)
- Shared values
- Integration and fulfillment of needs
- Shared symbols of membership that have meaning.

In the reciprocity between individuals, family, community, spirit, ancestors, and nature, how are these elements present in rites of passage strategies? Should they be present, and if so, what are the existing conditions that limit their presence? Where do these conditions already exist?

Although these elements are related to the concept of a psychological sense of community, they are not fully present or at equal strength in the Huichol group, nor are they likely to all be fully present or at equal strength in other settings. There is an important theme that runs throughout each of the elements in the psychological sense of community. Members in a community have an actual physical presence together, where members influence one another and share a set of values and expectations for behavior that explicitly accepts the interdependency of their ongoing relationships.

Common symbols, shared values, and *cohesion* are elements that can be useful to inform new designs for contemporary community-oriented rites of passage.

Common symbols include myths, rituals, rites, dress, adornments, ceremonies, and holidays (Warner and Associates 1949). Groups use dress and language as boundaries. These are all within the domain of symbols, which have common meaning and connect members of a community. When common symbols are displayed and embraced within a community there is identification and a sense of safety and connection (Charon 2004). Think about when you enter a new place. One of the first things you look for is something familiar, usually a familiar face or symbol. Even a familiar face, someone who looks like you, is a symbol. "The symbol is to the social world what the cell is to the biotic world and the atom to the physical world. . . . The symbol is the beginning of the social world as we know it" (Nisbet and Perrin 1977, 47).

Shared values serve as one of the cornerstones to the element of shared emotional connection. People are attracted to activities, feel a greater sense of community, and feel closer to each other when they reflect and reaffirm their shared values. Cohesion is especially reinforcing if the activities offer participants a feeling of success and when they are emotionally impacting, such as a crisis or occasions such as baptisms, coming-of-age events, weddings, and funerals—rites of passage.

The transmission of values that inform and guide expectations for behavior is a central purpose of initiation. What are the shared values in a community that are attractive to a majority of youth and compel them to interact with and feel more connected to their community? How are these values agreed on and then manifested in designs for more powerful youth and community development? Youth are seeking a pathway to come of age. It is their conscious and unconscious drive to grow up well that can fuel their interest in authentic initiatory experiences that connects them to essential, primal knowledge that impacts the formation of their identity and strengthens their connection to their culture, community, nature, and a sense of a sentient sacred Earth.

Reciprocity: Informing and Guiding Youth and Community Development

Deepening a youth's connection to the place they call home, the culture and community within the natural world were central to traditional initiation. Coming of age required a context in which to manifest the acquisition of adult values, expressed in behaviors, that served the survival of their culture and community. Within the Huichol group, individuals pursued connections with and membership in a community that included nature and the spirit world. It should be no less important for contemporary youth to experience that sense of connection with nature and the spirit world, which could help them to transcend differences in culture and socioeconomic status. A spiritual connection in a secular sense is not religious, but is a recognition of one's relationship to and connection between all things. It is remembering and reconnecting with that ancient knowledge that we knew when in the womb but forgot (Blumenkrantz 2007, Blumenkrantz and Hong 2008).

> *Mitakuye oyasin.*
> *We are all related.*
> —Lakota saying

The French philosopher and Jesuit priest Pierre Teilhard de Chardin in his work *The Phenomenon of Man* (1955) wrote, "We are not human beings having a spiritual experience; we are spiritual beings having a human experience." A key purpose of a rite of passage experience is to open the door to this change in perspective. The door leads all children on a path through nature, enabling a change in perspective to become human *beings* rather than to continue functioning in the physical plain as human *doings*. They are designed to bring a child from a consciousness of "Me" to a consciousness of "We," where "We" includes nature and Spirit, that fosters a sense of deep connection with that which is greater than one's own self all within the unfolding story of the Universe.

Among the most common achievements that respond to members' collective personal needs is the connection to nature. Rollo May (1953) in *Man's Search for Himself* writes,

> People who have lost the sense of their identity as selves also tend to lose their sense of relatedness to nature. They lose not only their experience of organic connection with inanimate nature, such as trees and mountains, but they also lose some of their capacity to feel empathy for animate nature, that is animals. In psychotherapy, persons who feel empty are often sufficiently aware of what a vital response to nature might be to know what they are missing. They may remark, regretfully, that though others are moved by a sunset, they themselves are left relatively cold; and though others may find the ocean majestic and awesome, they themselves, standing on rocks at the seashore, don't feel much of anything.
>
> . . . When a person feels himself inwardly empty, as is the case with so many modern people, he experiences nature around him also as empty, dried up, dead. The two experiences of emptiness are two sides of the same state of impoverished relation to life. (68–9)

One cannot feel a sense of community, a sense of connection to a place, unless one feels safe. Safety, trusting that one's needs for emotional and physical security will be met, is a prerequisite for a sense of connection and membership in a community. Feeling safe is a critical issue in contemporary society, where so many children may not have experienced a safe and secure early environment that nurtures trust. An individual is likely to develop tendencies toward mistrust when they do not have early positive experiences with trust in ways that assure them that their basic needs will be met. This could manifest itself later in fear—fear that their basic needs for safety, love, nurturing, and affirmation will never be met. Fear opens a pathway for anger to emerge from not having the necessary nurturing and affirmation of self-worth. Anger can either be directed inward on one's self or outward into the community and beyond. Entry into adolescence, departure from primary school, and entrance into secondary school occur simultaneously and are extremely stressful and vulnerable times for children. This is especially compounded where schools are not perceived as safe places, either emotionally or physically. Feelings of fear and anger can be mediated if rites of passage are potent enough and occur in the place that youth call home, community.

> *If we do not initiate the young they will burn down the village to feel the heat.*
> —African Proverb

Engaging in the community rituals, overcoming ordeals and challenges that are present in rites of passage, strengthens resiliency and evokes youth's sense of competency and potency, which supports their sense of safety. Within the safe space of a community-oriented initiation and rite of passage an individual is more likely to take risks, open themselves up to new experiences, increase the opportunity for transformation, and strengthen their sense of belonging and identification with the practices of the community.

David Reisman (1950) may have said it best when he wrote, "American young people have no such single ritual to assure personal or tribal success. However, one can see a similarity in the tendency to create rituals of a sort in all spheres of life" (279). Rituals serve to help the individual feel safe and a part of the process of group living through shared experience.

The enactment of a ritual can be powerful and can support an individual's desire to fulfill their personal needs and increase community cohesion and commitment. A unity of purpose can be achieved when individuals experience personal rewards associated with the fulfillment of their needs within their community. Sharing an encounter with the divine can create and maintain a positive sense of togetherness. Consider the experience of those who went on the vision quest. They have given their lives to connect with Spirit, with nature, and the Universe in order to bring back a vision for the community. This creates a strong bond through their shared ordeal. Facing death, or experiencing a great ordeal has been likened to an encounter with the divine. Was there a time in your life where you might have been in extreme danger, perhaps faced death and were with other people? You are probably able to vividly recall the experience and especially the people you were with. Perhaps the relationships with these people have been strengthened, or in some way changed as a result of the shared experience? Just think of 9-11—September 11, 2001. If you are American, or closely related to America most of the time, one only has to say "9–11" to conjure up clear recollections of that time and precise memories of who you were with and what you were doing. Some have said it was America's national rite of passage, which precipitated a palatable difference in the way we felt and interacted. Reports from New York City accounted for an extraordinary change in taxi cab driver behavior, which became courteous and compassionate.

While members of the Huichol community have unique and wide-ranging needs fulfilled through their membership, they are collectively committed to fulfill their needs to connect with nature. This is a part of a community that is life affirming and nurturing to each individual. Although this may be the overarching need of the community, in general it does not preclude an individual from satisfying personal needs.

A significant element that impacts a sense of community within the structure of a rite of passage is the shared emotional connection. This is the shared encounter with an ordeal that has been linked to an encounter with the divine. While community members may share common values, it is the continuous immersion in nature, shared emotional experiences, and ritual processes that solidify the members' connection with each other and the Spirit world. McMillan and Chavis allude to this in the comment that "future research should focus on the causal factor leading to shared emotional connection, since it seems to be the definitive element of true community" (1986, 14). Again, think of 9-11.

Given that the main thrust of this work is the relationship between initiation and rites of passage to a sense of community, it might appear strange and inconsistent, perhaps even contradictory, that the story told of the vision quest in chapter 3 did not take place in a community that was localized geographically. That is, it did not happen in anyone's home community. The experience was certainly powerful and transformative. The experience of my Bar Mitzvah remembered, especially related to returning home, depicted actual roles and responsibilities of adulthood and the honor, humility, pride and connections deeply felt. I was affirmed for being an adult within the religious community and required to fulfill adult responsibilities i.e. sitting shiva as part of a minyan and reciting Kaddish—the prayer of mourning. My stature and status was changed. I was an adult member of my community. In comparison, upon returning to my home community following the Huichol group, I experienced a sense of disconnection, disorientation, alienation, and depression. It is an emotion that many experienced upon leaving the group and illustrates the challenge of maintaining a consciousness of transcendence that strengthens one's sense of balance and connection once back in one's home community. These emotions are also frequently felt by youth who return from similar rite of passage experiences outside of their culture and community. This was brought home in a conversation with the Harvard psychologist and author of *Real Boys*, William Pollack:

> "David, you and I may be one of only a few people who are in the community and have to clean up the mess made when these youth come back from these rite of passage programs. Indeed, they do go through a powerful experience where transcendence and transformation frequently occur. Those undergoing a shared experience affirm, witness, and acknowledge the individual's transformation.
>
> "However, their parents, peers, and other people in their lives have no idea what they've been through. They do not understand, nor do they affirm or acknowledge the experience to have been transcendent and transformative. There is no change in their status or opportunity for them to demonstrate their new skills and engage in opportunities to live into their new role as emerging adults.
>
> "Some youth may be able to adapt and manage the resulting frustration and disappointment and integrate their transformative experience into a healthy identity. Others however experience disappointment, frustration, anger, and depression that leads to alienation and a disintegration of the vision of their identity unveiled during the experience. This leads to role confusion, and the seeds for continued challenges in their psychological development and overall life are planted."
>
> —Personal communication, June 20 2013,
> West Roxbury, Massachusetts

Alone, an individual may find it challenging, although not impossible, to reproduce the sunrise ritual, described in the story, in ways that bring the energy and spirit of nature and community into his or her life. Morning rituals within a tradition that forges a connection between others in the community, nature, and all our relations set the stage for acting in ways that fulfill our full potential as human beings. What are the morning rituals that many in western culture engage in to prepare us to fulfill our full human potential? How many awaken to the morning with a meal, drinking coffee to stimulate heightened awareness and actions on the way to human doings? I once read a sign that said, "Drink coffee. Do more stupid stuff faster." And, so it goes.

My purpose in this chapter was to establish particular criteria for understanding the relationship between rites of passage and a psychological sense of community. The chapter offered elements that can be used as design principles—a road map— to further explore their integration into viable community rite of passage practices. Establishing criteria for these concepts is intended to help make a discussion of these complex human phenomena possible. We are still confronted with the limitations of language, as Thomas Kelting (1995) notes: "We say we have 'explained' something when we have found and described the root phenomena from which it springs. But what has been gained? Have we not just deferred questioning to another domain?" (28).

If you have no psychological connection with a rite of passage—if it lies outside your paradigm, your experience or your way of looking at the world—you may consider this to be an interesting but irrelevant exercise. Or, if you have never considered several critical transition stages in life to be an integral part of the initiatory process, then much of this may be meaningless. It may be as foreign a concept as death. Rites of passage as well as a sense of community remain an integral and central part of life. When individuals can meet their own needs for affirmation, love, connection, and balance on the path for meaning, identity, and purpose in life, they can serve their culture and community, ensuring their survival.

I invite you to suspend disbelief and reflect on the story again. Consider the definitions of rites of passage and sense of community. Everyone is always somewhere in the process of initiation (Somé 1995). Reflect on what place in the initiatory process you may now find yourself. Are you just beginning, separating from, in the middle of, or at the end of a particular stage of your life? Have you ever been cast into the initiatory process reflected in a particular ordeal in your life? How might this be related to a sense of community? Do you remember where you were and whom you were with on September 11, 2001? Have you thought about your sense of belonging and identification with a group or community? How does your association within this community support the fulfillment of your needs while you help to fulfill the needs of others?

Again, I invite you to reconsider the story in light of the constructs that built the definitions of rites of passage and a psychological sense of community. I urge you to consider events in your own life that could reflect elements of a rite of passage and personalize a psychological sense of community.

I am reminded at this point of the old philosophical question typically explored in one's early college years: If a tree falls in the forest and no one is there to hear it, does it make a sound? Two similar questions are worth considering related to rites of passage and community: If a youth has a transformative experience on the passage to adulthood and no one is there to witness it and hear the story, is the youth able to really come of age? What is the sound of youth coming of age when no one is there to hear it? Weeping?

> There was a child went forth every day;
> And the first object he look'd upon, that object he became;
> And that object became part of him for the day, or a certain part of the day,
> or for many years, or stretching cycles of years.
>
> —Walt Whitman

6

On Rites of Passage

Symbols of Initiation

Comparison of rites from all over the world suggests that these initiation rites themselves possess an archetypal structure, for the same underlying patterns and procedures are universally apparent.
—Anthony Stevens

Describing and explaining human experiences like love, loneliness, thirst, and hunger always seem to fall short. For example, how do you explain to someone what an orange tastes like? Even more challenging is attempting to make generalizations from examining a few experiences and applying them to all future experiences. I knew when I began this work that I faced a formidable challenge. That is fitting. Entering into initiation is a formidable challenge, which is supposed to be in service of the greater good.

I began by taking the well-traveled path of van Gennep's (1960) tripartite structure. This seemed at the time to be a solid foundation for considering a structure for defining and understanding rites of passage. Some may find it inadequate in light of more recent literature on myth, including Joseph Campbell's contributions of the "hero's journey" and many other interpretations of initiation and rites of passage. However, van Gennep's structure can be a useful lens and point of reference to consider whether contemporary variations still uphold the original theme. In this schema there are distinct, albeit interrelated, structures of separation, transition, and reincorporation. van Gennep suggests that while a complete schema of rites of passage includes these three components, they may be more or less developed depending on the nature of the event and culture in which they take place. For example, rites of separation may be prominent in funeral ceremonies, rites of incorporation may be central to marriages, and transition rites may play an important part in pregnancy, betrothal, and initiation (van Gennep 1960). These rites of separation, liminal rites (transition), and postliminal rites (incorporation) are not always equally featured in each transitional phase nor attended to in ceremony or ritual. Those features that figure prominently in each phase are purposely crafted to meet both the transitional needs of the individual and the social and cultural needs of the community. Initiation is always impacted by context, which includes culture, place, ancestors, and Spirit.

van Gennep's paradigm presents an orientation, based on observation, to the human phenomenon of rites of passage. Although practically speaking it is somewhat imprecise for modern-day classifications, it still offers a valuable foundation. Least attended to in van Gennep's classification and documentation of observations is what Solon Kimball pointed out: inherent in the architectural structure is the concept of reciprocity and van Gennep's "basic thesis has direct relevance for theories of change," (Kimball, 1960 p. x). Unlike many other observations and theories related to initiation and rites of passage, van Gennep's was strongly anchored to context.

In general, the strength of a paradigm is related to its ability to uncover an element of *truth* in the world and to create a structure to explain it. A paradigm has a group of adherents in the scientific community who follow certain rules and are guided by the paradigm to the investigation of certain problems associated with that truth (Kuhn 1962). While this definition may hold true for the physical sciences, such as physics and chemistry, it is questionable whether such models can exist in the social sciences. Furthermore, it is unclear that problems that are *selected* in the social sciences are solvable in the same way that problems in the physical sciences are perceived to be solvable. This became clear in my review of the ethnographies describing rites of passage of cultures around the world, detailed in a later chapter.

Thus far we have not established a paradigm in the area of human development and mental health that sets forth rules to be followed that can effect personal change and eliminate psychological symptoms such as depression, for example. Nor have we developed a paradigm that organizes the principles of community change into established practices that when implemented guarantee specific desired outcomes. We seem to have a greater ability to understand conditions that precipitate individual symptoms and dysfunction and community problems than we do in linking the two.

The psychological sense of community may best be described as something you know you have when you have it and something you know you don't have when you don't. The same thing may be said about rites of passage, as we have not yet formulated well-crafted theories of personal change and transformation, which are at the heart of rites of passage. Jay Halley (1995) said:

> The field [of psychotherapy] has a problem. It is very good on why people do what they do, what's wrong with people and how to classify them and so on. If you ask someone about a case they can tell you at some length probably what caused the problem. What's missing is a theory of change, that's harder. There are very few theories of change and that is the whole point of psychotherapy, to help people to change.

While this highlights the limitations of imprecise theory, it should not alter our course of exploration. Indeed, it points toward the utility of exploring an important relationship between the principles and practices of initiation and their relationship to individual and community change. If initiation and rites of passage were our species' organic method for precipitating and managing individual and community change, then how can the essential elements in initiation inform and guide contemporary efforts to precipitate and manage change?

Focusing on the use of paradigms in the social sciences introduces another set of complex issues. Nevertheless, a paradigm shift could be useful if we uncover essential elements in initiation and rites of passage that can help us understand and manage the phenomenon of human behavior particular to an individual's period of transition. It could have implications for practice in how we view change related to individuals and large and small systems such as family, groups, organizations, and community.

Although some may challenge the preciseness of van Gennep's tripartite structure (see, for example, Lincoln 1981) his chief contribution of identifying a structure for considering rites of passage is useful. In later chapters we explore further several different approaches to rites of passage and, more important, set forth a structure for considering the development and ongoing adaptation of a new field of youth and community development through rites of passage.

A rite of passage is not something done alone. The Cartesian notion "I think, therefore I am" is thus incompatible with rites of passage. Hillman's (1992) conception of the individual, which places the community in the psyche of the individual would be more fitting. "I would rather define self as the *interiorization of community*. And, if you make that little move, then you're going to feel very different about things. If the self were defined as the interiorization of community, then the boundaries between me and another would be much less sure. I would be with myself when I'm with others. I would not be with myself when I'm walking alone or meditating or in my room imagining or working on my dreams. In fact, I would be estranged from myself," (Hillman p. 40). One cannot be transformed without a context and connection with the outside world. Personal and individual transformations may be considered possible, but they lie outside of the world of rites of passage. No one can change their status within a community unless the community recognizes that their status has changed. If van Gennep's structure is deficient at all it is because his observations were made at a time and in a place where individuals were inextricably tied to culture, ancestors, spirit, community, place in nature, and the Universe. One would not consider having a rite of passage outside of a community or village and devoid of cultural symbolism and spiritual involvement. If it takes a whole village to raise a child then it could be suggested that it takes a whole community to recognize an adult.

It is for the reasons stated above that our definition of rites of passage includes van Gennep's tripartite structure and the participation of the community. The definition used in our analysis can now be restated:

> The degree to which a series of activities are a rite of passage is directly proportional to a community's acceptance and participation in the activities and youth's perception and belief in the activities as fulfilling their conscious and unconscious needs for transformative experiences. That is, a modern-day rite of passage is achieved when parents (and/or their surrogates) and the community create and participate in experiences, which are perceived to be transformative by youth and in fact offer them increased status within the community and facilitate their healthy transition through adolescence. Equally important, the celebration of a rite of passage is renewing for the entire community. A youth's public expression of and commitment to a community's values and beliefs reinforces expectations for behaviors for the entire community. A child's coming of age presents an opportunity for the whole community to examine, adapt and recommit themselves to their social and cultural heritage. (Blumenkrantz 1996, 21).

In this light we say, "It takes a whole child to raise a village." That is, when villages focus on raising their children together through rites of passage there will be a strengthening of connections between people and a process that increases resiliency and adaptation for their survival.

Further Analysis of the Vision Quest

The traditional vision quest was "vital to the survival and well-being of both the individual and the extended family" (Cruden 1996, 20), helping to guide a youth on a path to their future while also bringing lessons to their people that helped them adapt for their survival. It was an intergenerational exchange of wisdom, reciprocity. Schlegel and Barry (1991) suggest that initiation practices in general increase social solidarity within the community and especially among the individuals who participate in the initiatory events together. "Through initiation, our tribe survives" is a belief among many indigenous people, including the Navaho and Apache. Ritual in general is "necessary for human social survival on the planet" (Grimes 2006, 142). Ritual is the only way certain kinds of meaning can be expressed and conveyed, especially related to transmitting essential values that inform meaning and guide expectations for behavior (Rappaport 1979).

The analysis continues through the filter of ritual and rites of passage unfolding in a process of youth and community development. The first stage of the tripartite structure of a rite of passage is separation. The narrative of the story in chapter 3 "The First Story—My Creation Myth" does not include many details about preparing for the vision quest. We believe that the "journey begins when you think about going." It is first in the mind of an individual that the process of separation begins. In other words, you start the journey when you make the decision to go. Slowly you prepare yourself through prayer and contemplation, continually moving out of your regular reality, shedding the layers of one's self. About a month before the vision quest I began to fast and eat fruit, cleansing and purifying my body, preparing it for the journey out of the profane and into the sacred. I cannot say with certainty, but the onset of traditional initiation was probably unknown to the initiate. They did not have time to prepare, although they undoubtedly were aware of their impending initiation through stories filtered down over years. Perhaps altered activities in the village were signals that something was about to happen. In any case what was about to happen marked a great change for the individual, their family, and the entire village.

This represents a change in paradigm. It is a critical element in an architectural framework for youth and community development through rites of passage. A paradigm shift is a complete revolution in the way you think and act. It transforms and changes a particular view or behavior in any given situation. You begin to mentally prepare for the separation by reflecting on what values and ethics are necessary to achieve the desired outcome through the ritual process. The outcome is in part the strengthening of relationships between you, community, ancestors, Spirit, your place in the natural world, and the Universe. Rituals are the methods, the design strategies or programs that can effect change in this way. Rituals enlist allies of spirit, programs enlist allies of science. This is amplified in another one of the essential elements or principles—that relationships are key to any successful outcome and not program practice. It requires a paradigm shift that moves away from the belief in "evidence-based programs" as centrally important and into the process of developing and strengthening relationships. These relationships not only are with the people in the "village" but also extend to "natural relationships" with all things in a person's world.

Rituals

As we move forward in extracting the core elements in rites of passage, several other characteristics emerge. A series of interrelated elements appear to represent contemporary rites of passage design strategies that are featured in programs. They are oriented to the liminal, or second stage.

These elements are *ordeal*, where some kind of challenge exists (we say that adversity introduces us to ourselves), and *silence*, or time alone for reflection. Silence nurtures a child's inner dialogue that matures to help them narrate their reality in ways that deepen meaning in life. *Stories* that include *myths* or *legends*, which in the vision quest narrated in chapter 3 was the entire cosmology within the Huichol traditions. In other situations one's culture and the community's history, symbols, and traditions are essential parts of the story that frame the rites of passage experience. Perhaps most significant is the potency that rites of passage have in contemporary culture when they are the overarching story within a community for raising their children. Everyone is on "the same page"—has a common language and expectations. Children know that there is a pathway for helping them navigate the journey to adulthood. Parents know that their roles will change and can expect elders and mentors within the community to become present as guides in support of their children's emerging adulthood.

It bears repeating that strengthening one's connection with nature is a central element in rites of passage and an important aspect of the Huichol vision quest. It is one of the primary purposes of initiation and is illustrated in the vision quest story. Ritual methods are used to energize and intensify the experience, helping to achieve maximum benefit for the individual and community.

When you feel the love of Mother Earth for an instance it will be sufficient for your entire life.

The Challenge of Separation

We return to the central questions: Initiation into what? By whom? and For what purpose? These questions invite a story to emerge that is in service of one's culture and community's survival.

A state of separation is a necessary stage in contemporary rites of passage. Traveling from my home in Connecticut, through several airports, on large and small aircraft, and finally in a van to the remote wilderness area amplified the physical separation. A number of events contributed to both the inner, spiritual, and outer (physical) separation. The degree of anticipation and anxiety that preceded the physical separation from the community cannot be overstated. During the months before the event I was periodically overcome with anxiety and dread as well as moments of eager anticipation. On several occasions I remember feeling more anxiety then I can ever remember. Not one day passed that I did not think about the impending vision quest with varying degrees of emotions ranging from fear to joyous excitement. Although I doubt whether any accounts exist, I imagine that early initiates understood the significance of their impending experience and had a wide range of emotions, which may even have included eager anticipation and fear, that preceded their actual initiation rites. I could not imagine that one would have a matter-of-fact attitude about an impending initiation. And that is the way it should be. An important qualification needs to be addressed. Traditional initiations occur once in an individual's life. Although the full process lasted for some time, the intense initiatory event was shorter. This was not my first vision quest. I do not recall the heightened sense of anxiety or dread in anticipation of my first (prior) vision quest.

One of the important features highlighted in the story was the completeness of the setting to evoke both the physical and spiritual separation. Besides the distance traveled to reach the location, the setting in a remote wilderness location was full of the potential to facilitate a transformation. The journey from suburban America to a tent in a remote wilderness area was the platform to move into the sacred space of the ceremony and ritual. The ritualized structure full of symbolism contained within the departure ceremony amplified the experience. Receiving strength, *Kupuri*, from the Shaman; being purified; leaving the world of the mundane behind and opening one's self up for the possibilities that exist in the universe; and joining with the Spirit world were empowering. Regardless of the feelings of apprehension I may have felt before that day of departure, I felt supremely ready to leave my life and enter the world of the sacred, to go on my vision quest to find my life.

My wife and family were all aware and assisted in my preparation. They understood and supported the quest as not just a remote individual experience but one that would serve to enrich and guide our family. On several occasions my young son accompanied me to the Huichol group and participated in ceremony and life in the "village."

The place was not chosen for me, but rather, I had to be *guided* to my place. This was not easy, and it contributed to the rigor of the experience. It also forced me to focus on the connection between the internal and external world, which came together and impacted the selection of a place. The place had to feel right. It had to be ritually cleansed and prepared to protect me. Once selected, the place had to be arranged in a prescribed ritual manner consistent with the tradition in order to open a pathway to the Spirit world and to support a transformative experience. Mastery of these protocols was essential for survival. This is no small point. Many programmed rite of passage experiences designate specific vision quest sites, usually within sight of a "buddy" or a guide who checks in. Finding one's place within the protocol of a traditional vision quest begins the process of releasing the conscious mind and entering into deeper connection with the natural world. You literally had to let go of all your typical ways of perceiving and open yourself to the "call of your place." It is both terrifying and exhilarating. As you venture out to find your vision quest place you are pitched out of your normal reality and reduced to a most primal state. You are on the path to reconnect with your authentic human being.

A person's complete separation from the familiar and the mundane sets the foundation for entry into the liminal experience. It comprises both symbolic and physical forms that signify the detachment of the individual from his or her past points of reference (Turner 1967, Foster and Little 1987). This is a prerequisite for the most significant phase of van Gennep's schema, the liminal or *betwixt and between* phase (Sullwold 1987). In this phase the person is in a period of ambiguity. They are not oriented in time or space and have no point of reference from their past or future. Turner's comments on this state are most fitting in his description of the vision quest for Plains Indians:

> Among many Plains Indians, boys on their lonely Vision Quest inflicted ordeals and tests on themselves that amounted to tortures. These again were not basically self-tortures inflicted by a masochistic temperament but due to obedience to the authority of tradition in the liminal situation—a type of situation in which there is no room for secular compromise, evasion, manipulation, casuistry, and maneuver in the field of custom, rule and norm. (100)

Liminality is a state of abandonment of the self and prepares an opening for the actions of the sacred to shape and mold the initiate. Their transformational energies (liminality) are for the individual and the community. "They provide social cohesion and personal consolation" (Grimes 2006, 12). Bruno Bettelheim (1954) described one facet of this in the area of sex distinctions within societies dominantly structured by kinship institutions. These societies symbolically assigned the initiates either genderless or bisexual roles, which were regarded as a kind of human *prima materia* as undifferentiated raw material. This description offers further evidence that the separation is directed toward opening the possibilities for transformation to occur. They are, in effect, setting the stage for the event to begin within the heart of the experience, the liminal state. The "opening" achieved in the liminal state makes accessible ancient wisdom and unveils to us who we are in relationship to this sacred knowledge guiding our connection to an identity in harmony, balance, and connection with nature and the Universe. Some would say it is accessing the place of the "soul."

The liminal state is present in a most pristine form during the vision quest. Above all, there is a focus on the shedding of self to become open to the spirit world. Eliade (1967) suggested that at the heart of initiation, more than anything else was the "revelation of the sacred." Initiation for early society was to place one's self physically at the threshold of the other world to achieve a spiritual awakening and to be introduced to the spiritual values of the culture. "Through initiation, the candidate passes beyond the natural mode—the mode of the child—and gains access to the cultural mode: that is, he is introduced to spiritual values" (Eliade 1967, p. 287). This is the heart of initiation and the place where essential knowledge is transmitted to the initiate.

Seclusion, isolation, altering the diet, and continuous spiritual practices in a setting specially designed within the traditional wisdom of a vision quest helped to achieve access to the spiritual world. The vision quest presented an abundance of opportunity for entering into the *Nierika*. This is the doorway to the other world in the Huichol tradition. It is a threshold place where one can become transformed by a direct encounter with Spirit. In many instances Spirit may teach through metaphor and symbolism. Lessons can be brought by spiders and fire, by extraordinary means, all requiring discipline and attention to focus on what you cannot see and listen for what at first you cannot hear. It is the enactment of "other ways of knowing." I was completely and totally divested of my regular thoughts, habits, and behaviors as I was thrust into contemplating the universe and my relationship with it. Turner (1969) characterized the state of liminality as one of *reflection*, which is another one of the essential elements in initiation. This was also illustrated in the details of the first vision quest and how our *prayers help to show our reflections to the Gods.*

For five days and five nights Tate Wari sang the songs from the creation, and the Gods would see their reflections from their hearts and these reflections would come back as part of their shields, the covering that they wore on their front and back. The shields were the dreams of the deer told to the Shaman. And Tate Wari saw his reflection in the fire. He looked into himself, and saw the circle of stones and the way it was to be for the Gods to be in physical forms. They go out on their vision quest so that they can remember the knowledge of who they are and how they are to live on the earth.

Bringing Lessons Home to the Place of the Heart

The third state that consummates the initiatory event, that of incorporation or aggregation, brings together the experience of the individual and incorporates it within both the personal and the collective knowledge of the group. Although the personal manifestation of the experience continues for a considerable time, the initial return to the community is quite special. The presentation of salt to the fire and a shared meal are several of the traditional symbols of incorporation. An essential element of initiation is when the community participates in the celebration of the participant's return. This is absent from most contemporary rites of passage programs where the individual does not return into their own community. There is reciprocity in the relationship. The people who go out on the vision quest thank those who remained behind and maintained a vigil and prayer, while the community thanks the people for giving their life for them and bringing back teaching visions for the benefit of the community. For those who went out on vision quest there is an increased status and regard from the group in the social context. Personally, an elevation of sense of self, mastery, and sense of accomplishment is pervasive and is incorporated into your life.

Visions and dreams presented symbols of the structure and form of traditional rites of passage. The events following my Bar Mitzvah reflected the stage of incorporation. The community called on me, as an adult member, to accept responsibility for and participate in the traditions.

Accompanied by the rabbi and cantor, the elders and I paraded the Torahs around the synagogue as the people rejoiced. For the first time I realized that I am one among them. I was carrying the Torah, which held the stories, traditions, and laws of the Jewish people. They had come to me. For the first time I walked among the rejoicing congregation as an adult in the minyan of my people. I felt as though they were rejoicing for me as they came forward, touching the Torah with their prayer books and tallis. They rejoiced in my becoming a Bar Mitzvah and they rejoiced as a community, with the satisfaction that the tribe of my ancestors, Abraham, Isaac, and Jacob, and all that is sacred and special in Judaism—will survive and continue.

I am someone among them. I have an identity that is connected to the community. This was not only community in the temporal sense of the present but community within the thousands of year's history of my ancestors. I am someone because of what I do in and for the community, and the community exists and is sustained because of my place in it. It is a reciprocal relationship anchored in and amplified through the ceremonies and rituals. I have an obligation to the larger community. An obligation to be of service to the larger community is an essential element in rites of passage. It was reflected in the vision of becoming a Bar Mitzvah and unfolded with the obligation as a Jewish adult to be part of a minyan and sit shiva. I had to fulfill my responsibilities, even if it meant giving up a beautiful day, sitting in a suit, and participating in the minyan, enacting the shiva ritual, enabling the ritual of mourning to occur within the tradition, as it has done for generations. I had to give up previously held attitudes and beliefs, just wanting to have fun all the time, and change my appearance to fulfill my obligations to the community. What teenager wants to sit around on a beautiful day in mourning with a group of adults—and wear a suit to boot?

The images and visions received on this vision quest journey compelled me to tell the story. The primary reason it was selected for analysis is that the images revealed so much material about the nature of rites of passage. It was a rite of passage within the Huichol tradition of a vision quest and revealed through symbols and patterns the essential elements of the initiatory experience that appear to be present within all rites of passage. The recurrent dream/vision in the cave presented a connection with the creation myth of initiation rites. This was confirmed to be part of the story of the vision quest within the cosmology of the Huichol Indians. The story within the vision of the Huichol children going out on vision quest and bringing spirituality back to their village again illustrated essential elements in reciprocity between the individual, culture and community in ways that serve survival. The children's skill in making the God's Eye's - *Ojos de Dios* then instructing the village in their placement was central to the renewal of spirituality within the village. What lessons might we learn and apply today within our world so full of people in need of remembering their connection to each other and the natural world?

While I received much more information, this was the only part I felt I could share. The images of my Bar Mitzvah portrayed another traditional approach to initiation. It also provided an opportunity to illustrate the role that community plays in the transformative experience. I was fully initiated into the religion, the Story, and the traditions of my ancestors as witnessed by the congregation. This conveyed to me a number of rights and responsibilities and set forth certain expectations for my behavior in front of my peers, other children and youth, and the larger community of adults. I not only had a place in the adult world, as evidenced by carrying the Torah during the holiday of Simchat Torah, but also had responsibilities illustrated by my role as a member of a minyan carrying out the obligations of community mourning.

The connection with community is critical and was acknowledged in the roles that I was able to fulfill immediately following the Bar Mitzvah. These roles affirmed my coming of age to the community and me. Just as my return from the vision quest was celebrated and witnessed by the group, the events that followed my Bar Mitzvah also solidified my change in status within the Jewish culture and community. Unless there are opportunities for youth to experience a real increase in status and responsibility, a rite of passage remains just a personal exercise. Increase in status and responsibility affirmed and expected by the community are two other essential elements. It is why initiation and rites of passage have always been conducted within a community.

Unless you are welcomed back to the village and honored for completing an ordeal you become sick. The transformation can only be complete when the initiates return home and are welcomed back into their community. The work of initiation is individual, while responsibility for its transformative potential belongs to the community.

7

Ritual Form

Design Elements

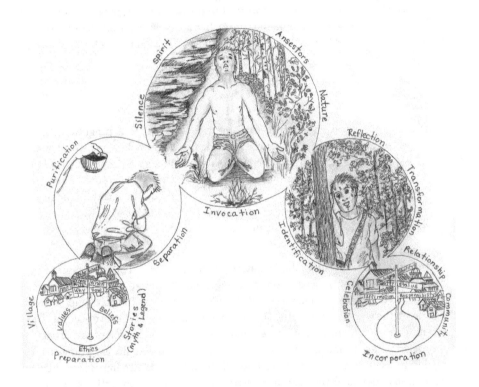

"*The human soul can always use a new tradition. Sometimes we require them.*"

—Pat Conroy

What is of particular importance in the entire initiatory event is the pervasiveness of the sacred rather than the secular. One leaves the physical territory in which one carries out one's life—the mundane world—and transitions into the world of the sacred. The connection of the individual within a community into the sacred world, the world of Nature and Spirit, is central. This is the place where wisdom resides, where lessons are learned, where visions emerge to guide an individual's life and are in service to the greater good of the community and nature.

The conditions that foster entry into this dimension of nature and spirit are frequently present in the "liminal" stage of rites of passage and are featured in many contemporary programs called rites of passage. It begins with rituals that help to create the conditions and container in which the transcendent experience can emerge and be held. It prepares the individual to enlist allies of spirit on their journey of transcendence and transformation. Let us explore the ritual form a bit further.

Rituals

Programs in education or youth work are a type of ritual. A program is performed in the same way, each time, intended to achieve some expected outcome. Rituals are similar: they are our ancient methods for deepening a sense of connection with and meaning in the world. Contemporary programs engage allies of science, while rituals engage allies of spirit. That is, scientific theories guide the formation and application of programs, while "other ways of knowing" inform rituals that relate to all things in the seen and unseen world.

The ritual form, evident in similar patterns throughout cultures, offers design strategies to foster authentic separation from the secular/material world and a potential for enhanced access to "liminality" and the domain of Spirit. In their simplest form, rituals are the way we transact the business of our daily lives. When we wake up every morning we usually engage in routine behaviors. This can be thought of as a ritual that is enacted to help us move from sleep to being awake. It makes life easy, almost automatic. This is one way of looking at ritual behavior. Ritual is also important in that it helps us to understand and deepen our sense of meaning and connection to all of life.

It is still an open question whether seeking and creating rituals is biologically ingrained in our brains and whether we are hardwired for ritual. Dr. Andrew Newberg, a pioneer in the field of neurotheology and Director of Research at the Myrna Brind Center for Integrative Medicine in Philadelphia, found that people engaged in spiritual practices and mytical experiences display unique brain functions. "When we looked at [subjects'] brain scans, instead of the frontal lobes going up, the frontal lobes actually went down [in blood flow]. Which makes sense in the context of what they are describing is happening to them," Newberg explains. "They don't feel that they're purposely making it [happen]. They feel that they are being basically overcome by the experience" (cited in Erickson 2012). Where ritual does not exist, we create it. We seek ritualized behavior as a way to craft and deepen meaning and emotional connection with the world. Rituals, in part, are what make

us human beings. They are the vehicle that can move us to a transcendent state—
and even to ecstasy.

What follows is a generic five-part structure in which a ritual process sometimes
flows, depending on the culture, context, and desired outcomes. I have used excerpts
from the vision quest story to illustrate each stage.

1. *Separation.* To be removed from one's regular world and placed in a position to
   experience things in new and different ways. One cannot discover new oceans
   unless one has the courage to lose sight of the shore.

   *We go out into the wilderness to seek a vision for our lives. To let the connection with
   the physical world and Spirits infuse with our soul. To become human again. We cast off the
   trappings of technology and the material world and become one with our natural selves—
   inseparable from the Spirit and the Universe. Within each of us is buried an indigenous
   heart. A heart knowledgeable of and connected to the natural world.*

2. *Purification.* Serves to help one become prepared to enter the new world. Sometimes
   considered to be a cleansing or washing away of the mundane and secular world, it
   prepares one to enter a different world, the world of the sacred.

   *It is just before sunrise. A mist hangs onto the morning, shrouding the village in a blan-
   ket of silent gray dawn. Clothed in ceremonial attire, we take our Huichol bags up to the
   ceremonial fire.*
   *The Shaman smudges me with kopal giving Kupuri, life force, and strength, as I prepare
   to follow in the tradition of the ancestors and go on vision quest. A new strength fills me;
   I am purified and prepared to meet my destiny.*

3. *Invocation.* Brings into the phenomenon a spiritual or quality of other-worldliness.
   There is an aspect of connectedness with a higher power, ecstasy, and the feelings
   of unity with the community. This could be considered part of the technique to
   achieve a liminal state. Some methods for achieving this include burning incense
   or taking in some kind of substance.

   We begin to shed our selves, leaving our past as we pray and make an offering to the fire.
   *A brightly colored cloth surrounded by flowers is set out before the Shaman's chair on
   which we place our prayer arrows for them to be blessed. We put our prayers, the seeds for
   change, into the arrows, as the ancestors have done for thousands of years. Now we are connected to them and the Gods through our prayers. The Mara Akame—Shaman—consecrates
   the arrows, dedicating them for their journey to the Spirit world, helping to bring forth our
   prayers. Now it is up to the Gods.*

4. *Identification.* In a transcendent state we connect with the message of the entity
   being invoked. In the spiritual sense one feels a deep sense of connection with
   God or Spirit. We begin to fully enter the initiatory experience and are *"pitched
   outside of ourselves"* (Campbell 1988, p. 84) and identify with something beyond
   our own ego. We may begin to know something more fully.

The departure begins. I solemnly lift my Huichol bag onto my shoulder, uncertain whether I will return, ready to cast my destiny to Spirit, ready to die in order to live more fully with a good heart. I avoid making eye contact with anyone or saying good-bye, fearful that my purified spirit will be diminished. I head out to the trail leading into one million acres of remote wilderness area of the Cranberry Wilderness Preserve.

5. *Transformation.* A change occurs. One is no longer fully in the same place they were when they entered the experience (psychologically, behaviorally, spiritually, etc.). The seeds of future growth are planted. One moves into another phase of life/development. It is similar to the stage of reincorporation in rites of passage in that one tries to integrate new knowledge and information into one's life. One can no longer be in the world in the way they were before.

After the morning ceremony we eat and then return to the fire to tell our stories. Each of us offers a tale with varying amounts of detail. Some offer emotional renderings of their journey complete with descriptions of extraordinary visions and experiences. All is taken in, like the water that brought us back to life hours earlier. We are connected in the physical plane by the encounter shared, the stories told, and the ritualization of the experience, wrapped collectively in our natural human identities. We bask in the security and comfort of our basic human fraternity of hunger, thirst, cold, exhaustion, and loneliness.

Our experiences are discussed; the Shaman offers some interpretations of the mysteries of the visions. But essentially we are encouraged to consider them during the unfolding of the rest of our lives. It is said that if you feel the love of Mother Earth for just one moment, it can fill you with love for a lifetime. The journey continues . . .

The ritual form aids our journey into the unknown in ways that help us to know ourselves more fully within the context of nature and the Universe. It creates a more potent way to be meaningfully connected with all of one's natural relationships. Rites of passage are enacted in the form of ritual. This is markedly different from the enactment of programs, which predominate secular life in education and youth development.

> "The human soul can always use a new tradition. Sometimes we require them."
>
> Pat Conroy

8

Which Write, Wright, Rite Is Right?

Knowing Your Rites from Your Rights

It's Reciprocity

Aristotle maintains that it is not necessary for the initiated to learn anything, but to receive impressions and to be put in a certain frame of mind by becoming worthy candidates.

—Groissant, 1932

Ritual is central to work in rites of passage. The preceding chapter introduced the topic and offered a generic framework for ritual to emerge in practice. This chapter explores ritual in greater depth. It offers a more thorough treatment of its history and invites consideration for its integration into contemporary use. At the end I also address the sensitive issue of the appropriation of cultural traditions and practices. Ritual has been considered a universal feature of our human existence (Alexander, Giesen, and Mast 2006). It is a distinguishing feature of our social interaction and "just as one cannot envision a society without language or exchange, one would be equally hard-pressed to imagine a society without ritual" (Carrico 2014).

The initiation of youth and subsequent public rites of passage appear to be primarily oriented to the individual, as expressed in more and more programs that offer this service. This is especially noticeable within the European/western practice, which gives preference to the individual. Other orientations and cultures place the collectivity of the group or village as the central most important entity of our species. This is an ongoing debate among evolutionary biologists. One faction believes that the individual is the single most important unit in our species. The other faction believes that the community is the single most important unit in our species. The reality, revealed in our collective human story, shows that the primary purpose of rites of passage was to ensure the survival of the community and this depends on the righteous and healthy way a community initiates their children. Providing prosocial, culturally relevant, village-oriented initiation for children increases the likelihood that they will in turn be of service to others and ensure the survival of their culture and community. It is not one or the other. It is reciprocity.

The position of the famed evolutionary biologist E. O. Wilson (1978) has been that *Homo sapiens* are predisposed through genetic wiring to congregate in groups of ten to one hundred adults, never just two. This feature of all primates is purposeful and directed toward the survival and continuation of the species. The human infant has a long period of dependency and requires a communal environment to learn society's traditions. Learning to get along with members of a community is an early primary task of the species and relies heavily on the strength of the bonds of community for survival. The initiation process is one of the most significant "educational experiences" the individual undergoes. This is done in groups for the purpose of binding the individual to his/her age group and connecting them with the traditions of the culture (Block 1974; Grimes 2006).

Of course, I am not an evolutionary biologist. During the preparation of this work I met with both anthropologists and community psychologists. Among the most hotly debated issues was which filter or lens should be used to look at the topic of rites of passage and the psychological sense of community. Would I look through the rites of passage lens of an anthropologist to examine and explain the sense of community, or through the sense of community lens of a community psychologist to consider rites of passage? I chose not to choose.

The struggle between academic disciplines was at hand. It illustrates the "silo" and the mechanistic, reductionist tendencies that can limit real knowing. Reconciliation of this issue will not happen anytime soon. If pressed to choose which chicken came before which egg (i.e., rites of passage or the psychological sense of community) I would have to pick neither. One of the chief propositions of this work is that you cannot have a deep sense of community without individuals engaged in ritual and you cannot have meaningful and productive rituals without a sense of community. It is reciprocity, designed by nature to be in symmetry, where one begets the other in a loving balanced dance propitious to the future of a society. Nature makes no distinctions within this particular orientation to levels of hierarchy and timing.

The Roots of Ritual

The first rituals laid a pathway toward art and religion (Taylor 1996). They arose out of an awareness of repetition in nature – the regular rhythm of the rotating earth moving from day to night; sun and moon; winter, spring, summer, and fall appearing with consistent regularity; the appearance and disappearance of the migrating animals; the fruit on trees; and wild foods. All life was in a rhythm that informed the emergence of ritual. Even the regular beating within the human chest presented a direct physical connection to the regularity of life. This *regularity* informed the enactment of rituals that preceded and welcomed each natural event as well as those that followed an event, which honored and gave thanks for its occurrence. Early ritual was enacted as a welcome and prayer for the expected. Humans were an important link in the cosmic order. When you pray that the sun rises, and it does, it changes the way you think about the world and your place in it. When you pray for a food source, like the buffalo, to offer itself for your life, and it does, the ritual recognizes the reciprocity of life and your connection to it. Early humans believed that through their rituals they had a direct connection with the comings and goings of life and the phenomenology of the natural world. They were in a reciprocal relationship with nature. They performed their rituals, and nature provided what they expected and needed to live.

One could suggest that we engage in rituals every day. They include daily activities that give us "a sense of the rhythm of our lives, help us in making the transition from one part of the day to another, and express who we are" (Imber-Black and Roberts 1992, 15). Rituals help us make the transition from sleeping to waking, they prepare us for meals and bedtime, they express a welcome to friends and family or the salutation offered for a sneeze—"God bless you." Rituals affirm and celebrate someone's birthday with chants of "Happy birthday to you. Happy birthday to you. Happy birthday dear. . . . Happy birthday to you." These examples point to the pervasiveness of the process of ritualized behavior that is part and parcel of our human experience.

While human ritual behaviors may not be genetically encoded, as many of them are in other parts of the animal world (Driver 1991), it is likely that we have innate capabilities to create and conduct our lives within the ritual process (Turner 1969; Sullwold 1987). The creation of rituals is, in a sense, part of the architecture of our soul; there is an almost primal need to be initiated (Stevens 1990). The ritual form has been a key ingredient in shaping our lives (Nelson 1986). They could be like metaphysical structures that give us safety and security in an uncertain world. They are the structures, not unlike the physical form of a home, in which we safely reside. In the absence of rituals we are naked in the cold world without a roof over our head. Mythical roofs can shelter someone quite well from the present atmosphere of our modern dilemmas of living.

> One becomes truly a man only by conforming to the teaching of the myths, that is, by imitating the gods.
>
> —Mircea Eliade, 1957

The origin of rituals is anchored in myth, from which they emerge and convey essential values, attitudes, and beliefs that inform and guide behaviors that serve survival. One of these central values is related to the promotion of a sense of community, which is achieved through rites of passage. Scholars such as Victor Turner, Mircea Eliade, and Joseph Campbell have devoted considerable attention to the structure, form, and purpose of myth and ritual. For our purpose, I narrow the focus to the connection between ritual and community: in the course of powerful rituals, consciousness itself is refined, and it is not rare to experience a "loss of self," where the feeling of individual distinction is replaced with one of unity with other members of the ritual community (Rappaport 1979).

This excerpt is consistent with Hillman's concept of the self, where no psychology of the individual can be viable that does not include the psyche of the individual within the psyche of the community, that is a self intimately connected with and dependent on a reflection of community—the "interiorization of the community"

(Hillman & Ventura 1992). We would no longer champion the Cartesian notion of "I am because I think," which gives psychotherapy the avenue to work on the interior self. It would be, "I am because of others and the world." Or, as someone once said to Hillman, "I am because I party," (40). *I am because I party!* This is central to an orientation where one's self is defined and only known in relationship to one's interiorization of the community and sense of place and connection to nature.

Community celebrations, like rites of passage, are an important socializing force for children. "Through their [children's] participation in community celebrations, children learn to participate in the construction and the consumption of their culture" (Smith-Shank 2002, 57).

In our attempt to bring youth into adulthood in ways that serve the greater good, wouldn't helping them achieve an interiorization of the community be warranted? They would only know who they are through their relationship with and in the community. And this community includes nature and the environment. In this way they will develop a sense of connection to and responsibility for the community of which they feel a part. They are in the community as the community is in them. And, the community would be the one in which they live, with all the prerequisite cultural and secular values and expectations for behavior essential to maintain the community's survival.

Rituals: The Reenactment of a Myth

"Myth" originates from the Greek word *muthos*, meaning a story or tale, or the plot of a play, or more basically just something a person said (Sharpe 1984). In modern usage, a myth is a story with ancient roots, often relating extraordinary or supernatural events or characters, that expresses the fundamental beliefs, yearnings, and worldview of a community and that often explains the natural world and/or the group's provenance.

Eliade (1957) speaks of myth within the model of paradigm, that is, as a way to view and live in the world:

> One lives by myths as a way of connecting with the beginning of time, "*illo tempore*" and the Gods. The myth relates a sacred history, that is, a primordial event that took place at the beginning of time, "*ab initio*." But to relate a sacred history is equivalent to revealing a mystery. For the persons of the myth are not human beings; they are Gods or culture heroes, and for this reason their "*gesta*" constitute mysteries; man could not know their acts if they were not revealed to him. The myth, then, is the history of what took place in "*illo tempore*," the recital of what the Gods or the semidivine beings did at the beginning of time. . . . Once told, that is, revealed, the myth becomes apodictic truth; it establishes a truth that is absolute. (95)

Myth speaks of the realities of what happened and was fully manifested in sacred time and space. This is one of the chief characteristics of myth, its ability to explain the origin and intricacies of sacred reality. Enacting the story of this sacred reality through rituals helps to guide the way we live. Is there any less need now, than in the past, for powerful stories that help us teach our children important lessons? Can the story of rites of passage serve as a more adequate myth for our time? Let us look at Sharpe's general properties of myth to see if and how rites of passage can serve as a more adequate myth, a story to inform and guide practices for living.

Sharpe (1984) reviewed a number of definitions put forth by distinguished scholars including Watts (1960), Leach (1967), Maranda (1972), Childs (1960), Lévi-Strauss (1978), Kirk (1970), Patai (1972), Eliade (1959, 1960, 1963), and Wittgenstein (1965) and synthesized several characteristics of myths. He culled from these previous definitions eight general properties of myths. They present a clear approach to the meaning and description of myth that is useful for informing and guiding practice. What follows are the eight general properties of myth Sharpe sets forth followed by their contemporary counterparts.

First, a myth is a story; this characteristic is present in nearly all definitions. The story has a plot as well as a beginning and middle where characters act out certain dramas, perhaps even parts of their lives. The characteristics of *story* are broad enough to allow for the inclusion of many different forms.

> The stories of rites of passage are evident in human history. We know something predictably happened throughout many cultures around the world, during transitional points in one's life. We call these happenings by many names, including baptism, initiation to adulthood, marriage, and funerals. Certain patterns and symbols of initiation and rites of passage have emerged. Literature abounds with themes of initiation and rites of passage.

Second, the characters in myths originally included *extramundane beings*, gods or superheroes, representing some form of the human experience in such a way as to captivate attention. The character represents a detail of the human experience that is important to illuminate and amplify in order to teach, inform, or convey a cultural value, belief, or tradition.

> Youth today are in need of more adequate models—superheroes—that illuminate more positive qualities. Even more, they need to be part of a story where they can be the hero and heroine on a journey fully immersed in lessons that transmit value and ethics essential to guide their lives.

Third, myths have important ties to time and space. They are often set in another time, what Eliade (1957) calls "illo tempore." The reenactment of myth through ritual can alter space and time, bringing the myth into the present for direct experience and benefit.

There are central principles, symbols, and patterns of initiation that can help youth to transcend their own sense of self-importance (characteristic of childhood) and guide them into another space and time for maturation to occur. The ordeal, common among many initiatory experiences and coupled with silence, time alone in nature, reflection, and fasting, is among a number of different patterns of initiation that alter time and space.

Fourth, myths offer ways of ordering experience (Barbour 1974). They provide a filter to look at the world and organize the way we structure reality. "Myth informs man about himself" (Barbour 1974, p. 20). Myths present the *ideal* form for the manner in which things came to be and the reason they exist. They form a link between the ancestors and the world today, furthering the bonds of community through their shared acceptance.

Rites of passage order experiences for the individual, the family, and the community. They signal to each that an important time is upon us and something special needs to happen. The individual, parents, family, and community need to reorganize themselves to make a place for the new adult to emerge. They invite the ancestors, Spirit, nature, and the Universe to enter into a sacred process to strengthen a sacred bond between all things.

Fifth, myths may be used as models for behavior. They illuminate a form to be imitated. A myth reveals the existence and the activity of "superhuman beings behaving in an exemplary manner, a manner to be imitated for the benefit of the community for eternity" (Eliade 1960, p.16). In this manner, myths serve an educational function as well as a deterrent function (Murray 1968). They set forth ideal ways to live and consequences for actions that are disapproved.

The hallmark of initiation is the transmission of values that inform and guide expectations for behavior. This behavior has to be in service to the health and wellbeing of the individual and the community as well as the natural world.

Sixth, myths convey meanings that are taken into the consciousness of an individual at a very deep emotional level. They become part of the architecture of a person's and culture's essential structure. They are lived as though real through the manner in which they organize the world. The myth anchors itself within the archetypal vessel of an individual, it is familiar and fits at a very deep level, and "in one way or another one 'lives' the myth, in the sense that one is seized by the sacred, exalting power of the events recollected or reenacted" (Eliade 1963).

More than any other youth development or educational practice, rites of passage resonate deeply with youth. Engagement in a community-oriented rite of passage has significant meaning for the child, parents, family, and community. When embedded into the structure of a community's education and youth-development efforts they become part of the architecture of a person's and culture's essential structure. They help to organize the world and offer navigational aids to the youth on their journey to adulthood and set forth the expectation that the family/parents and community need to adapt, change, and make a place for the new adult.

Seventh, this property links itself with the one before and is related to an absolute belief in the truth and authority of the myth. A myth is a "living reality" (Sharpe 1984). Myths are accepted as true because of the belief that they narrate something as if they really happened (Eliade 1960), and as such are reenacted to bring them into present reality and reaffirm their authority.

During a youth's engagement in the initiatory process, which last for many years, they come to know the values and ethics essential to their lives and the survival of their community. During their passage, in their home, at their school, within their peer group, community, and nature, they learn lessons and achieve specific competencies. They are provided opportunities to demonstrate their newly acquired competencies in ways that give them affirmation and recognition. They have been put on a path to adulthood, guided by elders who have been there before them and can show them the way. When rites of passage are provided in a community over generations, everyone knows them to be authentic and true paths to righteous adulthood.

Eighth, myths are often found in association with rituals. Rituals bring the story of the myth to life in the present time. They allow the participants in the ritual to become connected to the sacred space and time of the actual mythical event. They are able to take on the persona of the characters in the myth and exemplify the behavior in the sacred to enhance their lives in the profane world.

Rites of passage are special. They give youth a place and time to fully consider the end of childhood and the entry into adulthood. The ritual container makes it distinctive. It engages all the essential players, namely children, parents, family, community, ancestors, Spirit, nature, and the Universe in a sacred connection. It is a mythical event brought into present reality in the service of the future of all included. It enacts the story that going through the initiatory process and a community-oriented rite of passage is the pathway to adulthood. The child and everyone in the village knows this transition is a special and sacred time and provides design strategies within the guiding principles of youth and community development through rites of passage to convey honor and respect. It brings us back to the use of rites of passage as a more adequate myth, a story in the service of youth and community development and the survival of us all.

Properties of Myth

While these general properties present an architectural structure for discussion and helps inform our work with rites of passage, identifying universal properties of myths is impossible. After an exhaustive search Kirk (1975) declared, "There can be no common definition, no monolithic theory, no simple and radiant answer to all the problems and uncertainties concerning myths," (pp. 18–19). Perhaps all we can hope to achieve in furthering our understanding of myths is to catalog them and continue to understand their common properties, but, more importantly, consider how they can be useful for the problems of living today. Especially, how they can inform youth development through rites of passage that are anchored in a child's culture, community and the natural world in which they live.

Lévi-Strauss (1974) and Jung (1963) may have offered the most exacting possibility for considering the properties of myth by suggesting that there are unconscious structures of the mind that have an innate capability for the construction and reception of myth and their construction is supported by universally recognized symbols that serve as the building blocks of archetypal structures. Symbols provide shortcuts to endowing reality with meaning (Stevens 1990). Jung put it this way: "Cut off the intermediary world of mythic imagination and the mind falls prey to doctrinaire rigidities" (1963, 292). This is an important point. In Sharpe's sixth general principle I amplified youth's deep connection with and response to rites of passage. They "get it" because they deeply understand their need for it and are psychically available to engage in the process. They want to act out a central role as hero and heroine in their community's rite of passage story. Myths are not created without a function. And while the functions vary depending on culture, context, and circumstance, they all seem to answer many inquiries about the universe. "They are like an encyclopedia which covers different sciences. According to the ancient people, myths are the only source of knowledge, religion and social charter" (Alhaidari and Bhanegaonkar 2012, 6).

Biology and Rituals

In his consideration of ritual and ceremony as biologically based and comparable to animal ritual behavior, E. O. Wilson (1978) suggested that a comparison between the human and animal was inevitably "imprecise." While animal signals conveyed through ritual behavior are considered to be limited to discreet signals with limited meaning such as sexual advertisement or bond formation in birds (Wilson 1978), they fall short of others' (Durkheim 1964; Somé 1993) insistence that human rituals rejuvenate the moral values of the community. Human rituals are concerned with the active attempt to manipulate nature and the Gods (Wilson 1978). They include performance and sacred symbolism, convey forms of authority or rules, and represent tradition and ancestors (Bell, 1997). All known human societies engage in rituals (Brown 1991) as a way of ordering the world and making meaning out of chaos (Bell 1997). Early human rituals using animals were probably "sympathetic magic" derived from the notion that what is done with an image will come to pass with the real thing. Ceremonies were constructed to reenact the hunt and therefore concerned themselves with anticipatory action on the part of the hunters for a successful hunt.

Yet, later explorations into the purpose of myth and ritual link it directly to the long-term survival of our species. In his book *The Social Conquest of Earth* (2013), Wilson suggests that the evolutionary history of "the origins of modern humanity" holds clues to our survival such as the selection and incorporation of what he calls "eusocial" characteristics. This is where group membership is composed of multiple generations that are prone to altruistic acts, where employing a "defensible nest," a site for common feeding, communication, and protection contributed to long-term survival. These adaptations where "group selection drove the evolution of culture" contributed to the successful, long-term survival of the social insects as well as our species.

The anthropologist Roy A. Rappaport (1971) suggested that sacred rites of early humans appear to be directly and biologically advantageous. Rituals also regularize relationships in which there would otherwise be ambiguity and wasteful imprecision. "The rite of passage eliminates ambiguity by arbitrarily changing the classification from a continuous gradient into a dichotomy. It also serves to cement the ties of the young person to the adult group that accepts him" (180–81).

Myth and Culture

What is the underlying myth that we seek to reenact in support of our youths' transition to adulthood today? Campbell (1949) writes:

> And though many who bow with closed eyes in the sanctuaries of their own tradition rationally scrutinize and disqualify the sacraments of others, an honest comparison immediately reveals that all have been built from the one fund of mythological motifs—variously selected, organized, interpreted, and ritualized according to local need, but revered by every people on earth. . . . The comparative study of the mythologies of the world compels us to view the cultural history of mankind as a unit; for we find that such themes as the Fire-theft, Deluge, Land of the Dead, Virgin Birth, and Resurrected Hero have a world-wide distribution, appearing everywhere in new combinations, while remaining, like the elements of a kaleidoscope, only a few and always the same. (20–21)

Kluckhorn (1968) writes, "certain features of mythology are apparently universal or have such wide distribution in space and time that their generality may be presumed to result from recurrent reactions of the human psyche to situations and stimuli of the same general order" (46). He reports on a similar variety of consistent motifs that Campbell does and also includes creation, witchcraft, flood, slaying of monsters, incest, sibling rivalry, castration, and androgynous deities. The

Oedipus-type myths, and the hero-type myths many consider to be the two "proto-typical of all human myths."

Jung considered that, within the archetypal program responsible for the trans-formation of the child into adult, a major emphasis is on the descendence of the parental archetype and the ascendence of the *hero* and *anima* archetypes in the boy and the *haitera* and *animus* archetypes in the girl. These, Stevens (1990) writes, are responsible for the promotion of individual identity with one's own sex, awareness of one's attractiveness to the other sex, and support the weakening of parental bonds. The synchronized descendence and subsequent ascendence of these archetypal pro-grams are critical to the transformative process.

This view suggests that a transformation of the symbolic representation of reality within the individual is the foundation for the external psychosocial transforma-tion of adolescence.

The creative internal work of an adolescent must be supported by family and community processes—initiation rites—that are able to nurture the creative imagi-nation of the child on the threshold of transformation. It intentionally affirms the ascension of a child's emerging adulthood, the onset of adolescence, and the change in the parent's relationship with their child. This is an important design consid-eration that can only be enacted within community-oriented rites of passage. An essential aspect of initiation is it is a public process that affirms a collective agree-ment in the separation of the child from the parents and establishes an expected pathway for the separation to manifest.

This is not at all accomplished in one fell swoop with a dramatic change. Rather, the change commences at the beginning of the initiatory process and continues to increase with collective anticipation in the coming years. These public rites of pas-sage make explicit what is implicitly occurring at deeper levels of consciousness within both the youth and their parents.

One example is the orientation and subsequent integration of transitional strat-egies for parents while their children undergo a more extensive Rite Of Passage Experience—ROPE. ROPE for Parents amplifies the "collision of transitions." Parents are usually entering or in the period of midlife when they have adolescents. This can be a volatile time as the adult begins to reflect on how they have been doing over the past several decades of adulthood at the same time as their children are coming into an awareness of their impending adulthood. "Midlife crisis" has become a familiar situation. Put adolescent children into the mix and you can see why our ancestors felt it was so critical to have a clear strategy and marker to mediate the potential for the "generation gap" to manifest into disaster.

Stevens (1990) writes:

> Just as the child withdraws the projection of the parental archetypes from his or her father and mother, so the parents now have to relinquish their identification with these archetypes in themselves and to withdraw their own projection of the child archetype from the adolescent.
>
> Clearly, the most desirable outcome for all concerned is that both parties should withdraw their projections at the same time. Unfortunately, this is

unlikely to occur, since it is improbable that powerful archetypal constellations could undergo such radical change at precisely the same moment—unless some dramatic event should arise which affected them all equally. It was this event that the initiation rite so effectively provided in preliterate societies. (118)

Stevens's remarks affirm an essential ingredient of community-oriented rites of passage that must occur for both the individual child and his or her parents or guardians. Central to traditional initiation rites were design features that focused on the transition for both the children and their parents. This could only occur in community-oriented rites of passage. This is what the initiation rite so effectively provided in preliterate societies and it is why contemporary rites of passage must occur in and with a community. An example of this is offered in the "passing of the fence" ritual of the Masai, detailed in chapter 10, "Something Happened." Before the first son can be fully initiated and become a man, the father has to undergo a ritual that acknowledges that his change into elderhood must occur. Both father and mother have to experience a transformation in order for the child to enter into adulthood.

Myths can be taken into a person's life and help to provide balance, meaning, direction, and ways to live. Ritual can be a powerful event we use to reenact the myths and bring them into our lives. When community rituals reenact myths, stories that help us to know who we are as human beings, nourish our collective soul, and help us live well together, they can help us adapt and survive. Joseph Campbell examines one underlying myth generally accepted as an essential structure for the male initiatory story in *The Hero with a Thousand Faces* (1949). Within this framework there is a "call to adventure." The youth (the "hero") sets out from his bond with the parents. This is articulated in van Gennep's schema as separation. He moves across a threshold into a special or sacred space, where he is fully immersed in the experience of ordeal or testing. This is the place of betwixt and between, the liminal place of possibility and potentialities waiting to be born. This is the middle ground from which one cannot return home in the same form, but must continue forward on the journey to manhood. It is the place of becoming human. In the hero's journey, van Gennep's phase of reincorporation is articulated in the return home, where the hero is transformed into an adult and acquires the throne of the kingdom and the hand of the beautiful princess.

Stevens (1990) writes:

These myths express in symbolic form the experience of Everyman: to embark on the adventure of life, he must free himself from his parents, leave home and cross the threshold into manhood. If he is to win a bride, he must undergo a second birth from his mother—a final breaking of the psychic umbilical cord. Victory over the dragon-mother often involved entry into her. Then, after a period in her belly, he succeeds in cutting his way out or causes her to vomit him up. Failure to overcome the monster signifies failure to get free of the mother: the hero languishes in her belly forever, and the princess (the "anima") is never liberated from the monster's clutches. (125)

While this "story" offers structure for the boy's journey to manhood, it may not be adequate to represent the transformation of young girls into women. Bruce Lincoln (1981) suggests three other terms to adequately describe the female's transformation: "enclosure," "metamorphosis" (or magnification), and "emergence" (101). His formulations are based on observations, in which he noted the absence of the girl's "separation" from her place of residence. He acknowledges that while there is a period of "isolation" it cannot be "rightly called separation." This sets the foundation for Lincoln's view of the inadequacy of van Gennep's schema. Lincoln writes, "without a clear enactment of separation, one might question whether there can truly be a liminal period or a process of reincorporation, for nothing has been left behind and there is nowhere to which one can return" (101).

There are several aspects about Lincoln's reformulation of the structure of rites of passage that are important to consider. First, this is just one of several schemas alternative to van Gennep's structure that have been proposed for rites of passage. Like others it, too has three parts and emanates from observations of different indigenous practices. Second, gender differences seem to correspond to structural differences. That is, it depends on the cultural practices of the group and differences in male and female roles. Third, Lincoln's terminology comes directly from the metaphor of insect metamorphosis, which he noted in the Tukuna's description of their Moca Nova festival, where the initiand is likened to a caterpillar, who enters the cocoon and emerges a butterfly. He also relates this to the Tiyyar *pandal* and ancestral home or of the Navajo *hogan*. The basis of this metaphor is in the phenomenology of the natural world expressed through symbols (i.e., cocoon, metamorphosis, butterfly). When placed together, these considerations may lead one to acknowledge the universality of a three-part structure for rites of passage, although this could very well be conceived in a more simplistic structure that has a *beginning, middle,* and *end.* Surely a young girl's "enclosure" in a different place is a separation. The linguistic differences between *liminality* as a place of *betwixt and between* and *metamorphosis* as the central place of transformation are minimal, as they both have a sense of limbo or suspension for transformation. And, both *reincorporation* (van Gennep) and *emerging* (Lincoln)—like a caterpillar from a chrysalis—assume a new state. Both incorporate the necessary information, biologically and psychologically to manifest the new state or status.

Lincoln's contributions open the door for a discussion about the accuracy and relevance of the traditional schema of rites of passage, specifically in the area of gender. This discussion should be expanded to consider the relevance of a schema developed from observations of indigenous cultures whose social structure—values, beliefs, attitudes, and daily activities—is considerably different from modern western culture. For the most part, indigenous cultures may have greater connection to the creation myths, the stories that gave rise to their functional initiation rituals, than modern initiation rites presently being created. The symbols of indigenous initiation relate directly to culturally relevant materials, thereby making them unavailable and inappropriate to replicate in contemporary forms.

For example, symbols of the Tiyyar initiation, as described by Lincoln (1991), reflect the symbolic acknowledgment of the onset of menstruation through seclusion; marriage through tying the *tāli*; defloration through the initiate puncturing the leaf over the divinatory pot; pregnancy through the objects hidden within the pot; childbirth through the extraction of one of these objects; and lactation through the seat made of milkwood (104). In these actions the initiate experiences certain crucial moments of a woman's life and in doing so becomes a woman. Symbols from both the male and female world are introduced to the initiand to magnify and effect the transformative process.

Symbols of initiation are crucial to our understanding of the ritual process and its utility in our modern attempts to support the transition of youth to adulthood. These symbols must be related to cultural motifs and myths and anchored contextually or else they represent nothing of relevance and render rituals disingenuous and meaningless. "Only through metaphors can we express and still contain the turbulent events that change a life forever" (Meade 1993, 284). The symbolism within the initiation of Cuchulainn, discussed in both Meade (1993) and Eliade (1958, 1967), points toward the need for a "tempering of men." To quell the burning rage and anger, which accompanies the hero's journey, a place must be created to "extinguish the wrath."

During his return from the hero's journey, Cuchulainn is duped into being submerged into three vats of cold water. After Cuchulainn is finally cooled, he is able to return to the village and be accepted as an adult. Reducing and redirecting the fire within the souls of men for the benefit of themselves and their community is a central symbol and task of initiatory events. "When the inner heat cannot burn toward a symbolic expression that speaks meaningfully to a community, it burns toward destruction. If kept inside, it burns toward an inner destruction, tearing down the body through drugs, alcohol, stress, or literal suicide" (Meade 1993, 259). If the inner heat is not productively redirected it will burn down the community and destroy the culture.

Symbols are the language of ritual, especially in its reenactment of a myth. Dance, costume, song, prayer, and action symbolically reenact the mythical journey in the psyche. The drama is acted out in a ritual performance. The physical phenomenon of initiation and rites of passage, while apparent and important, is secondary to the symbols that impact the unconscious. Kluckhon (1959) points out "a comprehensive interpretation of any myth or of mythologies must rest upon the way in which themes are combined, (p. 268)." The recurrence of certain motifs, like Campbell's "hero's journey," in various areas separated geographically throughout history tells us something about the human psyche. Something happens between our internal biological processes and the external physical world that calls for attention and actions during times of transition. These transitions can be within the celestial realm, like sunrise and sunset, and over the course of the life cycle. At either end of this life cycle spectrum are birth and death, each with their own cultural customs and practices. These times of transition seem to ignite deep within our collective memory powerful images that are transformed into stories, symbols, and ritual forms. In the formulation of designs and strategies for contemporary rites of passage it is crucial to consider the integration of cultural symbols, stories, themes, dance, music, art, and other ingredients relevant to the context within the community and natural world and the process in which the integration occurs. Collective inquiry into the cultural and contextual symbols, in all forms of artistic expression present within the culture, natural world, and social and community context are essential to a community organizing process for rites of passage.

The Myth of Rites of Passage Enacted for Our Survival

What are the myths underlying the modern creation of rites of passage? Can the old stories in the myths be useful or must we combine the myths of science with those of antiquity to create a new story to support the mythology underlying our modern-day rites of passage?

Theories, which support modern science, are the stories about a particular part of our experience of the world (Sharpe 1984). Stories are an innate part of our evolution as *Homo sapiens*, and our capacity for "storied thinking" has probably not changed in the past 40,000 years (Marshack 1972). While fitting the general properties of myth established previously, science is inadequate as a mythology, especially in education and human services, because of its limitations in evoking "commitment to ethical norms and policies of action," eliciting "emotional and valuational responses," encouraging "decision and personal involvement," or offering "ways of life and patterns of behaviour" (Barbour 1974).

One could argue, in contrast, that social science "stories" serve to provide exactly those elements. I submit that they, too, fall short, as evidenced by the increase in problems of living associated with increases in individual, family, and community dysfunction and alienation. This may not be exclusively related to inadequate theory (story), but how it is reenacted within the context of policy-directed "programs" of human service. These programs become the rituals in their attempt to reenact the stories of psychology, education, sociology, and other "deities" that purport to interpret the phenomenology of the mysteries of the world. In other words, programs are the enactment of the myth we call science.

Stories not only have a substantial impact on an individual and their development but also they can have an impact on a nation and the world (Kottler 2015). It's not about the programs or the policies, it's about the stories that can connect with people and compel them to engage in collaborative actions for the highest good. In reflecting on his first years in office, President Obama said his biggest mistake "was thinking that this job was just about getting the policy right. And, that's important, but the nature of this office is also to tell a story to the American people that gives them a sense of unity and purpose and optimism, especially during tough times" (Hart 2012).

All agree that adolescence, coming of age, is a particularly volatile time in a person's development. This is not only for the child but also for their parents and/or guardians and the community, who have been challenged to figure out how to come together and raise their children. There is no more important time for a story to compel unity in the community and a collective purpose for helping to raise their children. Rites of passage have been such a story for thousands of years. The story of reciprocity in youth and community development through rites of passage can emerge again in service of our survival.

Although arguably inadequate, science is the mythology of our time. Some even consider it to be a religion (Eisley 1973; Barbour 1990). These scientific stories—secular mythologies—manipulate but do not direct behavior through virtuous principals that stimulate deep emotional involvement, connection between individuals, and identification with the sacred. We exist in a world surrounded and controlled by the results of scientific ritual. Experimentation is the reenactment of the myth of a deified discipline. Each discipline's story has its characters, whether they are atoms, cells, or psychological archetypes. The manipulation of these characters produces a change in reality that may have enormous impact on individuals and the entire globe. Think atom bomb. We participate in the results of scientific ritual. Scientific ritual offers the womb for much of our present reality. What is created in the laboratory (secular scientific temples) during the ritual of science becomes part of our reality through the technology created. If one of the general principles of ritual is the reenactment of a myth in order to relive and identify with the story, then technology enables us to live the myth of the virtue of science. "Better living through chemistry" (DuPont 1935) is one of the anthems.

Earl MacCormac (1976) suggests, "Future archaeologists may look back upon much of present scientific activity as empty ritual, research that had little purpose or direction other than to consume energy and funds." This "emptiness" is one of the greatest limitations of the social sciences. The present paradigm within the social sciences promotes practices like "programs," "therapy," or "interventions" (things professionals do *to* individuals, families, communities, and systems) that lay outside direct sacred experience. This is quite opposite to the traditional manner in which one regarded myth. People in the past "lived" the myth, in the sense that they were seized by the sacred, exalting power of the events recollected or reenacted (Eliade 1963), which informed and guided their lives. Seizing the "exalted power" of the scientific myths has left our culture empty and yearning for fulfillment through reconnection with the sacred. This is of particular importance in the lives of children who are seeking an awakening to the exalted power of the sacred; to reconnect and remember that essential knowledge they knew when in the womb. When science and technology are chosen as the carriers of tradition, our logical minds may be full and satisfied but our hearts and souls are left empty. Our lives crave real experiences that can support our transformation into human beings. This is the myth of rites of passage that can be integrated with contemporary science and reenacted in ways that offer our children, their families, community, and the planet the necessary information and adaptation for survival.

Space Flight: A Myth for Modernity

The story of human space flight has captured our imagination and attention for more than six decades. It offered the illusory opportunity to achieve greatness and power (especially in relation to other governments, i.e., the Soviet Union) and symbolically approach the place of the sacred. This was captured in the famous poem by an American-born British aviator, John Gillespie Magee, Jr.:

> *And, while with silent, lifting mind I've trod*
> *The high untrespassed sanctity of space,*
> *Put out my hand, and touched the face of God.*

Ronald Reagan referenced the line when he addressed NASA employees following the loss of the Challenger 7 crew: "We shall never forget them nor the last time we saw them, as they prepared for their mission and waved good-bye and slipped the surly bonds of Earth to touch the face of God."

Eliade (1959) notes "man desires to have his abode in a space opening upward, that is, communicating with the divine" (91). This scientific myth, aligned with religious symbols of heaven, told us that *sacred space* lies above our atmosphere and among the planets and stars of the cosmos. The myth created superordinary beings in the form of the astronauts and scientists who would help us all "touch the face of God" through space flight. The dramatic reenactment of the myth in the ritual and ceremony of space flight helped us order our experience to support the virtue and authority of the sciences, which contributed to the story of flight into sacred space.

If myths inform us about ourselves, the space-flight myth told us how great we were, that we could fly to other worlds and move beyond our mortal physical selves. We could become transformed out of our mundane existence and approach the exalted power of the sacred in outer space. The power of the myth was its initial ability to compel our belief in it. The first human space flights garnered tremendous attention as we watched, with breathless anticipation, the countdown and hung onto every utterance from Mission Control as if they were the words of Spirit. We sat around the electronic campfire and together heard the story as a nation. In our separate worlds we shared a ritual.

But this attention could not be sustained, underscoring the inadequacy of the myth for serving our human needs, and with greater frequency space flights became part and parcel of our everyday life. Unless there is a horrible catastrophe (e.g., The Challenger) or an incredible discovery in the future that once again captures our spiritual imagination, space flight's capacity to help us move into sacred space has been minimized or lost. At one time it held our nation's attention, but now it may not even receive mention on the evening news.

Peering through a filter of the general principles of myth described earlier, how do the stories of science enhance our lives and bring reasonable understanding to the great mysteries of life? Do these stories compel emotional involvement in a process that connects people to the potentiality within the sacred and offer healthy and humanitarian ways to live and support our continued transformation in the process of becoming human? Do they set forth positive role models, offer ethical guidance, and help us to live optimally in the world? How do they engage us individually, emotionally, or cognitively? Do the stories of science engage us in activities that promote community? How do they support or inhibit a sense of community in the way rituals performed this necessary task? How are our children doing transitioning from childhood to adulthood and populating the world in ways that are making it better? The absence of—or inadequate, inappropriate—rites of passage may be one of the factors contributing to the condition of our children, communities, and the world in which we live.

Responses to these questions may bring one to consider the inadequacy of modern science to serve as our current mythology, especially as it relates to our children. The newest mythology told in the story of "evidence-based" practice is one example. This myth suggests that there are proven ways of behaving together, couched in a program, that will produce the same beneficial predictable outcomes over and over again. Science, for many is the *gospel*, and those deified through degrees accorded by academia proselytize its virtues and contributions to humanity. These new saints and prophets, cloaked in the degrees of academia, create a proprietary language that builds a cosmology with a pantheon of gods anointed by and referenced in citations.

Sharpe (1984), building on Horton (1974), suggests that the models of science are the "intellectual furnishings of a very large sector of the population," and the acceptance of their models is more a function of the social status of their proponents. Power and prestige are linked to the creation and acceptance of scientific myths. This firmly plants these stories in the domain of the profane and inadequate to convey the ethical know-how to use the scientific know-how in ways that nourish life and help us know how to live together and in balance with our sacred Earth.

One of the functions of myth is to relate a "sacred history ... a primordial event that took place at the beginning of time" (Eliade 1959) that helps us to understand the mysteries of the world in relationship to the sacred. Science has placed a wedge in between the worlds of the sacred and profane. We are the first to experience a completely profane world (Sharpe 1984). For Eliade and others it is the direct experience of the sacred that is real, and this contributes to making us humans. In the absence of the sacred we become beings exalted by the power of exploitation and dominance, moving farther away from actualizing our *real* potential to experience the supreme joy and harmony contained within a sacred reality. This reality is supported through rituals, which continually immerse us in more adequate mythologies favorable to a healthy, life-affirming future society.

Obviously these realities are sacred realities, for it is the "sacred" that is pre-eminently the "real." Whatever belongs to the sphere of the profane does not participate in being, for the profane was not ontologically established by myth, has no perfect model. As we shall soon see, agricultural work is a ritual revealed by the gods or culture heroes. This is why it constitutes an act that is at once "real" and "significant." Let us think, by comparison, of agricultural work in a desacralized society. Here, it has become a profane act, justified by the economic profit that it brings. The ground is tilled to be exploited; the end pursued is profit and food.

Emptied of religious symbolism, agricultural work becomes at once opaque and exhausting; it reveals no meaning, it makes possible no opening toward the universal, toward the world of spirit. . . . What men do on their own initiative, what they do without a mythical model, belongs to the sphere of the profane; hence it is a vain and illusory activity, and, in the last analysis, unreal. (Eliade 1959, 95–6)

Ritual is Primal Prevention

Individual and community rituals tap into private and collective unconscious energies that support personal health and community cohesion and well-being (Somé 1993). Ritual includes the creation of a setting for inviting Spirit to participate in matters that humans need help with and cannot do alone. Rituals invite allies of spirit, while programs invite allies of science. It does not have to be an "either/ or" situation, rather, "both/and" is what is needed. Rituals provide an inoculation against the problems of living. They use symbolic representations that impact both the conscious and unconscious processes, while recruiting the inner energies of individuals and the collective resources of the community, and foster a connection with the divine, thus, achieving a greater opportunity for living in balance. Rituals offer a powerful resource, and when integrated with contemporary science they provide a synergy that would produce more effective design strategies for youth and community development, especially through rites of passage.

In his introduction to the translation of van Gennep's (1960) classic work in the field, Solon Kimball writes, "One dimension of mental illness may arise because an increasing number of individuals are forced to accomplish their transitions alone and with private symbols" (xviii). Rituals work at an unconscious level by speaking to our inner symbols in order to aid in our basic construction of reality. If you can adjust the underlying, inner symbols that build a person's reality, you can change their reality (Somé 1993). Rituals do not function like some preformulated program with component parts, constructed in advance and rigidly implemented. In fact, they are chaotic, informed by the setting and nature at that moment and intended to pitch the participants out of their mundane world into the world of the sacred. This calls for a reassessment of the present program paradigm—namely, program replication—and presents considerable challenges for applying the concepts of "innovation transfer," "emergence," and "emergent design" discussed in subsequent chapters. It also challenges the worldview, disposition, and personal orientation and needs of professionals, who would no longer hold deified positions but rather are in a "sacred partnership" with the people and communities learning together about initiation and rites of passage. Contrived and controlled rituals do more to serve the ego of the host than to invite Spirit into an honorable dance in order to "help in something that humans are not capable of handling by themselves" (Somé 1993).

If scientific theory is a modern form of myth (Sharpe 1984), the activities (programs) that are generated from these underlying stories are the rituals for enacting the myth. Yet, unlike traditional myths featuring characters with superordinary qualities whose origins are birthed from the divine at the beginning of time, all modern myths, that is, scientific theories, must have proper citations that pinpoint their human source. The superheroes are not only contained within the myths themselves but also are considered the creators of myth. Einstein became a deity to many because of his theories (scientific myth). The characters within these myths, wrapped in the jargon of the disciplines (atoms, protons, super ego, defense mechanisms, viruses, $E = MC^2$), besides being inaccessible to most, do not have superordinary qualities or convey any moral value. Technical advances aside, the myth of relativity did little to connect people to each other or the divine. Unless, of course, you consider what happened at Hiroshima or Nagasaki to reflect connecting people to the divine?

> Traditional myths beget rituals in the service of connecting with and honoring Spirit, accessing individual inner resources, and strengthening community bonds. "Life's major transition points, such as circumcision, entry into adulthood, and marriage are, above all, seen as milestones in one's deepening commitment to the community" (Shore 1992, 20). "One purpose of initiation is to awaken an inner authority in each person and to connect that force to the common ground of the community" (Meade 1993, 314).

It could be considered that myths within a context of social science beget programs in the service of creating bureaucracies and strengthening the position of adherents of those creation myths. Rituals enacted through social science programs, in many instances, connect the administrators and conductors of the rituals with power rather then opening inner resources within the participants and connecting them and the community to the divine. Somé suggests that poorly crafted rituals constructed in the service of one's ego are an insult to the divine. They will not only fall short of their intended purpose, but will more likely have unwanted and unpredictable consequences. What has been the impact of social-science-generated human-service programs? Have they achieved adequate advances in promoting individual well-being and a sense of community, or have they fallen short of our expectation? After thirty years of evidence-based programs are our children better off? Are they coming of age better? Have communities figured out how to become a village to raise their children? I believe we can do better.

The limitations of social science's progress in achieving sterling advances for individuals and communities may not rest in inadequate myth (theory) as much as in the absence of powerful and productive ritualized enactment. In other words, a ritual process is absent from human-service programs, which limits their ability to ultimately achieve their goals. In the foreword to *The Art of Ritual* (Beck and Metrick 1990), Angeles Arrien quotes Alvin Toffler's *Future Shock*: "We have the opportunity to introduce additional stability points and rituals into our society, such as new holidays, pageants, ceremonies and games. Such mechanisms could not only provide a backdrop of continuity in everyday life but serve to integrate societies, and cushion them somewhat against the fragmenting impact of super-industrialism" (ii). Arrien (1990) continues, "Ritual provides the bridge between inner and outer worlds, and creates a context for reconnecting to the seat of our souls. The end result of all ritual is increased balance, strength, energy, and comfort" (ii).

Enacting rituals in the service of promoting human-service goals requires an extraordinary paradigm shift. In a sense we have to go "back to the future." The routinized, mechanical delivery of "programs," especially for children, puts them to sleep, spiritually anaesthetizing them against their own humanness, distancing them from their own natural inner resources for resilience and adaptation. In the absence of a ritual process as the context for our existence, life becomes less sacred and meaning is derived from the manipulation and control of the external world. A central question for youth development should be: Development for *what*—to be beautiful human beings in the sacred or humans doing the mundane work in the profane?

Somé (1993) writes:

> Our role in ritual is to be human. We take the initiative to spark a process, knowing that its success is not in our hands but in the hands of the kind of forces we invoke into our lives. So the force field we create within a ritual is something coming from the spirit, not something coming from us. We are only instruments in this kind of interaction between dimensions, between realms. (50)

Ritual prepares us for engagement in the world in a way that permits our best performance. Ritual is transformative (Turner 1969), as it opens us up for deep learning and an appreciation of the universe and our connection to it. Driver (1991) suggests three major functions of ritual: "making and preserving order, fostering community, and effecting transformation" (71).

Golf in the Kingdom

Golf in the Kingdom (Murphy 1972) features a philosophical golfer, Shivas Irons, who considers golf a microcosm of the world. Our engagement with it, and how we play, serves as a mirror of our engagement and relationship with the rest of the world. "A round of golf partakes of the journey, and the journey is one of the central myths and signs of Western Man" (Murphy 127). Technical aspects of the game such as the stance and swing are secondary to the intention and manner in which one approaches the endeavor. I was reminded of this years ago when attempting to improve my own beleaguered performance on "Lucifer's rug."

After I demonstrated my swing several times for the golf professional who tried to perform the miracle of improving my game, he said to me, "You need to develop a consistent pre-shot routine."

"But what about my swing?" I responded, somewhat bewildered.

"You need to develop a ritual that will prepare you to perform the technique well. The technique will come when the proper preparations are made."

Still bewildered by this, I pressed on in my desire to improve my game, which, in my mind, meant attention to technique.

"But what about my swing, my stance, my position over the ball? Am I keeping my eye on the ball and my head steady?" I asked.

The golf pro just shook his head and responded, "The foundation of your game is built not on technique but on your intention and the manner of your approach. First, you must shift time, slow down and transform your existence from the mundane of the everyday world to the special place, the quiet place, the transcendent place of a *golfer*. One whose intention is impeccable and focused on connecting with the ball in a good way. A way that will direct it toward a goal you envision."

My puzzlement must have been obvious as I struggled to comprehend this.

"Look," he said, "you were not born a golfer, you have to become a golfer anew with each address of the ball. You cannot just waltz up to a ball and swing away. A ritualized address is the proper foundation for each golf swing. It is what you do before each swing that alerts the rest of your body to do what it knows how to do. Right now you have demonstrated your swing a dozen times. And, each time you approached the ball in a totally different manner. You were confusing your body by not sending it a consistent signal that would engage it to be a *golfer*."

With that preface, my lesson consisted of developing a preshot routine, a ritual that included specific body movements, and patterns of thought consistently repeated before each shot. Without any focus on technique these adjustments made a remarkable contribution to my play. What does this experience have to contribute to our discourse on ritual? Simply stated, achieving a technically superior performance in anything requires the proper approach and preparation. In the absence of this, our efforts will always be limited in relation to our full potential. Ritual gives us a way to slow down, focus on actively engaging in the affairs of the world in a purposeful way in order to achieve the goal of being human.

For those more attuned to basketball, just look at every player before they take a free throw after a penalty. They all engage in the same preshot ritual. What kind of preshot routine do we engage our children before we expect them to become students and scholars.[1]

Consequence of the Absence of Initiation and Rites of Passage

M. Duncan Stanton et al. (1982) suggests that themes of death stand out as a consistent feature in families with addictive disorders. Families view the transition of a child to adult as a loss of "their child." The child's movement into the larger world,

---

[1] For more information see the "Initiation of Scholars" design within the Rite Of Passage Experience─ROPE process at www.rope.org. Also, Blumenkrantz (2009).

forming new associations and dependencies, shifts a balance in the family, which produces not only addictive responses but also a myriad of other difficulties. The experience of loss and separation is pervasive in humans; it is part of the comings and goings that characterize our existence.

Writer and scholar Malidoma Somé (1995), raised within the Dagara traditions of West Africa, suggests that Western culture provides an inadequate vessel to contain and quell the grief associated with separation and loss, especially for men. The inadequacy produces antagonistic and hostile relationships with others and a propensity to engage in controlling and manipulative encounters with the planet. Somé designed a ritual for men, based on the traditions of the Dagara culture. This ritual is detailed in the next chapter, to illustrate the sequence of activities and the power of ritual. Even more than this it demonstrates the ability of rituals to be recreated in the service of enhancing our lives today. That is, we were not in a Dagara village when we experienced the ritual, nor were there any Dagara tribespeople there, except Somé. Yet, as illustrated in the story, the effects were profound and achieved the intended results of the indigenous ritual. This raises the very sensitive issue of transporting rituals from one culture to another.

Rites and the Right Way

There is substantial sensitivity and controversy surrounding the use of other cultures' traditional rituals in western culture. Some condemn the practice as stealing the soul of a people. Others implore that it is the final desecration of Native Americans and other indigenous people. Whether traditional ceremonies and rituals are led and used by people who are not blood relations to the ancestry of those rituals is truly a critical issue in this entire dialogue.

Someone asked me how I would feel about people using the rituals and traditions of Judaism who were not Jewish. The question personalized the issue of the appropriation of other's traditions. At first it hit me as strange. I thought, "Why would anyone want to use our rituals and traditions? Especially rituals, like Hanukkah that recreate our sacred stories of our ancestors." At my core I felt uneasy about the prospect. Then, I thought about it more. I began to consider the idea when I placed it within the context of the purpose of ritual and the intentions of the ritual leader. Was it intended to help someone or a group of people through some transitional period? Was it done for healing? Was it done as part of commerce? Was it done with integrity and honor, respecting the tradition and consistent with its ancestral roots? Did the participants and the leader truly understand the history and tradition of the ritual and believe in the significance of the practice? Did the ceremonial leader receive the information in a culturally appropriate way that included permission to be a ceremonial leader? Or, were they simply "playing" Jews? Is imitation really the best form of flattery? Or, is it just stealing? Within the criteria implied by the questions, one could consider the respectful transfer and use of rituals.

It is not an easy proposition to determine whether there is a "rite" way and a wrong way. I once heard it said, "appropriation is in the eye of the beholder." That is, if someone is using a cultural tradition from someone else's culture and someone from that culture objects then it is appropriation. It is likened to sexual harassment. The judgment of whether it is harassment or not rests mainly with the individual who is "feeling" harassed. It is in the eye of the beholder. But, what if that eye is seeing the world through a lens impacted by hostile or nefarious forces that shift perceptions for other motives or agendas that foster conflict? What is cultural appropriation, and who is the arbitrator and judge over when it occurs? Perhaps we need to search for better questions in this area to help guide us in our inquiry while on this shaky, controversial, and sacred ground. In one sense, we are addressing the essential nature of a pathway toward sacred ground. The way we navigate going from the mundane ordinary world to the world of the sacred and extraordinary. It has been said that all spiritual paths lead to the same place. I am uncertain if this is true. But what seems to be relevant is that there is a natural tendency, regardless of traditions and with different levels of intensity at certain times in life, especially the onset of puberty, that the existence of the extraordinary, the sacred, comes into our perception and we want to find a way to make a connection with this mystery. Paths to this connection emerged for those who came before us, our ancestors, which formed a basis for culture. What are the design features that might be similar among all people and helpful to guide us to remember this journey?

If we consider the structural form of the B'nai Mitzvah (the process for becoming a Bar or Bat Mitzvah), there are valuable design features that can, in fact, be transferable. In short, the process incorporates preparation for entry into a special status within the congregation. There is a separation from parents, who also engage in preparation to release their child. There is a gathering of the community in religious school, where lessons of the history and traditions of Judaism are intensified. Youth must learn the history, traditions, and all things related to Judaism, including reading and writing in Hebrew. They then must demonstrate these competencies in front of the entire congregation, their family, and friends during the public rite of passage—the Bar or Bat Mitzvah. Once this is complete, there are opportunities for them to take on the role of Jewish adult. They can be considered part of the adult Jewish community and be included in a Minyan, the quorum of ten Jewish adults required for certain religious obligations. There are elements within this process that are similar to elements within other ritual forms and rites of passage. When general principles or elements are made culturally and contextually appropriate, but do not replicate a particular cultural practice, is this appropriation? What are the similarities in core elements of cultural practices that work quite well to achieve the desired outcomes of increased community cohesion and perceived change in a youth's status?

Let me be clear. I am not suggesting that ritual practices and protocols from other cultures should or could be transferred and "used." I think cultural appropriation exists and understand, to the degree possible, how it is offensive. I am suggesting that there *may* be appropriate and reasonable ways to enact the core elements of traditional rituals that preserve the integrity of the practice and honor the ancestors of a people. I am reminded of the Lakota saying *Mitakuye Oyasin*—"We are all related" or "All my relations." Common to many traditional philosophies is this underlying connection between all things. In South Africa,

"Ubuntu" means a universal bond—sharing. The central prayer in Judaism, the Schema, relates to the connection between God and all things. In physics it is called nonlocality—or, as Einstein referred to it, "Spooky attraction at a distance." If the origin of many rituals resides in myth and is transmitted from God, Spirit, or a divine entity to humans for the enhancement of *all* life, then wouldn't all human use of rituals be appropriate, within a context that ensured its integrity? I believe that, given the extraordinary circumstances we face today, we must consider the ethical and moral use of ceremony and ritual in the service of saving humanity and the planet.

This orientation does not mean that I categorically support appropriation of cultural heritage or traditions. It is an invitation to witness what is important and present for many different people and to search for similarities and common symbols, patterns, and principles that can be imagined anew. Shabbat is the most sacred time for the Jewish faith. Many other faiths and spiritual paths resonate with it. Their practices are not identical to Jewish practices (e.g., lighting the Sabbath candles, saying Kiddush over the wine, reciting HaMotzi over challah). Rather each could think of ways to honor and reenact Shabbat's primary tenets: rest (*menuchah*), holiness (*kedushah*), and joy (*oneg*). Or, decide, name, and make real through rituals which "primary tenets" are important to celebrate. Why and how? Shabbat ritual practices affirm and sanctify the transition from daily life-sustaining ordinary and mundane activities and help us make a place for the sacred to emerge. It helps us transition from our human doings, transcending the mundane, to become human beings, and enter the province of the sacred and extraordinary. A relationship with the sacred is self-determined and evolves within the culture of a community. Shabbat is the grand organizing principle (the story) within which unique worldviews inform the enactment of general elements and guiding principles in the form of rituals.

The creation story central to the Jewish tradition of Shabbat is written in several sections of Torah. The central prayer that informs practice is in Exodus 20:8.

> "I have a precious gift in my treasure house," said God to Moses, "'Sabbath' is its name; go and tell Israel I wish to present it to them."

In Genesis 2:3 we are told that God rested (*shavat*) from His creative activity and set apart the seventh day as the memorial of the work of His hands. God called the seventh day "holy" (*kodesh*), which means set apart as sacred, exalted, and honored.

זָכוֹר אֶת־יוֹם הַשַּׁבָּת לְקַדְּשׁוֹ:
Zakhor et-yom ha-Shabbat l'kadsho
Remember the Sabbath day, to keep it holy (Exodus 20:8)

The word "zakhor" is translated as "remember." It means to recall or recollect past events and experiences and to assess, adapt, and renew them in the present in accordance with Jewish principles of living. Each week we are invited to reflect on our lives, to judge if we are in a right place within ourselves as it relates to our religion. Remembering gives us a regular time to "check in" with ourselves and to make adjustments, recommitting our lives to the primary tenets of our faith. On the Sabbath we read from Torah as a way to remember, to continue learning and adapting our lives to the never-ending changes. Helping people and communities remember the story of initiation and rites of passage is central to our work with youth and community development through rites of passage.

In the tradition of my ancestors I leave you with another story.

Rabbi Zusha used to say, "When I die and come before the heavenly court, if they ask me, 'Zusha, why were you not Abraham?' I'll say that I didn't have Abraham's intellectual abilities. If they say, 'Why were you not Moses?' I'll say I didn't have Moses' leadership abilities. For every such question, I'll have an answer. But if they say, 'Zusha, why were you not Zusha?' for that, I'll have no answer."

9

It Is a Long Journey to a Ritual

A person of Chinese descent was attending the funeral of a relative in Australia. He placed a bowl of rice on the grave and stood silently in prayer. When leaving the gravesite, an Anglo-Australian friend approached and inquired respectfully, "Will your loved one be eating the rice in the next world?"

The Chinese man offered in return, "When you lay flowers by the grave of your loved one, do you expect them to smell or benefit from their fragrance?"

Malidoma Patrice Somé was born in West Africa among the Dagara in Dano, Burkina Faso. Somé believes his destiny is embodied in his name "Malidoma," which means "friend of the enemy/stranger." He has spent the last several decades bringing the wisdom of his ancestors to westerners in ways that are healing for individuals and their community.

Malidoma crafted a ritual, based on the Dagara culture's funeral customs of his people, which he has been extending to western men with remarkable results. I was privileged to participate in the power of the ritual in the spring of 1995. Somé (1994) writes in his autobiographical work *Of Water and the Spirit*:

> It takes millions of tears to produce a flood capable of washing the dead to the realm of the ancestors, so refraining from weeping wrongs the dead. Rhythm and chanting crack open that part of the self that holds grief under control. But grief unleashed without the help of ritual drummers, musicians, and chanters runs the risk of producing another death. It is a force without a container. To the dead, it is useless energy, like food that is wasted while people go hungry. . . . An adult who cannot weep is a dangerous person who has forgotten the place emotion holds in a person's life. (57)

During that spring weekend retreat with Somé, I witnessed and experienced the power and magic of ritual and its ability to purify and cleanse even the most reticent and intractable demons from men. Fifty-five men came together, bound by a common pursuit of increased self-understanding and exploring their mutual connections. I went to observe and increase my understanding of the ritual process and quickly became swept up by the power and potency of ritual. We are hardwired as a species to respond. Even the most reticent and reluctant are compelled to return to the core of their human beingness and participate.

Each member of the community has a responsibility to help in the grieving process. Public grief is essential for the entire community. It bonds people together in their "natural human identity." Only by passionate expression of grief can a loss be productively assimilated into a form that can be lived with (Somé 1993). Community exists when there is a link to those who have died—the ancestors. What are the "arrangements" that can help shift consciousness from western, concrete, logical, and sequential thinking to intuitive, heartfelt, nonordinary perceptions of reality?

A process of gradual immersion subtly began. It was similar to entering icy water. Taking a quick plunge is one way, but might result in a shock to the system. Entering a ritual process of this magnitude required moving from and through one's familiar perceptions and behaviors to those that enable transformation and transition. Malidoma demonstrated a keen sensitivity to this requirement, frequently absent from western attempts to force ritual on unsuspecting participants. He extended an invitation for the men to organize themselves into birth years, the first invitation to begin the journey to a ritual. Nothing profound. Familiar and easy to do. The men were assigned by birth year into groups representing fire, water, mineral, nature, and earth. Each group began to learn and take on their responsibilities for each of these elements essential for the ritual.

Somé set forth that a ritual is to be experienced, not explained. "Your psyche will explain it to you. Explanations cloud the reality of your own experience. It is best when you enter into something physically to keep awake and connect with each other." These cautions echo in my mind and again suggest a central limitation of language to adequately convey the essence of an experience, especially a ritual. This narrative attempts to provide an example of the ritual structure described in chapter 7. It is offered here to illustrate some of the essential elements of ritual, put into practice and considered as design features for village-oriented rites of passage. Another distinguishing feature is the relationship between death and its *containers*—funerals—as an aid to this transition and the adolescent transition and its containers—rites of passage. These two life cycle events are related. Initiation rites mark the death of a child and the birth of an adult, while funerals mark an individual's death in the physical realm and birth into the spiritual, nonphysical realm. In the absence of a ritual container and process to manage emotion and the physical separation and changes, not only individuals but also the entire community is impacted. This was discussed earlier citing the work of M. Duncan Stanton et al. (1982), who wrote that the transition of a child to adult is experienced by parents as a loss of "their child." The experience of loss and separation is pervasive in humans; it is part of the comings and goings that characterize our existence.

These days it is a long journey to a ritual. Space and time need to be purposely shifted, helping to shed the cloak of our mechanically woven garments. It is a battle to cast off the mantle of modernity. The tightly woven threads of our lives fix our attention on the masks that hide the true dimension of nature, especially our own human nature and its ultimate life-affirming and sustaining connection to the Universe.

We yearn to find our place, to return home, to make the longest journey of all—from our head to our heart—and arrive at our true place of being human.

Separation

The first challenge of ritual is the separation from the profane to the sacred world. We left our hurried worlds and worked hard to transcend mundane modernity to enter the sacred place of the heart. We arrived in our steel chariots—our unconscious minds—opening to the power of the ritual, making the preparations long before we physically began the journey.

The journey begins when you think about going.

I did not know with certainty why I was there. In my exploration into the human phenomenon of initiation rituals I engaged in different activities in the hope of achieving some keen insight that would enhance my work. And by this I mean offering me not only new knowledge received from books but also the wisdom that comes from incorporating powerful experiences and strengthening personal authenticity and other qualities, such as attunement, to bring that wisdom into service on behalf of the children, youth, families, and communities with whom I was in relationship.

I was thoroughly impressed by Somé's writings and intrigued by the path that brought him to be such an authority on matters of ritual, community, and the heart. His writing conveyed a deep understanding of these matters and validated my actual experiences, unlike most of the purely academic treatments of the topic. Raised in a village in Burkina Faso, West Africa, Somé was initiated in the ancestral tribal traditions, and is a medicine man and diviner in the Dagara culture. He holds three master's degrees and two doctoral degrees from the Sorbonne and Brandeis University, and teaches at universities and leads group experiences throughout the United States. He is acclaimed by scholars such as James Hillman, Robert Moore, Robert Bly, and Michael Meade as a "bridge" between the worlds of the ancestors and modern people. His writings on ritual and community convey an understanding of the delicate balance between the needs of individuals and their collective responsibility for community.

Somé's writing set the stage for this encounter, but to a certain extent made me ill-prepared to initially engage in the experience. That is an example of the conscious, "intellectual mind" attempting to process and understand the actual phenomenon of a real ritual experience. Our need to know something before it is experienced, in the hope of reducing anxiety from encountering the unknown, undermines our ability to be truly in the experience. What is mediated and explained by the mind tends to become the experience, rather than the experience appreciated as it authentically emerges into existence.

My expectation was to be in a didactic workshop, interacting with Somé and "being taught" about ritual. It was immediately clear that this was not to be the case. The meeting room filled with men. As the noise of friendly banter grew, the beating of drums invaded the space. A growing sense of awkwardness crept into my consciousness as more and more men drummed, shook rattles, and connected with one another. This was not familiar territory. Why are there only men here? What had I ventured into? A nervous smile etched itself across my lips as I peered around the vibrating room, half expecting Robert Bly to enter in wild man motif reenacting a mystical *Iron John* saga. This was not the workshop I signed up for or what I expected. I felt myself being pulled into a world in which I was not prepared to enlist.

Entering into a ritual is to approach the unfamiliar, to shed the cloak of personal history, to separate from the known into the unknown and open the doors of unordinary perception inviting transformation. There we were, in the recreation hall of the retreat center, beginning to craft a space that could contain the ritual. Somé entered the room, distinguished by his elaborate hat and colorful embroidered cloak, in the tradition of his people. He called the men to join hands in a circle, teaching us a traditional Dagara song to honor the ancestors.

*Bora Somé—Bora Somé—Bora Somé—Bora Soméé é é—**OH!***

"Come on," he chided us. "What kind of singing is that? This is supposed to honor the ancestors, not insult them!" Somé laughed as he encouraged us to fully enter into the chant. Once again voices rose, only this time the rafters shook. Humor and laughter are Spirit's way of moving into and through one's armor and protection, piercing the cloak of insecurity, opening one's heart to the possibilities of self-discovery in the reflection of the Gods. It is still one of the most potent ways to quickly bring people together. That and yawning . . . except laughter is so much more invigorating!

"Good!" Malidoma erupted in obvious joy, "Let's do it again." Together we chanted, louder and stronger. With each repetition powerful vibrations moved deep within us, echoing beyond the hall, carrying us back into time. Malidoma's penetrating gaze through his sparkling brown eyes and his inviting smile circled the group, initiating a connection between himself and each of us. Chanting in an unfamiliar language shook our unconscious, stirred our souls, and awakened the possibility of an encounter with the divine.

The journey toward the ritual began to unfold. Malidoma charted the territory he hoped to open up to us. His discourse on matters of ritual helped return me, albeit momentarily, to a familiar place—a place of logic, filtering and diluting the experience in words within the safety of my mind. Upon reflection, he was careful to gradually immerse us into the ritual process. An immersion that was too rapid would have been overwhelming and terrifying. Many would have battled to maintain a grip on their present reality, insulating their mind with logic, filtering the intrusion of this altered state of reality, losing the potential for transformation. He outlined the tasks of the weekend and set forth our objective to reenact a Dagara funeral rite.

Somé explained that the resolution of grief is "unfinished business," especially for men. We can resume the traditional methods for connecting with each other and reinvigorating a sense of community through dealing with loss and grief. This is an important part of initiation. "We are always in a stage of initiation," Somé said, "moving into something, being in the middle of something, and ending something, and then moving on to begin something anew. You always are in the process of initiation, which is repetitive and ongoing and needs successful closure for each state (beginning, middle, and end) in order to successfully move into another productive initiatory process. When an individual is not acknowledged at a stage of initiation, recognized for the completion of an initiatory cycle, and welcomed back to the village, they have to undertake another ordeal that will finish and complete that portion of life's journey. The worst part of initiation is getting used to it."

Somé's descriptions depicted a world where people are disconnected from the natural elements of the earth, fire, water, and air and, as a consequence, have no sense of place, no home. Disconnection fosters a frantic search for rootedness and relatedness. Failed attempts at establishing these essential life connections result in engagements of dominance, control, and manipulation over others and the planet. The results are wars, sorrow, and a planet whose soul and life are deteriorating.

Somé presented a compelling case for the connection between the absence of ritual and our pervasive sense of disconnection and loss. His carefully crafted presentation established a reality that fostered a connection between the men and called for our engagement in a ritual journey that he had prepared for us. We were drawn together, brothers in the grief and sorrow of our present condition. As the first evening came to a close, Malidoma invited us to call out and invite spirit guides, our ancestors, and others to come among us, for we needed all the help we could enlist for our work ahead. We stood, and the men called out the names of deceased parents and grandparents, animal spirit guides, and a host of names familiar only to the voice that called in the night.

Something was building. I could feel a charge in the atmosphere as we were divided into "clan" groupings by the year of our birth. Clans were symbolically oriented in fire (red), water (blue/black), mineral (white), nature (green), and earth (yellow) symbols and contained properties related to these elements and colors. We were receiving a constellation of symbolic materials, colors, elements, words, and chants, from which to construct an inviting Universe into which we would move from our present reality into the transformative power of ritual. These preparations were at the level of the heart, the place that knows how to be in and learn from rituals.

The Clans moved into their own separate space and were given the task of discussing losses and the clan member's position within the initiatory process (i.e., beginning, middle, and end). Within the context of the symbolic elements of the Clan—the heat and power of fire, the cooling nurturing qualities of water, the memory of the minerals—and with a rising tide of sorrow, we told our tales of loss and described our place in the initiatory process. This furthered the connection with each other and revealed the depths of emotions related to our personal experiences of loss.

Malidoma spoke to both our conscious and unconscious. The Shaman connects people with the natural world and, thus, with their real human beingness. The constellation of symbols he presented helped to connect our conscious and unconscious worlds. They served as the vehicles of induction to bring us out of our regular realities and into an "extraordinary state of reality." It is no easy task to unleash the bonds that anchor us in our present reality. We need a firm bump to shove us off our moorings and into a more receptive state, available and open to transformation. A key characteristic conducive to entering the receptive state is chaos. Chaos produces confusion and an opportunity to be inducted into the formless void, assisting in the suspension of disbelief and casting open the pathways to transformation. In a sense, it is related to the "confusion technique" or "paradoxical intention" used as a method of induction in Milton Erickson's *utilization* practice of hypnosis (Haley 1993). When a person is confused, the conscious mind is occupied trying to resolve the confusion. It leaves room for accessing the unconscious to engage with learning and different ways of knowing. Confusion leads people into a trance of their own making, which makes them more ready to enter the trance enacted within a ritual without resistance.

The chanting and drumming combined with the information Malidoma presented flooded my mind. I had difficulty comprehending it all and anxiously felt myself being drawn away from the familiar and into another world. A growing uneasiness intruded into the pit of my stomach as I searched in desperation to find familiar ground, something or someone to assist me in understanding what was going on and why I was there. Once again the struggle resumed between my logical, analytical, scientific mind and the phenomenology of the experience unfolding before me, which offered to transport me out of myself, if I would relinquish the reins of control and enter into the abyss of initiation.

No one goes into initiation willingly. No one wants to disrupt the equilibrium in his or her life, which is the purpose of initiation.

I went to sleep that night both excited and anxious about the events of the next day. "Your psyche will explain it to you. Explanations cloud the reality of your own experience. It is best when you enter into something physically to keep awake and connect with each other. Drop your profession at the door; your gut will tell you what to do." Somé's remarks echoed in my mind as I drifted off to sleep separating from the conscious to the unconscious—moving further away from my present reality and deeper into the liminality of the ritual process.

The next day, we quickly resumed the preparations for the Dagara funeral ritual. Malidoma gave further instructions on the construction of the shrine, the doorway to the other world. It will serve as the repository of the men's grief. The construction of the shrine is part of the ritual. The process continued to unfold, deepening our immersion into the abyss. Doing the work to build the shrine is part of the ritual itself. In a sense it is the embodiment of the Ericksonian utilization technique of induction. One part of the self is in the linear world, and one part is in the nonlinear world. Your conscious mind is engaged in the very masculine act of construction while the unconscious begins to experience, learn, and remember. You are releasing control by your conscious mind and accessing the resources and lessons in the unconscious. I was included in the Fire Clan, which was responsible for the architecture of the shrine. The other clans were responsible for collecting the materials associated with their Clan (i.e., nature, water, earth, minerals).

Throughout the morning the Clans worked to collect the materials necessary for the construction of the shrine. The tempo and *heat* of the ritual was building as the men began to chant as the shrine was being erected.

*Bora Somé—Bora Somé—Bora Somé—Bora Soméé é é—**OH!***

Small and large limbs of pine and maple trees rose within the ten-by-ten-foot alcove in the recreation hall that was the container for the shrine. The fragrance of pines penetrated the air and mixed with the earthy aromas of the other natural elements, engaging our senses and aiding in the release of our conscious mind. Tree trunks, logs, and boulders were wrestled into place, buttressing the limbs whose pine needles and leaves completely disguised the walls and ceiling. Moss, dirt, and grasses were carefully arranged by the Fire Clan on the shrine floor, making a lush green and brown carpet. A large mound of dirt, surrounded by candles, covered with moss and a large flat stone with a water-filled crater in the center, served as the altar in the center of the shrine. The entire flora and fauna of the surrounding ecosystem was brought in to construct the sacred space, the place we would make our offerings and leave our grief.

*Bora Somé—Bora Somé—Bora Somé—Bora Soméé é é—**OH!***

This was the place to which we would make the final journey, completing a process of grieving begun for each of us in our own specially crafted personal crucible. Here, collectively, we would share and shed our grief and be welcomed back to the village, with one heart, successfully completing an initiation.

*Bora Somé—Bora Somé—Bora Somé—Bora Soméé é é—**OH!***

"A ritual adjusts something inside of us for healing," Malidoma said. "It opens the knowledge which allows us to come home to the place of community. How you feel during a ritual is what home feels like. Ritual makes life worth living. Repetition of these rituals across generations anchors those coming after us to a greater connection with what they already have—the experience of their ancestor."

In an instance the chanting came to an end. Silence engulfed the room. We gazed in amazement at the shrine, dark and forbidding. Cloaked in the mystery of the great beyond, it lured us deeper into a region of possibilities. A chill ran through my body. It was inexplicable. The shrine was extraordinarily beautiful yet terrifying. It was an unborn entity waiting to come alive and devour us, looking like the gaping jaws of some primordial monster. I was clearly captured, suspended in the moment. My conscious, linear mind was being drawn across the threshold of the shrine and into another dimension.

Malidoma instructed us to repeat the process of building Clan shrines at an old church near the recreation hall. Placing personal artifacts on the altar, the Clan shrine would represent our village and be the place to which we would return after successfully depositing our grief and sorrow on the altar in the jaws of the community shrine. Bundles of colored cloth, symbolic of our clan, were laid out. Following Malidoma's instructions I took a red piece of cloth and went off to collect earth, minerals, and wood. Alone in the woods, I focused on moving deep within myself and extricating the remaining vestiges of these burdens of grief, transferring them to the earth, minerals, and wood, and wrapping them purposely in the red cloth. It would hold my grief and sorrow. I was alone in the woods as the sun moved toward the horizon and twilight silently entered the forest. I sat quietly in the growing shadows cast by the trees, holding my bundle of grief.

Purification

The men filtered back into the recreation hall and quietly stood in front of the shrine. Pacing nervously in front of the shrine, Malidoma became very solemn as he warned us about the power of the shrine.

"Once this shrine is charged up, *purified* with the smoke, it is alive. I cannot know what will happen. We must be careful and do exactly as I have instructed. The power is immense; it can draw you into it. Once, I remember, a man, drenched in his sorrow, abandoned his senses and plunged into the abyss, never to be seen again. I can't promise that this won't happen again. Please—you must do your job and help me to keep us safe."

I couldn't believe what my ears had heard. Yet, instinctively I knew it to be true. My conscious mind was losing the battle for logic as the linear world began to drift away. I had a most peculiar sensation. *All things are possible*, I thought, *if you let the experience enter in.*

The men, herded together in front of the shrine, watched and listened carefully as Malidoma made the final preparations. "I need several drummers. They must be good drummers, able to maintain the beat, impeccable drummers. They keep the beat of the ritual. The beat is the container for the ritual. It must be precise. It is very dangerous if we lose the beat. We could all be lost." Several men volunteered to be drummers. Each Clan was instructed in their role within the ritual. The Fire Clan was the guardian of the threshold to the shrine. They protect the mourners, who, consumed with grief and out of control may try to hurl themselves across the threshold and into the shrine.

Tension and excitement filled the air, breeding on itself, growing and enveloping us. "You enter a ritual in order to give, not to get," Malidoma said, "If you are in a "fix me" mode, nothing happens. You cannot adequately prepare yourself for becoming the person you are about to become. You will stand naked without your mask and be in the natural world. The world your ancestors were born into. Remember, we live in a culture where it is not okay to be real; you are expected to wear a mask. You are about to take off your masks. I warn you, your nakedness will be a shock to many of you who will experience your true selves for the first time. Are you ready?" Malidoma finished, peering out among the men, silently gazing into the eyes and the souls of each of us, pouring in his wisdom and strength. "Yes!" we responded in unison.

Malidoma once again burned sage in a seashell, purifying and cleansing us, as he had done the first night. We stood in absolute silence. Candles surrounding the altar within the shrine were lit as Malidoma carefully laid a narrow mound of silvery wood ash across the threshold of the shrine. He burned something else in another shell, waving and fanning the smoke into the shrine and chanting.

Invocation

"There, it is done. The spirits have been invoked. They have been called to join us and be allies in this ritual. The shrine is charged up and ready to go," Malidoma said. "Go back to the village," Malidoma pointed to the other side of the room. "Fire Clan, you come first to the threshold and toss your bundles upon the altar. There is no time for grief now, be quick about your task, then walk back to the village. Water, Earth, Mineral, and Nature Clans follow in order and do the same. This is your offering to the shrine. You are feeding the shrine, honoring it, *invoking* its help." One by one, the Clans approached the threshold and the men tossed their bundles onto the altar.

The candles in the shrine radiated tentacles of light into the room with an inviting orange flickering glow. The men returned to the village and stood in silence. Malidoma led the drummers to their position. I remained at the threshold of the shrine waiting and wondering what task lay before me. Would the men really try to hurl themselves into the shrine? Could I be lured into the mouth of the abyss? Would I get pushed in by the grieving men? It looked so incredible and mysterious, like the womb of Mother Earth herself. What was going to happen?

We were all perched on the edge of a cliff, ready to leap. Malidoma again reminded each of us of our roles. Mourners approaching the shrine must be followed closely and protected by other village members so they do not leap into the abyss. The Nature and Mineral Clans chant to help keep the beat. "Remember," Malidoma said, "this is your opportunity to cast off your grief, to give it a proper funeral."

The drumming began.

Standing guard at one end of the ten-foot-wide threshold while another member of the Fire Clan stood at the other end, I felt the muscles in my legs tighten as I prepared for the unknown. I looked at the group of men who stood before me. They looked like tall trees swaying in the wind of the beat. I saw something move out of the corner of my eye. Half expecting to find something alive in the cave behind me, I nervously glanced over my shoulder into the shrine.

Identification

For the first time I felt that something was in there, alive, pulsating with the beat of the drums. I became a part of it—*identifying* with and connected to the mysterious entity. I kept turning toward it in fascination, trying to watch it and the men at the same time.

The first man approached the threshold, closely followed by two others. Their faces were intense, eyes concentrating on their brother. The first man stared intensely into the shrine, the two protectors staring just as intently at him. I crouched in a defensive stance. The drumming was loud and powerful as the men approached the shrine. The mourner stopped inches away from the silvery line of ash, his protectors, inches behind him, arms outstretched with open hands ready to snatch him back from the abyss. The mourner suddenly jerked forward, his protectors and I became rigid, ready to embrace and block his advance as he fell to his knees at the threshold and yelled into the shrine. The blood-curdling scream mixed with the drum. Over and over again he sucked in long breaths and exhaled in long ear-piercing wails. In a few moments it was over; he stood and walked calmly back to the village.

Slowly, the next man peeled away from the village mass and approached the shrine with his protectors in tow. The drama was repeated. Each man expressed grief, unloading his personal burden, which resonated from a place deep within him. Some men walked to the threshold, gazed into the shrine, turned, and walked back. At first the progression was orderly, men took turns approaching and depositing their grief into the shrine. They identified with and became the carriers of the ritual, dutifully performing its structured tasks. The mourners mourned while the protectors protected, the drummers drummed, and the chanters chanted, all with choreographic precision.

Time seemed suspended, although I was wearing a watch and trying to monitor its passing. The slow flow of men approaching the shrine began to elevate in pace and intensity. Each disbursement of grief begot another of heightened intensity. Men began to race up to the shrine, their anxious protectors frantically trying to guard their charge's every move. They cursed and screamed, directing their emotional declarations to a lover who scorned them, a spouse who divorced them, a father or mother who was not available for them, and an abundance of other sorrows they had labored to carry. I was astonished at the growing intensity and voraciousness of the men's screams of delivery as they placed their grief and sorrow into the shrine. Some men laid face down, prostrate on the floor, kicking and screaming, sobbing uncontrollably. Several men abandoned their clothes and repeatedly charged into the shrine, demanding that their protectors and I physically restrain them.

Transformation

The scene escalated to pandemonium. Groups of men approached the shrine in packs, screaming and crying as they delivered their grief and mourned their losses, their abandonment, their failures, consumed by their sorrow, awash in their pain. "You left me, you bitch," one man screamed into the abyss, tears streaming down his contorted face. "You took everything I had, my money, my children, my house, my heart, you took everything—even my manhood—you left me with nothing, you fucking bitch."

The men screamed and cried in wild fury while their protectors and I desperately tried to keep them from being sucked into the shrine or accidently falling across the threshold. Bodies banged together in a shaking mass along the threshold of the shrine. I was quickly becoming exhausted from maintaining such a heightened state of vigilance and continually holding these men back. The drumming seemed to become louder and more intense, corresponding to the growing chaos. I was relieved by another member of the Fire Clan and returned to the village. I was torn between the emotion of the experience and trying to observe and consider the incredible events that were unfolding before me. I rested on one of the support pillars, trembling as my body withdrew from the vibrations of the threshold and shrine. I felt suspended in the moment and could not move, frozen against the pillar. I felt a great sadness begin to flood my consciousness. This struck me, since I could not connect to the origin of this sadness. I was not consciously thinking of anything to be sad about, yet the feelings of sorrow and grief became overwhelming. There was no escape from the power of the moment and I became consumed by the experience, suddenly finding myself walking slowly toward the shrine. I peered down from someplace above and saw myself standing and gazing into the shrine. The room became dark, the drums muffled in the distance, and for a fleeting moment I was a tiny speck on the altar, dwarfed by the huge ferns and moss surrounding me. The flame of the candle was like the sun. I was drawn to it like a moth and saw a bright blue, violet, and yellow light surround me. My eyes filled and grief rolled down my cheeks as I began to unite with the collective grief in the room. Time was suspended until I found myself in the physical world of the threshold in front of the shrine. I turned and walked back toward the village returning to the pillar for support. I had a sense that something was different but I did not know what. The drumming went on, the men continued to approach the threshold and be consumed by the experience and their grief.

I resumed my position as a guardian at the threshold, helping the men deliver their grief and protecting them from falling into the abyss.

The proceeding continued on for almost three hours, gaining and losing intensity as in some cosmic dance. The men left the village and journeyed to the shrine where they unloaded their burdens. The procession tapered to a trickle, and the intensity of the delivery waned; there were long lapses where no one journeyed to the shrine. The drumming stopped—and there was silence.

There was very little talking as the men left the hall. The next morning we prepared to reenter our clan villages at the church down the road and perform the closing ceremony at our own shrines.

The business is not done until we have been welcomed home and honored.

Once again we were purified with sage and invoked the spirits to help us in the closing ceremony. We asked the spirits to guide us home while the other clan members prayed for our safe return. As each of us moved into the center of the shrine the men called out, telling the spirit and us that we were needed back in the village. We acknowledged the completion of our journey and honored the end of this initiation.

Malidoma said, "Unless you are welcomed back to the village and honored for completing an ordeal you become sick." The transformation was complete when we returned and were honored and welcomed back into the community. The work of initiation is individual, while responsibility for its transformative potential belongs to the community. We have all come a long way to experience the journey back to ourselves.

The description of the ritual reflects the stages of ritual: separation, purification, invocation, identification, and transformation. It also provides an example of the community's participation in the transformation of an individual, which is the essential intent of an initiatory event. Although language is significantly limited in transmitting the power of an experience, it should be evident that the ritual required complete participation. Over 75 percent of the men actively and emotionally engaged in the procession to the shrine and deposited their grief with unmitigated emotion. Bonds were tightly woven among many of the men, who have gone on to continue these meetings and engage in the ongoing process of community ritual. Malidoma said, "A village is a village because it is held together by a shrine." The Shrine is part of the ritual.

A village is a village because it is held together by their rituals.

Lessons

What are the underlying myth and lessons of this Dagara rite? Somé never disclosed this directly, but alluded to it in the opening conversation, which I included earlier in this chapter. There were two essential lessons transmitted in the ritual for the Dagara people to remember that Somé said were relevant, especially for people in the western world.

The first lesson was *It takes millions of tears to produce a flood capable of washing the dead to the realm of the ancestors, so refraining from weeping wrongs the dead.*

"Millions of tears" reflects the role of the community in the funeral ritual. If it takes a whole village to raise a child, helping the child cross over to adulthood, then it takes a whole village to help the dead cross over into the realm of the ancestors. Not only are the tears important but also the very act of crying, which in this situation was a shared emotional release. "Refraining from weeping wrongs the dead." It is pretty clear that a collective release of emotions is essential for the welfare of the village. Crying is one way. Laughing is another way that feels much better. Rituals, called rites of passage during times of transition in the life cycle, are likely to evoke heightened emotions like laughing and crying and frequently both.

Rituals immerse us together in the task of being human. They powerfully engage us in a full body, heart, and spiritual experience in which we must be totally committed and submerged. We experience a collective drowning in our grief for us to emerge as a nurturing and caring community able to thrive and survive together.

The second lesson was woven into Somé's admonishment: "An adult who cannot weep is a dangerous person who has forgotten the place emotion holds in a person's life" (57). Sharing emotions together is one of the most authentic ways to be human beings together in community. It is very difficult to be disingenuous when really crying. The kind of crying where your shoulders shudder and whole body convulses.

The power of the ritual does resides not only in the underlying myth but also in the reenactment of the myth in the performance of the ritual. Ideally, the underlying story of the myth conveys values, beliefs, customs, or traditions that are important to remember. The ritual Somé designed provided a safe, consecrated space for the men to remember how to feel deep emotions, weep, and connect with and cast off their grief and sorrow. They were burying memories mourning their losses, their abandonment, their failures, consumed by their sorrow, awash in their pain and grief. Sharing their sorrows and millions of tears producing a flood that collectively washed their losses, their abandonment, their failures, their sorrow, their pain, and their grief away. It was a collective emotional release. A village of men held together and strengthened by the ritual.

The transition through adolescence is a time of loss. What would our world be like if we had no funerals to serve as a container for grief and loss? Funerals are the ritual vehicle that helps transport our grief and anger to positive energy built on the remembrances of the ancestors. Funerals act as containers for loss and grief in the same way that coming of age initiation rites accomplish this. Although this may be difficult to imagine, its consideration may help the reader understand the impact of the absence of rites of passage for today's youth and their families and communities.

The previous chapter, as well as this one, focused on the construction of ritual and its link to myth. A question arises: What myths are today's rites of passage trying to reenact? I suggest that the concept of a *meta-myth* may be helpful to consider modern efforts to establish rites of passage. The word "meta" in front of another word has been used to mean "about." For example, in statistics meta-analysis is a compilation of different studies that analyze data collected on the same subject in the hopes of identifying similar patterns that reveal some underlying theme to increase our understanding about a particular subject. In other words, it is a story about a story that collects elements from many similar stories.

We know there have been stories about rituals in general for seventy thousand years and stories of rites of passage, whether in birth, coming of age, funerals, or weddings, for a very long time. We know through stories that there were rites of passage that appear to be central for supporting a child's transition to adulthood, strengthening the bonds of community, fostering resiliency and adaptation for survival. Contemporary rites of passage can be most potent when they capture the central elements in the stories of all rites of passage from all cultures. A meta-myth brings together from different places information and practices that offer an overarching view of rites of passage.

This orientation recognizes the important link between myth and ritual. Myths previously reenacted in other culture's initiation rites frequently related to that culture's creation myths or other stories related to their history. They would not be appropriate to reenact in today's secular initiation rites, because they would not have the same kind of symbols or associations that anchor the rituals, making them authentic and powerful. Furthermore, our conscious reality—our belief system—may be far removed from the ethos of the early myths.

> It was the common belief in Athens that whoever had been taught the Mysteries would, when he died, be deemed worthy of divine glory. Hence all were eager for initiation.
>
> —Scholiast on Aristophanes

Belief systems play an important role in shaping our construction of the world. James Borhek and Richard Curtis define a belief system as "a set of related ideas (learned and shared), which has some permanence, and to which individuals and/or groups exhibit some commitment" (Borhek 1975, 5). Cultural belief systems are created to organize and direct our interaction with the world. They help us to structure and give meaning to the world and offer values and goals that shape our behavior.

Traditional rites of passage were integrally incorporated within the belief system of the people who practiced them. They conveyed in powerful ways the central values and beliefs essential for survival and held as supreme truth the conception of a rite of passage as transformative for the individual and propitious for the continuation of the culture and community. For example, a number of traditional initiation rites required physical alterations of the body. Circumcision, scarification, and subincision were all used to "create" and mold the adult out of the child. The child's body needed external alteration to become an adult. These practices would be totally unacceptable today. Yet, their symbolic significance should not be lost.

Currently, our technologically oriented culture believes that following an educational path and engaging in "positive youth development programs" provides the structure for the transition from youth to adulthood. We have to find other, more acceptable ways of using relevant symbols of initiation and designs that transmit essential values and expectations for behaviors and exact a similar result (i.e., a powerful opportunity for transcendence and transition to adulthood).

I propose that the myth we are trying to reenact, one that encompasses the eight properties of myth introduced earlier, is that a story of rites of passage existed and was helpful for the transition of children to adult. The story that rites of passage existed is the myth underlying the creation of modern secular, community-based rites of passage.

The myth has a form of van Gennep's tripartite schema, further crafted in light of Campbell's (1949) description of the journey in *Hero with a Thousand Faces*. I realize that Campbell's structure is male oriented, and suggest that Bruce Lincoln's (1981) structure, in *Emerging from the Chrysalis*, may offer a more suitable form for the myth for girls/women. I am not certain that reenacting traditional rites of passage processes would be advantageous to our current situation of building a sense of community and helping with the transition to adulthood, especially where these strategies occur outside of a youth's community. Remember Malidoma's caution:

"Unless you are welcomed back to the village and honored for completing an ordeal you become sick." The transformation was complete when we returned and were honored and welcomed back into the community. The work of initiation is individual, while responsibility for its transformative potential belongs to the community. We have all come a long way to experience the journey back to ourselves.

Rites of Passage as an Adequate Meta-Myth for Our Time

Is the logic and resulting formulation of a meta-myth sound and potentially useful? Let us briefly consider how rites of passage fulfill the properties of myth introduced earlier.

First, rites of passage are stories deeply carved in almost every culture from the beginning of recorded time. Each story has a beginning, middle, and end that both van Gennep and Lincoln's tripartite schema address well. Campbell's hero's journey and other permutations of the story of rites of passage have similar structures that include a beginning, a middle, and an end. The characteristics of a rites of passage story are broad enough to allow for the inclusion of many different forms supporting an infusion of multicultural, ethnocentric, and secular elements.

Second, the story contains superordinary elements in a way that captivates attention and illuminates and amplifies portions of the human experience in order to teach, inform, or convey a cultural value, belief, or tradition. Robert Hinkel's (1987) filmography reflects works whose themes encompass initiation, rites of passage, and life crisis or transition. Films and literary works contain themes of rites of passage that have been beneficial for both youth and adults. Culture, whether spiritual or popular, offers examples of heroes and heroines. During the initiatory process, youth enter the hero's journey. They seek out their own heroic model, which they identify with, emulate, and then become as their life unfolds.

Third, the stories of rites of passage are set in another time. Modern-day rites of passage help connect both the community and initiate with the ancestors, offering a foundation to move more successfully into the future. One of the central elements important to the creation of modern-day initiation rites is the alteration of time and space for the initiates. These have been manifested in contemporary forms during programs featuring time alone in nature, mental and physical challenges, and designs that guide children to find their bliss.

Fourth, rites of passage offer a way to order the experience of transition. They provide a filter to look at the world and organize the way we structure reality. Rites of passage can help inform the community and children about the proper structures necessary to build clear pathways to adulthood. These structures can serve as design principles and inform the creation of a community's rite of passage experience. Over the course of a child's development there are skills, competencies, and knowledge they are required to acquire. Transitions throughout their academic career, that is, primary to middle school, then to high school, offer opportunities to demonstrate competencies and receive affirmation for their achievement and movement to another level on their way to maturity and adulthood.

Fifth, traditional stories of rites of passage illuminate models of behavior, which are woven throughout the enactment of their contemporary counterparts. Rites of passage serve both an educational function and a deterrent function for children. They set forth ideal ways to live and consequences for actions that are disapproved. They establish clear values and expectations for behavior. One example is that a community that offers a rite of passage provides an opportunity for their children to move successfully into a productive and healthy adulthood while a community that does not offer one reduces this desired outcome.

Sixth, rites of passage offer a powerful way for youth to learn. They engage both the community and initiate at a very deep level. Experiential activities, by design, are directed to the unconscious and produce emotional learning—learning through the heart rather than the head. Ordeals and challenges are key in the initiatory process; adversity introduces us to ourselves and to our potential for meaningful engagement in the physical and spiritual world.

Seventh, rites of passage powerfully convey a truth—that their reenactment can produce a successful passage from childhood to adulthood. They have the capacity to be authoritative, especially in a world where extraordinary difficulty exists during this transitional time. Rites of passage can be accepted as powerful and viable because they have been proven to be so in the past.

Eighth, rites of passage help connect the individual and community to a special place and time. They are able to suspend the participants in a sacred event connecting them with the potentiality that exists in their humanness. This is an essential ingredient for positive youth development—to promote a connection between children and their internal resources in ways that serve the families, schools, peers, community, and nature.

Questions That Matter

I can hear my colleagues in youth work and other practitioners on the front lines wondering, "What's the point? Is this not just an intellectual exercise with little to no practical value?" From a practical perspective, what utility does youth and community development through rites of passage have as a meta-myth? How is it supposed to influence practice? These chapters, and in fact the entire book is designed to raise questions about our existing "story" that informs and guides efforts at educating and helping children come of age. Remember, "when we get our story wrong we get our future wrong." I am suggesting that if we remember our shared sacred story of initiation and rites of passage and understand its fundamental elements, it will help us get the story right for educating and helping our children come of age.

*When we get our story **rite** we get our future right.*

Inherent in the title of Kevin Sharpe's book *From Science to an Adequate Mythology* (1984) is the notion that while science has given us considerable know-how in the form of technology, it has not offered enough in the way of knowing how to use technology for the highest good and in a way that nourishes life and contributes to a world that works for all. He writes, "What we need is a living of the sacred and the profane at the same time, a *mingling* of them as though they were part of a long, continuous spectrum" (1984, 1). Spiritual values of altruism, compassion, and forgiveness have been usurped by secular values of individualism and allegiance to specific groups oriented around power, prestige, and control. Revisiting and compiling the essential elements of initiation and rites of passage into a different story can lead to a different way we educate and help our children come of age, ultimately leading to a better future.

I began making a case that science was an inadequate story—as manifested in one-size-fits-all programs, especially those within the paradigm of "evidence-based practice." They are not potent enough to compel individuals and groups, like a community, to come together in sustained actions that are adaptable and able to raise children as well as we would like. Furthermore, I have seen no evidence that contemporary approaches to youth development or education, as good as they may be for some people in certain situations, can capture the attention of children and youth in ways that respond to their inner yearning for initiation.

The purpose of the last several chapters and the ones to come is to set forth design elements that can inform the "mingling" of the sacred and profane, the worlds of spirit and science, in ways that guide the emergence of rites of passage for individuals and communities. The eight properties of myth, as set forth by Sharpe, can stimulate one's creative imagination to think about questions that matter when considering designs for youth and community development through rites of passage. In the end, it is about conversations that engage people about the important questions more than a formula or recipe exported from somewhere else to be replicated in another's home.

The following are such questions:

1. What are the rituals and stories related to transition within each culture and community that can inform the creation and design of culturally specific, developmentally appropriate, and shared secular rites of passage? What stories influence our children? What are the values conveyed through these stories?

2. Who are the cultural and community "heroes and heroines" that serve as models for adults and children? What are the values inherent in their behaviors and acts that guide and inform their behaviors?

3. Where are opportunities already present for youth to engage in a healthy alteration of time and space, of reality? What are the culture, group, and/or community doing to guide children and youth into healthy forms of play, which are not "adulterated" into organized sports, but viewed as *secular spirituality* (Blumenkrantz 2000)? How can children and youth be intentionally guided to find their bliss, their inner genius?

4. Where are there presently times of transition in the lives of children and youth that can be organized within a rite of passage experience, for example, birth, entry into education, acquisition of essential knowledge and skills and demonstration of this competency, transition to new school, and so forth? And, what are the central skills, attitudes, and behaviors that demonstrate competencies illustrating growth and maturity, for example, between primary and secondary school, learning how to learn well, and so forth?

5. Where are the transmissions of values that inform expectations for youth's behavior already occurring, for example, home, school, peer group, culture, and religion? What are the ways this occurs? Who is or can be engaged in this process, like older youth mentoring younger youth? Are they effective?

6. What currently exists in a group and/or community that engages youth in powerful emotional experiences where values are transmitted and a shared common experience occurs?

7. What would we be doing when children, their parents, and the community believe that the *rite* way to educate and help children come of age is through youth and community development through rites of passage? How would we explore and craft our own community rites of passage experience?

8. What programs presently exist that feature a ritual component and/or could be enhanced for the integration of ritual structures? Where are there opportunities to ritualize particular events in a child's life to foster more meaning that leads to a deeper connection with nature, spirit, and ancestors and include their parents, guardians/surrogates, and families?

This brings us to the importance and potency of rituals, especially for children and youth seeking adventure and a mystical experience. Considerable evidence exists on the propensity adolescents have for engaging in risk-taking behavior (Casey, Getz, and Galvan 2008; Nelson et al. 2002; Steinberg 2008; Romer 2010). "This maturational gap in development of PFC-based [prefrontal cortex] control relative to more advanced motivational circuitry is said to result in an inevitable period of risk for adolescents. Furthermore, it is suggested that interventions to reduce this period of vulnerability will inevitably have very limited effectiveness" (Romer 264).

In chapter 7 I offered a generic structure and design features for thinking about and designing rituals. The case study narrative presented in the previous chapter provided an example of the application of design features and the potency of rituals to impact behavior and create a powerful shared emotional experience. I cannot stress strongly enough the potency of the ritual form to engage children and youth. Through these shared emotional experiences that rituals in general and initiation and rites of passage offer, children learn essential values and ethics that convey expectations for behaviors essential to their own growth and maturation and strengthen a sense of community. We have seventy thousand years of evolutionary evidence to illustrate that the ritual form has been within our shared experience (Vogt 2006). No species will maintain a behavior for this long unless it serves their survival. In my own fifty years of work in youth development, education, and community organizing, I have found no other technique that can engage and teach better than ritual. This transcends any setting from a juvenile justice training school for adjudicated delinquents, residential mental health facilities, group homes, and educational settings. In this way, youth and community development through rites of passage offers a more powerful story, the *rite* story, which *mingles* spirit and science, the sacred and profane, in ways that nourish all life and help us to cocreate a future that works for all.

Mangling Mingling

"Mingling" is not as easy as it sounds. For years, people who have been in partnership with me in codesigning rites of passage have said, "The little things are so big." Yes, they are. Its elegant simplicity masks the true challenge in the authentic enactment of the sacred and profane in the confluence of spirit and science. Walking in these two worlds is a dance of balance between intuition and the intellect. Each strives to lead in the dance of constructing one's reality. Building bridges between these two worlds in the service of youth and community development through rites of passage is a delicate process that requires a keen understanding and attunement of both worlds. One can not just show up, without the rigor, history, and indepth exploration of the breadth of western knowledge and acquisition of wisdom obtained through experience. It is why I dove deep into the exploration and still I am amazed and in wonder about the phenomenology of the human experience of initiation and rites of passage. I offer these artifacts of my exploration that came to be the central materials in this work and leave it to you the reader and practitioner to consider what is necessary for developing the capacity to become "thought partners" with others in the application of this story for getting our future right.

At times like this I am reminded of the stories of my own tribe. Those are the myths—the stories from which we learn the central values that have helped us adapt, live, and thrive for thousands of years.

> One day a rabbi, in a frenzy of religious passion, rushed in before the ark, fell to his knees, and started beating his breast, crying, "I'm nobody! I'm nobody!"
>
> The cantor of the synagogue, impressed by this example of spiritual humility joined the rabbi on his knees, saying, "I'm nobody! I'm nobody!"
>
> The *shamus* (custodian) watching from the corner couldn't restrain himself either. He joined the other two on his knees, calling out, "I'm nobody! I'm nobody!"

At which point the rabbi, nudging the cantor with his elbow, pointed at the custodian and said, "Look who thinks he's nobody!"

(Kurtz & Ketcham 1992).

The next chapter helps provide food for these dreams. It reviews a sample of ethnographies from the Human Relations Area files at Yale University. These files offer descriptions of cultures throughout the world. One component in the description is devoted to initiation rites.

All I can do is to tell the story, and this must be sufficient.
And it was sufficient.
For God made man because he loves stories.

—Frenaye (1972)

10

Something Happened

Stories to Dream By

*When a father is in truth a father, and a mother a mother. When a son
is a son, and a daughter is a daughter when the older brother and sister
are an older brother and sister, the husband a husband, and the wife a
wife, then the house is in the right way. When the house is set in order,
the world is set in order; the world is set on a firm course.*
— Adapted from the *I Ching*

Rites of passage have helped to set the world on a firm course throughout human history. By initiating each of us into our life's pathways and roles within a community and the natural world we are able to fulfill our destiny as a father, mother, son, daughter, older brother and sister, and husband and wife. Each house is set in the *rite* way. And, each house and all who reside within are linked through a common initiatory experience for the community to be set in order. When the community is set in order, the world is set in order. The world is set on a firm course. The Universe is in balance.

Exploring accounts of these important human experiences can help guide and inform the emergence of more potent and viable contemporary forms of rites of passage. Our human history is rich with stories of ritual and rites of passage spanning almost seventy thousand years (Vogt 2006). One of the great repositories for stories of rites of passage is contained in the ethnographies of the Human Relations Area Files (HRAF) Archive at Yale University. George Peter Murdock and his associates began to develop the HRAF Archive in 1949. In the year I reviewed the Archive, 1994, they had over 3.9 million file pages on over 340 different cultural, ethnic, religious, and national groups around the world. They are classified into eight major geographic regions as follows: Asia, Europe, Africa, Middle East, North America, Oceania, Russia, and South America.

The headquarters for the HRAF Archive is in an old house on a tree-lined street in New Haven, Connecticut. I found the files located in the damp, dimly lit basement. Ethnographies were typed or hand written on 5 × 7 cards in old wooden library card catalog files.[1] (If you are old enough to remember, card catalog files that stood on legs with little brass knob handles.) A small brass frame held the hand-written notation identifying the range of the file's content. I spent long days over many months

---

[1] The organization of the material in the file was on cards that did not include page numbers.

like a miner panning for gold, sifting through the cards trying to make sense of it all, searching to find the nuggets of gold in consistent themes, symbols, patterns, and processes of initiation and rites of passage among diverse cultures around the world. Were there central elements consistent among all rites of passage? Could these golden nuggets become guiding principles used to help rites of passage emerge in communities?

The Search: A Dance with the Intellect

My original review and report included thirty-nine different cultures in eight geographic regions and focused on Archive number 881—"Puberty and Initiation." The Archive description read as follows:

> Ideas, beliefs, and practices associated with first emissio seminis and first menstruation; rites of passage at or near puberty; prevalence of special initiation rites for each sex; ceremonial sponsors; function and purpose of ceremonial; mystery and seclusion; taboos; ordeals and test; inculcation of secret lore; special instruction in sex life; ideas of death and rebirth; etc.

This chapter is a substantial reduction and synthesis of the initial document, which included almost 25,000 words in 75 pages. The review and report was part of my own initiatory ordeal for entry into the Ph.D. culture and community! The ethnographic stories used here were selected because they provide more descriptive information than most and help to illustrate similar themes, patterns, symbols, and processes that emerge throughout many of the archival narratives on diverse cultures.

What Can We Really Know?

There are several questions and qualifications that need to be raised and discussed that impact the investigation and its results. People who were not from the different cultures wrote the ethnographies, the stories of other people's lives. What could those who wandered in the cultural wilderness almost a hundred years ago really know about the cultures they witnessed but were not a part of? How can we accurately and, more importantly, ethically come to interpret and make conclusions about the meaning, symbols, and structure of other people's values, ways of knowing, and lives? Can common symbols, themes, and patterns of initiation be appropriately integrated in contemporary rites of passage without disrespect and the perception of appropriating another culture's sacred rituals and practices?

Anthropologists and others describe things they see. But what did they really see at a level of consciousness in concert with the natural rhythms of the people they were observing? Could their (mostly) western-oriented male (Pelto and Pelto 1987) belief system allow them to understand the symbolic meaning of the acts and "feel" their deep meaning and hence know their true significance? Ethnographic writing is increasingly viewed as less than completely factual (Clifford 1988; Clifford and Marcus 1986; Clifton 1990; Fikes 1993). The ethnography of the Delaware people reviewed later in this chapter presents a clear illustration of how the observer's values and lens create a disconnection of consciousness, leading to disrespect and preventing real understanding.

The interpretation of cultural symbols has been addressed in the investigations of Turner (1967, 1969), Campbell (1949), Eliade (1957, 1958), Ortner (1984), McGee and Warms (2004), and others. Each discusses the importance of symbols. Turner says, "The symbol is the smallest unit of ritual which still retains the specific properties of ritual behavior; it is the ultimate unit of specific structure in a ritual context" (1967, 19). Symbols act as vehicles of culture (Geertz 1973). Even with his extensive investigations into ritual, Turner expresses doubt about an outsider's ability to fully understand and interpret the symbols unique to a culture. He quotes Professor Monica Wilson, who stresses, "Interpretations of rituals, for anthropological literature is bespattered with *symbolic guessing*, the ethnographer's interpretations of the rituals of other people" (Turner 1967, 6). Symbols are important and powerful to the extent that all the participants in the ritual acknowledge the symbols' meaning and use and believe in the desired outcome intended. "The symbol becomes associated with human interests, purposes, ends, and means, whether these are explicitly formulated or have to be inferred from the observed behavior" (1967, 20). He adds, "The significant elements of a symbol's meaning are related to what it does and what is done to it by and for whom. These aspects can only be understood if one takes into account from the beginning, and represents by appropriate theoretical constructs, the total field situation in which the symbol occurs" (1967, 46). In other words, an observer from outside of a culture would never know the history, depth, context, spirit, and ancestral connection that contribute to the multifaceted meaning of a symbol. Hence, the outsider, a foreigner, would engage in "symbolic guessing" that makes any interpretation limited and potentially inaccurate. The observer is always influenced by their own internal world and its symbols and is challenged to differentiate external symbols and internal dispositions (Asad 1983). Symbolic anthropology, while describing social conduct and symbolic systems, does not attempt to explain these systems, instead it focuses too much on the individual symbols themselves (Ortner 1984; Des Chene 1996).

In the absence of a complete understanding all of the diverse facets and nuances of a culture, thorough and accurate understandings of the ritual will always be limited and imprecise. While these challenges create a dilemma and are a cause for concern, they should not detract from the central purpose of this review—to uncover common elements that undergird the process of rites of passage and to see if and how these activities are related to and strengthen a psychological sense of community. Some interpretations are offered, but they are done with full respect for the limitations considered here. Also, while some may feel entitled by academic privilege to promote their views and pretend to thoroughly understand a culture, I am more reluctant to take such a lofty position. Furthermore, how accessible are a culture's initiation rites anyway? These rites are the access points for inclusion into a culture. They are the doors one walks through into a culture's adult world. How guarded these worlds are remains unanswered and therefore brings into question the complete picture of the observations described. In my relationship with the Huichol people, for example, I know first-hand that they purposefully do not share essential information with outsiders, especially those who align themselves with academia and disciplines that investigate cultures.

Selection of Stories

There were two criteria for selecting material from the Human Relations Area Files to include in this chapter. First, it had to have a narrative detailed enough to illustrate themes, use of symbols, and patterns that were similar in other cultures' initiation and rites of passage processes. Second, the details revealed common design principles that could be useful to inform and guide the emergence of contemporary community rites of passage. In light of the cautions raised, I have limited any analysis, refraining from "symbolic guessing" and interpreting for meaning, which would places us on shaky ground. While I have included details for the above reasons, I am not suggesting that they should be copied, transferred, or appropriated in other settings. This has been addressed elsewhere and again at the end of this chapter.

I have kept the original title for this chapter, "Something Happened," because that is about the best and most accurate thing I could say after reading the ethnographies, other commentaries, and personal experiences about rituals, initiation, and rites of passage. The only thing I could say with certainty is simply that something happened and something needs to happen to affect a child's transition to adulthood. And that what happened was as important for the larger collective, the family, community, culture, ancestors, and Universe as it was for the individual. Just as with the other rites of passage across the life cycle (i.e., birth, marriage, and funerals), the process of coming of age (going from childhood to adulthood) was always done within a larger context. Consider these questions: Are rites of passage conducted exclusively for an infant to bring them fully into the physical and spiritual plane? What about funerals? Are they most important for the deceased or for the family and community that must reorganize in the absence of the departed? And in the rite of passage ceremony for the dead are we not celebrating and remembering important values for life?

After reviewing ethnographies and more than six decades of a deepening relationship with rites of passage, three primary questions emerged. The questions have become more relevant now with the dramatic increase in programs offering rites of passage. They are: Initiation into what? By whom? and, For what purpose?

Responses to these questions emerged from the stories that follow. In effect, this is the way it has always been. Stories have always been the central way we handed down essential information that has served our survival. Perhaps by remembering the central elements and key lessons in these rites of passage stories we can help our children to make a better world. In helping our children to make a better world, we are not only helping them now but also helping them to make a better world for their future and the future of their community and the earth and all who reside on her.

Stories from the Teda People of the Middle East

The first excerpt is the exact file as it appears in the Archives from the Teda culture in the Middle East. It provides an example of how the files were written, giving facts and descriptions of observable behaviors and physical features, but is limited in terms of explaining with any accuracy much of its meaning. Many of the files were not organized with page numbers, which is reflected in their absence in the reference section.

> "In Teda society girls undergo lip piercing when they are about ten to twelve, usually around the time of the date harvest (Kronenberg 1958). For seven days the girls remain in seclusion in a hut. They rub the wound with an unripened date and soot. The purpose of their operation is to enlarge the upper lip and color it bluish.
>
> Boys are circumcised around their fifteenth year. The boy chooses a married couple to be his sponsors. He refers to them as "my mother" and "my father," while his parents stay in the background during the ceremony. Prior to the ceremony the boy shaves his head."
>
> "Circumcision among the Teda is a genuine ritual of transition, for the moment the cut is made, the boy becomes a man and must therefore also be addressed as such (Kronenberg 1958). This is illustrated during the procedure when the operator says to the candidate: "little boy, look up" and when the cut is made he says: "man, look down." They congratulate the initiate and say: "You have become a man and that is good" (LeCoeur 1950).

Reports indicate a consistent age cohort for circumcision.

> "However, parents sometime postponed the event until a boy was 14 and even up to 20 because they did not like the emancipation which followed the circumcision of their children and because the festival was expensive and they may not have had the money. Boys, however, were impatient to attain the adult status conferred by circumcision, indicated, for example, by shaving their heads and the right to wear a turban, and some even tried to circumcise themselves" (Chapelle 1957, 268–9).

The desire for initiation is so strong that in the Middle East Teda culture boys were observed to circumcise themselves.

Some may grimace at the thought of this. But, how different is it from American youth who ravage their lives and the lives of their community in their attempts to find meaningful initiatory experiences? In the absence of community-oriented rites of passage, youth will find ways to initiate themselves, to mark their passage to adulthood. Something has to happen! The narrative illustrates several themes consistent in other ethnographies. Seclusion for girls was common. The event occurred in relationship to symbols of fertility and birth. In this example, the girl's initiation occurred sometime around the date harvest. Nature signaled the beginning of the initiatory process, which was related to the harvesting of dates, which also featured prominently in the ritual. It is unclear what the significance was of the lip piercing or coloring (bluish), but it certainly was of symbolic significance within the culture. Parents had strong emotions about the initiation and subsequent emancipation of their children. Not dissimilar to many parents' sentiments today. There was always some kind of community festival. The purpose of this will be addressed in other narratives.

Exploring these stories revealed themes, symbols, patterns, and processes of rites of passage that can help inform contemporary practice. Most important, the stories underscore the reciprocal nature of rites of passage. They did not just focus on and support a child's transition to adulthood. They appeared to always be in connection with and service to the initiate's family, community, their ancestors, the spirit world, and nature. The stories also illustrate that one person does not provide initiation and rites of passage to another person. Rather, it is a dynamic arrangement of relationships with the initiate, who is coming of age into their place in nature and within their family, ancestry, culture, and community. Each of these entities participates directly or through a symbolic surrogate. They also acknowledge a cosmology that integrates their history with the history of the Universe. All are in relationship. This is a subtle yet potent constellation of factors that is mostly overlooked in the ethnographic reports. These reports focused on concrete observable behaviors without understanding of the context, cultural, ancestral, and cosmological dynamics that undergirded the entire process. This is where the "symbolic guessing" that Wilson alluded to might creep into the narrative.

For example, if one were to take the above story at face value, one might think that the circumcision was a "genuine ritual of transition." Yet, in most cultures, the boy or girl does not take on the status of a man or women immediately following a part of the initiatory process (e.g., circumcision for the boy or seclusion for the girl). Rather, circumcision and seclusion are points of transition within an initiatory process, where the boy can no longer return to being a boy-child and the girl can no longer be a girl-child. Both are not yet fully adults as they relate to responsibilities, reproduction, and status within their culture and community. It is the beginning of the end of their childhood. These are dramatic events designed to signal to the youth, their family, community, ancestors, spirit world, and Universe that the initiatory process is commencing.

There is a collective call into the universe:

AH - HO! Look here Great Spirit; we are beginning the transformation of our children to be in your service—to be strong and in service to all their relations.

What is more compelling and evident in most other stories is the section related to the relationship of the family, initiation, and the community: "However, parents sometime postponed the event until a boy was 14 and even up to 20 because they did not like the emancipation which followed the circumcision of their children and because the festival is expensive and they may not have the money (Chapelle 1957, 268–9)." Herein lie two golden nuggets from the Teda culture in the Middle East introduced earlier. First, the parents did not want emancipation. This gives historical credence to a long-standing and substantial challenge in human development. Today we refer to it as "letting our children go to grow." The separation of children from their parents and/or guardians and surrogates as they get older is a central task of community-oriented rites of passage, where parents play an essential role. We discussed Jung's contributions in this area earlier, and in a subsequent story, we'll see how the Masai mediated this challenge and exemplified how rites of passage are so essential to help children separate from the "infant/child" status to which the parents are likely to cling. Furthermore, the Teda story illustrates a central characteristic present in almost all other rites of passage. That is, there is a reciprocal relationship between the family and community. While it takes many different forms, there was considerable evidence that something happened between the family and other significant relationships in what I am referring to as the initiatory constellation. The initiate is coming of age into their place in nature, and within their family, ancestors (culture), Spirit world, and community—all within a cosmology that integrates their history with the story of the universe. Elders are attuned to the initiatory constellation in ways that inform the overall design of the initiatory process.

In the story from the Teda culture in the Middle East we find a strong desire to undergo the initiatory process. Even though it is unimaginable that a boy would inflict that much pain on himself, the pull for increased status, as with western youth, is overpowering. The symbolic or literal alteration of the body, which symbolizes a change in status, is a consistent theme in initiation. Likewise, western youth today have continued the practice with body piercing, hairstyles like shaved heads, and other measures to differentiate their physical form of a adult from that of a child. Rather then the community honoring them and welcoming them into adulthood, youth today are self-initiating, satisfied with recognition and congratulations from their peers to mark their transition to adulthood.

I wrote previously, "It takes a whole child to raise a village." We have an innate understanding and orientation to come together to raise our children. Our evolutionary story suggests that a central reason humans formed groups is to collectively raise their children. It is ingrained in us as a species. We do this to survive. A village comes together to enact their collective story of rites of passage. It is what we have been doing for thousands of years. The collective efforts of a village are essential to raise a whole child who is healthy, life affirming, and civic- and nature-minded. A child who has a sense of connection to all things and is able to balance the competing demands of satisfying their own needs and those of the greater collectivity makes a community resilient and strong. Equally important, relationships in the village are strengthened, able to continually adapt to meet the changing needs of each member, which aids their survival. It is reciprocal. Initiated adults, serving as elders, must be able to respond to a child's inner need and hunger for initiation.

In the absence of village-oriented initiation and rites of passage, children will continue to initiate themselves with health-compromising behaviors whose consequences have and will continue to threaten our survival and the survival of the planet.

Lessons Learned for Modernity

What are the lessons learned from the story of the Teda culture's rite of passage? One passage speaks volumes and can inform contemporary practice:

The boy chooses a married couple to be his sponsors. He refers to them as "my mother" and "my father," while his parents stay in the background during the ceremony.

A child undergoing initiation frequently has other adults, besides their parents, who are committed to guiding and supporting them in their transition. It appears that one's biological parents are not among the central players, nor are they in the forefront of their own child's initiation. Someone else is there to cut the psychic umbilical cord, to lift the child out of the life-sustaining parental bond and into relationship with his or her community, spirit world, ancestors, and nature. In the Teda story, as in all other stories that follow, other adults take on a surrogate and guiding role and the community features prominently in the process. Equally important is the child's role in choosing their sponsor. It opens a pathway to their sense of autonomy and self-determination. Knowing the central elements in rites of passage, listening to other people's stories from their culture and community, and engaging them in conversation can help rites of passage emerge within their culture and community.

Obligation to the Community

The community featured prominently in all of the stories about puberty and initiation rites. In the Teda narrative, families had to consider the expense of the public celebration that always accompanied these rites.

Community celebrations, as we will see in all other cultural stories of initiation and rites of passage, are central to the process. Why? One reason is that we like to have fun, play, and recreate, which are all part of having a party. Laughter is a common, desirable, and healthy thing we do. I imagine if our ancestors were like us then they liked to party and laugh as well. In fact, laughter is thought to have predated human speech, perhaps by millions of years (Menting 2010). It was our earliest species form of communicating, "We are safe—let's bond" (2). What better occasion or excuse would there be to party than a major life-cycle event like a birth, wedding, funeral, or the celebration of someone coming of age? There is more to it than this. Rejoicing together in common celebration of an important life event, seasonal and celestial transitions, and religious or cultural occasions serves survival. We revisit the reason for the celebration and the values related to the events. We honor our relationship to nature in seasonal and celestial celebrations. We remember the stories and myths of our ancestor during religious and cultural events. We are drawn to reflect on the values and ethics underlying each event and affirm and/or adapt them for our survival. As detailed in the previous chapter, rituals offer a setting and the conditions ripe for sharing emotions, whether they are sadness expressed in crying or joy expressed in laughter. The shared emotional experience strengthens the bonds between people. Just think of your own experiences sharing in a celebration of a milestone event.

This part of the story captures what the psychologist James Hillman meant—as discussed in chapter 8—that no psychology of the individual can be viable that does not include the psyche of the individual within the psyche of the community. We would no longer champion the Cartesian notion of "I am because I think," which gives psychotherapy the avenue to work on the interior self. It would be, "I am because of others and the world." Or, as someone once said to Hillman, "I am because I party." *I am because I party* is central to this orientation, where one's self is defined and known in relationship to one's interiorization of the community and sense of place and connection to nature. Rituals in general and rites of passage specifically help us continually reaffirm who we are and the righteous way to behave within a community connected nature.

The Kanuri

Something happened—and it didn't just happen to and for the initiate.

Stories from the Kanuri people of the Middle East represent the ethnographies that illustrate the relationship between rites of passage and community.

Puberty and adolescence are important milestones in the Kanuri culture, yet clear lines of demarcation between childhood and adulthood in one rite of passage event are not evident. Cohen (1960) writes of the Kanuri: "Puberty is not an age-grade in the same sense as childhood or adolescence. Yet it deserves some special attention because it is a marker that separates these two life periods" (63). "Even for girls there is no sharp break between child and adult. Even after marriage she may not be considered a full woman" (63).

Cohen goes on to remark, "The important thing is not the readiness of the boy" for initiation. "Rather it is the auspiciousness of the occasion in terms of the family's relationship to the rest of the community." For the Kanuri, it is propitious for families to have their boys circumcised with high-ranking members of the community. "Usually the higher the rank of the leading families involved in a circumcision the greater the number of boys who are likely to be cut at the same time" (64). Just as with other initiatory practices, a strong bond is created not only among the initiates themselves but also between their families.

How is this similar to the prestigious colleges and universities that are highly desirable as much for their academic reputation and prestige as for the "high-ranking members of the community" whose children attend? The similarity extends down to early child development centers in urban areas that enroll high-ranking members of the community to which others want to be in relationship.

Initiation into What?

Cohen reports that the major function of the initiatory event is related to community connections.

> Certainly it marks publicly the opening of the gates on the road to manhood for the young man, but, much more importantly, it validates, strengthens, and dramatizes the relational network of ties that the family and the household maintain and attempt to promote in the society. (1960, 65)

> As with many cultures around the world the Kanuri regard the circumcision ceremony as a mark of approaching manhood, and even though the boys are often quite young the ceremony still dramatizes their adult or approaching adult status. (Cohen 1960, 65)

Cohen's observations point toward a continued unfolding of activities following circumcision which flows toward a truer status of adulthood, a status that includes the concomitant responsibilities of marriage, fatherhood, and increased economic responsibility. Following circumcision, boys approximate their adult status by brandishing whips and chasing young girls who pay them off with pennies.

> The girls must "buy off" such treatment by giving the young boy a few pennies. This ritual was left unexplained by informants who answered questions about its meaning by saying," We do this because it is our custom." (65)

What is of interest here is the continuation of the ritual in the absence of reports of a thorough understanding of its origin or meaning. "We do this because it is our custom," they say. In other words, the history and meaning of the ritual may not be the most critical features. Importance lies in repeating a ritual that had been performed by one's ancestors, within a context of initiation that achieved a desired outcome. In this case, the "boys approximate their adult status." They do it to maintain a link with their ancestors. In the performance of the ritual they are honoring and remembering their ancestors and accepting that what they did then, in the ritual form, helped them in the same way it can help them achieve their desired outcomes now. In effect they are saying, "When our ancestors did this the boy or girl became an adult. We do this now to achieve the same ends." This is similar to the observations and reports of other cultures, especially the Okayama in Asia. Something happens that is consistent with what has happened before. This illustrates the concept of a meta-myth. What has come before, the stories of initiation and rites of passage, can be retold through the reenactment of certain essential design elements, symbols, protocols, prayers, dress, and so forth, in the form of rituals. The story of rites of passage provides a context for our children's adulthood to emerge in a meaningful way that is connected to and connects children with their ancestors, Spirit, and nature and strengthens the bonds of people in a village.

Contemporary social learning theory would consider this within social (successive) approximation (Skinner 1953; Miltenberger 2012). A child engages in behaviors they perceive to be characteristic of adults, like smoking, sex, and drinking, that make them feel more like an adult. Acting in this way is perceived by the child to get them closer and closer to the desired status of "adult." This is related to Bandura's (1986) notion of "reciprocal determinism," where a person's behavior is both influenced by and influences their environment. In the absence of community-sanctioned socially and culturally appropriate initiation, children engage in behavior they perceive to be self-initiating and for them represent entry into adulthood. When children think smoking or drinking represents adult behavior, they engage in this and influence each other to think that is the way to become an adult.

There is an economic component to the circumcision ceremony. As with other cultures (Masai, Javanese, Samoan, etc.), gifts are exchanged. The initiated youth usually presents a gift to his godfather or sponsor, and members of the community present gifts to the initiate and their family. These activities have several benefits. It maintains the importance of honoring elders and giving thanks. It promotes the importance of reciprocity—that giving and receiving combine to maintain a balance in society and hence the universe. It also helps to establish the youth economically. Giving him gifts of animals, land, and other material items increases his status, making him a good provider and hence more suitable for marriage. It underscores the dynamic aspect of rites of passage. After the ceremony of circumcision the boy does not immediately become a full adult. Rather, he is seen as crossing an important line on his continued journey to adulthood. Adulthood is progressively conveyed through the activities associated with that status (i.e., marriage and economic self-sufficiency), which are given authority by and within the community. Something happened and it happened in relationship to others and the community.

Celebrations, Shrines, and Ancestors

Just as with the festivals reported in the Teda culture previously, coming of age is cause for a community celebration among the people of Okayama, Takashima, Japan. The focus of the celebration is on the construction and parading of a shrine, called a *sendairoku*, through the village. The members of the procession go from house to house early in the day to collect contributions. These contributions are related to the construction of the shrine and may include personal and family artifacts as well as money to purchase sake for members of the Seinendan, the initiatory group. The description reports, "this ceremony may have originated as a combination of puberty rites and a ceremony of induction into a formalized young men's age group" (Norbeck 1954).

Contributions of money are usually fairly large, and the total is sufficient to purchase ample sake to get all members of the Seinendan drunk, the purpose for which the money is intended. This is the one occasion of the year when young unmarried men (from about sixteen years of age upward) may, without censure, become thoroughly drunk. It is said also to be a day when all differences and dislikes between individual members of the Seinendan are forgotten.

> After the portable shrine has been set down the young men, many of them weaving from drink and all sweating profusely, convene at someone's house where they continue drinking until the sake purchased is consumed. In former days most young men became very drunk and very boisterous (but not quarrelsome). (Norbeck 1950)

Members of the community, even those that have had disputes, come together in celebration. The celebration is fueled and orchestrated by drinking, which alters the participant's consciousness in ways that increase a sense of connection. It is notable that although they are drunk, there is no evidence of quarreling. Perhaps the values of the observer make them predisposed to think that when young men drink they become "quarrelsome." Nevertheless, in this report, it is notable that all are deepening their connection with each other in ways that foster a sense of community.

> In the celebration they are maintaining a tradition, which has lost its meaning. Neither the decorations of the portable shrine nor the ceremony connected with it convey much specific meaning to members of the Seinendan or to most other persons of the buraku. If put to it to find an explanation, they may state that the ceremony is some form of respect for Kojin-same, one of their gods. (Norbeck 1950)

Just as in Cohen's account of the Kanuri, the origin and meaning of the Takashima custom has been lost, but they maintain their tradition. There is a relationship between the ceremony, a group of boys similar in age, and an initiation rite. The community participates through their contributions and witnessing the proceedings. Some kind of physical transformation takes place when youth paint their faces, altering their appearance, and parade, in an altered state of consciousness (drunk), in front of the community. There is reference to offering respect to the hidden god(s). The meaning for much of the ceremony has been lost or forgotten; yet the ceremony continues. This speaks to its continued utility both for the individual and community. Once again we see that a story of unknown origin is remembered and reenacted as a ritual. At this point, the story becomes the myth that if engaging the parents, children, and community in a reenactment children can become adults. There is a place for them within the community. "The house is in order; the world is set in order; the world is set on a firm course" (I Ching).

It must be quite an event to see scores of young people, happy and boisterous, weaving around the community, carrying a shrine composed of individual and family artifacts. Elders watch from a distance, grinning with the memory of their own youthful time of initiation and celebration. By linking the memory of the elder's past experience with the ritual engaged in the present by their children, both elders and youth share and are connected by the ritual experience of initiation. The youth who celebrate together in this fashion may be able to contribute collaboratively to the work of the community throughout the remainder of the year. It also speaks to the importance of festival and "party" as a central way for people to connect with each other with a sense of the spirit. It is no accident that we refer to liquor as "spirits." Its use here as a "social lubricant" in helping to enhance one's sense of connection to their ancestors and spirit world is evident.

Is it too much of a stretch to consider similarities with the widespread celebration of St. Patrick's Day? After all, in America and elsewhere, do people who participate in parties celebrating the day recognize that St. Patrick was responsible for driving paganism from Ireland and converting people to Christianity? Born in England in 387 A.D., he was forcibly brought to Ireland as a slave. His escape back to England, where he heard the voice of God, and his subsequent epiphany could parallel an initiation compelling his actions and devotion in life. The myths underlying celebrations may long be forgotten, but their utility lies in bringing people together, in levity and laughter, which is likely to strengthen the bonds of community. Might there be a rather simple, if not pedestrian reason for rituals that lay in our basic need for affiliation? "Throw a party and they will come!" Festivals, community meals, and gatherings are the central ways of gathering that ultimately serve to strengthen the bonds between people. As James Hillman said, "I party therefore I am."

Connection to Spirit and Ancestors

There may be no greater ethnographic evidence of the importance of the initiate's connection to the spirit world and their ancestors than in the descriptions of the Hopi people. It is evident from Titiev's (1944) descriptions that the entire Hopi community immerses itself in the tribal initiation. Elaborate costumes, songs, and performances mark the nine-day event in which the four tribal divisions come together. Through chanting and dancing, the ritual reenacts the life of the Hopi as well as the life cycle of the individual. Tribal divisions, usually segregated, come together and divide up responsibilities for essential elements of the ritual. This includes lighting fires, dance, night patrols, and public performance, all designed to link the initiate with the ancestors, the spirit world, and impending adulthood while strengthening the bonds of community between the different divisions.

As with other initiations, the boys are separated for portions of the rite and engage in symbolic behavior related to the culture. Hopi youth are considered "little chicken hawks" (133-A) and have hawk feathers tied in their hair when they enter the seclusion kiva. For three days they must remain in the kiva, because "their quills are not strong enough." They imitate chickens during feeding and are given a wooden scratcher, which they use as a bird uses a claw.

> The candidate for initiation has a sponsor from the division they will ulti-
> mately join. The "ceremonial father weaves for his "son" a special poncho-
> like garment, daubed all over with white clay and wider in front than
> in back. The entire garment is said to represent the feathers, wings and
> tail of a hawk. These outfits are given to novices on the fourth day of the
> Wuwutcim initiation and are worn by them on their first public appearance
> as members of the society. (133-B)

Perhaps most revealing and illustrating the concept of death of the child and rebirth as an adult is the following description:

> The Hopi village prepares a feast for their dead ancestors. Much elaborate
> preparation is undertaken. During the day the women prepare large quan-
> tities of food for the expected "guests." The feast is set out after sunset and
> all the tribe moves to one side of the village leaving the feast for the spirits
> on the other side. Much activity occurs with guards confronting spirits and
> I would imagine the entire village remains awake much of the night. Not
> only does the entire village participate in the ritual, but also this portion
> establishes the inclusion of the spirits and ancestors.
>
> To perform its part in the ensuing ritual, each spirit is supposed to enter
> the particular kiva with which it was associated while alive. At some time
> prior to the arrival of the dead, four of the Kwan men who had been inducted
> into the society at the preceding Tribal Initiation are delegated secretly to
> visit the local graveyard and to strip four recently interred corpses of their
> burial garments. There the four Kwan members dress in the foul smelling
> grave-clothes, and soon after, they appear before the startled neophytes in
> dimly lighted kivas where they are readily mistaken by the terror-stricken
> novices for the very dead men whose apparel they wear.
>
> What befalls the initiates in the presence of this weird assembly of liv-
> ing Hopi, visible "dead," and unseen spirits, no white man can tell with
> assurance; but from the general context I think that we may reasonably
> conjecture that in some manner the novices are ceremonially "killed," their
> boyish lives are terminated, and they are reborn as men. At the same time,
> they are introduced to the "society of the dead" and thus made certain
> of occupying their proper places in the other world, for there are special
> "homes" to which only the shades of Kwan, Al, Tao, or Wuwutcim men may
> go. (136-A)

Titiev synthesizes his observations into an analysis of the Hopi's tribal initiation to have three related aims: "First, to confer manhood on the boys; second, to establish coordination between living and dead members of the societies; and third, to renew the contacts between the populations of this world and the next" (137-A). While these may be valid interpretations, within the limits and cautions set forth earlier, another result is the reconnection of tribal divisions or clans and the strengthening of bonds between the adult members of the tribe. The different clans within their tribal society cooperate in order to conduct the tribal initiation ceremonies, helping to maintain balance and order. It also illustrates a connection between a conscious mundane physical reality and a spiritual reality including all of their ancestors.

Connection with ancestors may be a challenging concept for some in contemporary western society. Voluntary and forced migration and slavery over hundreds of years have created large gaps in relationships between present and past generations. Even more challenging is the concept of connecting with the Spirit world, or the world we do not see. These are complex yet important issues to be grappled with in contemporary community rites of passage. More and more youth development experts are recognizing the importance of the spiritual development of children and trying to figure out how to respond to this in practice within a secular multicultural society (Benson, Roehlkepartain, and Rude 2003; Benson et al. 2012; Kimball, Mannes, and Hackel 2009).

All Are Connected—All Must Change

The next ethnographies provide material that informs us of the importance of making a place in the family and community for the initiate. The extensive material on the Masai culture depicts a central rite called "The Passing of the Fence," which coincides with the initiation of the oldest son.

> A Masai child cannot be circumcised until the father has observed a custom called *the passing of the fence*.
>
> The man who wishes to have his eldest child circumcised brews some honey-wine, and calls his neighbors together while it is being prepared.
>
> A hut is then built for him outside the *kraal*, and he stays there for four days alone. He also sleeps there, and his food is taken to him.
>
> During these four days he only approaches the *kraal* to look after his cattle when they are grazing outside.
>
> He must don the clothes, ornaments, and weapons of a warrior—the sword, the spear, the club, and the shield, the cap made from the stomach of a goat, the head-dress of ostrich feather and the cape of vultures' feathers, the anklets of colobus-monkey skin, the arm-clamp, the garment of a calf-skin, and the piece of goat's skin fastened to the waist.
>
> When the four days have elapsed, some of the elders go and bring him back to the kraal.
>
> He has to stand by the door of the hut where the honey-wine, which has previously been prepared, is kept.

One elder then says to him "who is passing the fence? Go, become an old-man."

The latter replies: "Ho! I shall not...!"

The order is repeated, but he still refuses.

On being told for the fifth time, he says: "Ho! I have gone then."

He then enters the hut and puts aside the warrior's paraphernalia; the honey-wine is drunk; and he is called by his son's name, thus: The father of so-and-so.

When he replies to this name, he is told to go and make a profit.

He answers: "Herds and flocks."

This is repeated four times, and the ceremony is over.

After this any of his children, whether girls or boys, may be circumcised." (Hollis 1905, 294–5)

Bernardi (1955) also describes the passing of the fence. He adds to the previous description:

The ceremony is performed only once in a man's life, namely when he "wishes to have his eldest child circumcised." This particular circumstance shows that by "the passing of the fence" a man obtains a special elderly status, which gives him a right to have all his children initiated.

Thus, there is a relationship between the father's social status and the initiation into the age-class of his sons. None of these may be initiated unless the father has reached the proper status. The personal status of the father is reflected on his children. Therefore the "passing of the fence" is not in itself part of the age-system initiation, but a condition which must have been observed before a man is allowed to have his sons initiated. (272)

What golden nuggets can be extracted from this rich story that can inform the emergence of community oriented rites of passage? First, once again we see that rites of passage are central to a family and community. Arrangements are made within the family and community in order to enact the initiation of an individual. The social and cultural context needs to be well established for an initiation to result in real transformation. The narrative describes that both local and regional preparations are established throughout the land of the Masai. This prepares the elders to be elders and provides a structure for and context to incorporate the initiates into their adult role. The house needs to be set in order.

One of the great challenges in childrearing today is "letting go" of one's child and allowing them to learn self-reliance in a world full of self-indulgence. Recall in the story of the Teda people that parents did not want their child initiated because they did not want them emancipated. There are real reasons in today's world for protecting and ensuring the security of our children. A fine line exists between fostering independence and keeping a watchful eye on our children.

One central purpose of rites of passage was to formally begin the process of separation between parents and their children entering puberty and adolescence. Without a formal and public expectation for separation, both parent and child are challenged to do this well.

The process of separation was dramatically depicted in one segment of the acclaimed 1977 miniseries based on Alex Haley's *Roots*. In the scene of separation, an "Elder" male sneaks up behind the unsuspecting Kunta Kinte, right in front of his mother, places a hood over him, and takes him away to the initiation camp. His mother, played by Cicely Tyson, says, "My boy is taken. A man will return." It is swift and clean. There is no confusion that the boy must leave his home to become a man.

So, too, in the Masai custom of passing of the fence, where the father, who wishes to have a son initiated, must first move himself out of his existing social order. He even enacts not wanting to go, having the elder repeat the command to move over. Is this not similar to contemporary western parents' ambivalence and anxiety about releasing their children for them to enter adulthood?

> One elder then says to him "who is passing the fence? Go, become an old-man."
> The latter replies: "Ho! I shall not…!"
> The order is repeated, but he still refuses.
> On being told for the fifth time, he says: "Ho! I have gone then."
> He is called by his son's name, thus: The father of so-and-so (Hollis 1905).

In this ritual, the family hierarchy is adjusted to make room for the new initiate to become a man. And both the father and son are linked by their names. The father becomes known as the "father of …" This is similar in the Jewish tradition. During my Bar Mitzvah ceremony I was publically introduced as David ben Herschel, the son of Herschel, which was my father's Hebrew name. In other cultures, the initiate takes on another name to identify his/her changing status. These cultural and contextual processes of publically altering the family structure, facilitating the separation of a child from their parents, guardians, and/or surrogates, aid in meeting the historic challenge of letting go of one's child for them to grow.

The Call to Adventure: Drugs and Sex

Over the past several decades, teenage drug use, including alcohol, and their sexual behavior have occupied adult attention. Out of a national concern for our children we have declared war on drugs and spent billions on the prevention of teenage pregnancy. *Just Say No!* has been a big part of both campaigns. How has that been working?

Adolescence is a time of awakening to the possibility of a great adventure. All youth, coming into increased power, physically, mentally, and spiritually are seeking ways to engage in an inquiry into the great mystery, the meaning of life and their place in it. As revealed in a story told earlier, at the time of puberty they are awakened with a memory of a knowledge they need to remember. They seek to reconnect with that sacred primal knowledge they had while in the womb. One path they perceive as open to this knowledge is through experiences with nonordinary states of reality, which drugs produce quite well. For many youth both sex and drugs, veiled in mystery and taboo, have become a part of the adolescent experience (Scheer, Gavazzi, and Blumenkrantz 2007). They are attractive to youth who are seeking to explore boundaries and limits and experience adventure. Youth are looking to feel alive within their emerging potency. Drugs do work to produce nonordinary states of reality, and sex feels good. These are some pretty good incentives for teens to engage in experimentation with each. While some may suggest that youth engage in drug use and sex as part of their own self-created rite of passage, which has merit for them, something else is at work here.

Some suggest that humans are *hardwired* to experiment with nonordinary states of reality (Weil 1983). When a toddler is just learning to stand up and walk they experiment with altering their reality. In a sense, they are learning how to alter their reality or, you could say, "get high." Here is how they do it. They spin around in circles, get dizzy, fall down giggling, and then get back up having learned that they can control their perception of the world, alter their consciousness, and feel good. They are learning that they can control their world, especially how to feel pleasure. They are beginning to learn that different states of consciousness are fun and pleasurable. After falling down giggling what do they do? They do what you'd expect. They get up and do it again!

History is rich with accounts of human "intoxication," and the production of wine and beer go back to antiquity (Charles and Durham 1952; Chrzan 2013). This is not to mention the psychotropic plants and mushrooms ingested by indigenous people around the world (Siegel 1989; Sullivan and Hagen 2002). Without getting too far astray into the fascinating topic of our relationship with nonordinary states of reality, let us look at several initiation rites that incorporate this into their practices.

Hardwired to Experience Altered States of Consciousness

Ethnographies from South American cultures are rich with accounts of the use of psychoactive plants to effect a nonordinary state of reality on the initiate. The narratives from the Jivaroan people of the Ecuadorian and Peruvian Amazon reveal this well.

In Jivaro, Karsten (1935) reports, "when the first signs of puberty appear, an important epoch in the life of the Jibaro girl begins" (236). Upon the first menstruation, around the age of eight to ten years old, the girl's mother takes her down to the river, where she washes her with a big leaf. "She has now to submit to certain taboos for four days. She is not allowed to pass the night in the house, but sleeps in a small shelter specially made for her in the plantation in the neighborhood, whither she is accompanied in the evening by the other women" (236). The girl is not required to stay there during the day and may return to her house, where she is not allowed to touch anything. She has to observe a strict diet and is given repeated doses of tobacco water with only a small quantity of manioc. The tobacco medicine is supposed to fill her with power and to protect her against evil spirits who are attacking her, but it is also calculated to produce dreams for her. These are supposed to relate to her future as a woman (Karsten, 1935).

Boys engage in a lengthy process of initiation also involving strict taboos, dietary regulation, and more intensive intoxication with maikoa and tobacco. When the boy reaches the age of puberty (no age is given) he engages in a drinking ceremony. Karsten (1935) describes the ceremony:

> The oldest men of the family or tribe arrange themselves in two parallel rows facing each other. Each man holds a pininga containing a small quantity of maikoa. The novice must now go from the one to the other in due order and take a sip from each pininga, starting with the oldest member of the family. . . . It is considered absolutely necessary . . . that the novice should receive something from the clay vessel of each man.
>
> When the young man has finished drinking the oldest man asks him: "Do you know now why you have drunk maikoa?" "Yes" the youth answers, "It is in order that I may become a real man and a brave warrior and that I may be able to marry." (241–42)

This description depicts the relationship between the novice, the elders, and the spiritual world. The men of the village have to participate in the transition of the novice to adult by symbolically sharing their wisdom through the sacred maikoa. The boy passes through the "tunnel" or pathway set by the men. Along the way, the boy is getting vital substance, in the physical form of maikoa, which opens to the realm of the spiritual world, to help unfold the mysteries of life and adulthood. Another valuable design feature is illustrated here when the men form a "tunnel," which serves as a pathway for the boy to travel. During the passage through the tunnel the elders reveal important information.

The young girl also experiences segregation from the community and engages in activities prescribed within tradition by her elders. In almost all traditions there is a clearer signal for females to begin the initiatory process. A natural biological marker and order of change and transformation occurs with the onset of menstruation. There is ritual cleansing; cloistering with other elder females, not including the biological mother; exchange of information related to sexuality and other essential knowledge for their entry into adulthood, marriage, procreation, and their role as an adult in the community.

On the occasion of initiation for young boys around fifteen or sixteen, a three-year process begins with the preparation of a feast. A new plantation must be built, and animals must be bred to feed the celebrants two or three years later. Karsten (1935) reports that several months prior to the feast the youth undergoes extreme privation. He has to wear special garments, and is not able to keep his long hair untied. During the four-day festival the youth goes through a series of rituals that center around ingesting tobacco water and smoke. Although Karsten does not interpret any similarity to the use of this substance in girls, I would suggest that tobacco and other medicinal herbs could be considered an ally of the Jivaro.

The tobacco produces very strong effects on the boy, including a "narcotic sleep" intended to produce visions and connection with spirits who "give him advice and information concerning his future" (Karsten, 238–41). This is a time of considerable volatility for the boy, who awakens in this intoxicated state and has to be physically contained by the elders who are standing watch. Sometimes the boy and old men retreat into the forest, where they stay for three days and nights performing the ritual. Harner (1973) reports that the youth, around the age of sixteen, retreats into the forest and kills a tree sloth, making a *tsantsa* (shrunken) of its head. All accounts place great importance on the dreams, which may decide their whole future.

Once again we see the inclusion of a feast for the community. Intoxication produces dreaming and visions for both the boys and girls. One of the reasons for the ritual intoxication is to make ancestors' wisdom accessible. During the narcotic sleep ancestors and Spirit visit the initiate. There is an exchange from which the youth has a vision:

> It is the acquisition of this vision [*arutam*]—or "audition," strictly speaking— which gives meaning and direction to life for most Jivaroan men. Individuals who have undergone several successful arutam quests are immediately recognizable by their forceful manner of speaking, their self-possession and obvious confidence in their own moral authority and strength. (Taylor 1993, 661)

Dreaming and visions are key ingredients in the initiatory process. "It is the acquisition of this vision which gives meaning and direction to life." This is the quintessential reason for the questing and ordeal element in the initiatory process. Helping youth acquire a vision, which gives their lives meaning and direction, is critical. Altering one's consciousness into a nonordinary state of reality places the youth's mind in the desired state of perturbation. Perturbation is a mental state of disturbance or agitation. It can serve as the pathway for dreaming and having visions. In astronomy, perturbation is a deviation of a celestial body from a regular orbit about its primary heavenly body, like the moon's orbit around the earth. It is caused by the presence of one or more other bodies that act on the celestial body. Youth are seeking a way to move out of their regular orbit of childhood and into adulthood. Having a vision and dream for their future aids in this transition. We know that when youth have hopes and dreams for their future the chances of growing up well are markedly improved. Dreams and visions help propel us forward. They give us something to reach for and journey toward.

These cultures placed great importance on having a rich spiritual life. The onset of adolescence coincides with a dramatic shift in consciousness and maturing cognitive development of children. They begin to think differently, moving from concrete to formal operational cognitive abilities (Piaget 1983). The famed developmental psychologist Jean Piaget (1977) observed that a child before the age of around 11 sees and thinks of things in logical concrete black and white terms. Somewhere around puberty they can begin to think logically about abstract propositions and test hypotheses systematically. They become interested in philosophical thinking and inquiry into meaning, the future and ethical and ideological problems. This is the time during which they are seeking an awakening and are deepening their immersion in wondering about themselves, the Universe, and their place in it.

Supporting Wonderment

From a very young age, children—even toddlers—are enchanted with wondering about the universe and their place in it. Indeed, this wonderment and a yearning to make sense of and connections with the Universe are part of our essential human nature. This nature is the foundation of our spirituality, which is having a deep, joy-filled sense of connection with and wonder about the world and Universe.

We see this in the old Yiddish story by Rabbi Adin Steinsaltz (2005), shared earlier and worth repeating. While we are in the womb, we know everything there is to know about the universe, but we forget it all at birth. After a number of years of wondering about it around the time of puberty there is a special opportunity—and a need—for an *awakening* to that original wisdom. He says:

> Around the time of puberty, in late adolescence, . . . I hear a knock and I know it but I may not be ready. Later on I feel the void . . . If I miss it I can go on a quest . . . If this call is missed and the opportunity for "awakening" to this inner wisdom passes, then there will always be a void. (27)

This is consistent with Piaget's conception of cognitive development. Around the time of puberty a child is beginning to perceive and experience abstract thought. This leads to wonderment. Wonderment is the awakening to a sense that there is some kind of "original primal wisdom" that needs to be known. Young adolescents are searching for opportunities for "awakening." This, in part, is the attraction to drugs. It gives them a sense of awakening, but this is not an awakening, guided by adults, that ensures a spiritual and healthy growth experience.

> If children are given no occasion to become awakened during their coming of age, then the void of missing wisdom becomes increasingly painful and must be filled. Young people may learn to fill the void with violence, with cynicism, or with drugs, alcohol, and other forms of acquiring, ingesting, and abusing anything they can have a pseudo-relationship with.

The narrative from South America describes the Jivaroans' way to respond to youths' need for awakening to a deep connection with their ancestors, Spirit, and things that are greater than themselves. And, this connection brings the power of love. In the Huichol tradition it is said:

> If you feel the love of Mother Earth, even for just an instant,
> it will be sufficient for one's entire life-time.

Another distinguishing feature in these initiatory practices are youths' deep engagement with the natural world. Although the stories are from cultures that were tightly connected to the land, there are repeated accounts of taking the children deeper into the woods or forest. They describe the elders as taking the youth on "retreats into the forest," where other important activities occur. Connection with spirit, ancestors, and nature are all central to the initiatory experience. Once one has a deep sense of connection with these elements, something transformative happens.

Females, Procreation, and the Future of a Species

Thus far, the majority of information presented has been about male initiation. Circumcision was a consistent tradition along with a number of other observable details. It is less clear what information elders communicated to the female initiate; there is very little written evidence about this. Assumptions are that values, attitudes, and skills essential for survival are conveyed, along with information about the spirit world and ancestors. But there are no transcripts or detailed reports. As discussed at the onset, this leaves us on shaky ground when discussing the initiation of females.

There are fewer observable behaviors and activities for females than for males, and therefore much less information is known about female initiation. One thing is constant. At the onset of menstruation something happens. Nature signals when to begin the initiatory process. This is much more overt for females than males, which points toward the relationship of the elements in the "initiatory constellation," discussed previously. There is some evidence that information on conceiving and bearing offspring, the essential task in any species, is conveyed. If initiation served survival, then one of the most important pieces of information conveyed would be about procreation. There is little direct information that reports how information on procreation was transmitted. There is some veiled evidence that it was important but not directly addressed. This is alluded to over and over again, although there are no details. While activities related to the initiation of boys are more fully known, there must have been some cultural reason why women's initiation was more discreet and secret. Perhaps the wisdom shared was too powerful for men to know?

An example of this is reported in the archive of Okayama, Matsunagi, in Japan, by Hall, estimated to be from the early 1960s:

> Most young people who do not go past middle school receive no instruc-
> tion in sex matters except what they get from reading modern novels and

romantic stories in popular magazines. For girls in particular, since they have become widely published in numerous postwar American-style magazines, stories of romantic love and marriage are important forms of sex education. A pubescent individual, whose sexuality is gradually heightened by growing sex knowledge, reaches the age of marriage with a basic understanding of the nature of sexual relationship without any explicit parental instruction. (Hall 1966)

Another report from Norbeck (1954) on the Okayama, Takashima, in Japan, offers similar references without much detail, context, or explanation:

> She has learned about relations between the sexes from the same sources as her brother, with the addition of a brief, practical, and unnecessary explanation from her mother just last year at the time of her first menstruation. Yuriko is well aware of the premium placed on chastity in her community. The rare girl in the buraku who makes even one mistake of this kind is almost certain to be found out. She is then known as damaged goods, and there are serious problems when it is time for her to marry. Yuriko expects to enter marriage as a virginal bride, and, until marriage, she is content with the company of other girls. (Norbeck 1954)

Opler (1940) reports that Ute girls reach puberty around fourteen to fifteen and are "capable of entering into adult economic life to the fullest extent" (132).

> At first menstruation, a girl was taken an eighth or a quarter of a mile from the family camp and segregated in a brush wickiup. Her grandmother or the older female relative who accompanied her made a cedar bark wickiup in cold winter weather. There she was instructed in sexual affairs and told of the dangerous potency of menstrual blood to things masculine. (139)

The seclusion of girls after first menstruation appears to be present in many cultures. It is unclear what occurs during this time of seclusion. The descriptions refer to the initiate being ritually cleansed, surrounded, protected, and taught by other adult women in the village. Details do not reveal whether the girl's mother is present. Understanding is further compromised by the fact that men did all of the observations and reports. Even when direct reports are second-hand, the informants were other men from the village. With some reservation and without judgment, analysis, or understanding, I offer the following description of the Lozi tribe from Africa, written by Turner (1952):

> There are no initiation ceremonies for boys, nor age-sets, though most boys and girls served the king in his capital or other village for a time.
> Girls, at first menstruation, are secluded in the bush in a hut with two or three companions, married women, spending the day there and returning to their fathers' homesteads at night to sleep. During this period the

married women dance and sing round the girl, beating her with sticks, or alternatively instructing in the physical and psychological aspects of married life. This "rite de passage" (mwalianjo, Stirke) is terminated by a purificatory rite, in which the girl is washed in the nearest water by the elder women. (44)

Gluckman's (1965) contributions on the initiatory practices of the Lozi appear to also focus on fertility and preparation for reproduction:

> Girls, too, grow gradually into family activities, but they have a sharp break at first menstruation. Then a girl is secluded for two or three months, spending the day in a hideout in the bush in the charge of older women, and returning in the evening to the village. At the end of this period the girl is finely dressed and decorated and sits downcast and tearful surrounded by women. Later in the day, escorted by her male guardian and a substitute for her mother, she emerges under a blanket, which the man removes with a hoe and the woman with an axe. The girl fetches water and then she chooses a new name. The people present dance. The girl is now ready for marriage. (84)

In Turner's further account of the activities within the Lozi life cycle, he notes that the bridegroom gives gifts to the parents of his intended, a variety of goods and objects such as oxen, a hoe, and a wooden dish, while the father-in-law is given a shirt and loincloth. The hoe is also used in the mwalianjo procedure (rites de passage). The hoe as an object has both symbolic and functional purposes. On one hand, it is an instrument used in the cultivation of food. It scratches the ground, making way for new growth. Symbolically, it may also be considered to be related to fertility. Gluckman noted that following the period of seclusion the girl emerges from a blanket, which is removed by a man with a hoe. A woman who helps expose the new woman with an axe assists him. Both of these are instruments of transformation, one applied to the earth and the other to what grows above it.

Information on reproduction is also provided about males. This is included in Merker's (1910) description of the Masai. His commentary on the source of ritual is important and is similar to other accounts, which suggest the origin of the ritual is not remembered. The ritual reenacts a sacred story and is in service of the greater good. This has implication for helping communities remember and co-create contemporary rites of passage.

Merker (1910) reports, "According to the belief of the Masai, circumcision was introduced by a command of God." This important note, not qualified or elaborated on, seems to reflect the divine nature of these rituals. They are the bridge between the secular and nonsecular worlds that connect the sacred with the mundane existence.

Merker suggests a close association between the ideas of circumcision, conception, and birth: "Therefore circumcision is regarded here as a means, even though not necessary for conception, nevertheless desirable for it and promoting it." We find the same thought in the Bible, where God, in Genesis 17:6, when he announces to the 99-year-old, childless Abraham the sign of the covenant (i.e., circumcision) says, "And I will make thee exceeding fruitful, and I will make nations of thee."

Each of the above descriptions is steeped in cultural values and myths that are probably beyond understanding from anyone outside of the culture. This is frequently the way it is when outsiders observe and try to understand the cultural practices of another culture. This is especially true with initiation, which is the culture's practice that allows access and entry into their whole world. As will be seen in Heckewelder's disrespectful and offensive report on the Delaware people, one's own values are a critical lens for viewing the world.

One cannot understand the Lozi practices through the lens of a contemporary western observer. We know the young girls were secluded, for varying lengths of time, surrounded by older women—some reports say married women, others are unclear. This is very common in many other cultural initiatory practices with girls. Is it too far of a reach to suggest that the transmission of information on sex, reproduction, and the relationship between genders was paramount? The above description from the Masai, at face value, could lead one to believe that circumcision originated from the divine, as with the Hebrew tribe, and was specifically intended to ensure procreation. Perhaps less valid is an interpretation that these initiation rites also had something to do with the relationship between men and women during married life. Yet, going back to the first stories from Okayama, Takashima, evidence exists where it specifically says, "She has learned about relations between the sexes from the same sources as her brother, with the addition of a brief, practical, and unnecessary explanation from her mother."

The separation of males and females for initiation was reported to be universal among all of the cultural practices. These practices were at a time, place, and within cultures where clear distinctions were made between the roles and responsibilities of a man and a woman. That is not usually the case within contemporary secular western culture. This creates a dilemma for how to adapt initiation processes for modernity. There is no easy or clear answer or pathway. More discussion of this issue is taken up briefly in a subsequent discussion in the next two chapters.

The Delaware Nation

The following account, of the Delaware Nation, also illustrates how one focus of initiation was to alter the consciousness of the initiate. The sentiment expressed by Heckewelder, who was an ethnographer and United States Indian Agent, is a striking example of the limitations, misunderstanding and disrespect of a culture by the observer. Even though it is almost two hundred years old, it reflects the issues raised earlier about the lens and orientation of the observer that limits the ability to truly understand the events observed or recounted.

Heckewelder (1819) writes of the initiatory activities of the Delaware people:

> I do not know how to give a better name to a superstitious practice which
> is very common among the Indians, and, indeed, is universal among those
> nations that I have become aquatinted with. By certain methods which
> I shall presently describe, they put the mind of a boy in a state of perturba-
> tion, so as to excite dreams and visions; by means of which they pretend
> that the boy receives instructions from certain spirits or unknown agents
> as to his conduct in life, that he is informed of his future destination and of
> the wonders he is to perform in his future career through the world. (245)

Heckewelder, who lived among the Delaware people, appears to be in disbelief at the rich spiritual life, referred to as "superstition," of the Delaware and
other indigenous people. His suggestions that they "pretend that the boy receives
instructions from certain spirits" disregards and disrespects the spiritual world
of the Delaware people. What are the implications of these descriptions if we
accept them as true?

Newcomb (1956) describes the vision quest of young Delaware Indian boys as the
"climax of the more formal aspects of the educational system [which] served to usher
the boy over the threshold into adult life." He reports, "When a boy was about ten
years old, or when his voice began to change, he began what can best be called a series
of ordeals" (35). He refers to Heckewelder's description, noting that the boys are put
under an "alternate course of physical exertion and fasting, either taking no food
whatever, or swallowing the most powerful and nauseous medicine, and occasionally
he is made to drink concoctions of an intoxication nature, until his mind becomes sufficiently bewildered, so that he sees or fancies that he sees visions, and has extraordinary dreams, for which, of course, he has been prepared beforehand" (245). These
dreams became the architectural blueprint for their lives (Newcomb 1956).

Putting the boy in a state of perturbation, so to excite dreams and visions, is a
very important part of initiation. Heckewelder claims this is "universal among those
nations that I have become acquainted with" (245), substantiating earlier reports
and suggesting the importance of the practice during initiation. While less dramatic,
all of the previous accounts describe the creation of settings in which the initiates,
both boys and girls, are placed in a state of perturbation, frequently through induc-
ing nonordinary states of reality. This is the sense that something is different and
one has lost their bearings. Put in this novel place, the initiate is positioned to figure
out new navigational aids to gain a new sense of direction. In this state there is a
cultural expectation that their visions will inform and guide their lives and in many
instances serve the survival of the tribe.

The Emergence of Initiation

The account of the Delaware people is of particular interest to me. In 1965 I was
initiated into an "honor society" at a summer sleep-away camp. Lore had it that the

initiatory practice used was based on the Order of the Arrow initiation used by the Boy Scouts, which was based on those of the Delaware Nation. In 1915, as the Boy Scouts were forming in America, there was an initiative to recognized those scouts who exemplified the best in Scout virtues. E. Urner Goodman, founder of the Order of the Arrow, became director of a Boy Scout camp in Philadelphia. It was located on Treasure Island in the Delaware River. Goodman and the Assistant Camp Director Carroll A. Edson researched the lore and language of the Delaware Indians who had inhabited Treasure Island. They combined characters from James Fenimore Cooper's *Last of the Mohicans* with the Delaware materials to develop dramatic induction ceremonies for the "Order of the Arrow," as the fledgling honor society was dubbed.[2]

The following excerpts from the *Order of the Arrow Handbook* and the *Order of the Arrow Manual for the Ordeal* are informative and included here.

From the Foreword of the *Order of the Arrow Handbook*, which E. Urner Goodman wrote in 1915:

> The Order of the Arrow is a thing of the outdoors rather than the indoors. It was born in an island wilderness. It needs the sun and the rain, the mountains and the plains, the woods, the waters, and the starlit sky.
>
> We pick up the lore and traditions of the American Indians and honor them today. The Indian respected the open air, and his culture is ours to preserve.
>
> From life in the open country comes a precious ingredient that our country and any country needs if it is to survive—self-reliance that makes men strong in any time of stress. (6)

From the *Order of the Arrow Manual for the Ordeal*:

> The founders devised the Ordeal to give them this inspiration in the form of an experience involving the ideals they were to follow.
>
> Eat you nothing but the scant food you'll be given. Learn by fasting, sacrifice, and self-denial, to subordinate desires to the spirit's higher purpose.
>
> Your directions are the whispers, urgings, promptings, deep within your hearts and spirits. Therefore, till you take the Obligation, strictly keep a pledge of silence.
>
> Spend the day in arduous labor, working gladly, not begrudging, seek to serve, and thus be faithful to the high ideals and purpose of the Order of the Arrow.
>
> All your strength will be required when you face the isolation, which a leader often faces. So tonight beneath the heavens sleep alone upon your groundsheet. (3)

Almost fifty years later, I remember being taken from my bed in the middle of the night and brought into the woods. There, around a fire, were all the elder members of the "tribe." Stern faces glowed in the flickering light of the fire. I was transfixed and pitched out of my normal existence into another state of awareness. There,

---

[2] http://www.scouters.us/oahis.html—History of the Order of the Arrow.

surrounded by the elders, with the black of night behind them, I was told what the values of the tribe were and the expectations for behavior of its members. The initiatory process of the week was detailed, including a day of fasting and silence and community service. I was taken to another place, deeper into the woods, there to remain alone for the night, reflecting on my destiny to be a member of the tribe. To be strong and in service to the camp community.

These excerpts illustrate several major issues in contemporary rites of passage. One is the perception of appropriation of indigenous traditions and practices, discussed earlier. The description of their "birth" appears to give full credit to its provenance, or where it came from, and respect for the native people of the place:

> It was born in an island wilderness. It needs the sun and the rain, the mountains and the plains, the woods, the waters, and the starlit sky.
> We pick up the lore and traditions of the American Indians and honor them today. The Indian respected the open air, and his culture is ours to preserve.

From the onset, there is deep admiration and respect for the people who first inhabited Treasure Island. Might it be considered that Goodman and Edson, who loved the island, heard the voices of these First Nation people who wanted to share these practices for the purpose of the preservation of their memory and also the preservation of their sacred Earth? Goodman and Edson did not say that they "created" the protocols in the Order of the Arrow. They said it was "born in an island wilderness." What if the land and nature can speak to others besides those first people to inhabit the area who can also hear nature's voice?

The practices used in the Order of the Arrow ordeal are very similar to those described by Heckewelder in 1819 and later by Newcomb in 1956. The Boy Scout's adaptation uses the symbols, themes, and patterns of initiation of the Delaware people, but these are very similar to designs used by other cultures. For example, Jews fast on Yom Kippur, and are dedicated to service by the major tenet of Tikkun Olam—repairing the world; similar traditions are followed by many other cultures and religions. It is the same with time alone in the wilderness and periods of reflection. Remember the stories of Moses and Jesus? They, too, experienced wandering in the wilderness, periods of reflection and ordeals. What is the appropriate modern adaptation of these common symbols, themes, and patterns of initiation?

Service is the rent we pay for the privilege of living on this earth.
                                                        —Shirley Chisholm.

Transmission of this ritual from the Delaware Nation to the Boy Scouts Order of the Arrow to an initiation rite in a summer sleep-away camp is quite a legacy. For his part, Goodman implies that the protocols and ritual "emerged from the land." Clearly, Goodman and Edson knew something about initiation, perhaps through military service. Otherwise why would they have incorporated it as part of the Order of the Arrow? Whatever knowledge they had presumably helped them to understand something about the central elements essential to the initiatory process and helped them extract what was already present in the information perceived and born in an island wilderness. In other words, they knew at a conscious and/or unconscious level what the core elements of initiation were and sensed their presence on Treasure Island. Combining what they already knew with what they felt from the place fostered the *emergence* of the Order of the Arrow initiation. This is perhaps the single most important feature uncovered in reviewing the initiatory processes. It is not created by anyone in particular, but it emerges through an interaction with the place, its ancestors, and Spirit and within the culture and context of the people responsible for initiating their children. Perhaps it could be said that someone was attuned to and sensed the initiatory constellation in ways that enabled them to hear how all of the elements within it were related and understood how they were to be enacted in the initiatory process. Emergent design, as discussed in a previous chapter, occurs when we are attuned to all that is seen and unseen, especially that which gives voice to nature, Spirit, and those who have come before. Coupled with the traditions of western science, the enactment of this attunement, with righteous intentions in rites of passage, can have particular potency for individuals as well as their family and community.

The famed first people's historian, scholar, and wisdom keeper Vine Deloria Jr. (Deloria 2006) and others affirm attunement to all of the elements in the natural world as part of one's "lifeways." By our very nature, human beings are organically predisposed to be in relationship with all of nature and the earth. These relationships were reciprocal, and communication was a two-way proposition. "The earth was full of sounds which the old-time Indian could hear, sometimes putting his ear to it so as to hear more clearly. The forefathers of the Lakotas had done this for long ages until there had come to them real understanding of earthways. It was almost as if the man were still a part of the earth as he was in the beginning, according to the legend of the tribe" (Bear 1933, 192). People were able to learn directly from the earth (Deloria 2006). There was a time when we were all receptors of and in relationship with a sentient being capable of giving and receiving love. That is why the old people "sat or reclined on the ground with a feeling of being close to a mothering power. It was good for the skin to touch the earth and the old people liked to remove their moccasins and walk with bare feet on the sacred earth" (Bear 1933, 192). Might another central purpose of rites of passage, especially those that occur for youth coming of age is to help us remember the power of love? After all, it has been said, by many different faiths and spiritual paths that "love is the most powerful force in the Universe." What if another central task of adolescences is to grapple with and balance the equal and opposite forces of the power of love and hate?

Rupert Sheldrake contributed to this orientation. "Knowledge gained through experience or plants and animals is not an inferior substitute for proper scientific knowledge: it is the real thing. Direct experience is the only way to build up an understanding that is not only intellectual but intuitive and practical, involving the senses and the heart as well as the rational mind" (Sheldrake 1991, 213). Morris Opler, in *An Apache Lifeway*, quoted an old Apache regarding the feeling toward the earth, and the sentiment is similar to that expressed by Standing Bear (Deloria 2006).

Some say that the earth talks to them. They get their ceremony from that. Some say the wind has life. Some say the mountains, like that San Andreas, have life. Anyone who gets power from it says, "That mountain talks to me." The old people tell stories that show that all things have life—trees, rock, the wind, mountains. One believes that there is a cliff where the Mountain People stay and they open the cliff and talk to him. (Opler 1996, 206)

I am reminded of what George Carey, 103rd Archbishop of Canterbury, said in preparation for the funeral of Princess Diana, September 6, 1997: "We've never done this before. We'll have to make up the ritual as we go along."

In light of the wisdom of Vine Deloria Jr. and others cited above, might all of these esoteric design considerations still be taken as just some white man's interpretation to justify what other nonnatives may think? Could the "initiatory constellation" and other formulations with references to the wisdom of First Nation people be considered another insult and prime example of the appropriation of indigenous customs, rituals, and protocols? Within the human experience exist possibilities that lay outside of the boundaries of contemporary science. Great artists like painters and songwriters frequently describe their creative process as extraordinary and influenced by their environment and other sources. An interview with Bob Dylan illustrates this point. "Now for me, the environment to write the song is extremely important. The environment has to bring something out in me that wants to be brought out. It's a contemplative, reflective thing" (in Zollo 1991).

From another perspective, one might have the opinion that here again is one more example of the appropriation of indigenous knowledge and rituals. With humility and respect to those with that opinion, I offer humble apologies. Yet, I cannot help but think of all the young boys in scouting and elsewhere over the past one hundred years who were brought into deep relationship and respect for nature, honoring and remembering the first people of this place actually were able to hear and be in authentic relationship with nature and deeply felt connected to a sacred earth. And who as a result were helped to come of age with a sense of self—inseparable from and responsible for the care of themselves, their family, their community, and a sacred Earth. These boys had no idea of insults or cultural appropriation and, like me, probably would feel uneasy, perhaps embarrassed or guilty, about their experience if they knew others had this view. Is that truly what Mother Earth would want for her children? Or, does a loving and sacred earth differentiate and segregate certain people, banishing them from being in relationship together in ways that nourish life in a world that works for all? What if rites of passage were to help us all remember the power of love?

It is a continuing conversation, to be sure. And, if done in full respectful partnership with our indigenous brothers and sisters, it will hopefully come to a place of humility, gratitude, and grace. For all our ancestors knew the central life-affirming and nurturing relationship we must have with nature and this sacred Earth and recognized its place in the initiatory process.

Authentic initiation comes from the place of and through those who are attuned to sacred information that enables them to help the initiatory process emerge and manifest itself on behalf of individuals, the community, and nature. I once heard it said that nothing is really created. Everything already exists. We just remember it and help it to reemerge.

11

Making Something Happen

Community Institutions as Places of Initiation and Rites of Passage

In the preceding chapter I relayed stories of initiation and rite of passage practices from different cultures around the world. They illustrated that something happened near the time of puberty that impacted far more than just a child's transition into adulthood. Something happened between the family and other significant relationships in what I have called the initiatory constellation and emergent design. Features in the constellation include the individual youth (initiate) and the family, community, ancestors, spirit world, and nature. The initiate comes of age in relationship to each element of this constellation. This is all within the uniqueness of each culture's creation myths, symbols, belief system, rituals, and celebration forms and stories that integrate their history with the larger creation story of the universe. Elders and other attuned to that which is seen and unseen, stories and theories in western science and traditional wisdom, bridging the sacred and profane, engage in a process of emergent design where the elements of initiation become clear and then are manifested in practices. Practices are not anchored in cement, but are respectful of traditions and adaptable to be potent for the people in a specific time and place. There appear to be common themes, practices, patterns of initiation, and purposes among diverse cultures around the world. These themes, practices, and patterns are part of the primary resources and materials for the emergence of rites of passage. Perhaps these themes and patterns are part of the archetypal symbols floating around in our unconscious that keep emerging in the form of youth's attempts at self-initiation and also as elements in contemporary rites of passage programs. Initiation was always in relationship with the initiatory constellation of elements. Evidence of their existence goes back over thirty thousand years. The length of their existence and prevalence in diverse cultures around the world is evolutionary evidence that they served our survival.

What important questions, if answered, could help make something happen in communities that would help guide our children into healthy, fulfilling, joyous, and connected adults today?

What did these stories shared in the last chapter reveal? What was the purpose of initiation and rites of passage? Who were the initiators? What were youth being initiated into? And, were there common themes, practices, and patterns of initiation among diverse cultures around the world? Exploring these questions was intended to reveal key elements that could be used as design principles for guiding the emergence of community-oriented rites of passage.

Initiation into What?

Initiation is the process of individual transformation from one state of being into another. Rites of passage are the public processes prescribed within the culture and community that affirm and effect this transformation within the social context. The rites take the form of performance and ceremony that are unique to the culture and place. Many have fundamentally similar underlying structures. The initiate is coming of age and initiated into their place, that is, nature, their culture and community, and the world of their ancestors and Spirit. It integrates their own personal, family and ancestral history, myths, and stories with the history of the Universe in ways that foster in the initiate a strong identity with a sense of connection and belonging to something greater than themselves. Initiation and the public rite of passage bring these elements (nature, culture, community, ancestors, and spirit) together to inform and guide the coming of age process. Collectively they energize and affirm the transition within the entire Universe.

You can only bring someone as far as you've been yourself.

By Whom?

Initiation was always by elders from the community who had been down a similar path of initiation. They were informed and guided by nature and the other elements in the initiatory constellation. Witnessing and affirming this transformation were their family, village, ancestors, and Spirit. Initiation is a process that occurs over time and began in response to signals from the individual—namely, puberty and menses—and nature. Those aunts, uncles, and elders who have a direct role in the initiation are ambassadors of the ancestors. They transmit the values, beliefs, and expectations for behaviors that give youth a sense of self within the history of their people and a connection with their place—nature—that is essential for them to live in ways that ensured the survival of their tribe. It is essential that elders are always present in the initiate's lives in order to continually guide, ensure accountability, and affirm the initiate's ongoing passage to adulthood.

For What Purpose?

The work of initiation is individual, while responsibility for its transformative potential belongs to the community.

The purpose was to transmit essential values, ethics, and skills that informed expectations for behaviors necessary for the initiates' own health and happiness and the survival of the tribe. Initiation effected a transformation in youth, bringing them into deep connection with their culture, community, and the natural world. The public rite of passage presented the entire community with an opportunity to revisit, adapt, and recommit themselves to life-affirming and -sustaining values and behaviors. It strengthened the bonds of people to each other, their culture, ancestors, the Spirit world, and nature. Initiation and rites of passage served survival.

What's the Story?

Each feature of the constellation plays a starring role in the initiatory process. They bring together important relationships that are central in the life of a child. A context was established within the family and community so that initiation and rites of passage were seen as the way children were guided into adulthood. It was the way a community taught and prepared their children to live in balance and respect with all their relations and helped to ensure the survival of their people. Within the context of culture and community, parents could engage in their own transitions necessary to make a place for their child's emerging adulthood. Rites of passage were not an isolated program for a select group of children conducted outside a community or culture by elders who were not from the community. It was done to strengthen everyone's relationship and the community's commitment and capacity to raise their children. In these stories we witnessed the central role that parents played and how they needed to acknowledge that something happened, not only for their child but also for themselves and their village as well as the ancestors, spirit world, and nature.

The stories revealed that a child undergoing initiation almost always had other adults besides their parents. Parents, guardians, or other family members selected "sponsors," who were committed to guiding and supporting their children on their journey, their transition to adulthood. Elders were referred to in family relationship terms (e.g., grandparents, aunts, and uncles). It may very well be that within these cultures, as I have seen elsewhere, everyone was in a family relationship with everyone else. Elders were always an *auntie* or *uncle* to everyone who was younger. All in a community were considered to be family, in relationship. It appears that one's biological parents were not among the central players in these experiences, nor were they in the forefront of their own child's initiation. Someone else was there to cut the psychic umbilical cord, lift the child out of the life-sustaining parental bond and into relationship with his or her community, Spirit, ancestors, and nature. It was an expectation within the culture and community that this happens, which made it acceptable. Rites of passage were their paradigm, their story for youth development. This is the way in which the village came together to raise their children. And "the village" may, in fact, be represented by only a few people that were central to the initiatory process and represented by the sponsors.

We all have the ability to creatively imagine how to use symbols and craft ritual experiences that aid in our children's transcendence and transformation to adulthood. As human beings, one of our essential assets is our ability to imagine stories that help us understand the complex mysteries of life. Stories inform the emergence of rituals that bring all of our relationships together into joyous experiences that enhance the meaning of life. Through initiation we die and are born again into our adult identity that is inextricably linked to culture, community, and nature. The concept of the self includes not only the psyche of the individual but also the psyche of the community and nature. As we discussed earlier, one's self is defined and only known in relationship to one's interiorization of the community and sense of place with and connection to nature. In the process, we remember our purpose as physical and spiritual beings. We need to be reborn into our full potential as sentient beings.

A central ingredient in traditional rites of passage was making explicit the change in the role of parents and/or guardians. There was a public affirmation that change was commencing. Something big was about to happen for the child, their family, and the community. When a child comes of age, a place needs to be set—the order of things needs to be changed.

> *When the house is set in order, the world is set in order, the world is set on a firm course.*
> —from the *I Ching*

The change in a parent's role is very important and another challenging part of our children's transition to adulthood. It was one of the primary reasons for community rites of passage. Within them everyone expected that certain changes would occur, which aided in the transition of children to adulthood. What follow are some examples to fuel the creative imagination. All of these designs emerged from participation of elders and within their unique culture, place, and nature. These examples illustrate what is possible when a village comes together to raise their children and that initiation and rites of passage were the ways this was accomplished.

Madrinas and Padrinos

Several decades ago I was in relationship with a Latino community interested in youth and community development through rites of passage. As with many communities, parent and adult involvement in their children's coming of age was important but frequently challenging to engage. One of the primary ways I enter into these kinds of community relationships is to exchange stories. In the case of adult and parent involvement, I asked how this has occurred in other situations: "Where are the parents or other adults already involved in the lives of children?" In sharing stories the organizing agency remembered their *baptismo* (baptism) ceremony and thought about reconstituting it within a coming-of-age process. Thus was born the Madrina and Padrino rite of passage for this community.

With their parent's consent, a child selected a man and woman to become their *Madrina* and *Padrino*—their Godmother and Godfather. Similar to the Teda people and other cultures, the child chose their sponsor. During the public rite of passage ceremony the *Madrinas* and *Padrinos* would stand up with the initiate and declare their commitment to help support and guide their "child" through adolescence and into adulthood. Initiation is an ongoing process. One of the most important and powerful things we can do is enact a public ceremony at the onset of this process of passage. In this way, all of the primary partners are alerted and acknowledge that a change of status is at hand. It makes visible and public for all to witness that something happens.

During the ritual process, a child identifies particular traits of childhood they need to leave behind and certain qualities of adulthood they need to master. Identifying certain skills and competencies they need to master is a central part in the initiatory process. Demonstrating competencies and skills can be ritualized and celebrated over the years in which the initiatory process unfolds within a community's rite of passage experience. Public ceremonies affirm and acknowledge important times during the initiatory process. They could celebrate a commitment to learning and becoming a "scholar," or to demonstrate some accomplishment or competency. During public celebrations roles and responsibilities for becoming part of a village that raises children together are made explicit. They continually renew a commitment to their guiding principle: "All children are our children."

Madrinas and Padrinos were already present within the Latino culture's *baptismo* ceremony. Mentors and surrogates were in their cultural repertoire. *Quinceañera* is a rite of passage at the age of fifteen. It publically recognizes that something important needs to happen to mark a girl's departure from childhood and part of a process for entering adulthood. Both the *baptismo* ceremony and the *quinceañera* engage other adults, in concert with parents. These cultural resources were already present and able to be integrated within the initiatory process and public rite of passage in ways that would engage parents and other adults.

> You hear your own voice when you tell a story: "Everything you need to know you already know." It is powerful and unlocks memories of what is already known, which can be an invaluable resource for health and survival. When stories are shared, something happens. Each story holds threads of gold, and when these are woven together with the threads of stories from other times, places, and cultures, a new story emerges. This new story integrates individuals' existing resources, cultural symbols, and practices that capture the spirit of a place with design features that are universal. This new story becomes their story. It is their initiatory constellation. There are powerful distinctions between adopting someone else's story, like those told as "evidence based," and remembering one's own story. When you gaze up to the heavens and see your own constellation you are connected with the Universe in ways that can be transforming.

The emergence of Madrinas and Padrinos offers an example of how sharing stories and having knowledge of important design elements in the rite of passage process become integrated into a community's rite of passage strategy. It was not a prescribed program brought into a community from outside, or replicated as something "evidence based." Nor was it a program outside and apart from a community that featured rites of passage, which youth participated in. Rather, it uses the time-honored process of bringing people together, exchanging stories that inform the emergence of designs for their rite of passage experience. Evolutionary evidence collected over thousands of years documents that sharing stories was always the way we helped to overcome challenges and survive in the midst of grave dangers. It also serves as an illustration for how design principles from one culture, like the use of surrogates by the Teda, can guide and be incorporated into contemporary rites of passage designs in service to another culture. Over twenty years later, Madrinas and Padrinos is continuously evolving and adapting to changing conditions and still features prominently in this multifaceted youth and family community agency.

Rites of Passage for Parents

One contemporary rite of passage design strategy creates a context for parents to make a place for their children's emerging adulthood. Making a place for an emerging adult in the family and community is a central ingredient for contemporary rites of passage. This was illustrated in the Masai practice, "passing of the fence." ROPE for Parents is a contemporary example that coincides with the child's entry into the first phase of their community's Rite Of Passage Experience. This is when children are around 11–12 years old and typically transitioning from primary to secondary school. It is oriented around and makes explicit a "collision of transition." One important personal attribute to have in parenting a teenager is a sense of humor. We say to parents, "The great spirit has a sense of humor because they have given adults teenagers right at the time they are typically entering the midlife period of their lives. This situation is ripe for a 'collision of transitions.'"

As their children enter adolescence, parents grapple with the challenges of their own transition and entry into midlife. Who does this easily? The "passing of the fence," installed by the Masai, is an example of a rite of passage strategy designed to manage this universal challenge. Accepting their own change of life and accommodating these changes in ways that foster their child's resiliency, self-reliance, and emerging adulthood is a challenge and desire for all parents. Reconciling a "collision of transitions" is an important consideration for contemporary rites of passage.

Here is a story of how this is accomplished. Parents and their children engage in a community rite of passage experience known as ROPE. In the first phase of ROPE, children begin the initiatory process within the context of their community and culture. Parents are invited or "summoned" to a "very important meeting" by the superintendent of schools, principal, head of the parent/school organization (PTO/PTA), and frequently even the mayor or chief elected or appointed official. At this meeting, a ceremony of separation begins the process for an entire elementary school's sixth graders. Children are symbolically separated from their parents and brought into a special place of initiation. Community elders, including high school students, lovingly express their care and affection for them and let them know that they are at the beginning of the end to their childhood. Parents go into a separate place and receive an orientation to the rite of passage—a youth development process that will unfold over the next six years.

This powerful community event is a marker for the parents, children, school, and community to understand that something happens. The details of the process are described. Parents take an oath to keep the details secret from their children. There is an explicit expectation that changes will happen and important roles need to be fulfilled in the process. Parents are expected to sign up immediately following the orientation to participate in a rite of passage experience with students who are not their own children. Parents are not directly involved in the initiatory experience for their own children, but come together as a village for other people's children. It exemplifies a guiding principle that "all children are our children." They also participate in ROPE for Parents, which helps them to begin the separation process with their own children and explore values and ideals related to their own transitions. Parents are encouraged to reflect on the dreams and aspirations they had as teenagers and assess how they have been doing to achieve their dream as an adult. Have they maintained the values and achieved what they thought they would when they were teenagers? During ROPE, children explore what it means to be an adult and the different skills, competencies, values, attitudes, and behaviors that are important.

Conversations continue by asking the parents questions:

What are the values, attitudes, skills, competencies, and behaviors that have served you well as an adult?

What values, attitudes, and behaviors toward your child will you need to give away in order to affirm your child is moving to adulthood?

What new values, attitudes, and behaviors will you have to take on to foster resiliency, self-reliance, and other health-promoting qualities in the service of your child's emerging adulthood and in service to your own health, resiliency, and self-reliance?

In ROPE, students are asked similar questions:

What are the qualities of childhood you have to give up, or move into the background in order to be a healthy, happy adult?

What are the qualities of adulthood, values, skills, competencies, behaviors, and attitudes, and so forth, that you need to pay attention to and work on or develop in order to be a healthy, happy, successful adult?

What would you be doing to prepare yourself to be the kind of adult you'd want to become?

Coming of age presents an opportunity for parents and children to engage in a different kind of conversation. This is a challenge mediated by ROPE for Parents that coincides with ROPE for their children. In a sense, they are both going through similar experiences, but at different transition points in the life cycle. What is important is to amplify that both the child and parents are going through a necessary transition, which must be navigated successfully in order for a child's emerging adulthood to be nurtured and welcomed.

Another series of questions encourages the kinds of conversations that help children and their parents learn together about transitions and how to be helpful to each other.

For children:
What are problems and concerns you "heard" teenagers have?

For parents:
What are problems and concerns you "heard" people in midlife have?

The responses from children to this and other questions are put alongside the parents' responses in the ROPE for Parents session. Parents are fascinated and struck by the similarity of the "problems and concerns they heard people in midlife have," with the "problem and concerns" that their children heard teenagers have. For example, children are concerned about their looks—the onset of puberty creates self-consciousness at their physical appearance. Parents entering midlife are grappling with physical change and diminished potency and power. Children are experiencing the waxing of their physical power and potency, and parents are experiencing a waning in the same area. Both experiences of change precipitate a certain degree of anxiety, which in a typical family might be part of what is called a "generation gap." Most of the areas identified as "problem and concerns" have similar themes for both children and their parents, but seen from a different developmental vantage point in their lives.

> Themes for the child: Who will I become as an adult? What will I do for a living?
> For their parents: How have I been doing as an adult for the past twenty or so years? Have I lived up to the goals and ideals I had as a teenager?
> For both children and parents: Am I likable and lovable? Who are my friends?

Responses from these conversations are charted and shared during subsequent sessions with children and their peer's parents, who also have children in a rite of passage experience. Again, parents are in conversation with other children, not their own, to help each group navigate their own individual passages and transitions.

Some communities incorporate the child and parent responses into a public ceremony as part of their rite of passage experience. It is the contemporary form of "the passing of the fence." The parent and child have to do something different and they are declaring this publicly in front of the community. Something happens. Other design strategies feature opportunities for parents to talk to their own children at home as part of their child's ROPE experience. Adolescence is typically a frightful time for parents, who feel alone and frequently overwhelmed. A community rite of passage gives parents comfort. They are relieved to know that they will have other parents to talk with about their child's adolescence. They are not alone. They now understand what it means to have a "whole village to raise a child" and are grateful.

Lessons from My Ancestors

Making something happen within the family, that affirms the transition for the parent and child can be accomplished through a ritual occasion within many different settings. It could be included within a traditional family holiday or celebration around the New Year or birthday. It can be a part of a special occasion, or as part of an overall initiatory process.

In Judasim there is a parent's blessing, typically during the Bar/Bat Mitzvah that thanks G-d for being with them and helping them reach this auspicious moment. For contemporary use the prayer is generally considered to be one of thankfulness and acknowledgement of the transition of the child into a different stage of life. It is a prayer of releasing the parents from a level of responsibility accorded a child. It recognizes the young person as a full-fledged member of the Jewish people, and as such, responsible for his/her own actions. It is said that until this point the parents could claim credit for their child's accomplishments, but they also had to take responsibility for their mistakes. This prayer/blessing expresses this transition.

This is the prayer in contemporary form: "Blessed be He who has released me from being punishable for this (child)."

> *ROPE gives us something to hold onto during this difficult time of parenting adolescents. It gives us a common language to speak with our children and other parents.*
>
> —Richard Keane, 1983
>
> Parent of five children engaged in ROPE.
> Killed in the World Trade Center – September 11, 2001.

In my review of the stories on initiation and puberty rites from around the world I saw no evidence that parents were the primary navigators or guides in their own children's passage to adulthood. Something happened publicly to mark the beginning of a separation between parents and their child. It was expected that aunties, uncles, grandmothers, and grandfathers—the whole village—became more involved in the process of raising children and the process of initiating children into their culture and community.

> *Children must have at least one person who believes in them.*
> *It could be a counselor, a teacher, a preacher, and a friend.*
> *It could be you.*
> *You never know when a little love, a little support, will plant a small seed of hope.*
>
> —Marian Wright Edelman

What Would We Be Doing if We Believed That Everything Was Related?

Over the past four decades programs featuring rites of passage have exploded around the world. A number of them have come together within an association called Youth Passageways (http://youthpassageways.org/), which promotes program opportunities for youth. The seeds for many of these early programs were planted and germinated around the same time. During the cauldron of unrest and social change in the sixties, many individuals began to seek changes and envision a new paradigm for a more civil and just society. They recognized the seriousness of the problems facing nature and a growing global population, which were all seen as connected. They appreciated that real lasting change would have to focus on raising children and helping them cross the threshold from childhood to adulthood with a consciousness of compassion, caring, empathy, and one deeply connected to their community and nature. The seeds for change would have to be planted in the next generation.

Early rites of passage program pioneers explored pancultural wisdom, anthropology, psychology, philosophy, sociology, history, initiation, the architectural structure of ceremony, and ritual. While they were spending periods of time alone in nature, their ideas were marinating in an interdisciplinary stew, merging into a vision for what possibilities would stimulate changes for healing and health to individuals and all their relations. Knowledge cultivated from scholarship combined with their immersion in nature's wisdom informed the emergence of their own self-generated ceremonies and initiation practices. These programs continually matured and adapted over time to the robust and powerful rite of passage programs presently provided for tens of thousands of children, youth, and adults around the world.

Many of these programs have integrated the central elements identified in the stories of initiation and rites of passage presented previously. A new organization, Youth Passageways has begun to catalogue these rites of passage programs and promote them on their website: http://youthpassageways.org/ (Youth Passageways 2015). Many of these programs are oriented around wilderness experiences that bring the initiate into deep connection with the natural world. Others are concerned with their ancestors and culture. They believe that a person must see themselves as part of a distinct group and that this group must first recognize and affirm itself before it is able to successfully interact and appreciate others. Focusing on culture and ethnicity is a response to contemporary society, which is viewed in ways that compromise the health and security of their own people's culture and ethnicity. Still other rite of passage programs are oriented around creative somatic movement, the arts, service learning, music, poetry, gender, and a vast array of human interests and experiences in the service of helping youth creatively imagine who they are and what their future might hold. Each of these programs holds valuable lessons and experiences that can be truly transformative for individual participants. They are powerful and poised to become part of a network of resources for community-oriented rites of passage.

Through Initiation the Tribe Was Saved

Another story comes to mind that was told to me in 1993 by my friend Louise Carus Mahdi.[1] As she told it to me I share it with you:

> I've seen documented evidence from the 1890s about a tribe of Omaha Indians who were facing a major problem. They sent a group of young boys out on a vision quest. When they came back the boys sat with a group of elders and shared their visions. From the boy's stories the elders were able to figure out a solution to their problem. And the tribe was saved.

[1] L. C. Mahdi was the editor of two books on rites of passage; I worked with her on the second book, *Crossroads: The Quest for Contemporary Rites of Passage*, 1996.

Since 1966 I have participated in and organized experiences to enrich the human spirit. As a trained community psychologist, therapist, youth worker, educator, and community organizer I have humbly been in caring relationships with individuals, helping them through situational crises or hanging in there with them during longer-term mental health issues. I was in relationship with families and couples to support a process of awareness, reconciliation, change, and growth in ways that enhanced and improved their well-being. Facilitating group experiences in a wide variety of settings addressed the needs of individuals within the larger context of the group. My earliest experiences, fortified over decades, continues to strengthen my belief that organizing larger groups to stimulate change, like schools and communities, will be the most potent way to affect beneficial adaptation for the future. Youth and community development are inseparable. One's development depends on the development of the other. This is deeper work engaged in at the level of the heart that affects people's souls.

What do the ancient stories of initiation and rites of passage have to tell us that can help to save our global tribe of people and all our relations on and with this sacred place that in English is named Earth?

Initiation provided a unique opportunity to harvest a child's adaptive intelligence in ways that served our survival. It established a systematic context to continually revisit a group's shared values, attitudes, and behaviors to assess whether they still serve to ensure the health and well-being of individuals and the survival of the group.

At the end of the previous chapter we discussed initiation practices that originated with the Delaware Indians and then emerged from a place, Treasure Island, to inform the Boy Scouts Order of the Arrow initiation practices. There are many considerations and challenges surrounding contemporary rites of passage. Almost everything about them requires a substantial paradigm shift from our present beliefs and practices. We need to reflect on how traditional initiation and rites of passage emerged and were continually adapted within an initiatory constellation and how the primary design elements, patterns, and themes worked together.

We Know the Way—Do We Have the Will?

The way programs in education and youth and human development are created, transferred to or replicated in another setting, and evaluated are inadequate. The process attempts to parallel the scientific or medical model. There is a fatal flaw in this orientation. Unlike the elements or component parts that go into scientific experiments or medical procedures, human behavior is dynamic, variable, and beyond control and our ability to predict outcomes at a level of confidence that is present in the "hard sciences."

Presently one person or a group typically creates a program. They have component parts, which are supposed to be repeated in the same way each time (fidelity) and as a result achieve a high level of predictability pertaining to the outcome. This is at odds with how people behave in reality and how rites of passage are coaxed into emerging within a community, as I have described previously. We have to change our paradigm in order for rites of passage to become potent and fulfill their central purpose for individuals, their community, their culture, and all their relations. Rites of passage are not programs in the traditional way we view programs. They are more like an innovation that could be transferred and adapted to other settings in which the people and place have great influence. This gives rise to another set of navigational aids.

Emergent Design Eludes Random Clinical Trials Evidence-Based Evaluation

Authentic community-oriented rites of passage informed by an initiatory constellation that engages both traditional wisdom and western science within an emergent design are beyond the capacity and outside of the paradigm of evidence-based methods of evaluation using random control trials (RCTs). Beechler and Trickett (2011) "examined hundreds of papers across multiple disciplines (psychology, nursing, social work, public health, speech pathology, etc)" (2) and found that "the current push to design, test and disseminate evidence-based interventions in psychology represent an ideological movement with more potential to benefit commercially and politically than scientifically" (3). In other words, proponents of evidence-based practices are advertising more than they can and have delivered.

They uncovered at least four problems:

1. The relationship between the "intervention" and the actual delivery setting and people in reality has too much variability to adequately track and account for outcomes within an RCT model.
2. Intervention as "technology" cannot be applied exactly the same way and achieve exactly the desired outcomes as may be possible within a medical model.
3. Technology is always an advancement over local innovations, however recent research reveals many of the practices deemed "evidence-bases" fail to live up to their advertised efficacy. This is more a result of flawed approaches or theories than to inadequacy of local implementation.
4. Science is not apolitical but is politicized to "consolidate" power (11) by those who develop, test, and disseminate evidence-based interventions and have convinced funders and policymakers of their idea of "truth" and imposed their evidence-based interventions on others.

In an attempt to shift the paradigm, Trickett offers three ecologically based themes to provide alternative questions about the evidence-based practice movement's role in complex community interventions: (1) What is the intervention in complex community interventions? (2) What are contextual criteria for assessing the external validity of programs? and (3) What are the unintended consequences of focusing on the question "What works?" rather than the more contextual question "What works for whom under what circumstances with respect to what set of outcomes for how long a period of time?" (Trickett 2015, 177).

Themes generating the general area of inquiry reflected in these three questions are a movement in the right direction. But, there is still an overarching issue related to power and control, alluded to in Trickett's fourth problem above, that leads to another area of inquiry related to evaluation. What is the purpose of evaluation? Is it to justify the expenditure of funds or to prove a particular program achieves a desired expected outcome or is it to provide feedback for continuous improvement to citizens and "consumers" impacted by the intervention? Who designs the methodology and controls the information and data? How can one adequately and accurately account for the variability in delivery of the "intervention," the likelihood of different conditions and population dynamics that ultimately impact outcomes, which cannot be predicted with any degree of reliability? Perhaps most important and relevant to the emergent design emphasis of community-oriented rites of passage is the essential need for and potency of local engagement.

Research by Joanna Levitt Cea and Jess Rimington at Stanford University's Global Projects Center is identifying benefits of applying best practices in crowdsourcing and codesign to the planning, design, and evaluation of projects for social impact—and finding that superior innovation and insight are generated when "endusers" (i.e., people from the beneficiary groups) are at the center of creating these plans and designs and provide feedback.[2]

Reality always astonishes theory.

Again we are confronted with a challenge in the confluence of science and spirituality, of the profane and sacred. Language is consciousness, and the way it is used to frame evaluation and science within the providence of power and control by institutions with political or other agendas has made a substantial impact. Others discuss challenges within an evidence-based RCT methodology and suggest that real science would be within a framework of a community process (Rapkin 2011). In reality there is no evidence that RCTs, the gold standard in evidence-based evaluation methodologies, is sufficient to accommodate the complex factors within interventions, either at an individual, group, or community context. The reality confronting the implementation of interventions is sufficiently complicated by local history, staff enthusiasm, relationship with citizens/participants, variability and individual differences, differences in delivery technique and context, and other subtle variables to impact both input—namely, intervention delivery—and outcomes.

---

[2] Personal correspondence July 18, 2015; Cea and Rimington.

Green (2000) suggested,

> It is undeniable that health promotion requires a strong evidence base. However, if this derives solely from the accumulation of empirical evidence of effectiveness, there is a very real danger of ending up with little more than a menu of proven interventions from which to select and without a rational base to guide that selection. Of more relevance to the practitioner are general principles together with an understanding of context-specific factors, which will allow adaptation to suit different situations. (128)

The twenty elements in the architectural structure for youth and community development through rites of passage offer design principles that guide the adaptation of rites of passage within the unique context and culture of each community. The word "evaluation" by its very nature has historical meaning and "baggage" that becomes a burden for individuals and citizens within communities, especially communities with cultures that are not oriented within western science conceptions of reality. Most people do not have a positive, warm and fuzzy feeling when they hear the word "evaluation." Questions related to obtaining feedback to help citizens know what is going on, what is happening as a result of agreed on designs, that is, "intervention," and how to use the feedback for continuous improvement to help citizens, recipients of the intervention, achieve the outcomes they desire move in the direction of citizen-centered feedback. It is more aligned with Cea and Rimington's notion of "crowdsourcing for social impact." Community-oriented rites of passage, like any other "interventions," occur within a living dynamic system. When the shared interests within a community bring them into the realm of rites of passage, a learning community of practice becomes an adaptive learning system that continually engages in inquiry, actions, review, and adaptations that lead to refinement of key ingredients for continuous improvement in the intervention (Rapkin 2011).

Confluence of Art and Science

Helping rites of passage emerge in communities and other settings is a challenge. In reality, programs cannot be replicated in one setting exactly as they appeared in another setting. It would be nice if they could, but they can't. Everyone who works in these settings knows this. When moving education and human service programs into different settings than where they first began, we need to think in terms of *innovation transfer rather than program replication*. And, even that term, "innovation transfer," is inadequate, but it moves us in the *rite* direction.

There are significant differences in rites of passage program orientations and practices. When coupled with the complexity of community dynamics, the practice of innovation transfer is more viable than program replication as championed in an evidence-based paradigm. Innovation transfer is more in the domain of art than science (Blumenkrantz 1992). Martinez-Brawley (1995), Smale (1993), and Rogers (1983) offer useful guidelines for the transfer of innovations to other settings. Schorr (1993) suggested that context matters significantly and "figuring out what's working in human services is not like figuring out what's working in the physical sciences" (11). Transferring innovations depends on the ability of the outside partner to become attuned to what is not visible within a setting or community and to help people remember rites of passage. Just as with the limitations cited in the ethnographies in the last chapter, intelligent observation must unearth what is obvious, but more important is what is hidden in the particular local context and culture. The outside partners needs to divest themselves of authority and step away from the mantle of expert. They must help their community partners articulate a vision for youth and community development through rites of passage in ways that can connect deeply with a broad constituency and compel them into action. It also has to do a lot with luck and *zeitgeist*, the spirit of the times.

Martinez-Brawley (1995) may have said it best when she wrote, "Knowledge use generates new knowledge, and the process of diffusion, which is itself a process of transformation, begins again. In the human services, knowledge application and use generate new knowledge. Any program generated through replication is, in the end, a new program that can again be disseminated" (679). In a sense, ideas take on a life of their own when applied in new settings. How does this fit, or not, with the evidence-based paradigm, which suggests that you can replicate a program in the exact same way in any situation or context?

Unlike a strategy to produce some predictable outcome in the physical sciences, human service strategies do not lend themselves well to adoption through replication but rather work best within a context that promotes adaptation through information exchange. "Compatibility between the new idea and the values and beliefs of the organization is crucial to success. Compatibility becomes one of the major negotiating items as new ideas enter new organizational domains" (Martinez-Brawley 1995). Initiation and rites of passage focus on compatibility and integrating people, ideas, programs, or anything new into a setting. Sensitivity to the initiatory process can make a great difference in any setting or within any organization. Remember, the fundamental focus of initiation has to do with people's sense of being included or excluded from a group.

Rogers (1983) suggests that human service agencies fail to recognize the importance of what an innovation is called. "The perception of an innovation is colored by the word-symbols used to refer to it. . . . It is the potential adopter's perception of an innovation's name that affects its rate of adoption" (228).

Uttering the phrase "rites of passage" in some communities can set off an explosion of unintended consequences. Initiation is a highly personal process for transmitting a culture's sacred information to the next generation. It is a very delicate situation, which in some instances does not yield to an outsider's involvement. Asking, "How are the children?" and talking about youth development in general can lead to new ways for a community to think about raising their children. Listening to and exchanging stories can be a first step. It shows respect and at the very least one might be able to learn the nuances of a community's language and culture. At best, conversations might open a door through which members of a community can bring in rites of passage ideas. Many times something happens not even remotely related to rites of passage, like the death of a teen from drunken driving, or mean bullying behavior in school, that moves a community into productive action on behalf of their children. Drinking becomes seen as a rite of passage, and bullying is viewed as some kind of initiation related to hazing. The incident becomes the agent for changing the story to one related to rites of passage.

Having been described in the early eighties as the "Johnny Appleseed of rites of passage," I have witnessed seeds planted, nurtured by a community, and harvested into rich and powerful rites of passage that feed a community's spirit for decades. This has happened even when there were only one or two conversations. Seeds were planted. New possibilities emerged that would not have been perceived before.

There are no new paradigms, only the activation of old memories:

> The very nature of innovation in the public sector has changed drastically in recent years. In the first part of this century, human-service agencies were innovative largely because they were new, and were addressing social problems that had not been responded to before by any kind of organized effort. Now, these institutions have matured in somewhat the same way that American manufacturing has matured—there isn't room for brand new service programs. The fertile ground for innovation, therefore, is enhancing, rethinking and expanding existing service programs. (Backer 1988, 18)

Communities have the capability to help their children grow up well. They have been doing it for millennia. Over the last several hundred years, huge changes have created many distractions from our central purpose of raising children. We forgot that all children are our children and it truly takes a whole village to raise them. No matter what the new program of the day is, it cannot replace the health-promoting relationships that children need to have with another person. Helping us to remember this and what our authentic assets, talents, and innate abilities are to use rites of passage is essential. People do not want to be told what to do or how to raise their children. They want to be respected and included in an authentic process of creating a better place for themselves and their children to grow up well. Children want and need to be part of the process. They say, "Don't do anything about me without me" (Schiller 2012). Through educational experiences, community members can be introduced to the essential ingredients of contemporary rites of passage. Engaging them in a broad array of activities related to the initiatory process strengthens their understanding and sense of ownership to what emerges. "NIH—Not Invented Here" is a syndrome leading to the death of programs created in one place and replicated in another. Research (Blumenkrantz 1996; Woodard 1996) has documented rites of passage's potential to serve as a community-mobilizing vehicle on behalf of contributing to the positive development of children and the health of their community. That's the way it has always been.

What Would We Be Doing if Institutions That Mattered In the Lives of Children Were Reframed as Places of Initiation?

There are many institutions that influence our children in large and small ways. Families, religious and cultural organizations, schools, government, nongovernmental organizations (NGOs), and civic and recreational organizations are all "institutions that matter in the lives of children." They are present in communities and each has its own story in the form of a mission and services. Frequently the stories are the same, like the story that schools are to educate youth. The story of many NGOs is that not-for-profit community agencies aim to foster positive youth development and prevent and/or intervene in the problems of children and youth. There are many more, such as media, namely music, movies, and news outlets, although I am not referring as much to these institutions. Each has its own mission, purpose, and way of going about rearing, educating, and contributing to the positive development of children and youth, helping them come of age. The question in the heading invites you to creatively imagine what each of these institutions would be doing, together, if they understood and codesigned their community rites of passage experience. What would be possible if youth and community development through rites of passage were a common story that unified all of the existing institutions that mattered in the lives of children? United within the common story that "all children are our children."

There have been islands of opportunity where citizens from communities have worked collaboratively on behalf of raising their children all within a common story, more or less. Genuine collaboration is a function of time spent together. It cannot be achieved quickly for expediency to meet a requirement in a grant for organization and community cooperation. Getting to authentically know someone is the only way to lay the foundation for genuine collaboration. A tall order? Yes. Pie in the sky? Possibly. What are the alternatives?

A framework of youth and community development through rites of passage provides opportunities for individuals to remember and reconnect with their own initiatory experiences. Developing a learning community unique to each setting is intended to build a collaborating "core group" within a community. A group where individuals can have their own needs met without compromising the needs of the group to be of service to the community. Through the shared emotional experience of their common initiatory training, the relationship between members of the core group is strengthened to such a great degree that they become the central agent for organizing change in a community. It is people in authentic strong relationships who become the real force for change and the central element in supporting and enacting activities within a rite of passage framework. It has never been about "the program" that was at the core of "what works"; it has always been about the relationship between the people and institutions that really matter. They turn service into caring and connect diverse segments of the community together to realize the enactment of the proverb "It takes a whole village to raise a child." Unrealistic? No. Easy? *No!* Not only is it complicated and difficult work but it also takes a very long time to learn to build a foundation and bring to fruition a community's rites of passage. It is not as easy as a simple slogan, like Just Say No! We believe in Just Say Know! The work lies in acquiring the knowledge and wisdom through in-depth learning together, in community, about youth and community development through rites of passage. Actually, it has already been done! Read on . . .

> If you want to go fast go alone. If you want to go far go together.
> —African Proverb

Island of Opportunity: Small Models Illustrate Big Possibilities

Thus far we have covered terrain exploring the relationship between rites of passage and a psychological sense of community. We discovered reciprocity between an individual and their community through community-oriented rites of passage that serves our survival. In this chapter we will travel to a place where public policy endorsed the emergence of youth and community development through rites of passage. An island of opportunity existed for a brief period of time. Amazingly it resulted from a State of Connecticut grant program. Initial funding was offered from the Connecticut Alcohol and Drug Abuse Commission (CADAC). They released a Request For Proposal (RFP) for a new grant category: "Community Mobilization: A Program to Promote Collaboration and Build Essential Skills by Focusing on Identified Community Substance Abuse Problems." A regional substance-abuse planning agency, the Capital Area Substance Abuse Council (CASAC), received funding through this State program for "an innovative approach to building a collaborating community."

In July 1994, CASAC in turn released an RFP. It invited sixteen communities within its purview to use rites of passage design strategies to promote broad-sector community engagement and galvanize mentors to participate in developing and offering community-based rites of passage. Twelve communities expressed interest, generating eleven initial responses to the RFP. In October 1994, ten projects were notified of their grant award followed by three to four months of technical assistance, orientation, and training of community elders. Activities for over 6,500 youth and adults were initiated between January and May of 1995, and lasted for several years of funding, with increasing citizen participation.

The project was called Paths to the Year 2000 and became known as Project 2000. The RFP from the regional agency (CASAC) included the following:

> We are looking for programs that bring together varied resources in creative ways to achieve significant change in the way communities view

adolescents. We also seek to help communities focus energy and resources on the substance abuse problem by altering the conditions that contribute to it and other destructive behavior.

One condition is the absence of modern day rites of passage . . . The absence of modern day rites of passage has seriously limited our ability to help youth successfully make the transition from childhood to adulthood. (Johnston and Blumenkrantz 1994)

Five things stand out. First, a message from the State trumpeted a new approach to the public that shifted the paradigm from program replication to innovation transfer and emergent design focusing on engaging and building citizen capacity. Second, it did not focus on professional experts but on engaging and empowering youth and adults in a whole-community approach. Third, it affirmed the importance of rites of passage and amplified public education that focused on the consequences of its absence, which was related to teenage substance abuse. Fourth, there was an explicit expectation and requirement that a whole-community approach was necessary for funding. And there were design principles that fostered genuine collaboration necessary for a whole-community approach to rites of passage. Fifth, it affirmed the uniqueness of each setting and acknowledged and respected the diversity of cultures devoted to raising their children within their own values and customs. From the outset, the community-organizing process recognized that patterns, themes, symbols, and practices of initiation and rites of passage already existed and we just needed to find, enhance, and link them together. Where they were not present we helped them to emerge within the context and culture of the community. Finally, and perhaps most important, the executive director of CASAC, David C.-H. Johnston, understood the value of rites of passage, the consequences of their absence, and their ability to mobilize a community into action. His vision, leadership, and ability to explain and advocate for Project 2000 to CADAC was invaluable not only to obtain the grant but also to carry out the tasks necessary for it to be a success.

We again return to the public education literature that accompanied the RFP.

Adolescence is a time of opportunity as well as peril. There is no greater challenge than the development of community sanctioned and individually meaningful rites of passage for our young people and their families. It is about "community-building." . . . Most important is the context in which rites of passage occur. **The commitment of parents, community officials and agencies, schools, and youth is critical. The community must come together to examine values, attitudes, behaviors and beliefs and then determine which of these they should transmit to their children and how best to do it.** (emphasis in original)

Rite of passage designs were to be formulated within a "collaborative evolutionary process," which was the overarching theme of the entire project. The consultants from CASAC were in "partnership" with members of the community to support the development of community-oriented rites of passage. The program's focus was on different ways youth and adults, representing the diversity of their organizations and community, could come together in conversations that explored questions that matter related to youth and community development through rites of passage.

Even though funding for this project came from the State's substance-abuse agency, one of its greatest achievements was that it did not focus on a single problem area. Right from the onset, it sought to put into practice a new paradigm promoted by CADAC, which changed its name to the State of Connecticut Department of Mental Health and Addiction Services the following year. The paradigm promoted engaging communities in a collaborative evolutionary process, which recognized that power, expertise, and leadership resided within the members of the community, who shared responsibility for helping rites of passage strategies emerge from their own vision. The project promoted inclusive decision-making and emphasized diversity and community participation. The rites of passage concept and design principles were used as a mobilizing agent intended to bring the members of a community together and engage them in new ways to prevent substance abuse and other youth problems by promoting more positive and socially sanctioned rites of passage.

Helping to Make Something Happen

We learned a tremendous amount from decades of this kind of experience with communities engaged in rites of passage. First of all, from the onset, certain expectations were made clear and mutually agreed on by all of the partners. Second, people had to come together in their organizations and communities. Third, this was not your typical program already fully developed within a traditional training-of-trainers model. Fourth, there were things that we all had to learn and experience together in order to understand rites of passage and the process of innovation transfer (i.e., how we can help rites of passage emerge in their organization and/or community). Fifth, a set of guiding principles was presented and was expected to be adapted, highlighting design features for the development of rite of passage experiences for the organization and/or community. Sixth, it was a "collaborative evolutionary process," which means it was never complete and always in need of adaptation to meet the continually changing needs of their children and community. Seventh, this was not a traditional "consultant for hire" situation. It was a partnership between the organization/community and us in a process of colearning for the codesign of the rites of passage experience. Eighth, roles, responsibilities, and outcome objectives had to be clear and mutually determined. Ninth, there had to be a feedback system for continuous improvement and evaluation to ensure that what was agreed on for outcomes was actually being achieved. A mechanism for objectively assessing and making the necessary changes had to be put into place from the outset. The central purpose was for feedback to the community and not the funding source.

Finally, and perhaps most important, was the relationship developed between all the partners within the community and from outside the community, especially the regional and state agencies that sponsored the grant program. At the end of the day, it was all about relationships. A multicultural partnership team was engaged on behalf on the granting organization. It was composed of two powerful, articulate, bright, creative, and playful women—one Latina and one African American—plus a white guy, me. We were a dynamic team and reflected almost all of the main ethnic constituency groups in the partnership communities. We genuinely liked each other and got along very well, which was evident in our frequent bantering, joking, and creating general mayhem wherever we went. It was like a three-ring circus within a party disguised as a community gathering for investigating questions that matter related to children. And, who doesn't want to come to a party? Once people experience these efforts as fun and within a party atmosphere, why wouldn't they want to attend another one? This is a key ingredient. From the outset, each community event was designed to promote the conditions that would likely lead to participants being open to the possibility that changes in the way children were being educated and raised could be considered. Building relationships is a very challenging and time-consuming prospect. It needs to be done carefully and within the cultural and con-textual protocols of the community and not dictated by some distant administrative timeframe that lay outside of the community. In reality this is a delicate balance and failure to not manage it carefully will undermine any chance of success. Reports and data can be "fudged" to demonstrate success for funding to continue, but what has really been accomplished will be questionable.

"Subject matter expert" (SME) is the latest label and jargon for bolstering the perception of professionalism of high-quality consultants hired to execute grants. An SME brings an important level of expertise to a project that is essential. Yet, a pathway built on relationships needs to be present in order for the SME's talents and assets to be accepted by the community. Our work was made much easier because of the multicultural team that helped reduce the natural resistance and reluctance citizens have toward people perceived as "outsiders" coming into their community to tell them what to do and how they have not been doing well by their children. The goal is to always enlist as many allies from the setting before any large group gathering. Building citizen's capacity, both youth and adults, to be comfortable with the material and to take an active leadership role right from the outset is a key to a strong foundation. We always approached our partners with the attitude that "everything they need to know they already know." We are just there to help them remember. And we designed an atmosphere like a party, where people can come together in conversations for new ideas to emerge and be harvested for the benefit of the community.

We always have to keep in mind that this was a real paradigm shift. It meant that there would be discomfort, disbelief, and a desire to maintain the existing circum-stances regardless of how much people thought they wanted things to change. These sentiments had to be respected and handled with sensitivity.

It was not about replicating a program, but about "community building," as stated in the grant requirements:

The commitment of parents, community officials and agencies, schools, and youth is critical. The community must come together to examine values, attitudes, behaviors and beliefs and then determine

which of these they should transmit to their children and how best to do it.

While words help to convey ideas, they are mostly inadequate (even when in bold!) to convey a real paradigm shift in education and human services. A paradigm shift in these arenas is not the same as one in the physical or hard sciences. Words, either spoken or in writing, no matter how elegant and clear, are still in the old paradigm of communicating (in written or oral form). A new paradigm to awaken memories stored deep within our bones must be communicated and transferred at the level of the heart. This can only be accomplished through actual initiatory experiences that are then enhanced, affirmed, and clarified through language. While "language is consciousness," as the saying goes, it is not as likely to change behavior as experience is. Nothing changes behavior like an emotional experience. That is what rites of passage can offer. Used in a process of community capacity-building, rites of passage bring people together and deepen their understanding of initiation through actual experience. Sharing in a common initiatory experience strengthens the bonds between community members, enabling them to transcend individual differences on behalf of raising their children. They also see what it is like to go through an initiation. One of the guiding principles in this work is, "You can only bring someone as far as you've been yourself."

Part of the grant process required an intensive period of learning together. This included a multiday retreat with adults and youth that enabled them to dive more deeply into and share a rite of passage experience. The benefits achieved for fostering deeper more authentic relationships between the participants were immeasurable to the overall success of the project. One last important detail; as the famous Huichol shaman and teacher of Brant Secunda, Don José Matsuwa used to say: "At the end of the day if you can't leave them laughing what good have you done!" In other words, laughter and play are among those little details that are so big.

Design Principles Guide the Village

Design principles for community-oriented rites of passage were set forth in CADAC's RFP. Developed from over forty years of research and practical experience they were the cornerstones for community members' initial orientation to rites of passage. If "it takes a whole village to raise a child," as the ancient proverb states, then how do you think the village raised their children? As we said before, initiation and rites of passage with and for a community were probably part of the process. This is one of the guiding principles discussed throughout this book. Project 2000 did not want people in communities to adopt and replicate a program that was developed elsewhere. An important element in a community-oriented rite of passage initiative was obtaining the commitment and engagement of parents, community officials and agencies, schools, police, houses of faith, and youth. This had to be demonstrated by members of these groups scheduling time to come together.

Conversations and experiential activities are central to a design where rites of passage are used as a catalyst and vehicle to mobilize a community into action. First, the community is convened and hosted in intentionally designed settings that are hospitable and support conversations among community members, who explore and respect each other's "stories" about growing up and educating and raising their children. Right now the national story is about academic achievement—"Common Core," or "Race to the Top." In the past the national story has been "No Child Left Behind" and "Just Say No!" and "War on Drugs," to name a few. Second, through shared stories people examine their values, attitudes, behaviors, and beliefs that inform and underlie these stories.

Third, experiences need to be designed so that people could transcend any historic or perceived differences in order to determine which values, attitudes, behaviors, and beliefs they share and how they could transmit them to their children and how best to do it. Then, they assess whether their current "story" is working to achieve the outcomes they desire. If not, then a paradigm shift may be in order to dramatically transform the story and change the future.

First we ask, "What's the Story?" Second, "What are the values and ethics that underlie the story?" And third, "Is the story working for us? Or, do we need to do things differently, undertake a paradigm shift?" This is what I call the "trinity of inquiry" and it is part of the design principles incorporated into the requirements for the grant to foster the emergence of new design for rites of passage in their community.

Roy G. Biv

We approach the development of community-oriented rites of passage more in the manner of art than science. That is, we introduce certain key design principles used to inform the development of specific activities that can be integrated into their community's rite of passage experience. In a sense, the key design principles serve as a rainbow of colors—the set of ingredients—red, orange, yellow, green, blue, indigo, and violet (Roy G. Biv), for the creation of the art of rites of passage. We share techniques and strategies for integrating and applying the design principles, such as the generic structure for ritual and the separation of parents and their children. We were also mindful of many other orientations, approaches, and programs that existed in communities, or passed through a community as the latest "flavor of the month," or favored approach. We asked, "What's the story with your existing approaches to educating and helping children come of age? What are you already doing?" We quickly found out what approaches and programs had already been tried and were present. Youth and community development through rites of passage can be an overarching story that integrates all other education and youth development approaches. And, it is THE story that captures youth's attention with the promise of an initiatory experience that they are seeking. We talk about existing models and theories familiar to most communities, such as social and emotional learning, developmental assets, character education, and resiliency. Our stories and language related to rites of passage weave together what already exists in their community. For example, we talk about the "social development model of youth development" development by David Hawkins and Richard Catalano form the University of Washington (Hawkins and Weis, 1985; Catalano and Hawkins 1996; see Figure 11.1).

We introduce community members to a concept of youth development that involves connecting and enhancing environments and building competencies, which promotes the positive development of children and youth in their families, in their schools, among their peers, and in their community and with a strong connection to the natural world. Youth come of age through initiation into these environments, which are connected, nonsequentially, within a systems framework that promotes whole human beings and strong, resilient, and adaptive communities.

Guided by the twenty elements in the architectural structure for youth and community development through rites of passage, and within an "emergent design" process, activities intensify focus on particular values, attitudes, and competencies expected within each environment. Demonstrations of competencies, family and community celebrations periodically mark special times in a child's development. Designs include the Initiation of Scholars, which supports and strengthens a child's connection to school and the skills necessary for competence (Blumenkrantz 2009). Initiation into Play focuses on a child's coming of age within the environment of the community and with peers (Blumenkrantz 2000). Giving back and community service is another design feature that instills values of caring and compassion, which are demonstrated during service to others in the community (Blumenkrantz 1993). This includes mentoring younger youth as they move through the coming of age process within each environment (Blumenkrantz 1998).

When a community embraces a common story of rites of passage and uses the language of this story in education and youth development a foundation is laid to help engage youth and their families in therapy if problems arise. Within this orientation therapy is reframed as another "ordeal" within an ongoing process of initiation. And, given the skills and experiences of both youth and their parents, both are enlisted as allies and "co-researchers" in partnership to overcome this initiatory ordeal. Their shared experience with rites of passage offers considerable information to guide conversations, and shared skills such as problem solving and multiple examples of attitudes and behaviors necessary to overcome challenges. Caring and compassion come back into play within the lives of people living together in community (Gavazzi & Blumenkrantz 1993).

Personal stories of initiation and other tales are shared to help nudge the unconscious to remember initiation. We build appreciation for the concept of rites of passage and orient community members to the skills necessary for constructing and refining their community's own initiation and rites of passage artistic processes. In this way, people develop an intrinsic appreciation for initiation and the skills to move forward and together design their own masterpiece—their community's rite of passage. We are nurturing and growing a cadre of public artists to move the story of rites of passage into a work of performance art and onto center stage in a community.

This is not your typical run-of-the-mill education or human service program, where we bring in experts, who know, to train citizens who don't know how to help

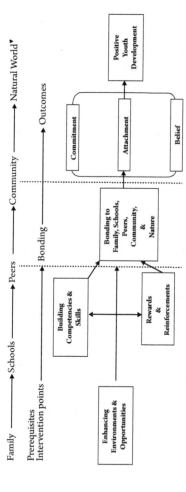

Family ⟶ Schools ⟶ Peers ⟶ Community ⟶ Natural World ▸

Prerequisites
Intervention points

Bonding ⟶ Outcomes

Enhancing Environments & Opportunities

Building Competencies & Skills

Rewards & Reinforcements

Bonding to Family, Schools, Peers, Community, & Nature

Commitment

Attachment

Belief

Positive Youth Development

Figure 11.1 The Social Development Model.

▸ Adapted and modified for Youth and Community Development through Rites of Passage by: D. G. Blumenkrantz, Ph.D, 1986.

THE SOCIAL DEVELOPMENT MODEL©

Drs. J. David Hawkins and Richard Catalano at the University of Washington. Youth development involves connecting and enhancing environments and building competencies, which promote the positive development of children and youth in their families, in their schools, among their peers in their community and with a strong connection to the natural world. Youth come of age through initiation into these environments, which are connected, non-sequentially, within a systems framework that promotes whole human beings and strong, resilient and adaptive communities.

Guided by the 20 elements in the architectural structure for youth & community development through rites of passage and within an " emergent design" process activities intensify focus on particular values, attitudes and competencies expected within each environment. Demonstrations of competencies, family and community celebrations periodically mark special times in a child's development.

Designs include: Initiation of Scholars© - Initiation into Play – Parent/Child change of status - Giving back & Community Service – Therapy as Initiation and more.

Impact of major systems/environments on child development = *Initiation opportunities*.

their kids to grow up well. It is a new way of mobilizing a community. Citizens invited to learn and share rite of passage experiences become initiated into an authentic community that can commit to design, provide, and continually adapt these powerful experiences with and for their children and their entire community. Making rites of passage a reality requires considerable focus, skill, and frequently luck. Part of creating luck is offering a structure that people can grasp and in which they can begin to work to expand their understanding of the complexity of rites of passage.

Roy G. Biv of Rites of Passage

The following are the design principles that were included in the grant material to inform the development of designs and activities that could be integrated into a community's rite of passage experience. They are the primary materials in the creation of the art we call community-oriented rites of passage.

1. An initiation/orientation event for both parents and their children. It usually takes place when children are in grade 6, ages 11–12. This is typically the transitional year between primary and secondary school. The event is dedicated to dramatically and appropriately shift the initiates' and their parents' attention to focus on the children's entry into adolescence. It enlists parents, community, and schools in strategic activities throughout a multiyear process. Through public ritual and ceremony children are separated from their parents and go with high school students and community elders. Both youth and parents are given a set of expectations for their roles in the initiatory process, which begins here and now and continues for the next six years, culminating with the youths' graduation from high school. It dramatically states to everyone that "something is happening—changes are commencing that will help our children make the transition from childhood to adulthood."

2. Several years of planned integrated and sequenced educational, physical, and mental challenges for youth, which are age appropriate and developmentally sequenced, including breakout experiences by gender and culturally relevant. These activities are designed to increase competencies in skills for living, like problem-solving and decision-making; promote autonomy, self-determination, empathy, and compassion; foster a connection with a "spiritual self"; and promote a shift in consciousness and a belief in and sense of their own transformation. They include:

   a. Skill building for positive youth development. Examples include activities that promote good mental and physical health, healthy diet, problem-solving and decision-making, ability to achieve insight and recognize a connectedness to nature and that which is greater than one's self, resulting in empathy and caring for others.

   b. Integrated designs that promote mastery and competency in essential attitudes and skills for life, such as learning how to learn well and engaging in health-promoting play. The Initiation of Scholars and Initiation into Play within ROPE are examples. Along with the acquisition of these skills is the demonstration of their mastery and public affirmation in ceremony and ritual.

c. Linking youth with positive leisure time activities and an understanding of the importance of having fun through positive play rather than more self-destructive activities like drinking and drug use and sexual experimentation. "If you help a child find their bliss it's the best protective influence you can give them and way to promote healthy life-style decisions."

d. Developing capacity for people to engage in mentorship relationships, peer counseling, or other youth empowerment and engagement activities. Community elders are prepared to mentor older adolescents (high school students), while older adolescents are prepared to serve as mentors for youth entering the initiatory process (transition from primary to secondary school). School and community systems are organized in ways that help develop and sustain mentoring relationships. A circle of life is connected.

e. Systematically guiding youth into identified and coordinated community service. Provide youth with opportunities to demonstrate their newly acquired skills in a setting that affords them higher status as an emerging adult in the community.

f. Celebration event(s) that mark significant transitions between elementary, middle, and high school and where the initiate demonstrates some form of competency in academic pursuits, recreation, or play related to their initial rite of passage experience. This could be the demonstration of some skill, a presentation, or public declaration of commitment to the obligations of an adult in the community.

g. Presenting multicultural and ethnically sensitive opportunities for youth to explore and gain an understanding of their own culture of origin. Create a setting for them to share and teach—exchange with others—cultural history and significance to increase multicultural understanding.

h. Providing some type of symbolic experience of death of the child and rebirth of the new youth.

i. A succession of increasingly difficult physical and mental ordeals or challenges where youth have to demonstrate a competency in skills learned in order to accomplish a challenge and move on to a higher order of ordeal. The challenges may range from ropes course, rock climbing and rappelling, to vision quest and other solo experiences where youth have an opportunity for self-dialogue and reflection.

j. An encounter with nature that strengthens a sense of connection and belonging.

k. Periods of isolation and alone time for reflection and the maturation of ideas into ones' own internal dialogue to inform and guide health-promoting values and lifestyle choices.

l. Stories that anchor youth in the historical and mythological context of their culture and community, their people, and their place in nature, while giving them references, heroes and heroines—models for their own lives and the creation of their own internal initiatory stories in which they can become heroes and heroines.

3. Parents need to learn:
   a. The importance of rites of passage as a framework for youth and community development and the expectations for their involvement in their children's initiatory process.
   b. Information about adolescent development and how to parent adolescents.
   c. Information that increases their understanding and sensitivity toward developmental milestones of midlife and the potential *collision of transitions* between adolescence and midlife.
   d. How and when to participate in planned and agreed on activities that support youths' rite of passage experiences.
   e. A variety of strategies to interact with children around themes of rites of passage during and following the proposed project.
   f. What the initiatory experience "feels" like so they can "walk the talk" and have had an intimate encounter with the initiatory process. This way they can serve as helpful and engaged community elders and mentors for youth.
   g. Learn how to put separating from their child into action, letting them go to grow, and how to consciously engage in their own "transition" to another stage in their life that enables their child's emerging adulthood to find a place in their family and community.
4. The community needs to:
   a. Identify and link community resources to support the youth and parent component and mobilize the community to develop and coordinate such resources.
   b. Promote collaboration between schools, community agencies, and other resources, such as cultural, religious, civic, recreational, and family, that are put into action through the development of a "core group" that represents the diversity of the community.
   c. Offer financial commitment to secure the necessary programmatic materials, insurance, space, and so forth.
   d. Secure policy endorsement from the school board, local governmental body, or governing authority for using a framework of youth and community development through rites of passage.
   e. Offer an administrative structure to provide a process for program development, implementation, modification, and adaptation for continuous improvement and relevance.
   f. Promote an authentic sense of community by supporting activities, gatherings, parties, and educational experiences that are designed to foster fun, mutual connectedness, interdependency, and responsibility.
   g. Establish strong and clear community standards for youth to learn and accept while providing positive and healthy elders as role models that guide youth on their rite of passage.
   h. Provide opportunities for markers that affirm and celebrate people coming in and out of the community's rite-of-passage process. Establishing protocols for people who enter and depart from the rite of passage project that models the initiatory process.

What Happened?

At this point you might be wondering what happened as a result of using rites of passage as a framework and story for mobilizing communities. Measuring multiple outcomes of such a complicated community intervention was explored. First, there were personal aspects of the intervention that could have been assessed within youth and parent participants and those community residents who volunteered to participate. Second, we could have focused on the relationship between networks of individuals and institutions as we sought to examine the story of rites of passage as a potent way to galvanize people into an organized response that promoted positive youth development. Third, we could examine the concept of reciprocity between youth and adults, individuals and community, and institutions. Finally, a larger order of analysis could focus on the attempt by government to change a paradigm, shifting policy away from focusing on single solutions toward adopting a whole systems approach.

The focus of research was made easier for two reasons. First, the project was funded by the State of Connecticut before the full force of federal evidence-based requirements dictated programs that education and community-based organizations had to provide. Besides, there were very little funds for any extensive research and data analysis in the first place. At the onset of the project, the State cut all funds for research. That helped to make the decision easier. In hindsight it also foreshadowed the challenges and limitations of large-order systems, like governments, when it comes to change. Second, the primary purpose of the grant was to achieve community mobilization. Community mobilization became the primary focus of research efforts. The focus of analysis was on the number of people and networks of people engaged, barriers to participation, and what stimulated people to become involved in a community mobilization project. While not the central focus of analysis, there was substantial qualitative information obtained from both youth and parent participants related to individual outcomes.

The Paths to the Year 2000—Project 2000 focused on seeking programs and methods that brought together varied resources in creative ways to achieve significant change in the way communities view adolescents. It also sought to enable communities to work in concert, focusing energy and resources on substance abuse problems by altering the conditions that contribute to it and other problems.

Community mobilization, in this situation, is broadly defined as enhancing a community's capacity to investigate a particular set of problems by facilitating their ability to collaboratively join together to identify and address their problems and concerns. In other words, it means creating an environment conducive for building a critical mass of people motivated to identify the variables that contribute to problems and through a collaborative evolutionary process implement designs to mitigate the problems. The details of the design and process were provided earlier.

Community mobilization, community empowerment, and building community collaboratives have become key ingredients in recent grant requirements. This particular project centered on using the history and story of rites of passage, coupled with established design principles as a method for mobilizing a community. Rather than selecting a particular community problem to focus on, like preventing substance abuse, this approach identified the absence of a particular community process for health or a potential protective factor, namely, rites of passage. This is a different orientation to community organizing and has acknowledged limitations. It could be viewed as manipulative and compromising authentic community empowerment and engagement that traditionally taps into citizens' own interests, attitudes, orientations, and particular issues and problems that they desire to focus on.

Our justification considered the question, "How would you know what you need and are missing if you never knew it existed in the first place?" When we introduced the history of rites of passage, evidence of their existence, their purpose, and consequences of their absence, it was not difficult for youth and adults to see the need and utility of a community-mobilizing process for helping rites of passage emerge in their location. Furthermore, there were no outside forces, political pressure, or even great economic incentive for community's to participate. Several communities that had never participated in regional projects before joined in, a further indicator of the potential of the story of rites of passage to capture attention and compel action.

In the design of the community-mobilizing process we offered general principles to guide community members organizing around the concept of rites of passage from which they designed their own interventions—community-oriented rites of passage. A participatory action research method was used. From the onset, youth and adults were engaged as "coresearchers" in the project. The outcome of all research was designed specifically to provide feedback to help them continually improve their project.

Perhaps most significant in the design and community organizing process were frequent "rite of passage experiences" as part of people's exposure to rites of passage for learning key concepts and processes. Some experiences were organized just for individual communities, and some were for the all ten projects within the region, which included two projects within a medium-sized city that were culturally and ethnically based and eight projects within surrounding suburban ring communities. These shared emotional initiatory experiences were intended to usher participants across the threshold of a changing paradigm, helping them to separate from past beliefs about education, youth development, and a single-solution silo orientation. It also was designed to accelerate and strengthen relationships in ways that would serve to unify and mobilize participants—within their own setting and together in a regional learning community—so that they would be able to share lessons learned, helping to adapt and enhance each other's projects, with everyone achieving the goals of the project together. In a sense, there was a big cheerleading component built in within and between projects that energized and sustained the effort. While many professionals believe that community engagement, mobilization and collaboration are important (Wolff 2010) few designs actual focus on impacting the conditions in which authentic collaboration is possible through strengthening genuine relationships. This is also the case with the current belief in the importance in spirituality as a key element in community interventions.

Central Findings

The central findings were best summed up in a newsletter from the Capital Areas Substance Abuse Council—CASAC (July 1996):

> Over 4,000 students and 2,800 adults were served through this project from its inception in 1993. A majority of the programs have identified other sources of funding and will continue the program in the coming years.

Another illustration of the community-mobilizing potency of the rite of passage story/framework was reflected in the fact that eleven out of sixteen communities within CASAC's purview decided to participate in the grant initiative. Historically, three of the communities had never participated with CASAC previously. One was not accepted.

Each of the projects was provided the general principles to inform and guide their project's development. Several chose the name of an existing approach, adapting it to their setting, and others created completely different designs and names: Avon, *Rite Of Passage Experience, ROPE*; E. Granby, *REACH*; Granby, *Realm*; Hartford, Mi Casa, *Padrino & Madrina*; Hartford, First Baptist Church, *Nyonca*; Newington, *Rite Of Passage Experience, ROPE*; Simsbury, *CHOICES*; West Hartford, *Leadership Project*; Wethersfield, *Rite Of Passage Experience, ROPE*; and Windsor, *Passages*.

There were twelve classifications of participant groups mobilized, for a total of thirty-five participant groups, with an average of seven participant groups per project. Participant groups included civic organizations, parents, church members, town leaders, business leaders, chambers of commerce, retired citizens, school faculty, town departments, community-based agencies, youth, and community professionals.

Following are a few of the responses to survey questions. The first are related to who was mobilized and the initial phase of the process. These reflect many other responses and reveal a common sentiment about people becoming involved in the project and its potency to unite people.

> "It basically mobilized everybody in our church in every category and demographic—it ranged from housewives working with professionals such as doctors, principals, teachers. You will find young people under the age of 13 and 14 working together with people over the age of 50 and 60. There was a wide demographic of people coming together and mobilizing for the betterment of the community."
>
> "I consider the mobilization more of a motivation to get the program to work toward mobilizing and enriching the youth, enriching the community.
>
> "From my experience there's a more cohesive group and we did move differently and forward where no one had been involved in. To me, mobilization meant putting it into action. Whereas I've been in one where we plan and plan and we have ideas and we never get our foot out the door.
>
> "It mobilized the schools. The schools are kind of a territorial type thing. This is the first program that the town ever coordinated together, we shattered barriers."

"I know of parents that want to do a Passage Club for the kids that just finished and the parents are going to do it themselves and run it. Lots of other activities have been spawned and are engaging more and more people. Also, a group of parents that want to do the experience themselves."

"You have a lot of egos in some of the other ones where you have to satisfy egos or satisfy personalities that want to control it. Here there was no control—there was not a controlling ego—it was really more of a cohesive team. Everyone's ideas we listened to and heard and everyone shared with each other and helped to carry out each other's ideas."

Another series of questions focused on inclusiveness, for example, "How reflective was the *core group* of the diversity of the community?" Here are some of the responses:

"There's a wide demographic—being a church-based organization, we have a tendency to be in a position where we can attract a wide range of people. This ranges all the way from—Professionals/teachers, doctors down to a housewife or just a regular plain old child who has no aspirations except to just have fun."

"The Core Group of elders is very reflective of the community. We have a good range of young and not so young people who have been in town for a long time and people who have just moved into town and looking for a way to be a part of the community."

Another response noted the significance of the group experiences:

"Our elders group is pretty diverse, but the problem is our elders group is hard to define exactly who's elder and who's not. We know that they need to go through common experiences—be brought in with some training. Who we have to choose from is very diverse. It's excellent but we need to expand it quite a bit, bring more people in. Eventually the goal would be to have the whole community being elders.

The concept of "community elder" was important and a central feature in the design of the rites of passage. Community organizing was intended to recruit "elders" who would serve as mentors to youth. As part of the community education-feedback process we asked people about their definition of a "community elder."

Their responses were the topic of community conversations that continued the learning process and capacity-building to strengthen their community-organizing and rite of passage activities. The concept of "elder" and "mentoring" are growing in importance, and these responses are informative in guiding future efforts in this area and affirming our orientation that an "elder" can be anyone just a bit older and further down the path of life than someone else. Many of the responses reflect a degree of reciprocity in the way adult's benefit and consider their participation to be a growth-enhancing experience.

Here are responses to the question "What is your definition of a community elder?"

"A volunteer who has a significant interest in acting in a mentoring and teaching capacity specifically in the rites of passage program from helping the kids get involved in participating in the activities to helping the kids get from where they were to where they want to be, and in the process they themselves participate in a learning and growth experience.

It also is a good experience for the elders. As a by-product they also go through an initiation and growth along the way. I neglected to say trained. That is important."

" If we're trying to get these kids from adolescence into adulthood, we have to show them some sort of role to pattern themselves after."

"What was most important was how these people would develop a good rapport with the kids to be a positive role model. What would make them positive are people that are behaving according to what is expected in society. Younger people who have been in trouble before, even people who are keeping very good with their own family, these are positive things in the community."

"A citizen who is concerned and thus active on issues pertaining to youth and families in their community. An elder is someone who commits some amount of time and energy or focus on rites of passage programs/ concepts."

"I don't think there's really one set definition for what a community elder is because they can take so many different and varied roles."

"I'm going to go traditional and say a keeper of the wisdom, someone who in the community has experienced certain things in the past and has certain knowledge about these experiences whether it be in terms of the community or an individual person. But more along the lines of the values and beliefs of the community and so a keeper of the community history so to speak."

"An elder does not have to be someone much older. I think people get hung up on elders. Sometimes, I think ROPE III students (high school) can be elders for the sixth graders because they've had similar experiences that they can compare. Anyone that may be a little bit older, but have similar experiences can guide someone through that. You don't have to have gray hair to be an elder."

In general, responses reflected a belief that community elders could be almost anyone, who would be a role model as determined by their behavior in the community, which exemplified the positive values, beliefs, and attitudes. Age did not appear to be a determining factor, but rather a degree of experience that could be passed on and be helpful to someone else. It did matter that elders were located in the community and available in both formal and informal ways to youth.

Several responses noted the value and need for common experiences and training. A follow-up question asked most of the interviewees to focus on whether the community elders needed some kind of training or orientation. In general, there was agreement that community elders needed training.

These responses reflect that general theme:

> "People need to go through some kind of an experience—what it is we're not sure—just to tie them in—we can do it for you but then it's not an ownership to them, it's an ownership to us. If they make the moves, write the letters, do the work they'll own it and buy into it more. Some experience is for an ownership."

> "There has to be an orientation so that there is team building—to become part of that team—a group feeling. And an ongoing orientation—team building all of the time for a sense of continuity."

The community-mobilizing process intentionally builds shared emotional experience into the design as a way to strengthen people's sense of connection to each other and hence the project. The strength of relationships transfers into feelings of ownership and responsibility for the project, which essentially is responsibility for raising their children. This is the saying "It takes a whole child to raise a village" put into action. As people explore and experience rites of passage together, relationships are spawned and strengthened, and in reciprocity they contribute to the overall vibrancy, resiliency, and sense of connection throughout the community.

Why are people motivated to participate? Responses to these questions ranged from a sense of personal gain to altruistic motives. Parents indicated that by working with other young people they hoped to get a better understanding of their own child and how to be a better parent. The opportunity to give something to the community and how it makes you feel was a theme, as reflected in this statement:

> "We definitely get fulfillment out of the opportunity to run this program and to contribute to the betterment of our children and community."

Many responses focused on people being "part of something that is bigger than their individual role" in the community. A significant number of the responses focused on the positive aspects of the program, as illustrated in this comment from one project:

> "I think there's such a negative view of the world out there, violence, gang, etc., that they feel like they're making a positive change and that they do have some kind of say in what goes on."

Participants' comments may be uncovering an element of personal and community empowerment, a belief that they have an ability to make a significant contribution in the community and have a positive influence in the lives of youth. A participant from one project responded:

> "What could be more worthwhile than trying to help a kid get started into adulthood in a positive way?"

"For me the program is incredible. It's an incredible program to bring together children with people who do care. There needs to be a positive sense and a sense of being proud of their community."

Almost every project offered responses that surfaced the issue of the lack of connection in a community and the opportunity the rites of passage projects presented to build connections and become involved. For example, from one project we heard this:

"People are in the 'rat race,' people don't have the time to build partnerships between groups and it becomes that much more difficult. More difficult because people don't have the time to build the bridges to make those bonds in between the organizations."

While a youth elder from another town offered this:

"There are a lot of things to do but you have to be willing to include yourself. We're giving people the opportunity to see what there is to do. It's a program that's saying, 'Here is what you can do.' Forcing them to see it, but not forcing them to do it. Opening the door to say, 'Come in—do something.'"

It gave adults in the community an opportunity to impact the lives of children, as an adult from one project offered:

"[There are] adults who have always wanted to serve the community, but they never had an outlet."

In another area, attention was given to the projects' connecting people with their heritage, as one of the projects' participants reports:

"I'm getting reconnected with those cultural values that give them a sense of belonging and commitment and sincerity."

Several respondents touched on the issue of building a "community ethic" for volunteerism and leadership and its decline over the last decade. Here is one of several comments referring to volunteering and parent involvement:

"It becomes a community ethic. . . . Because it is a community ethic, you create peer pressure and if you get a phone call and you get told this is something we need to do, and you need to call two or three other people to get them involved. You have a telephone linkage."

Paths to the Year 2000 offered a unique opportunity to focus on the community-mobilizing potential of rites of passage. One of the chief issues related to engaging and sustaining adults and other volunteers in the project was the lack of time. One response summed up the attitude of many:

"It really amazed me that those people could take that amount of time off of work and do what they do. I could never take the time. I would hope our society would move closer to allowing us the time."

There is a need to explore the potential of community-based rites of passage to mobilize a community and the multiple outcomes associated with mobilization. Clearly there were many people engaged in activities that provided positive youth development and educational benefit that were valued, as attested in participant responses. One adult commented, "However, whether or not they achieved being a rite of passage remains a question." This might be the $64,000.00 question. It can only be answered over time, as the rite of passage design elements emerge and become part of the social, cultural and political fabric of a community. Several of the respondents addressed this question:

"I personally, and I have a consensus among the elders also, hope that this project could expand. Expansion is a key element. In a society today where positive things are not expanding and are getting smaller, to me that's a very important point. I would like to see it reach more into the community and develop a sense of a permanent base, if possible."

"I hope that the community wakes up and realizes that they need to come together to help our youth because if it doesn't happen, the problems of youth are going to get worse."

"One of the key components is community involvement. We've just scratched the surface of what we can do to get these children in high school more involved in the community. There's a big benefit in having more inter-action of people of all ages."

"I would hope this actually does become a rite of passage. Because right now I don't think it is, it may build into one. I would really like to see it become a real rite of passage so a child expects that they have to pass through this to become an adult. I mean town wide, city wide, it's a good program."

The last response, "I would hope this actually does become a rite of passage," is significant. Inherent in this response is recognition of the complexity of rites of passage and the time required for the process to develop authentic community rites of passage. We were clear from the outset about the length of time necessary for authentic rites of passage to emerge and become a part of the fabric and rituals of a community. By definition rituals are rituals because the same activities occur over a period of time and result in desired outcomes. Only over time would the activities within a community's rites of passage achieve the desired outcome of fulfilling youth's need for transformative experiences and offer them increased status recognized within their community. At the same time, the celebration of a rite of passage, over time, becomes renewing for the entire community, which includes earth and all our relations. As I wrote previously, "a child's public expression of and commitment to a community's values and beliefs reinforces expectations for behaviors for the survival of the entire community and health and well-being of all our relations. A child's coming of age presents an opportunity for the whole community to examine, adapt and recommit themselves to their social and cultural heritage". This occurs over a period of time.

How Are the Children?

Qualitative and some quantitative reports from this and other previous and subsequent community-based rites of passage projects, especially the Rite Of Passage Experience ROPE, have all revealed similar results at an individual, family, school, and community level.

Qualitative and quantitative evaluations of ROPE have been conducted since 1982 (Blumenkrantz and Gavazzi 1993). A series of studies with five cohort groups totaling 410 participants revealed positive gains at both the individual and family levels. In terms of involvement with family, the ROPE group showed significant increases of involvement as compared with the control group. Also, the ROPE group reported more positive attitudes toward school than the control group. For drug use, ROPE participants decreased their drug use by 60 percent, while the control group increased substance use by 57 percent. Finally, the ROPE group reported significantly greater levels of connectedness and belonging after ROPE, while the control group had increased levels of alienation. Qualitative findings from youth and parents revealed common themes in the areas of self-confidence, decision-making, and commitment to school. Comments included "I can make decisions on what to do and not worry about peer pressure" and "This is the first year my daughter insists on going to school even when she's ill" (Blumenkrantz and Gavazzi 1993).

Since 1981, it is estimated, over 200,000 youth and their parents have been engaged in ROPE in Connecticut alone, while countless others participated in projects influenced by ROPE's guiding principles and philosophy. Other comments by children, parents and teachers include:

"ROPE is the best thing to come along since comic books."
                                    —Student

"My son brought home his experiences and new knowledge every night he had a ROPE class. And we discussed them for days."
                                    —Parent

"I learned to have confidence in myself and other people and treat others as I would want to be treated."
                                    —Student

"I can make decisions on what to do and not worry about peer pressure."
                                    —Student

"After participating in ROPE, students came to school more regularly and attacked problems in a new, more positive way."

—Teacher

"ROPE taught me not to judge people until you really get to know them, and it's easier to get things done when you cooperate with those around you."

—Student

"The Rite of Passage Experience provides a unifying force enabling students to work together for a positive goal."

—Teacher

"I learned to accept challenges without backing out."

—Student

"I learned to work in a group and even with people I don't like."

—Student

"ROPE students learn about their potential and ways to achieve it, gain self-confidence and problem-solving skills, and have more respect for their peers."

—Teacher

What if Human Evolution Is the Ultimate Clinical Trial?

In contemporary behavioral science, the randomized clinical trial (RCT) has emerged as the gold standard for evaluating the efficacy of medical and social interventions. Indeed, today, an intervention that is not "evidence-based" is largely excluded from most funding streams. But are there other ways we can judge the viability of potential interventions? What behavioral forms have stood the test of time and span cultural differences? What archetypal features are consistently found in all human communities that presumably contribute to the survival of our species? If such patterns do exist, should these processes and underlying principles become the touchstone of our efforts to develop interventions intended to improve individual and community life?

The questions regarding the presence of common features across the panorama of cultural practices that exist in our species that have to do with puberty and initiation were discussed throughout this book, especially in chapter 10, "Something Happened." We introduced how Arnold van Gennep's classic work *The Rites of Passage* (1909/1960) identified one such commonality: the presence of community-centered rites of passage to mark important life transitions, found in nearly all cultures. While the manifestations of these rites of passage (phenotypes) vary across cultures, van Gennep argued that they all contain an underlying process sequence (genotype) of three stages: separation, transition (liminality), and incorporation.

So what if evolution is the ultimate clinical trial? What if our millions of years of evolution as a species have led to the development of cultural forms that can help sustain us? We need to learn from that history and recognize the wisdom that is part of our past. Our heavy emphasis on "evidence-based" interventions may preclude us from seeing the evidence offered by the 2-million-year-old clinical trial called "human evolution." I am not suggesting we abandon contemporary science. Humankind has benefited and will continue to benefit from such intellectual endeavors. We need to adapt our methods to be in service of people and not politics.

Public Policy Prevents Communities from Initiating Their Children

It was clear to me in the early eighties, when the epidemic of evidence-based RCT began to invade the education and human service scene, that something profound was beginning. As discussed earlier, the RCT evidence-base paradigm is inadequate to gauge the real impact of community-based rites of passage. Its pervasive invasion into communities, mandated by the federal government, actually usurped people's desire and capacity to provide rites of passage to their children.

Between 1981 and 2001 there were dozens of communities throughout Connecticut and hundreds more around the country bringing rites of passage into the lives of their children. Parents received efforts at more rigorous evaluations combatively. They objected to the possibility of their children being in the "control" group and not being included in their community's rite of passage. One community that did agree to participate in an evaluation project, did so after parents were offered a day at an amusement park for their children. "Reality astonishes theory"—you can't make this stuff up! One by one schools and community agencies were forced by government mandates and funding requirement to abandon their rites of passage, which were replaced by programs on a list deemed evidence-based. Indeed, communities were left with little more than a menu of proven interventions from which to select with no rational base to guide that selection (Green 128). Children and their communities were not getting what they needed but rather what the government and others with vested interests decided they should get? In every state national policy precluded the emergence of home grown designs for rites of passage and other education and youth development programs.

While it is important to understand the ingredients and protocols that contribute to the success of interventions it is equally important to recognize the limitations of the existing model and explore alternatives. "By calling into question the 'tyranny' of the RCT, we level the 'playing field' for other research designs and methods, such as natural history studies, case studies, intervention process analysis, health service research, qualitative research, and participatory action research. All these research methods need to be used in tandem to open up the "black box" of the randomized experiment (Rapkin and Trickett 2005, 258).

The "tyranny of the RCT" and misguided, silo attempts to declare war on specific problems has usurped communities' natural desire and ability to provide rites of passage with and for their children. In doing so, these approaches unwittingly have undermined our greatest natural resource—rituals and rites of passage to strengthen citizens' sense of belonging to a place and community. All of these would have contributed to fostering communities of compassion and caring that would have been a natural asset that could intervene with authenticity and potency in many of the situations we hear about on the nightly news.

In the end, Newton's laws of motion affect human behavior. An object will stay in motion until and unless another object of equal force or velocity alters that motion.

What is interesting to consider organizationally is that the ability of a state agency to precipitate multilevel and sustained change at a local level is based on its own willingness to undergo substantial change. Whyte, Greenwood, and Lazes (1991) write, "In situations of major social change, the prevailing ground rules are likely to block the path to creative solutions of serious new problems. Creative solutions will depend upon the ability of the organization to change the organizational and intellectual ground rules" (42). In the previous narrative it was clear that the State of Connecticut was unprepared to "walk the talk" and support a paradigm shift operationalized through its own grant to a local agency. While it articulated the need for a paradigm shift it could not have fully considered nor practically accepted the consequences of a "revolution" (Kuhn 1962) in the way things were perceived and done. No bureaucracy wants to turn itself upside down, in spite of the potential benefits.

Human service organizations that promote a paradigm shift have to fully understand and embrace concepts and support activities that help achieve the desired goals, in spite of the potential to unbalance the organization and shift power and authority. Mobilizing a community may be directly related to the individual's and organization's perception that their involvement will have some direct positive benefit to themselves and failure to become involved would produce some unwanted, negative consequences. Behind altruism there may always be self-interest, even if the self-interest is the good feeling one has from giving to others.

Emergence Revisited

In the previous chapter I shared a story about the Delaware tribes' initiation practices and how they came to be part of the Boy Scout's Order of the Arrow initiation. The concepts of emergence and emergent design are central to the field called youth and community development through rites of passage.

Emergence assumes that something has been present, but is out of view. It comes into existence, into the light, through an interaction with forces seen and unseen. These forces are contained in the initiatory constellation, that is, individual, family, community, and ancestors, Spirit, Nature, and the Universe. It is a delicate dance that acknowledges all the forces and entities necessary to enact authentic initiation and rites of passage. In an age when the common story is

replication of evidence-based programs, the concept of emergence is revolution-
ary and requires a paradigm shift to put into action. The example of Paths to
the Year 2000 was provided to share how these concepts can and have been put
into practice. In contemporary western science it is best aligned with what I refer
to as innovation transfer. Yet, even this term and construct are inadequate and
controversial.

The Twenty Elements as Guiding Principles

Authentic initiation comes from the place where the initiates, their families, and
their ancestors live. It is a living drama choreographed by those who are attuned to
sacred information that enables them to help the initiatory process come into the
light, emerge, and manifest itself on behalf of individuals, the community, nature,
and our destiny within a living Universe. At the heart of the design principles woven
into the grant material, shared earlier, were the essence of initiation culled from
literature and life experiences. Twenty elements emerged to form the architectural
framework for youth and community development through rites of passage. The elements are used as design principles from which initiation and rites of passage practices emerge. The *rituals are made up as we go along*, but always informed by guiding
principles.

As discussed previously, many of the current programs featuring themes of
rites of passage include some of these elements in varying strengths. I suggested
that most of the present programs in youth development feature some version
of the patterns, symbols, and themes of the initiatory process that have been
lodged deep within our collective unconscious. For example, character education, resiliency, and values education have all been widely accepted and central practices in contemporary education and youth development. Aren't these
related to the central focus on initiation, that is, the transmission of essential
values to the next generation? How about community service and volunteering?
This is identical to the expectation during traditional rites of passage for the
initiate, as they move into adult status to make a contribution to their family
and community.

Embedded within the twenty elements are those that attend to van Gennep's three
stages of rites of passage. These are outlined in what follows and will be described
further in a subsequent book. The first three make up the "trinity of inquiry" and
begin a process of assessment that could lead to changes in the way we view and then
act in a situation, especially education and youth development. Together with the
next four they relate to the stage of "separation" in rites of passage. This is especially
relevant to an individual's separation from previously held ideas and behaviors that
have not enabled them to fulfill their dreams and aspirations. These elements are
central to community organizing and mobilizing for a change (Blumenkrantz and
Goldstein 2014).

They are:

1. What's the story?
2. Community values and ethics
3. Paradigm shift
4. Relationships are key
5. You can only bring someone as far as you've been yourself
6. It must happen in the home community and nature
7. Community fosters expectations for socially appropriate behaviors

The middle eight are aligned with the stage of liminality and, as discussed previously, are features included in many rites of passage programs.

They include:

1. Rituals and ceremony
2. Ordeals—"Adversity introduces us to ourselves."
3. Silence
4. Connection with Nature
5. Time alone for reflection
6. Connection with ancestral roots
7. Play—secular spirituality
8. Nonordinary states of reality

The final stage of incorporation is based on these principles:

1. Giving away one's previous attitudes, behaviors, and other relevant symbolic and/ or physical material possessions that are aligned with and represent childhood.
2. Obligation of service to the larger community
3. Changes of appearance that express/reflect a new status
4. Demonstration of new competencies and change of status in meaningful roles within their culture and community
5. Celebration and affirmation of status change within the culture and community

The twenty elements are used as a basis for community-organizing processes as well as designs for integrated activities within a community that is enacting its shared rite of passage story.

Separation

"Separation" is the first phase of rites of passage within van Gennep's schema. In this framework the first seven elements serve to guide a community's explorations into the present conditions for education and youth development approaches and their outcomes. One way, among many, to begin the conversation is through the traditional Masai greeting, "Kasserian Ingera?"—"And how are the children?" This invites conversations that use the first three elements as a "trinity of inquiry." Community conversations that explore present conditions and outcomes of their children's education and development may lead to decisions to "separate" from previous ways of viewing education and youth development. This could lead to a paradigm shift that adopts the whole systems approach of youth and community development through rites of passage as a community's shared story—their framework for youth development.

What's the story? "What's the story in the way we educate and help our children come of age?" Stories, myths, and legends passed down from previous generations convey values and ethics that serve survival. Everyone has a story, these stories inform the worldviews or paradigms that guide lives and actions. "What's the story?" is an invitation to explore what we are doing to educate and help children come of age and the other elements.

Community values and ethics. The hallmark of community-based rites of passage strategies is to address the values and expectations for behavior that youth must acquire to ensure the future success of the community. There must be deliberate structures that foster community conversations about mutually agreed on expectations for behavior and values. This process must precede the creation of experiences that foster youths' understanding, appreciation, and commitment to these expectations. Values and ethics that underlie, inform, and guide all education and youth development approaches also need to be explored and assessed to judge whether and how they serve the entire community, or whether they represent just one orientation and one culture that may unwittingly negatively impact others?

Paradigm *shift*. Adolescent development is connected to a community development process rather than being seen solely as an intrapsychic phenomenon. Interventions are ecological rather than individually oriented. Exploration of the present situation—asking *What's the story?* and assessing the *values and ethics* underlying the story—leads communities to assess whether a change is needed and accept the possibility that changing views— a paradigm shift—might be necessary.

The next four elements offer central design principles to guide the "emergence" of actual program activities.

Program success relies on relationships. Meaningful outcomes depend on the quality of ongoing relationships between youth and adults, between all of the adults together, and between all of the adults and the "program." In other words, all the adults should be "initiated" to, understand, and commit to rites of passage as the overarching education and youth development framework. Positive outcomes occur only when people within a setting are intimately connected to the creation and ongoing adaptation of a strategy. A process of feedback for continuous improvement must be designed with and for community elders as well as youth. Citizen input in the "emergence"—codesign and continuous improvement and adaptation—is essential. It is only then that a strategy can be implemented with sufficient commitment and creativity to make it adaptable, potent, and successful over a long period of time.

You can only bring someone as far as you've been yourself. When relationships are key, those who are initiators of youth need intentional training, personal and professional development to build their own awareness, and internal resources necessary to fulfill this critical role in their community. Initiators of youth need to undergo their own initiatory experience and rite of passage similar to what they will guide the children through. They must travel down the path they will guide their children on, modeling maturity in order to successfully mentor children through the initiatory process.

It must happen in the home community. We saw in the social development model of youth development, discussed earlier, how children come of age within a number of different environments in which skills and values are needed in order to achieve competencies within each environment. Children grow up, by and large, in communities that are defined by geographic boundaries and real live interpersonal interactions. Connection to an actual geographic place, especially when there is deep contact with nature and a psychological sense of community is critical to a sense of self and security for children. Effective rites of passage establish a safe place for intentional conversations to occur between citizens of the community, that is, youth and adults. These ongoing conversations hold people responsible and accountable over a long period of time to expectation for behaviors essential to strengthening the bonds of community to raise their children.

Rites of passage create expectations for socially appropriate behaviors. Coming of age in a rites of passage experience involves creating and supporting intentional environments that transmit essential values and ethics that guide and inform expectations for socially appropriate behaviors. This is true for individual youth, their parents, and other adults in the community as well as institutions and agencies that matter in the lives of children and youth. When everyone is on the same page in the shared community story of rites of passage, a common language serves to strengthen a whole systems approach to creating the conditions in which children come of age to become healthy, civic minded, and socially responsible adults who care about themselves, others, and the environment.

Liminality

The next seven elements, from "rituals" to "nonordinary states of reality," make up the core of liminal experiences and are central to the transformational potential of initiation and rites of passage.

Rituals. Previous discussions offered rationales and protocols for the purpose and strength of rituals within initiation and rites of passage processes. Ritual, as part of a rites of passage experience, can set a more powerful context and impact the atmosphere for interactions where learning can emerge and become embedded deeply within individuals.

Ordeals. *Adversity introduces us to ourselves.* Experiences that challenge the individual emotionally and/or physically present opportunities to learn values and/or skills that increase self-awareness and the ability to be in health-promoting relationships. When individuals participate in shared emotional experiences within a group, it increases the bonds between them. This fosters more compassion and altruistic behavior, which serve to strengthen a broader sense of community and contribute to a community's adaptation and survival.

Silence. Children and youth grow up in a cacophony of sound that makes the "call to adventure," the internal alarm clock awakening them to the coming of age process, almost inaudible. Silence helps a young person develop an internal dialogue for narrating and making sense of what is going on around them.

Connection with nature. Central to the initiatory process and a foundational feature in many rites of passage programs is the immersion of youth in experiences that help them realize and appreciate their connection and interdependence to the natural environment. Making these connections as close as possible to where youth actually live strengthens the possibility of an ongoing relationship with the "natural places" that youth call "home." These natural relationships then can become a resource for youth as they come of age. These places can become refuges and allies for youth when they need a period of silence and alone time to help them narrate and understand their emerging adulthood, the world, and their place within it.

Time alone for reflection. Contemplation helps foster balance in our connections and relationships. Time intentionally set aside for a person to reflect on his/her personal values, actions, and beliefs is critical to one's sense of identity and to find meaning and purpose in life.

Connection with ancestral roots. The opportunity to learn, value, and appreciate one's connection to those who went before and the values and ethics their heritage embraces is central to human development. Coming of age within one's cultural heritage and guided by adults who reflect and embody that heritage offers a resource for adolescents that can't be replaced.

Play. The opportunity to help individuals find their "bliss," those activities that they can immerse themselves in with great passion, and from which they receive unbridled joy is central to youth and community development through rites of passage. Play is secular spirituality and a primal, organic way for essential learning, laughter, love, and sense of community. This has been noted and referenced previously.

Nonordinary states of reality. We saw in chapter 10 that *something happens* around the time of puberty that is necessary and responds to a child's yearning for access to other ways of knowing and an encounter with the "great mystery" to answer the question "Where do I fit in the great expanding story of the Universe?" Experimenting with drugs, alcohol, and tobacco are contemporary patterns of behavior that attempt to satisfy this primal curiosity. The use of sanctioned behaviors such as vision quest, meditation, yoga, movement and dance, and playing 'in the zone' with sports and hobbies offers more health-promoting outlets to experience nonordinary states of reality.

Incorporation

This next stage is incorporation, and these five elements are arguably the most essential for a series of activities to be considered a rite of passage. A central purpose of initiation is to guide a child across the threshold to the adult community. The stage of incorporation addresses the question "Initiation into what?" Initiation into the culture and community of one's ancestors and where one lives is a central characteristic of authentic rites of passage. As we discussed earlier, unless you are welcomed back to the village and honored for completing an ordeal you become sick. Transformation is complete only when one returns and is honored and welcomed back into the community. The work of initiation is individual, while responsibility for its transformative potential belongs to the community.

The final five elements guide activities that help the initiate achieve a sense of incorporation and affirmation of their transition and are apparent in the ethnographies of cultural puberty and initiation rites in chapter 10:

Giving away one's previous attitudes, behaviors that may be attributed to childhood. The coming-of-age process through rites of passage includes giving up and/or giving away some aspect of childhood. It could be some behaviors, attitudes, or cherished items that characterized their former status. This process conveys a reality that change—leaving something dear in the past behind—is an integral part of the transition.

Obligation of service to the larger community. Through a community-based rite of passage, expectations for service are "institutionalized" as a central value. Adolescents are oriented to recognize that service to the community is an essential part of becoming a fully functioning adult in society. It also represents increased maturity and a sign that they are, in fact, becoming an adult.

Change of appearance that expresses/reflects new status. As recognition of their transition to a new status, initiates may adorn themselves with some external sign or marker that symbolizes this attainment. This might include special cloths, adornments, and badges that are awarded during the public rites of passage.

Demonstrate new competencies and change of status in meaningful roles within their culture and community. We saw within the social development model of positive youth development that the acquisition of new skills in different environments is part of the process of coming of age. There also must be opportunities in one's family, at school, with peers, and in the community and the natural world to demonstrate newly acquired skills; and the acquisition of new skills and the change of status that coincides must be publically affirmed in ceremony.

Celebration and affirmation of status change within the culture and community. Community celebrations that affirm and celebrate the initiate's new status and *welcomes them back to the village* as changed are the capstone of the processes within the stage of incorporation.

These design principles and related activities help to build a strong foundation for the emergence of a community's rites of passage experience through a collaborative evolutionary process. They help people join together to understand and accept rites of passage as important and a process for them to adopt it as the framework that becomes their "Story" for education and youth development policy and practice. It is a process that needs continued community involvement and regeneration. As previously stated, rites of passage are not only transformative for youth but renewing for the community. In this light, we say, "It takes a whole child to raise a village."

12

End Notes: Reflections of a Public Artist

A Call to Inquiry and Action

Figure 12.1 When in the womb everything to be known about the Universe we know–At birth we forget.

I have sat with children for decades. Several generations of them, in fact. I have looked into their souls, and they have looked deeply into mine. Our conversations kept reminding me of their brilliance, determination, and resiliency, their yearning to be in the world in a good way.

All are born with the possibility for altruism and grace. The conditions so necessary to nurture and affirm our children's lives have deteriorated. I have witnessed their growing despair. In the absence of a clear pathway to adulthood coupled with an increase in their perception of life-threatening problems, it is no wonder that the children of today feel the way they do.

Can we continue to ignore the condition of our children? Could we ignore a major environmental catastrophe? Ignoring an environmental catastrophe would place the planet and us at risk. Ignoring the plight of our children condemns them to a marginal existence in the future and risks grave consequences for our entire species and the planet.

And, how are the children? This question is an invitation to share stories about our children. As I noted at the beginning of this book, if the children are indeed our future, then the stories about how we educate and help them come of age are the most important stories to get right. When we get those stories wrong, which it seems we have, than we get our future wrong. The stories about how we educate and help our children come of age for generations have produced the world we have today. How are the children? They and we could be much better. What are the stories we tell about raising our children? What are the values and beliefs that form the foundation of our education and youth development efforts? What do our children need to grow up into healthy, responsible civically engaged citizens? Are the answers to these two questions in alignment? When we get out story *rite* we get our future right.

What's the Story?

What's the story? And what are the values and ethics that underlie and inform the story, leading to behaviors and actions? These are the first two essential elements in the architectural framework for youth and community development through rites of passage. The questions serve as a "call to inquiry" for analyzing any situation and help focus our attention on questions that matter related to our children. Citizens come together in conversations about these questions. Over the last several decades, large group conversation methods have been refined and codified into helpful processes that support youth and community development. The World Café (Brown and Isaacs 2005), Appreciative Inquiry (Cooperrider and Whitney 2001), and other programs have offered useful design methods that nurture the sprouting of collective intelligence and harvesting it for the greater good. At the core of our work is conversation on questions that matter related to youth and community development and its relationship to rites of passage. Small and large groups come together in conversations that examine the existing story that we created for educating and helping our children come of age. Is the story working for us? Decisions are at hand. This brings us to the third essential element in this "trinity of inquiry," a paradigm shift. If the story is not working for guiding our children to come of age well and helping their families and community make adaptations necessary to affirm and make a place for their emerging adulthood, then something has to change. A paradigm shift is necessary.

Humans are story-making creatures. We have a strong urge to organize our perceptions of the world through stories that attempt to explain the mysteries of life and help us feel safe and secure. Story making comes from our natural inclination to have an internal dialogue with ourselves that narrates our experiences in the world. We creatively imagine ourselves in relationships with the world in ways that provide meaning and make distinctions between the sacred and the profane. Our values, beliefs, and expectations for behavior begin to emerge and mature through these inner narratives. Story making serves survival by allowing us to be placed in situations, through our imagination, that would otherwise not be practical, allowing us to work things out as if we were really there (Gazzaniga 2008).

Just because we create a story to help us understand and explain a mystery does not mean we get the story right. It is one thing when our personal internal values and the stories they generate are not aligned with the external reality. But when we get the story wrong at larger levels of policy, social justice, economics, and the environment it can be devastating for us as a species, the rest of our planet, and all of our relations (Korten 2015). This is especially true for the story we make up about our children's development, their education, and the values that inform and guide these stories to become reality. These stories are told to our children in the form of scientific theories and enacted in evidence-based programs.

In chapter 8 we explored the operating principles behind myths, their relationship to ritual, and how scientific theories are contemporary myths. Theories are stories that attempt to explain and narrate our world. However, as pointed out earlier, the present stories that inform and guide our actions in education and youth development are inadequate because they are devoid of values essential for living.

Stories from our DNA

The story of initiation and rites of passage has always been within my ancestors' tradition. It was inextricably tied to community. My orientation to initiation and rites of passage as reciprocity between the individual, community, nature, a sacred Earth, and all our relations was not solely an intellectual exercise. It flowed through me, carried in my blood and DNA from my ancestors. I just could not see it any other way.

> When rites of passage unfold as "The Story" that a community adopts for raising their children, they lay a foundation for a common language to talk together and a set of beliefs and expectations for a whole village to raise their children. It reframes service delivery within the culture of a caring and connected community where citizens expect to be partners with other people, those whom we now call professionals.

Children are initiated into a community with values and expectations for them to be responsible and engaged citizens. They join adults who are responsible for their own lives, capable, caring, and willing to help their neighbors and fellow citizens. Over years and generations, more and more adults will grow up within a community's story of initiation and rites of passage. They will become the guides and initiators for their community's children and grandchildren. It will be remembered in their DNA. The elders will have been initiated and can then initiate their children. This also applies to older students, like high school students who mentor and initiate younger students.

This also aids younger student's transition into and through middle and high school, which are typically vulnerable times for youth. This is aligned with one of the twenty guiding elements: You can only bring someone as far as you've been yourself.

Through a common language, the framework for change also serves as the basis for subsequent involvement and therapy, reframed as another "ordeal" in the ongoing process of initiation, when youth development doesn't go as planned, which is frequently the case (Gavazzi and Blumenkrantz 1993). It offers strategic design opportunities, seamlessly integrated across the traditional spectrum of service delivery, from prevention and health promotion to identification, intervention, treatment, and aftercare.

When all youth in a community engage in a common initiation, their experiences inform lessons continually strengthened by community elders, who can be of service to them throughout their journey to adulthood and the rest of their life. Everyone engaged with children shares a common language to talk with each other and their children. This common language enables people to build a network of support, encouragement, and a mechanism for accountability. Problems, symptoms, and other behaviors formerly labeled and stereotyped are reframed as another natural part of the initiatory process, a time of change and transformation during which many opportunities exist.

When members of a community immerse themselves in the initiatory experience and engage in learning together about rites of passage, a new unifying story can emerge. The story serves as a kind of linguistic scaffolding, holding together the architectural structure of youth and community development through rites of passage. A common language holds together the story that becomes their community's "myth" for raising children. Powered by the interaction of myth and science, values that inform and guide expectations for behavior are transmitted to the next generation.

As discussed earlier, initiation and rites of passage have great potential to become a powerful meta-myth for this time of transition. As a meta-myth, youth and community development through rites of passage incorporates a collection of myths into one story with a theme that transcends each of the individual stories and deals with the most fundamental elements revealed in each of the stories. It offers an architectural structure for integrating and nurturing a deep connection among individuals, families, community, ancestors, culture, nature, and the Universe.

These are the central entities that make up the initiatory constellation. Rites of passage are the compelling story that can galvanize a community into actions that will continually strengthen the connection between citizens in a community. Over successive generations the "story" becomes stronger and more adaptive and evolves into more favorable conditions for individuals, their community, our sacred Earth, and all our relations.

> When one has no stake in the way things are, when one's needs or opinions are provided no forum, when one sees oneself as the object of unilateral actions, it takes no particular wisdom to suggest that one would rather be elsewhere.
>
> —Seymour Sarason

Professor Sarason's words are a poignant reminder that a broad diversity of citizens from a community needs to be intimately involved in the process of discovery to uncover their initiation and rites of passage story. When professionals enter the scene with their "evidence-based" myths, without input or consent from citizens, who become the object of unilateral actions, the problems facing our children, their communities, and our sacred Earth will only increase.

If we do not engage people in the process of initiation for inclusion, transcendence, and transformation, they will become alienated and disconnected from their own lives and their culture, ancestors, Spirit, community, and our sacred Earth. In the absence of a unifying story, like rites of passage that emerge from individuals collectively immersed in initiation and engaged in a collaborative evolutionary process through conversation, it takes no particular wisdom to suggest that one would rather be elsewhere.

Change the Story—Transform the Future

We need a unifying story that conveys values and exemplifies behaviors more favorable to strengthening climates of civility, respect, and civic engagement in a form that includes earth and all our relations. For thousands of years among diverse people throughout the world something happened around the time of puberty. Handed down from generation to generation, the story of rites of passage told us how values and ethics were transmitted to children. Rites of passage can once again be a unifying story. They provide the common language for a community's institutions and agencies to be in relationship with citizens. In fact, the word "relationship" comes from the Latin *relatio*, which means "to tell." At root, relationships are about making and telling stories.

Through the unifying story of rites of passage children would be initiated in ways that strengthen cultural identity and affirm their connection to community, nature, and all things. Values would be conveyed for community adaptations that support cooperation and attunement with culture, ancestors, and place. All would be initiated into a consciousness that considers Earth as a sacred sentient being in a interdependent destiny between all our relations in communion for nurturance and survival.

Individual and community rituals tap into private and collective unconscious energies that support personal health, community cohesion, and the well-being of the earth and all our relations (Somé 1993). Rituals offer a powerful resource that, when integrated with contemporary science, provide a synergy that could produce more effective design strategies for youth and community development, especially through rites of passage.

Youth and community development through rites of passage offers a language with design principles for this new story. It reflects reciprocity between the community, the individual and all their relations. The twenty design principles serve as navigational aids to inform and organize new ways of thinking. Within each setting, a new unique story emerges that guides individuals and their community to develop their own initiation and rites of passage practices. They incorporate individual and community resources, cultural symbols, and practices that embrace the spirit of their place. This new story becomes their story. There are powerful distinctions between adopting someone else's story, like those told as "evidence-based," and remembering one's own story.

Rite of passage stories can weave together elements of the sacred in secular forms that convey values and ethics essential to the survival of the Earth, all our relations, and ourselves. Children are a product of their thoughts and dreams. What they hear and see they remember and become. The stories our children hear today will fuel their dreams for tomorrow. Children are our dreams for the future. How we raise our children will determine the future.

In Search of Questions That Matter

In closing, I propose a pathway for using rites of passage to foster a more life-affirming future for our children, their families and communities, and all of us. First, one needs to address the question of policy. What is the focus of our public policy related to education, human services, and child and youth development? Is it about raising test scores or raising children? Do public policies provide a context for strengthening a psychological sense of community? Public policies reflect the values and beliefs in which the people who promoted them were raised. Are existing policies born from politicians who have been initiated, or at the very least raised in a collaborative environment that treasures empathy and compassion rather than power, control, and competition? What are the values and beliefs reflected in the structure of our existing education and human service programs?

What can we learn from the disaster at the Fukushima Daiichi nuclear plant? Years after the incident, workers are left to clean up the mess caused by the disaster. They didn't cause it, nor were they responsible for it, but nevertheless they are the ones responsible for cleaning it up—if that is even possible. The decision to use nuclear power is not in the hands of those who work there. Rather, the decision to use nuclear power is in the hands of government and businesses that have a vested financial interest in using this commodity. Again, commerce has a great influence on how we conduct the business of being human. We have chosen to see all things as unrelated, and the known threat of nuclear contamination was dismissed. How has this narrow focus, where nothing is related, working for us now?

Can we draw any comparison to our policies related to public education and youth development? Let's see.

The Busyness of Raising Children: Are We Nourishing the Lives of Our Children?

Language is consciousness. The Swedish word for "business" is "närings liv." It means "nourishment for life" or "nurturing life." In English, the word "business" means "to be busy"—"a state of being much occupied or engaged," or "what one is about at the moment" (comes from *bisignes* in Old English).

What are we about in every moment we are in the "business" of education and child development? Yes, business. What has happened over the past 100 years is a burgeoning of business (busy-ness) in education and youth development, which some have termed the "child industrial complex"—a far cry from the idea of business as "nourishing life."

More on Language

The term "homo sapiens" comes from the Latin for "wise man," or "be wise man." Are we as a species really becoming "wise"? One of the most controversial questions facing evolutionary biologists is whether the individual or the community is the single most important entity of our species. Is our primal story about the survival of the fittest and rugged individualism or is it a story asserting that all things are related and "it takes a whole village to raise a child?"

Nourishing Life in a World of Survival of the Fittest

Many of the challenges and problems we face today are generally related to how we satisfy our basic and essential needs without destroying the psychological sense of community: the sense that there is a network of and structure to relationships that strengthens rather than dilutes feelings of belonging (Sarason 1974). The earth and everything in nature are part of the community in which we need to have *feelings of belonging.*

When the individual is considered the single most important entity of our species, the idea of business as nourishing life becomes segregated into isolated service delivery silos by specialty, problem, and solutions. Programs spring from disconnected service providers who are oriented within their own narrow specialty to focus on the individual.

A powerful and pervasive service delivery industrial complex, driven by commerce and survival of the fittest (agency) considers everything in the environment as a resource for unbridled use in their service to satisfy human needs. All of this has mediated our biological inclination to be in authentic natural relationships that nourish life.

No one has articulated this better than John McKnight in his classic work, *The Careless Society: Community and its Counterfeits* (McKnight 1995). McKnight tells the story of "John Deere and the Bereavement Counselor,"[1] where the invention of the tractor, the "sodbusting tool," and a new "grief technology," altered the relationship of people both with their

---

[1] "John Deere and the Bereavement Counselor," http://www.centerforneweconomics.org/publications/authors/McKight/John

land and to each other. The profession of "bereavement counseling" was born, and a "new service technology" was established based on a belief that one's family and neighbors did not know how to help someone deal with the grief over the loss of a loved one.

Only through a "new service technology, forged at the great state university, could the needs of those experiencing the death of a loved one be met. This innovative technique was the only tool that could 'process' the grief of the people" (McKnight 1995, 5). "Service" began to be seen as another vehicle for commerce—or, a way for a small group of people to make money at the expense of a larger group. "The tools of the bereavement counselor make grief into a *commodity* rather than an opportunity for community. Service technologies convert conditions into commodities and care into service" (12).

The "new service technology" believes that the individual is the most important single entity of our species. One individual has unique specialized and sanctioned information and skills (technology) that have been affirmed (diploma, credentials) by those in power to be preferable to past practices. It disempowers a majority of the population and places little value on the historical practices of people helping people, ignoring that a neighborhood and community had all the skills and resources necessary to nourish life.

Rugged individualism and survival of the fittest permeates our consciousness and manifests in all of our systems and organizations. Agencies within large systems, like education, health care, youth and human services, and so forth, see themselves as independent organisms—single entities within the larger web of life in a "service delivery universe." Each entity is immersed in commerce as the central focus for their survival. Given limited funding and resources to maintain each independent organism, agencies are unwittingly pitted against each other, and only the strongest survive. Silo service delivery is not sustainable. There is no economic or practical way we can provide a service to everyone for everything. Services do not provide nourishment for life. People in meaningful, authentic relationships do.

Natural relationships with others and with our environment, on the other hand, can provide authentic nourishment for life. Professional service delivery has usurped these natural relationships, which occur everywhere and which can be brought to bear on the challenges of living in a complex world. There may be no greater challenge than raising our children and grappling with the problems of living in a complex world.

What can we do? We can remember the traditional wisdom of rites of passage. They guide everyone in a community to come together to nourish life and to raise children in such a way that they develop deep feelings of connection and belonging to all their relations. In this way, as a species, we may truly become "wise."

Public Policy and the Future

One can only bring someone as far as they have been themselves.

There will never be enough money to pay for all of the care, education, and services people need and have more and more come to expect. The present paradigm of service delivery for all is economically unsustainable. We need to balance the real need for services where technical skills are a necessity, as in medicine, with how we can reconvert "conditions" into opportunities for caring with and from people in authentic relationships.

What are key issues that need to be addressed if we are to adopt and enact a new story of youth and community development through rites of passage? Shifting the paradigm to embrace the underlying principles and practices of initiation and rites of passage is essential. It is crucial to have trained and initiated community elders who can help the story emerge and be put into practice as their community's contemporary rites of passage. As discussed previously, the "training" of practitioners in a new paradigm must itself be altered in ways that reflect the new paradigm and the "mingling" of the sacred and profane, traditional wisdom integrated with contemporary science and practice technologies. This is no easy task.

What public policies are already present, or need to be put in place that would support parents and other adults to be engaged in the lives of children? Raising children together was one of the central reasons communities came into existence in the first place. Children are in schools, out of the mainstream of adult society, while most responsible adult role models are sequestered at work by economic demands and a society that has incompatible family-oriented policies. It is not possible for a whole village to raise children when the entire village is away at work. Of course, villages are much larger than when the proverb first emerged, and we really wouldn't need a "whole village to raise a child," but still there are insufficient numbers of adults and mentors in appropriate roles in the lives of children.

I'm not suggesting that conventional big brother/big sister or mentoring programs alone are the answer. While these programs and others like them are valuable, we need elders, mentors, and guides within a framework of initiation and rites of passage who are steeped in the language and experience of initiation and can deepen their support of youth, especially during times of crisis and stress. And these must be elders who live in the community with the initiates and be present in their lives on a regular basis.

They Really Are Custodians

The best teachers are those who show you where to look, but don't tell you what to see.

—Alexandra K. Trenfor

There are many different kinds of adults who could fulfill the role of community elder and support the initiatory journey of young people to adulthood. Police, social workers, psychologists, youth workers, clergy, senior citizens, members of community civic organizations and clubs, and custodians are just some of the different adults who could be oriented to support the initiation of children and youth. Public school teachers, the largest group of adults traditionally engaged with children, can also play an important part, but only if they have both the academic foundation and actual positive personal initiatory experiences that would support their role as initiators for our communities' children. Over the past several years, increased attention to social-emotional learning and teaching methods that recognize the essential nature of relationships and promote holistic youth development have been gaining traction. This is a great addition for supporting the advancement of community/ school-oriented rites of passage and was not the case when we began forty years ago. "Engaged teaching" (Weaver and Kessler 2011; Weaver and Wilding 2013) is the new language for this form of teaching and along with the long-standing work of Rachael Kessler and colleagues at PassageWorks Institute and the Collaborative for Social Emotional Learning (Weissberg et al. 2007) have provided substantial resources. Again, the key is that a community or group adopts the story of initiation and understands and uses design principles to guide their practice.

The necessary paradigm shift reframes the story and all the characters within the story. For example, when institutions are seen as places of initiation, roles and titles change. Those formerly called "janitors" would be renamed as "custodians." Most schools may already employ "custodians," whose job it is to maintain school cleanliness and related tasks. In the new story, their role as "custodian" would make them "responsible for something valuable and upholding the values of the school."

All students within a school would have different roles and increased responsibility for taking care of all aspects of the physical structure. The custodian would be more like the traditional role of guidance counselor or social worker. Yes, there would need to be people who really do know how to take care of the school facility, but students would perform the majority of the work.

One of the best ways to change the climate of a place to one of caring, respect, and civility is to change the nature of people's relationship to the place—both the physical structure and the environment. Children must learn to love the Earth and consider it sacred before we expect them to pick up trash, recycle and care for nature. The same holds true for schools and other public places where both children and adults go. Engaging people in the design of public buildings and spaces strengthens their relationships to these places. This helps to create meaningful connections between people and the places they live and work. Public places, especially schools, should be designed, built, and cared for by the public in measures that are appropriate and within practical consideration of necessary safety and technical knowledge. The structure we presently have in place to design public spaces may unwittingly alienate people from these public spaces rather than connect them in ways that can nourish life (Blumenkrantz 2013).

We Are All Elders to Someone Else

Having said all of this, we still need to grapple with what we mean by an "elder" and how one can successfully fulfill this role. In the new paradigm, the role of elder is altered from tradition.

An elder has traditionally been defined in the context of a relationship between two people that is directly related to age. One person has seniority, or higher rank, or is a more influential member of a tribe or community than another, younger person. In contemporary form, the functional role of elder is not exclusively defined by age.

In contrast to traditional societies where elders were established almost exclusively by age, youth in western society frequently select their own elders. This selection is based on a youth's perception of someone as able to provide useful information that they perceive as necessary for their survival in the adult world. Elders also behave in ways that are appealing to the youth. Many youth select elders who are sports and music figures sustained by the media; they are not necessarily people who have been initiated in a positive way or live and work and share their lives with the community.

Elders have traveled further along the path of life than those who are looking up to them. They have gained a certain level of wisdom and knowledge from their journey on the path of life and possess a level of comfort and certainty about themselves, their place in the world, and their connection to the Universe. They are able to effectively communicate important information that is useful to others. Elders are able to share wisdom, gained from experiences, that can help other people understand the path of life that they are now on and that lies just before them.

The fact remains that insufficient numbers of adults are participating in raising America's children. The village seems to be too preoccupied with other matters, preempting their responsibility for raising their children. Our research during Paths to the Year 2000, discussed previously, indicated that many adults who had been interested in the rites of passage project did not participate because of a perceived lack of time. Priorities will need to change. We need more elders. That may seem like a daunting challenge until we realize that elders can be young!

The Child Is Father of the Man

In the proposed paradigm, where institutions are reframed as places of initiation, all children can become guides and mentors for other children.[2] Some students have traveled further along the path of life then other students within the context of school grades. In this way they have acquired a certain level of wisdom and knowledge from their journey on the path of life just a bit beyond a younger student. They are thus able to mentor and teach a younger student who has not traveled as far along the path of life. She or he is able to effectively communicate important information that is useful to another.

We have found that younger students often perceive someone a bit older, perhaps three to four grade levels, but even as close as one to two grade levels, as attractive role models able to provide useful information which they perceive as necessary for their survival in the adult world. Older students are also "real" people, in close

---

[2] The heading repeats a line from a poem by William Wordsworth (1802)—*The Rainbow*, or *My Heart Leaps Up When I Behold*.

> *My heart leaps up when I behold*
> *A rainbow in the sky:*
> *So was it when my life began;*
> *So is it now I am a man;*
> *So be it when I shall grow old,*
> *Or let me die!*
> *The Child is father of the Man;*
> *And I could wish my days to be*
> *Bound each to each by natural piety.*

proximity to younger students—not distant celebrities. They act in ways that model socially appropriate and healthy behavior for younger students. Within an initiatory culture, central values transmitted include caring, compassion, cooperation, empathy, respect, and support. Everyone within the culture of a school has the capacity to be responsible for themselves as well as other people.

This design works the same way with entry and "initiation" into the world of play and *re-creation* (Blumenkrantz 2000). There are always older students already on the path to finding their bliss. They can guide younger students along this path. If we can help a child find their bliss, it would be the best we can do to help them become human beings and mediate the potential problems of adolescence.

This is not a new idea. Many consider the "one-room school house" to be a quaint relic of the past, but such schools embraced, or at least facilitated, the concept of older students serving as models for and mentoring younger students. The advent of the modern model of grouping children of roughly the same age in separate grades actually started the process of separating us from one another, at least in the academic sphere.

Conveying values to the next generation that are favorable to individual and community adaptation and survival are the essential tasks of a community. A rite of passage story enacted within the design principles set forth in this book not only strengthens people's bonds to each other, hence fostering a sense of community, but also aligns with the health-promoting and healing benefits of self-help and support groups. It uses the social-psychological principle of retroflexive reformation (LeBel 2007), which posits that someone who helps others receive as much or more benefit than the person they help. The information conveyed in teaching others is deepened within the teacher. In the act of mentoring younger students, older students strengthen not only their own academic achievement but also their sense of self-efficacy, empathy, caring, and social responsibility. It is another illustration of the reciprocity within the initiatory process. Individuals within the initiatory process are participating in the transformation of themselves and others while contributing to a sense of community and at the same time strengthening a culture of respect and caring.

Memories of lessons learned are seared into a child's consciousness through initiation and affirmed in their community's rite of passage. Coming of age within a culture of initiation helps youth connect with values for being human with the brightest opportunity for "self-actualization" and sense of connection—communion with a sacred Earth and all in relationship to it. Childhood experiences make us who we are as adults. The children that we were have given birth to the adults that we are. *The child is father of the man.*

Lessons from Swimming

If the concept of retroflexive reformation seems remote, or the meaning and significance of young people as resources for mentoring each other seem implausible, then consider this story.

Many people who have taken swimming lessons, whether from the American Red Cross, YMCA or any organized institution, will know the term "buddy." The "buddy system" is widely accepted as essential to safeguard against drowning. "Always swim with a buddy; do not allow anyone to swim alone. Even at a public pool or a lifeguarded beach, use the buddy system!" (American Red Cross 2015). At the most basic level, the story of community-oriented rites of passage is to install and practice the principles of the "buddy system." Everyone today, not just children, is experiencing significant challenges in living. "Life is difficult" (Peck 1978, 1) was the beginning of Scot Peck's famous book *The Road Less Traveled*. Not only is life difficult but also these days it is dangerous for more and more children. Danger in the sense not only of physical safety but also emotional and psychological safety. Just as with swimming, if we institute systems where everyone has at least one other person who can look out for them, be there during good times and bad, be a "buddy," dangers of drowning would be greatly reduced. I'm not just talking about a buddy system for children and youth but also one where adults and parents within a community have a buddy. Feelings of loneliness, alienation, and disconnection are insidious and subtle consequences of contemporary society (Putnam 2000). Community-oriented rites of passage strengthen the bonds between people in community through reciprocity between the individual and community that serves survival. Although the above lessons from swimming might appear trite and simple, wouldn't this modest change in consciousness and practice promote the kind of compassion and caring that could contribute to communities that nourish life?

At the End We Find the Beginning

Throughout this book I have attempted to set forth through stories and scholarship that initiation rites, once common to most early societies and absent in contemporary American culture, are an essential ingredient for our children's healthy development. In a sense, they help to organize a group and/or community within a "buddy system" frame of consciousness. While this may remain inconceivable to some, our collective quest for a psychological sense of community is beyond denial. How can we transfer what we *know* into what we *do*?

I have learned much over the past six decades in my journey of caring and service and relationship with youth and community development through rites of passage. The lessons learned call for changes in both public policy and the way we conduct the business of education and youth and human services.

First, public policy must lay a foundation for practical approaches that enable the village to raise its children. It can do this in several ways. As discussed in the last chapter, we can promote funding opportunities that offer incentives for community participation in the lives of children. We've already begun to do this through adoption of the Family and Medical Leave Act of 1993. Funding opportunities can be set within a framework of youth and community development through rites of passage. That is, communities can be given the opportunity to construct rites of passage through the use of specific guiding principles. Youth and adults in communities can be oriented to the concept of initiation and guided to help them emerge through activities that respond to the conscious and unconscious needs for initiation. This design strategy was successfully used in the State of Connecticut and described in the previous chapter.

As my friend and mentor Louise Mahdi (1987) pointed out, "the need for some kind of initiation is so important that if it does not happen consciously, it will happen unconsciously, often in a dangerous form" (xiii). And, as my student who's become my teacher, Leah Beth Maille, asked, "Why do people keep trying to reinvent the broken wheel over and over again?"

There is a marked distinction between those who guide wilderness or other rites of passage programs and those guiding youth and community development through rites of passage. Those of us on the frontline of youth and community development through rites of passage for children and their families are essentially community organizers, who need to be steeped in the traditions, wisdom, and experience of initiation and rites of passage.

All communities are capable of raising their children by providing the developmentally appropriate resources and education. Considering a new paradigm begins with people assessing their existing story and deciding what is and is not working to give them their desired outcome. As part of this process, community members can be introduced to the essential ingredients for contemporary rites of passage and can engage in a broad array of activities related to the initiatory process. Research (Blumenkrantz 1996; Woodard 1996) has revealed the significant potential of rites of passage to serve as an agent for mobilizing and organizing communities on behalf of contributing to the positive development of their children. This orientation recognizes the value of youth in partnership with adults in the process of community development for changing the conditions that prevent problems and promote health among all citizens. Janet L. Finn and Barry Checkoway describe this in "Young People as Competent Community Builders: A Challenge to Social Work" (1998). They suggest, "Community is a unit of solution," and "when young people have the opportunity to develop and demonstrate their competence, they help themselves and develop their communities" (342–43).

"Don't do anything about me without me." (Schiller and Cooper 2012)

Participatory action research is a valuable vehicle for engaging communities in the design, emergence, and use of viable initiation and rites of passage strategies. The participatory action research method (PAR) suggests, "it is important both for the advancement of science and for the improvement of human welfare, to devise strategies in which research and action are closely linked" (Whyte 1991, 8). It is also a major focus of the PAR process for citizens, youth, and adults to be actively involved in all aspects of the inquiry. We've found teenagers to be exceptionally good researchers and adept at formulating innovative research questions and methods of inquiry. The Teen Action Research project of the Institute for Community Research in Hartford, Connecticut, has been a leader in this area. Their "Participatory Action Research Curriculum for Empowering Youth" (Sydlo et al. 2000) is a great asset.

Through the ongoing exploration and adaptation of rites of passage design principles, a community can craft a story that provides a solid foundation for community-oriented rites of passage. Over years of adaptation it will grow stronger and become a powerful initiation and rite of passage story that can be put into action for children, their family, and the entire community.

Whose Rite of Passage Is It?

Funding programs must be modified to adequately recognize the challenges of developing real, viable community collaboration, essential in a new paradigm for community-oriented rites of passage. Collaborative relationships should not be determined by signed agreements obtained within weeks, but by deeds and actions revealing authentic commitment built over years. Present funding cycles do not permit this. They require concrete actions within time frames that are too short to realistically achieve significant advances in promoting community collaboration. They precipitate pseudo-relationships based on convenience and each member's desire to get the money. It is like speed dating that has to result in marriage. The seeds for disingenuous relationships are unwitting cast right from the beginning.

Grant awards should be for four to six years with diminishing funding. This would allow for the formation of real community collaborations; sufficient recruitment, orientation, and training of community elders; and the construction of solid foundations for viable contemporary village-oriented rites of passage initiatives. Outside agents, such as federal, state, or private foundation grant givers, should not assume primary responsibility for the ongoing support of a community's rites of passage. They can be invaluable allies by offering incentives for community change that supports multicultural partnership teams to help nurture the process.

One of the central hurdles that needs to be surmounted is the insufficient number of adults available to become meaningfully involved in the lives of children, especially in community-based rites of passage. Even though the new paradigm recognizes that many children and youth can mentor others younger than themselves, public policy should be directed to make incentives available to all businesses to encourage adult work-release programs. Public policy should permit, and in fact set strong guidelines for, adults to make contributions to the work of the community, especially in the area of youth initiation. Adults should be permitted to be released from work, with pay, to participate in prescribed roles within the community's initiation and rite of passage process. They could serve as guides for youth in the orientation and skill-building phase of a contemporary rite of passage. They could be sponsors, encouraging and guiding youth into positive leisure-time activities and community service. They could be a bridge for youth to observe and experience the adult world of work. They could be positive role models and mentors. The key is to have a broad array of adult roles available in the initiatory process and to set incentives for adults to return to the essential work of their community (i.e., raising their community's children). Individuals returning from military service, who need to feel a sense of affirmation, respect and reconnection can participate in the initiatory process, helping them transtion from warrior to citizen, through participation in their community's rite of passage project.

In the absence of public policy that endorses, encourages, and/or makes it a standard expectation for all citizens to return to the work of their communities, individuals will always be frustrated in their quest for a psychological sense of community; our essential responsibility of raising children will never be successfully accomplished. Furthermore, without a large proportion of a community's adults becoming involved in the lives of its children, no amount of money, supporting any program, will win the war against any of the problems that our youth face. We can no longer afford to believe that we can exclusively hire other people ("professionals") to parent, initiate, teach, counsel, and support our children's journey through the turbulent waters of adolescence to the shores of adulthood. This is our collective responsibility as a species. They are our children; we all share the future.

Once again I return to a question asked in the Introduction: If it takes a whole village to raise a child, as the ancient proverb says, what is the consequence of not having villages anymore? Village, as the place where people felt connected to each other and shared their lives and stories. Village, as a place that was built on, housed, and nurtured by the concept of a psychological sense of community.

The evidence is overwhelmingly clear—if we do not have villages, we cannot successfully raise our children. The connections between people in a village were and will always be contributing factors in how successful we are at raising our children. That is not to say that the village usurps the role of parents or that an entire village should or could be engaged in this civic responsibility. It is to recognize that parents and families do not exist in a vacuum. They do well and grow best when planted firmly and nourished in the soil of community. And we take literally "soil" to mean nature as inextricably tied to a sense of community and sense of connection to the natural world; the world that reciprocates its love by giving clean air, fresh water, and all the other essential nutrients to nourish life.

We can now answer another fundamental question posed at the beginning of the book: Can a society have a psychological sense of community without community rituals like rites of passage? Can rites of passage exist in a society without a sense of community? The evidence is clear that community rituals are inextricably linked to a psychological sense of community. Without shared rituals, our collective sense of community is diminished. The pursuit of community-based, secular rites of passage should be a central quest if we are to survive. As Leslie Silko (1977) writes, "the only cure I know is a good ceremony" (3).

College as a Place of Initiation

There is another important place we can look to in pursuit of our goal to help the next generation through community-oriented rites of passage—institutions of higher learning. Surveying curriculums at universities and colleges in 1994 produced very little evidence of academic attention paid to rites of passage in any of the disciplines that train students in human services and education. Twenty years later, there is still relatively little information on initiation and rites of passage, especially viable contemporary forms within communities. If initiation and community rites of passage are a central structure for organizing ourselves in villages and communities in order to help children transition to adulthood, then why is there little or no formal instruction in rites of passage at universities?

Rather than focusing on the answer to this question, it would be more productive to propose ways to expose college students to rites of passage and the initiatory process. Universities themselves are places of initiation. In his autobiography, Tepilit Ole Saitoti (1988), a Masai warrior who traveled to America and engaged in university study, said of his Harvard University experience, "In a way I was repeating the night of initiation I had gone through. College was similar to treading the rigorous path of achieving manhood in Maasailand. I compared where I was to where I had come from" (129).

Among its many roles, college is a place for students to come of age, a place for rites of passage. While we acknowledge this to be true, as many have done, rarely do we intentionally capitalize on the natural power of college as a place for rites of passage to positively affect students and the rest of the college community.

A new infrastructure for human development involves transforming institutions, such as higher education, into places of initiation for supporting a large portion of the population undergoing transition. New terminology will have be crafted to adequately define and operationalize what rites of passage are and how they can positively impact youth and community development outcomes, as detailed by Blumenkrantz and Goldstein (2014).

Universities could serve as a great hub for initiatory activities. After all, every student entering college is in a transition that could be reframed as a rite of passage. First-year student orientation could be formulated within initiation and rites-of-passage design strategies. Colleges and universities could have "Centers for the Study and Advancement of Initiation and Rites of Passage." This interdisciplinary place could serve not only as a training ground for all undergraduate and graduate students entering education, youth work, and other allied fields in youth, family, and human services but also as a regional training center for communities. Students could serve internships in communities that are reestablishing rites of passage. Within each discipline related to youth development there could be a "strand" that includes rites of passage. Students could study the literature related to rites of passage as well as be given the opportunity to participate in initiatory experiences. They could help bring the story of rites of passage into communities and be part of an initial community organizing process. As part of the freshman orientation, as well as at a number of other points within the student's university experience, the initiatory process can build a foundation for promoting health and providing subsequent therapeutic intervention if problems do arise (Gavazzi and Blumenkrantz 1993).

Rites of Passage as Public Art

Rites of passage take form more in the arena of art than of science (Blumenkrantz 1992). They are not a program replicated in a community or one that children are sent away to participate in. Rather, they are "installed" in a community as a work of public art for citizens to engage with, share stories about, and extract meaning from. If we are to begin to set a foundation for the construction of rites of passage for the next millennium, we must consider training public artists rather than social scientists. If the story of rites of passage is to be kept alive, it will be done through artistic expression, not by program replication. Joseph Campbell (Campbell and Moyers 1988) wrote, "Myth must be kept alive. The people who can keep it alive are artists of one kind or another. The function of the artist is the mythologization of the environment and the world (85).

Initiation and community-oriented rites of passage are not a panacea. When provided by their community, they offer an opportunity for youth to cross the threshold to adulthood with the support, guidance, and wisdom of their elders. Youth can take their places as adults within their culture and a community that has adapted and recommitted itself to values essential for survival. After all is said and done, there are no easy formulas to strengthen a psychological sense of community or design contemporary rites of passage. We have taken so many paths that have led to nowhere in our attempts to really help our children. Perhaps now we can choose a path with heart and be a real help to our children, their families, and communities. Our lives depend on it.

In the End We Have People in Relationships and Stories

Programs don't help people, but people in meaningful relationships do.

There are dozens of valuable resources in the form of rites-of-passage programs throughout the country. Many provide youth with powerful transformative experiences, especially potent with young people who are experiencing some kind of challenge growing up and have limited support. What might be possible if these already-existing programs were linked in an intentional living system in reciprocity with and for people in community to be in relationship? These rites of passage programs become part of the community's initiation practices.

Before any youth is sent away to one of these distant rite of passage programs, a team of elders from the youth's community is exposed to the experience in an abbreviated multiday course similar to what their children will experience. The experience deepens their understanding of initiation and teaches them its values and the language needed to convey the experience to others back in their community. The seeds for initiation and rites of passage are prepared during this experience and brought back home to be planted and germinated in their own community garden. In this way, they would help nurture the emergence of rites of passage in their community as a foundation to a systems orientation to rites of passage.

More importantly, the team of elders would be able to adequately prepare their children to engage in the "liminal" portion of their community's rites of passage and strengthen the youth's family and community's ability to provide appropriate reentry supports. Upon the child's return home there must be a powerful way to honor and celebrate their experience. Providing a public community rite of passage with their family and where the child can demonstrate a competency, make statements confirming their understanding and commitment to important cultural and social values, and affirm their transition to a new phase of their lives would help them to reincorporate their experience. One of the ways communities can do this is to ensure there are adequate and appropriate new roles and responsibilities for youth in their homes and community.

> *Unless you are welcomed back to the village and honored for completing an ordeal you become sick.*
>
> —Malidoma Somé

You can only bring someone as far as you've been yourself—another design principle—recognizes that when adult ambassadors from a community immerse themselves in initiation and become part of their community's rites of passage they can be guides for others across a bridge to this new unifying story.

A central and sensitive part of our job is to open inquiries into people's stories and engage them in conversation. Questions that matter related to our children, their education, and youth and community development are key. We invite people to explore: How are the children? What is in the "field" of inquiry related to initiation and rites of passage that already exists and can be brought together, in authentic and meaningful ways, that has heart and can be of service to children, community, our sacred Earth, and the future of all our relations?

Across America and the world, many valuable resources exist in the form of rite of passage–related programs. Rather then exclusively being places we take our children for transformation, might they also be places of initiation for helping members of a community consider changing the story of how they educate and raise their children?

There are those who are presently talking about "building a field" of rites of passage. The field has existed for almost thirty thousand years. What are we in fact now fielding that can make the most powerful impact on the future of our sacred Earth and all our relations? We must notice what has not worked well, but instead of trying to design a program and fix it, we need to hospice the old and midwife the new. That transition in our culture would have the greatest effect. Of course, there is so much wrong and we have spent decades trying to fix things.

When stories are shared, something powerful happens. Each person's story holds threads of gold. When these are woven together with the threads of stories from other times, places, and cultures, a new story emerges. Our role as partners and guides in community-oriented rites of passage is to share stories that illuminate the golden threads of symbols, patterns, and processes of initiation. People's own stories of initiation are then triggered, and that, in turn, ignites their creative imagination. Design principles serve as navigational aids to inform and organize new ways of thinking that lead to innovative actions.

All change is local. It begins in the heart and is adapted at the level of the mind. The communion of heart, mind, and spirit manifests change out in the world. I have been discussing initiation and rites of passage as a framework for organizing change. It focuses on and fosters change within individuals, who can become agents for change and galvanize committed actions within groups and large systems. Initiating individuals to a consciousness of connection and interrelatedness in a living system is prerequisite to large-order, continually adapting change. Community-oriented rites of passage like the Rite Of Passage Experience are intentionally designed to stimulate large-order change. It does this by initiating more and more citizens within a setting to the new story of rites of passage as a framework for education and youth and community development. Only when people understand and accept change at the level of the heart will they be able to help the necessary conditions for change to emerge in their setting. Contemporary approaches to change are more mechanistic and intellectual, which distances individuals from becoming intimately engaged with and committed to putting into action the fundamental principles in the new story.

As the new story emerges, it incorporates individual and community resources, cultural symbols, and practices and assimilates the spirit of their place with design features that are present in (but do not disrespect or appropriate) other culture's ancestors or traditions. This new story becomes their story. It is their initiatory constellation. There are powerful distinctions between adopting some-one else's story, like those told as "evidence-based," and remembering one's own story. When you gaze up to the heavens and see your own constellation you are connected with the Universe in ways that can be transforming. It all begins by sharing a story and engaging in conversations. When we get our story *rite* we get our future right. And, that's the story.

A Sufi Tale

A Sufi story frequently begins with the end in mind. And so the story begins:

> *"Everything we need to know, we already know."*
> *Once upon a time in a village some distance from here, the people of that place were confronted with a grave problem.*
> *The people heard of a wise person several villages away. [They would have been called an "expert consultant" in our contemporary language.] The people sent word about their problem to the wise one and asked her to speak with them. The people congregated in the market square and anxiously awaited the words of wisdom from the wise one.*
> *The wise one asked, "How many of you know what I am about to say?"*
> *All of the villagers shook their heads from side to side affirming that no one knew what she was going to tell them.*
> *"You don't know what I am about to say, so I will leave you."*
> *The people were astonished. "If we knew what she was going to tell us why would we have invited her to help us with our problem?" The people lamented.*
> *Within a short while the problem grew worse and the people invited the wise one to return.*
> *Once again the wise one asked, "How many of you know what I am about to say?"*
> *The people were ready this time, and all shook their heads up and down, affirming that they all knew what she was about to say.*

"Well, if you all know what I am about to say, then there is no reason for me to say anything." And with that the wise one left, again, leaving the villagers with their mouths wide open in bewilderment.

But, the problem worsened, and once again the people in the village summoned the wise one. This time they were certain they would have the solution to their problem revealed.

The wise one ascended to the speaker's platform and once again asked the villagers. "How many of you know what I am about to say?" This time the villagers responded back, half of them shook their heads up and down affirming they knew what the wise one was going to say. The other half shook their heads from side to side affirming that they did not know what the wise one was going to say.

The wise one then said, "Will the group who knew what I was going to say tell the group who did not know what I was going to say." And she left.

A week later, a village elder convened the group. She told the group that she had a dream that made her realize the wisdom of the wise one's words. "Everything we need to know, we already know," she said. All we have to do is to talk with each other. So the group spoke among themselves and, lo and behold, they found the solution to their grave problem.

Initiation and rites of passage are within our collective memory; existing for tens of thousands of years in human experience, they transcend culture and place. Our ancestors have all sung their songs, said their prayers, and consecrated special places for the initiatory constellation to emerge in reciprocity and help something happen. The stories of our ancestors lie dormant in our DNA, awaiting an awakening. We know that initiation can emerge through reciprocity between entities in the initiatory constellation. Themes, symbols, patterns, and processes of initiation and rites of passage reside in our unconscious. We know the core elements within these patterns and processes. All that is needed is a catalyst to activate our memories and bring them into consciousness as a resource for healing our community, all our relations, and ourselves. Everything we need to know, we already know. We just need to talk among ourselves.

GRATITUDE

I end as I began, with a great sense of gratitude and grace for the bounty of blessings I have received throughout my life. Most of this book first took shape in 1994, informed by a lifetime of education and experience and put into form as a dissertation in 1996. The main ideas formulated and included in the initial work have only been confirmed by twenty additional years of experience. What has emerged in these pages has been an example of reciprocity between so many others and myself. Some are gone and others are still present in my life, especially nature and the abundance of love and wisdom shared.

I have preserved below the exact "Gratitude" section from the original work.

Gratitude—December 1996

No one is as capable of gratitude as one who has emerged from the kingdom of night.

We know that every moment is a moment of grace, every hour an offering; not to share them would mean to betray them. Our lives no longer belong to us alone, they belong to all those who need us desperately.

. . . And that is why I swore never to be silent whenever and wherever human beings endure suffering and humiliation. We must always take sides. Neutrality helps the oppressor, never the victim. Silence encourages the tormentor, never the tormented.

— From Elie Wiesel's Nobel Prize acceptance speech, reported in the *New York Times*, December 11, 1986.

There is much I have to be grateful for in my life. Those who have touched me with their joy and sorrow, love and anger, hope and anguish have all given me gifts. Many have made contributions to the benefit of this work. While I may omit the names of many from this acknowledgment, they all live in my heart.

This work began through Esther Sarason's encouragement and personal faith in me. I owe her a debt of gratitude for her persistent caring and nudging. Kevin Sharpe,

Jay Schensul, Louise Carus Mahdi, David Schwartz, Terry Fencl, Mel Embers, John Bierly, and the staff at the Human Relations Area Files all supported my efforts with their time, understanding, and guidance. Bethe Hagens made contributions of invaluable proportion. Ed Meincke's ongoing encouragement and friendship meant a lot to me. He is a true friend. Esther Kozak helped to bail me out when the deluge of information began to sink my boat. David Johnston leaped off a cliff with me. We both were able to safely land over the rainbow after bringing rites of passage to thousands of youth and adults in the Greater Hartford area. I am forever grateful for his faith and friendship. In the dictionary, next to the words "teacher" and "mentor," there should be a picture of Seymour Sarason. His support, wisdom, guidance, and friendship continue to enhance my life and work. He is a genius for bringing forth the truth and beauty in all things as well as being a real mensch.

I have been especially honored with the blessings that I have received through the Dance of the Deer Foundation—Center for Shamanic Studies. Brant Secunda, who guided my journey in the traditions of the Huichol Indians, has made a major contribution to this work and my life. I thank him and all of my brothers and sisters, especially Lori Antonacci, who has traveled with me on a *path with heart*.

Without my family, I would be a pauper. They have enabled me to obtain the fullest riches in life. My son, Michael, continues to be a source of inspiration for my work. For it is he who will inherit all I have done to help others. My mother, Renee, carried the seeds of my interest in initiation through her journey to America following the destruction of her home in Northern Ireland during World War II. Her love and support continue to fertilize my life. My brother, Steven, has made contributions to this work beyond his own knowledge. His encouragement and enthusiastic interest in my journeys kept my spirits high even when my energy was low. The spirit of my father and ancestors are woven into every word. How could they not be?

Most of all, I am indebted to my partner, friend, and wife, Louann. Her patience with my quest for learning and writing goes beyond the saintly. Sometimes, through great sacrifice, she has supported this work and my search for the really good questions. Her review of the manuscript has made most of this work readable.

Although many people have influenced my thinking, responsibility for the organization and content of this work rests solely with me. I have wrestled with the use of pronouns, mindful of egalitarian and sexist language. The use of "his/her" was too cumbersome. I have used the pronouns "his" or "him" for the sake of simplicity and ease of reading. I intended no disrespect to the female gender. In subsequent revisions I have used both masculine and feminine pronouns interchangeably. Another example of reciprocity.

> *At times our own light goes out and is rekindled by a spark from another person.*
> *Each of us has cause to think with deep gratitude of those who have lighted the*
> *flame within us.*
>
> — Albert Schweitzer

Continued Gratitude—2014

I did not create the Rite Of Passage Experience or the primary elements and ingredients in youth and community development through rites of passage in the traditional sense of making something out of nothing. Long before I came into being, all of the ingredients and elements in rites of passage that I discuss have existed since the great flaring forth of the Universe. The elements are always in a state of becoming, emerging into unique forms shaped by the culture and settings that called them forth into service. This work, as with my life, has been informed, guided, and blessed by all those I have encountered and engaged in learning together.

More than anyone over the years, Geoffrey Ben-Nathan, student of social anthropology from England, encouraged me to revise and publish this work. In 2000, he was preparing to write a book on rites of passage and contacted me for a copy of my thesis. He read the work and immediately said that it was inspirational. We began a relationship that lasts to this day.

In 2008, Ben-Nathan published his book on rite of passage, *"I'm Adult! Aren't I?"* *The Case for a Formal Rite of Passage*. The book included an entire section featuring my work, which he prefaced by stating, "Blumenkrantz has uniquely applied the idea of rites of passage in a contemporary modern setting and may thus be considered the father of modern rite of passage." That was humbling and energizing to say the least! Ben-Nathan's book had a small but dedicated following and made its way to British Prime Minister David Cameron's Government Advisor on Youth Development, Paul Oginsky, who was charged with the task of pioneering a program for National Citizen Service (NCS). Core concepts from the book were woven into the NCS blueprint. National Citizen Service has been a key component of Cameron's flagship "Great Society." It is designed to provide every British young person with a rite of passage that includes life-skills, life-experiences, and mission-challenge by way of volunteering. Over 100,000 young people per annum currently sign up for NCS. Oginsky commended Ben-Nathan's work as "a major contribution to thinking in the area of youth development."

It is difficult to really know the full extent of the power of words. Geoffrey is quite convinced that what was written almost two decades ago was central to informing and encouraging Britain's national citizen service as a rite of passage scheme.[1] His tireless efforts to foster a national rites of passage scheme in Britain has been an inspiration and has provided a decade of encouragement to publish this as a testament to his stalwart support of community-oriented rites of passage. Thank you, Geoffrey.

Since this was first written, twenty years ago, many, many more blessings have entered my life. Among them are the following:

Kenneth F. Heideman, Meteorologist and Director of Publications for the American Meteorological Society, showed up a few years ago after our initial meeting in the mid-sixties. He was among a group of ten bunkmates at a summer sleep-away camp where I was a junior and then senior counselor. Every summer for six years

---

[1] "Scheme" is used in the United Kingdom as the general name for program. I first thought it interesting and amusing, given how we use the word "scheme" in the United States.

I was his counselor. I did not realize then what he recently told me—that I helped him come of age. "Summer camp was my rite of passage," he told me. Ken brought to this work his understanding of initiation and a keen eye for organizing words in ways that could convey deeper meaning and broader accessibility. His editing was invaluable to updating the manuscript and integrating new material. To him and the Sleeper family, who began Camp Wamsutta, I am forever indebted, and to the woods, streams, ponds, lakes, and mountains in and around Charlton, Massachusetts, that taught me so much.

Nancy R. Wofford, illustrator and graphic artist, gave abundant energy, creative spirit, and the symbols and pictures that grace these pages and graphically bring to life the story in a way words could not. She was a real authentic partner who cares deeply about the welfare of children and all our relations.

There are a number of people who read parts of the manuscript, which helped it through its gestation: Rabbi Sarah Gurshuny, Rabbi Andrea Cohn-Keiner, Angela Duhaime, Len Fleischer, Bill Lavine, Stephen Gavazzi, and Marc Goldstein.

Rabbi Andrea was an authentic friend and ally in our efforts to enhance the B'nai Mitzvah process through Lech Lecha, which helped to reconnect me with my ancestors in a mitzvah-fulfilling Tikkun Olam, repair of the world.

Len Fleischer, long the lion and champion of youth and community development through rites of passage, frequently joined me on the adventure of seeing college as a rite of passage. His scholarship and practice in the area are substantial, and he and his wife, Erika, have been a blessing to me.

In 1990 my brother Steven and Seymour Sarason began the Center for Youth & Community, Inc. as the container for my work. There have been dozens and dozens of board members over the years who have provided valuable guidance and support. Only a few are mentioned here.

Marc Goldstein has been a consistent ally, friend, and esteemed colleague for many years and has always asked compelling questions that coaxed me into more thoughtful approaches to presenting the material. He and the other members of the Center for Youth & Community's board of directors have supported and consistently insisted that completing this series of books is the most important thing I could be doing, even in the face of "interesting distractions" that have continually grabbed my attention.

Board member Dr. William Lavine, a self-proclaimed "oral ecologist" and evolutionary biology scholar, provided keen insight and affirmation on a biological and evolutionary basis for the relationship between all things.

A longtime friend from "little kid school," Alan Daniels lent his unwavering support, legal advice, and continued wisdom on what's important and the "meaning of life." Lori Antonacci continually and energetically guided my reluctant entry into life in cyberspace and social media. John Sorrick—classmate and fellow seeker of what "truth, justice, and the American way," really means—continually supported inquiries that focused on the meaning of the "American way," and whether this isn't just another catchy phrase from Superman, who also doesn't exist. A longtime Board president and master ROPE facilitator and youth worker, Brian Evarts has always been there for me, during the good times and those times that challenged my soul. He and his wife, Deborah Winchell, are good friends and advocates for more conscious and sane ways of living and raising children. Their three children, Ben, Kaitlin, and Jessica, live the legacy of their lessons. Throughout the past several years Hyacinth Douglas Bailey has been a stalwart for clarity and practicality and shared her wisdom liberally. Leah Beth Maillie continues to prove the famous words of Art Linkletter, "Kids say the darndest things." One of my favorite *Leahisms* continues to make me smile: "Why do people keep reinventing the broken wheel over and over again?" Leah represents all the thousands of young people who have come into my life for learning and living together. She's grown into a wonderful talented woman, which continues to give me hope for the future.

Rabbi Eliot Baskin cheerfully escorted me on many walks in the woods and helped me to reconnect with my roots.

Tim Ravis, another one of my young professors, has been in my life for over fifteen years. I've watched him grow up since he was little. And, I do mean grow up, as he's over six feet four inches. Tim helped to massage the final manuscript and performed the miracle of ensuring that all the citations were included and organized. Only his caring and compassion exceed his inquiring intellect. Our wide-ranging conversations brought joy to my heart. Most of the time they were over food and drinks, which expanded the joy to my stomach.

There are many pioneers and second and third generations of guides and initiators of youth through rites of passage that I have met over the past thirty years. Each of them has brought their own ingenuity and enthusiasm to the growth of these rite of passage experiences for youth. Brett Stephenson, author of *From Boys to Men: Spiritual Rites of Passage in an Indulgent Age,* and I have had rich conversations about initiation and the role of community. He gets it more than most. Others in the field who have touched my life and brought so many blessings include Stephen Foster, Meredith Little, Stan Crow, Paul Hill Jr., Melissa Michaels, Malidoma Patrice Somé, Rachael Kessler, and Michael Meade.

For years I have always asked, "Does anyone have a good question?" Gratitude to my "Tocayo" and elder, David Isaacs, for affirming and giving a name to a method for helping really good questions to emerge and understand that the setting does matter. He and his wife, Juanita Brown, and the World Café community have helped affirm our focus on fostering designs that shape environments that are stimulating and fun for conversations that cultivate the collective wisdom of the group and the place.

For years Laurie O'Neil kept all the numbers in alignment and our financial records in order. Deep gratitude is owed to this mother of a ROPE alumnus, now a grandmother to the next generation of children who will hopefully be welcomed home to community through rites of passage.

The Norma and Natale Sestero Fund at the Hartford Foundation for Public Giving, Kalliopeia Foundation, Atlantic Health Systems and the Steven J. Blumenkrantz Memorial Fund have all made contributions to youth and community development through rites of passage and this book.

Jeff and Nedi McKnight hosted me at a beautiful place for writing and fed my body and spirit with their love and kindness. Gratitude also to my other temporary family on the Big Island of Hawaii, Julie Stowell, M. Kalani Souza, Chris Shaeffer, Jim and Kathy Love, Aric Arakaki, and Dave DeEsch.

For a number of years Dana Bliss, senior editor at Oxford University Press, and I have been in conversation about youth and community development and the concept of rites of passage. His understanding and enthusiasm grew as he had his first child and began to live the reality of our conversations. He has been a wonderful friend and editor who has guided the publishing process and has been a great ambassador for Oxford University Press. He and the team from Oxford University Press, Gregory Bussy, Daniel Petraglia, Emily Gorney, Stefano Imbert, Sylvia Cannizzaro and Devi Vaidyanathan have all made valuable contributions for which I am extremely grateful.

And, finally, once again to my best friend and angel among us all, Louann my wife, who has supported my quest to make a small contribution to humanity and gave of herself as well.

REFERENCES

Ahlbrant, R. S., and Cunningham, J. V. 1979. *A New Public Policy for Neighborhood Preservation.* New York: Praeger.

Albee, G. W. 1969. The relation of conceptual models of disturbed behavior to institutional and manpower requirements. In *Manpower for Mental Health*, edited by F. N. Arnhoff, E. A. Rubinstein, and J. C. Speisman. Chicago: Aldine.

Alexander, J. C., Giesen, B., and Mast, J. L. 2006. *Social Performance: Symbolic Action, Cultural Pragmatics, and Ritual.* Cambridge: Cambridge University Press.

Alford, K. A. 2003. Cultural themes in rites of passage: Voices of young African American males. *Journal of African American Studies* 7 (1): 3–26.

Alford, K. A. 2007. African American males and the rites of passage experience. In *Mental Health Care in the African-American Community*, edited by S.M. Logan, R. W. Denby, and P. A. Gibson (15–37). Binghamton, NY: Haworth Press.

Alford, K. A., McKenry, P. C., and Gavazzi, S. M. 2001. Enhancing achievement in adolescent black males: The rites of passage link. In *Educating Our Black Children: New Directions and Radical Approaches*, edited by R. Majors (141–56). London: Routledge Falmer.

Alhaidari, A., & Bhanegaonkar, S. G. 2012. Meaning, origin and functions of myth: A brief survey. *International Journal of Social Science Tomorrow* 1 (3): 1–6.

American Red Cross. 2015. *Water Safety: Take Steps to Stay Safe around Water.* Retrieved July 9, 2015, from http://www.redcross.org/prepare/disaster/water-safety

Apple, Jr. R. W. 1989. *Fighting in Panama: The Implications: War: Bush's Presidential Rite of Passage.* New York Times: New York, New York.

Arnett, J. J. 2004. *Emerging adulthood: The Winding Road from the Late Teens through the Twenties.* New York: Oxford University Press.

Arrien, A. 1990. Foreword. In *The Art of Ritual*, edited by R. Beck, and S. B. Metrick (pp. i–ii). Berkeley, CA: Celestial Arts.

Asad, Talal. 1983. Anthropological Concepts of Religion: Reflections on Geertz. Man (N.S.) 18:237–59. Clifford. 1973a. The Impact of the Concept of Culture on the Concept of Man. In *The Interpretation of Cultures* (pp. 33–54). New York: Basic Books, Inc.

Backer, T. E. 1988. Research utilization and managing innovation in rehabilitation organizations. *Journal of Rehabilitation* 54 (2): 18–22.

Bandura, A. 1986. *Social Foundations of Thought and Action: A Social Cognitive Theory.* Englewood Cliffs, NJ: Prentice-Hall.

Barbour, I. G. 1974. *Myths, Models and Paradigms: A Comparative Study in Science and Religion.* New York: Harper & Row.

Barbour I. G. (1990). *Religion in an Age of Science.* HarperOne: San Francisco, CA.

Barker, R. G. 1964. *Ecological Psychology: Concepts and Methods for Studying the Environment of Human Behavior.* Stanford, CA: Stanford University Press.

Bear, L. S. 1933. *Land of the Spotted Eagle.* Boston: Houghton Mifflin.

Beck, R., and Metrick, S. B. 1990. *The Art of Ritual: A Guide to Creating and Performing Your Own Ceremonies for Growth and Change.* Berkeley, CA: Celestial Arts.

Beehleer, S., and Trickett, E. (2011, June 17). *Contextualizing the Push for Evidence-Based Practice in Psychology.* University of Illinois at Chicago. Presentation at the Society for Community Research and Action, Division 27 American Psychological Association Biennial Conference. (Quotes from Powerpoint slides.)

Bell, Catherine (1997). *Ritual: Perspectives and Dimensions.* New York: Oxford University Press. pp. 138–169.

Ben-Nathan, G. 2008. *I'm Adult! Aren't I! The Case for a Formal Rite of Passage.* Herefordshire, UK: Kingston.

Benson, P. L. 1997. *All Kids Are Our Kids: What Communities Must Do to Raise Caring and Responsible Children and Adolescents.* San Francisco: Jossey-Bass.

Benson, P. L., Roehlkepartain, E. C., and Rude, S. P. 2003. Spiritual development in childhood and adolescence: Toward a field of inquiry. *Applied Developmental Science* 7 (3): 204–12.

Benson, P. L., Scales, P. C., Syvertsen, A. K., and Roehlkepartain E. C. 2012. Is spiritual development a universal process in the lives of youth? An international exploration. *Journal of Positive Psychology* 7 (6): 453–70.

Bern, G., Blaine, K., Prietula, M. J., and Pye, B. E. 2013. Short and long-term effects of a novel on connectivity in the brain. *Brain Connectivity* 3 (6): 590–600.

Bernardi, E. 1955. The age system of the Masai. *Annali Laternensi* 18: 257–238.

Bettelheim, B. 1954. *Symbolic Wounds.* Glencoe, IL: Free Press.

Berry, W. 1977. *The Unsettling of America: Culture and Agriculture.* San Francisco: Sierra Club Books.

Black, E. I., and Roberts, J. 1992. *Rituals for Our Times: Celebrating, Healing and Changing Our Lives and Our Relationships.* New York: Harper Collins.

Block, P. K. 1974. *Modern Cultural Anthropology.* New York: Knopf.

Bloomer, M., and James, D. 2003. Educational research in educational practice. *Journal of Further and Higher Education* (3): 247–56.

Blumenkrantz, D. G. 1992. *Fulfilling the Promise of Children's Services.* San Francisco: Jossey-Bass.

Blumenkrantz, D. G. 1996. *The Rite Way: Guiding Youth to Adulthood and the Problem of Communitas.* UMI Dissertation Services, Ann Arbor, MI.

Blumenkrantz, D. G. 1998. *Rite of Passage Experience, ROPE*: Guide for Promoting Youth and Community Maturation and Health.* 3rd ed. Washington, DC: Hummingbird Press @ The Center.

Blumenkrantz, D. G. 2000. Let's play: Initiating youth into the healthy world of play. In *Developing Competent Youth and Strong Communities Through After School Programming,* edited by Gullotta (pp. 67–114). Washington, DC: Child Welfare League of America Press.

Blumenkrantz, D. G. 2007. *Rites of Passage: Pathways to Spirituality for Adolescents.* Search Institute: The Center for Spiritual Development in Childhood and Adolescence.

Blumenkrantz, D. G. 2009. Rites of passage in a world that is not flat. *The Systems Thinker* 20 (8): 8–10.

Blumenkrantz, D. 2013. Organizing for a change: Part 1. *Paradigm Shift Blog.* Retrieved: May 29, 2013, form http://davidblumenkrantz.rope.org/?p=252#more-252

Blumenkrantz, D. G., and Gavazzi, S. M. 1993. Guiding transitional events for children and adolescents through a modern day rite of passage. *Journal of Primary Prevention* 13 (3): 199–212.

Blumenkrantz, D. G., and Goldstein, M. 2014. Seeing college as a rite of passage: What might be possible? In *In Search of Self: Exploring Undergraduate Identity Development,* edited by C. Hanson. San Francisco: Jossey-Bass.

Blumenkrantz, D. G., and Hong, K. L. 2008. Coming of age and awakening to spiritual consciousness through rites of passage. *New Directions for Youth Development* (Summer) pp. 85–94.

Blumenkrantz, D. G., and Wasserman, D. L. 1998. What happens to a community intervention when the community doesn't show up? Restoring rites of passage as a consideration for contemporary community intervention. *Family Science Review* 11: 239–58.

Blumenkrantz, D. G., and Reslock, B. 1988. 2nd. *Edition Rite of Passage Experience, ROPE*: Program Guide for Communities.* ACT Press: Glastonbury, CT.

Bonniwell, K. 1991. In: Cohen, D. *The Circle of Life: Rituals from the Human Family Album*. New York: HarperCollins.

Borhek, J. T., and Curtis, R. F. 1975. *A Sociology of Belief*. New York: Wiley.

Bowles, S., and Gintes, H. 1976. *Schooling in Capitalist America*. New York: Basic Books.

Brown, Donald (1991). *Human Universals*. United States: McGraw Hill. p. 139.

Brown, J., with Isaacs, D., and the World Café Community. 2005. *The World Café: Shaping Our Futures through Conversations That Matter*. San Francisco: Berrett-Koehler.

Buber, M. 1947. *The Later Masters*. Translated by Olga Marx. New York: Random House.

Campbell, J. 1949. *Hero with a Thousand Faces*. New York: NY Pantheon.

Campbell, J., and Moyers, B. 1988. *The Power of Myth*. Edited by Betty Sue Flowers. New York: Doubleday.

Carrico, K. 2014. Ritual. *Cultural Anthropology* website. Retrieved from http://www.culanth.org/curated_collections/4-ritual

Casey B. J., Getz S., and Galvan A. 2008. The adolescent brain. *Developmental Neuropsychology* 28 (11): 62–77.

Catalano, R. F., and Hawkins, J. D. 1996. The social development model: A theory of antisocial behavior. In *Delinquency and Crime: Current theories*, edited by J. D. Hawkins (149–97). New York: Cambridge University Press.

Carlson, R. 1962. *Silent Spring*. New York: Houghton Mifflin.

Chapelle, J. 1957. *Black Nomads of the Sahara*. Translated by F. Schutz. New Haven, CT: Yale HRAF.

Charles, P. H., 1952. *Alcohol, Culture, and Society*. Durham, NC: Duke University Press. Reprint, New York: AMS Press, 1970.

Charon, J. M. 2004. *Symbolic Interactionism: An Introduction, an Interpretation, an Integration*. Boston: Pearson.

Chedekel, L. 2015. Rising toll of mental illness. *Hartford Courant*, April 20, 1, 3.

Childs, B. S. 1960. *Myth and Reality in the Old Testament*. Naperville, IL: Allenson.

Chrzan, J. 2013. *Alcohol: Social Drinking in Cultural Context*. New York: Routledge.

Clifford, J. 1988. *The Predicament of Culture*. Cambridge, MA: Harvard University Press.

Clifford, J., and Marcus, G. E. 1986. *Writing Culture: The Poetics and Politics of Ethnography*. Berkeley: University of California Press.

Clifton, J. A., ed. 1990. *The Invented Indian*. New Brunswick, NJ: Transaction.

Cohen, D. 1991. *The Circle of Life: Rituals from the Human Family Album*. New York: HarperCollins.

Cohen, R. 1960. *The Structure of Kanuri Society*. Dissertation, University of Wisconsin. New Haven, CT: Human Relations Area Files.

Collinson, V., and Hoffman L. M. 1998. *High School as a Rite of Passage for Social and Intellectual Development*. Paper presented at the Annual Meeting of the American Educational Research Association, April 13–17, 1998. San Diego, CA.

Cooperrider, D. L., and Whitney, D. 2001. A positive revolution in change. In *Appreciative Inquiry: An Emerging Direction for Organization Development*, edited by D. L. Cooperrider, P. Sorenson, D. Whitney, and T. Yeager (9–29). Champaign, IL: Stipes.

Cron, L. 2012. *Wired for Story*. Berkeley, CA: Ten Speed Press.

Cruden, L. 1996. Thoughts on contemporary vision questing practices. *Shaman's Drum* (Winter).

Dance of the Deer Center for Shamanic Studies. 2012. http://www.danceofthedeer.com/about/huichol-indians

Davidson, W. B., and Cotter, P. R. 1986. Measurement of sense of community within the sphere of city. *Journal of Applied Social Psychology* 16 (7): 608–19.

Deloria, V., Jr. 1973. *God Is Red: A Native View of Religion*. New York: Putnam,

Deloria, V., Jr., 2006. *The World We Used to Live in: Remembering the Powers of the Medicine Men*. Golden, CO: Fulcrum.

de Mello, A. 1988. *One Minute Wisdom*. Image: Elkhart, Indiana.

Des Chene, M. 1996. Symbolic anthropology. In *Encyclopedia of Cultural Anthropology*, edited by D. Levinson and M. Ember (1274–78). New York: Henry Holt.

DeVoto, B. 1940. *Mark Twain in Eruption*. New York: Harper & Brothers.

Driver, T. 1991. *The Magic of Ritual: Our Need for Liberating Rites That Transform Our Lives and Our Communities*. New York: HarperCollins.

Durkheim, E. 1964. *The Division of Labor in Society*. New York: Free Press of Glencoe.

Einstein, A., Podolsky, B., and Rosen, N. 1935. Can quantum-mechanical description of physical reality be considered complete? *Physics Review* 47 (10): 777–80.

Eisley, L., 1973. *How Human is Man?* In Deely and Mogar, pp. 377–392.

Eliade, M. 1957. *The Sacred and the Profane: The Nature of Religion*. Translated by W. R. Trask. Harvest/Harcourt Brace Jovanovich, San Diego, New York, London.

Eliade, M. 1958. *Rites and Symbols of Initiation: The Mysteries of Birth and Rebirth*. Translated by W. R. Trask. San Diego: Harcourt Brace Jovanovich.

Eliade, M. 1959. *Sacred and Profane: The Nature of Religion*. San Diego: Harcourt Brace Jovanovich.

Eliade, M. 1960. *Myths, Dreams and Mysteries*. New York: Harper & Row.

Eliade, M. 1963. *Myth and Reality*. New York: Harper & Row.

Eliade M. 1967. *Essential Sacred Writings from around the World*. New York: Harper Collins.

Erdely, S. R. 2014. A rape on campus. *Rolling Stone* (November).

Evans-Pritchard, E. 1981. *A History of Anthropological Thought*. New York: Basic Books.

Fikes, J. C. 1993. *Carlos Castaneda: Academic Opportunism and the Psychedelic Sixties*. Victoria, BC: Millenia Press.

Finkerhor, D., and Ormrod, R. 2001. *Homicides of Children and Youth*. Office of Juvenile Justice and Delinquency Prevention, US Department of Justice, pp. 4, 7. Available at http://www.ncjrs.org/pdffiles1/ojjdp/187239.pdf

Finn, J. L., and Checkoway, B. 1998. Young people as competent community builders: A challenge to social work. *Social Work* 43 (4): 335–45.

Fisher, A., and Sonn, C. 2007. Sense of community and dynamics of inclusion-exclusion by receiving communities. *Australian Community Psychologist* 19 (2): 26–34.

Fisher, A. T., Sonn, C. C., and Bishop, B. J. 2002. *Psychological Sense of Community: Research, Application, and Implications*. New York: New York: Springer Science & Business Media.

Forster, P. M. 2004. Psychological Sense of Community in Groups on the Internet. *Behaviour Change* 21 (2): 141–46.

Foster, S. 1980. *The Book of the Vision Quest: Personal Transformation in the Wilderness*. New York: Prentice Hall Press.

Foster, S., and Little, M. 198). *The Book of the Vision Quest*. Englewood Cliffs, NJ: Prentice Hall.

Fox, R. 1971. The cultural animal. In *Man and Beast: Comparative Social Behavior*, edited by J. F. Eisenberg and W. S. Dillon (pp. 273–296). Washington, DC: Smithsonian Institution Press.

Freire, P. 1998. *Education for Critical Consciousness*. New York: Continuum.

Freire, P., and Donaldo, M. 1987. *Literacy: Reading the Word and the World*. South Hadley, MA: Bergin & Garvey.

Frenaye, F., trans. 1972. Les portes de la forêt. In *Souls on Fire*. New York: Summit Books. Wiesel, Elie.

Gavazzi, S. M., and Blumenkrantz, D. G. 1993. Facilitating clinical work with adolescents and their families through the rite of passage experience program. *Journal of Family Psychotherapy* 4 (2): 47–67.

Gayford, M. 2006. *The Yellow House: Van Gogh, Gauguin, and Nine Turbulent Weeks in Arles*. London: Penguin.

Gazzaniga, M. 2008. *Human: The Science Behind What Makes Your Brain Unique*. New York: Harper Perennial.

Geertz, C. 1973. *The Interpretation of Cultures*. New York: Basic Books.

Gluckman, M. 1965. *The Ideas in Barotse Jurisprudence*. New Haven, CT: Institute for African Studies, Yale University Press.

Glynn, T. J. 1981. Psychological sense of community: Measurement and application. *Human Relations* 34 (9): 789–818.

Goldstein, M. 2015. Personal Communication, August 1, 2015.

Gottschall, J. 2012. *Why Storytelling Is the Ultimate Weapon*. Retrieved from http://www.fastcocreate.com/1680581/why-storytelling-is-the-ultimate-weapon?partner=best_of_newsletter - May 2, 2012

Gould, S. J. 1977. *Ontogeny and Phylogeny*. Cambridge, MA: Belknap Press of Harvard University Press.

Green, J. 2000. The role of theory in evidence-based health promotion practice. *Health Education Research* 15 (2): 125–29.

Grimes, R. 2000. *Deeply into the Bone: Re-inventing Rites of Passage*. Berkeley and Los Angeles: University of California Press.

Grimes, R. L. 2006. *Rite Out of Place: Ritual, Media and the Arts*. New York: Oxford University Press.

Groissant, J. 1932. *Aristotle et les Mystères*. Paris. E. Droz.

Guber, P. 2011. *Tell to Win: Connect Persuade, and Triumph with the Hidden Power of Story*. New York: Random House.

Gusfield, J. R. 1975. *The Community: A Critical Response*. New York: Harper Colophon.

Haase, A. Q., Wellman, B., Witte, J., and Hampton, K. 2002. In *The Internet and Everyday Life*, edited by B. Wellman and C. Haythornthwaite. Oxford: Blackwell. http://www.mysocial-network.net/downloads/ng-8b1.pdf

Haley, J. 1993. *Uncommon Therapy: Psychiatric Techniques of Milton H. Erickson, M. D.* New York: Norton.

Hall, J. W. 1966. *Bizen: The House of Ukita: A Study Based on Bizen Province*. Princeton, NJ: Princeton University Press.

Halley, J. 1995. *The Process of Change*. Presentation at The Evolution of Psychotherapy Conference, Las Vegas, NV.

Harner, M. 1973. *The Jivaro: People of the Sacred Waterfalls*. Garden City, NY: Anchor Books.

Hart, D. (2012, July 12). Obama discusses his biggest mistake in office. Huffington Post. Retrived July 2012, from http://www.huffingtonpost.com/2012/07/12/obama-discusses-his-biggest-mistake_n_1669679.html

Hawkins, J. D., and Weis, J. G. 1985. The social development model: An integrated approach to delinquency prevention. *Journal of Primary Prevention* 6 (2): 73–97.

Heckewelder, J. 1819. *An Account of the History, Manners, and Customs of the Indian Nations, Who Once Inhabited Pennsylvania and the Neighbouring States*. Philadelphia, PA: Abraham Small.

Heinrich, K. T. 2001. Doctoral women as passionate scholars: An exploratory inquiry of passionate dissertation scholarship. *Advances in Nursing Science* 23 (3): 88–103.

Hinkel, R. 1987. Transition films: A selected filmography. In *Betwixt and Between: Patterns of Masculine and Feminine Initiation*, edited by L. C. Mahdi, S. Foster, and M. Little (489–98). La Salle, IL: Open Court.

Hillman, J., and Ventura, M. 1992. *We've had a Hundred Years of Psychotherapy and the World's Getting Worse*. New York: Harper Collins.

Hebb, D. O. 1974. What psychology is about. *American Psychologist* 29 (2): 71–77.

Henley, T., and Peavy, K. 2015. *As If The Earth Matters: Recommitting to Environmental Education*. Sarasota, FL: First Edition Design.

Hollis, A. C. 1905. *The Masai: Their Language and Folklore*. London: Oxford at the Clarendon Press.

Horton, R., 1974. *African traditional thought and Western science*. In Wilson, Chapter 7, pp. 131–171.

Hunt, J. 2011, Bullying Should Not Be a Teenage Rite of Passage: Five ways we an end discrimination and harassment against gay and transgender youth in schools. Washington, DC: Center for American Progress.

Ignatieff, M. 1984. *The Needs of Strangers: An Essay on Privacy, Solidarity, and the Politics of Being Human*. New York: Penguin Books.

Jenlink, P. 2003. Identity and culture work: The scholar-practitioner as public intellectual. *Scholar-Practitioner Quarterly* 1 (4): 3–8.

Johnston, D. C.-H., and Blumenkrantz, D. G. *Capital Areas Substance Abuse Council - Request for Proposal (RFP)*. West Hartford, CT: CASAC, 1994.

Jung, C.G. 1963. *Memories, Dreams, Reflections*. London: Routledge & Kegan Paul and in New York: Random House.

Karsten, R. 1935. The head-hunters of Western Amazonas. The life and culture of the Jibaro Indians of Eastern Ecuador and Peru. *Societas Scientiarum Fennica, Commentationes Humanarum Litterarum* 19 (5). Helsinki. Extracted in HRAF.

Kelly, J. G. 1966. Ecological constraints on mental health services. *American Psychologist* 21: 535–539.

Kelting, T. 1995. The nature of nature. *Parabola* 20 (10): 24–30.

Kett, J. F. 1977. *Rites of Passage: Adolescence in America, 1790 to the Present*. New York: Basic Books.

Kim, C., Losen, J., and Hewit, D. 2010. *The School-to-Prison Pipeline: Structuring Legal Reform*. New York: New York University Press.

Kimball, E. M., Mannes, M., and Hackel, A. 2009. Voices of global youth on spirituality and spiritual development: Preliminary findings from a grounded theory study. In *International Handbook of Education for Spirituality, Care, and Wellbeing*, edited by M. de Souza, L. J. Francis, J. O'Higgins-Norman, and D. Scott (329–48). Dordrecht, Netherlands: Springer.

Kimball, S. 1960. *In The Rites of Passage*. Translated by M. B. Vizedom and G. L. Caffee. Chicago, IL: University of Chicago Press.

Kingsley, P. 1997. Knowing beyond knowing: the heart of hermetic tradition. *Parabola* 22 (1): 21–25.

Kirk, G. S. 1970. *Myth: Its meaning and Functions in Ancient and Other Cultures*. London: Cambridge University Press.

Kirk, G. S. 1975. *The Nature of Greek Myths*. Woodstock, NY: Overlook Press.

Kluckhon, C. 1959, Recurrent themes in myths and mythmaking. In Daedalus, Vol. 88, No. 2, Myth and Mythmaking (pp. 268–279). MIT Press American Academy of Arts & Sciences, Cambridge, MA.

Knott, C. 2010. *Risking Rites of Passage: When Teens Control the Transition to Adulthood*. Retrieved from http://www.treatmentcenters.net/family-systems/risking-rites-of- passage-when-teens-control-the-transition-to-adulthood/

Korten, D. 2015. *Change the Story, Change the Future: A Living Economy for a Living Earth*. San Francisco: Berrett-Koehler.

Kottler, J. 2015. *Stories We've Heard, Stories We've Told: Like Changing Narratives in Therapy and Everyday Life*. New York: Oxford University Press.

Kristof-Brown, A. L., Zimmerman, R. D., and Johnson, E. C. 2005. Consequences of individuals' fit at work: A meta-analysis of person–job, person–organization, person–group, and person–supervisor fit. *Personnel Psychology* 58: 281–342.

Kronenberg, A. 1958. *Teda of Tiberti*. Translated by F. Schutze. Vienna: Horn.

Kuhn, T. *The Structure of Scientific Revolutions*. Chicago, IL: University of Chicago Press, 1962.

Kurtz, E., and Ketcham, K. 1992. *The Spirituality of Imperfection: Storytelling and the Journey to Wholeness*. New York: Bantam Books.

Laing, R. D. 1967. *The Politics of Experience*. London: Penguin Books.

Leach, E. R., ed. 1967. *The Structural Study of Myth and Totemism*. London: Tavistock.

LeBel, T. P. 2007. Examination of the impact of formerly incarcerated persons helping others. *Journal of Offender Rehabilitation* 46 (1/2): 1–24.

LeCoeur, C. 1950. *Dictionnaire Ethnographique Teda*. Paris: Librairie LaRosa.

Lerner, R. 2005. *Promoting Positive Youth Development: Theoretical and Empirical Bases*. Workshop on the Science of Adolescent Health and Development, National Research Council, Washington, DC. September 9, 2005. National Research Council/Institute of Medicine. Washington, DC: National Academy of Sciences.

Lerner, R. M., Brittian, A. S., and Fay, K. E. 2007. *Mentoring: A Key Resource for Promoting Positive Youth Development*. Promoting Positive Youth Development: The Research in Action Series, 1. Alexandria, VA: Mentor/National Mentoring Partnership.

Lévi-Strauss, C. 1974. "The structural study of myth" in *Structural Anthropology, New Edition*, pp. 206–231. New York: Basic Books.

Lévi-Strauss, C. 1978. *Myth and Meaning*. Toronto, CA: University of Toronto Press.

Lincoln, B. 1981. *Emerging from the Chrysalis: Rituals of Women's Initiation*. New York: Oxford University Press.

Lott, A. J., and Lott, B. E. 1965. Group cohesiveness as interpersonal attraction: A review of relationships with antecedent and variables. *Psychological Bulletin* 64: 259–309.

Louv, R. 2005. *Last Child in the Woods: Saving Our Children from Nature-Deficit Disorder*. Chapel Hill, NC: Algonquin Books.

MacCormac, E. R. 1976. *Metaphor and Myth in Science and Religion.* Durham, N.C., Duke University Press.

Madhubuti, H., and Madhubuti, S. 1994. *African-Centered Education: Its Value, Importance, and Necessity in the Development of Black Children.* Chicago: Third World Press.

Mahdi, L. C., Foster, S., and Little, M., eds. 1987. *Betwixt and Between: Patterns of Masculine and Feminine Initiation.* La Salle, IL: Open Court.

Malloy, E. A. 1994. *Rethinking Rites of Passage: Substance Abuse on America's Campuses.* Report from the Center on Addiction and Substance Abuse at Columbia University. New York: Columbia University Press.

Maranda, P. 1972 Ed. *Mythology: Selected Readings.* Harmondsworth, England: Penguin Books.

Marsh, J. A., Pane, J. F., and Hamilton, L. S. 2006. *Making Sense of Data-Driven Decision Making in Education.* Evidence from Recent RAND Research. http://education-2020.wikispaces.com/Data+Driven+Decision+Making

Marshack, A. 1972. *The Roots of Civilization: The Cognitive Beginnings of Man's First Art, Symbol and Notation.* New York: McGraw Hill.

Martinez-Brawley, E. 1995. Knowledge diffusion and transfer of technology: Conceptual premises and concrete steps for human services innovators. *Social Work* 40 (5): 670–82.

May, R. 1953. *Man's Search for Himself.* New York: Norton.

McGaa, E. 1990. *Mother Earth Spirituality: Native American Paths to Healing Ourselves and Our World.* New York: Harper Collins.

McGee, R. J., and Warms, R. L. 2004 [1996]. *Anthropological Theory: An Introductory History.* 3rd ed. New York: McGraw Hill.

McKnight, J. 1995. *The Careless Society: Community and Its Counterfeits.* New York: Basic Books.

McMillan, D. 1976. *Sense of Community: An Attempt at Definition.* Nashville, TN: Unpublished manuscript, George Peabody College for Teachers.

McMillan, D. W., and Chavis, D. M. 1986. Sense of community: A definition and theory. *Journal of Community Psychology* 14 (1): 6–23.

Meade, M. 1993. *Men and the Water of Life: Initiation and the Tempering of Men.* San Francisco: Harper Collins.

Menting, A. M., ed. 2010. Humor, laughter and those aha moments. *On the Brain: The Harvard Mahoney Neuroscience Institute Letter* 16 (2): 1–3. Retrieved from http://hms.harvard.edu/sites/default/files/HMS_OTB_Spring10_Vol16_No2.pdf

Merker, M. 1910. *The Masai: Ethnographic Monograph of an East African Semite People.* Translated by F. Schuze. New Haven, CT: Human Relations Area Files, Yale University.

Miltenberger, R. 2012. *Behavior Modification, Principles and Procedures.* 5th ed. Wadsworth. Belmont, CA.

Mohawk, J. 1997. *How the Conquest of Indigenous Peoples Parallels the Conquest of Nature.* Seventeenth Annual E. F. Schumacher Lectures. Williams College. Great Barrington, MA: E. F. Schumacher Society.

Moore, T. 1997. Schooling our intelligence. *Parabola* 22 (1): 6–8.

Mora R., and Christianakis, M. 2012. Feeding the school-to-prison pipeline: The convergence of neoliberalism, conservativism, and penal populism. *Journal of Educational Controversy* 7 (1): article 5.

Muchinsky, P. M., and Monahan, C. J. 1987. What is person-environment congruence? Supplementary versus complementary models of fit. *Journal of Vocational Behavior* 31: 268–77.

Murdox, G. 1945. The common denominator of culture. In *The Science of Man in the World Crisis,* edited by R. Linton (pp. 123–171). New York: Columbia University Press.

Murray, H. A., ed. 1968. *Myth and Mythmaking.* Boston: Beacon Press.

Murrell, P. C. 1997. Digging again the family wells: A Freirian literacy framework as emancipatory pedagogy for African-American children. In *Mentoring the Mentor: A Critical Dialogue with Paulo Freire,* edited by P. Freire, J. Fraser, and D. P. Macedo (pp. 19–59). New York: Lang.

Murphy, M. 1972. *Golf in the Kingdom.* New York: Dell.

Neihardt, J. 1932. *Black Elk Speaks: Being the Life Story of a Holy Man of the Oglala Sioux.* Lincoln: University of Nebraska Press.

Nelson, C. A., Bloom, F. E., Cameron, J. L., Amaral, D., Dahl, R. E., and Pine, D. 2002. An integrative, multidisciplinary approach to the study of brain-behavior relations in the context of typical and atypical development. *Development and Psychopathology* 14 (3): 499–520.

Nelson. G. M. 1986. *To Dance with God: Family Ritual and Community Celebration.* Mahwah, NJ: Paulist Press.

Newberg, A. 2012. Is the human brain hardwired for God? Video in *Is the Human Brain Hardwired for God?* by M. Erickson. Retrieved from http://bigthink.com/think-tank/is-the-brain-hardwired-for-religion

Newcomb, J. W. 1956. *The Culture and Acculturation of the Delaware Indians.* Ann Arbor: University of Michigan Press.

Nisbet, R. 1953. *The Quest for Community.* New York: Oxford University Press.

Nisbet, R., and Perrin, R. 1977. *The Social Bond.* New York: Knopf.

Norbeck, E. 1954. *Takashima: A Japanese Fishing Community.* Salt Lake City: University of Utah Press.

Nowell, B., and Boyd, N. 2010. Viewing community as responsibility as well as resource: Deconstructing the roots of psychological sense of community. *Journal of Community Psychology* 38 (7): 828–41.

Opler, M. 1996. *An Apache Lifeway.* Lincoln: University of Nebraska Press.

Opler, M. K. 1940. The southern Ute of Colorado. In *Acculturation in Seven American Indian Tribes,* edited by Ralph Linton (pp. 71–95). New York: D. Appleton-Century.

Ortner, S. B. 1984. Theory in anthropology since the Sixties. *Comparative Studies in Society and History* 26:126–166.

Park, R. E. 1924. The concept of social distance as applied to the study of racial attitudes and racial relations. *Journal of Applied Sociology* 8 (6): 339–44.

Patai, R. 1972. *Myth and Modern Man.* Englewood Cliffs, NJ: Prentice-Hall.

Peck, M. S. 1978. *The Road Less Traveled: A New Psychology of Love, Traditional Values and Spiritual Growth.* New York: Simon & Schuster.

Pelto, P. J., and Pelto, G. H. 1987. *Anthropological Research: The Structure of Inquiry.* New York: Cambridge University Press.

Perucci, R. 1963. Social distance strategies and intra-organizational stratification: A study of the status system on a psychiatric ward. *American Sociological Review* 28 (6): 951–62.

Piaget, J. 1977. *The Essential Piaget.* Edited by H. E. Gruber and J. J. Voneche. New York: Basic Books.

Piaget, J. 1983. Piaget's theory. In W. Kessen (ed.), *History, theory, and methods.* Volume 1 of the *Handbook of Child Psychology* (4th ed., pp. 103–126). Editor-in-Chief: P.H. Mussen. New York: Wiley.

Plotkin, B. 2008. *Nature and the Human Soul: Cultivating Wholeness and Community in a Fragmented World.* Navato, CA: New World Library.

Pollack, W. June 20, 2013. *Personal Communications.* West Roxbury, MA.

Potts, R. G. 2003. Emancipatory education versus school-based prevention in African American communities. *American Journal of Community Psychology* 31 (1/2). 173–183.

Putnam, R. 2000. *Bowling Alone: The Collapse and Revival of American Community.* New York: Simon & Schuster.

Proshansky, H. M., Ittelson, W. H., and Rivlin, L. G., eds. 1970. *Environmental Psychology: Man and His Physical Setting.* New York: Holt, Rinehart and Winston.

Rapkin, B. D. 2011. *Dissemination of Evidence-Based Interventions Using the Comprehensive Dynamic Trial Paradigm—Welcome to the Real World!* Paper presented at the annual meeting of the SCRA Biennial Meeting, Roosevelt University/Harold Washington Library, Chicago, IL.

Rapkin, B. D., and Trickett, E. J. 2005. Comprehensive dynamic trial designs for behavioral prevention research with communities: Overcoming inadequacies of the randomized controlled trial paradigm. In *Community Interventions and AIDS: Targeting the Community Context,* edited by E. J. Trickett (249–277). New York: Oxford University Press.

Rappaport, J. 1977. *Community Psychology: Values, Research, and Action.* Urbana-Champaign, IL: Holt, Rinehart and Winston.

Rappaport, R. 1971. The sacred in human evolution. *Annual Review of Ecology and Systematics* 2: 23–44.

Rappaport, R. 1979. *Ecology, Meaning and Religion*. Berkeley, CA: North Atlantic Books.

Reagan, R. January 28, 1986. State of the Union address. Washington. DC. Retrieved: NASA: http://www.nasa.gov/audience/formedia/speeches/reagan_challenger.html

Reason, P., and Newman, M., eds. 2013. *Stories of the Great Turning*. Bristol, UK: Vala.

Reisman, D. 1950. *The Lonely Crowd: A Study of the Changing American Character*. New Haven, CT: Yale University Press.

Rickel, A. U. 1987. The 1965 Swampscott conference and future topics for Community Psychology. *American Journal of Community Psychology* 15 (5): 511–13.

Riger, S., LeBailly, R. K., and Gordon, M. T. 1981. Community ties and urbanites' fear of crime: An ecological investigation. *American Journal of Community Psychology* 9 (6): 653–65.

Rites of Passage Wilderness. 2015. *About Us*. Retrieved from http://ritesofpassagewilderness-therapy.com/about-us/

Robers, S., Kemp, J., Rathbun, A., Morgan, R. E., and Snyder, T. D. 2014. *Indicators of School Crime and Safety: 2013* (NCES 2014-042/NCJ 243299). National Center for Education Statistics, US Department of Education, and Bureau of Justice Statistics, Office of Justice Programs, US Department of Justice. Washington, DC. Figure 1.2. http://nces.ed.gov/pubs2014/2014042.pdf

Rogers, E. M. 1983. *Diffusion of Innovations*. New York: Free Press.

Romer, D. 2010. Adolescent risk taking, impulsivity, and brain development: Implications for prevention. *Developmental Psychobiology* 52 (3): 263–76.

Roszak, T. 1992. *The Voice of the Earth: An Exploration of Ecopsychology*. New York: Touchstone.

Ryan, G. 1998. *Developmental Assets in Connecticut*. The Partnership Press: Connecticut Assets Network: Wethersfield, Connecticut

Saitoti, T. O. 1988. *The Worlds of a Maasai Warrior: An Autobiography*. Los Angeles: University of California Press.

Santayana, G. 1896. *The Sense of Beauty*. New York: C. Scribner's Sons.

Sarason, S. 1972. *The Creation of Settings and the Future Societies*. San Francisco: Jossey-Bass.

Sarason, S. 1974. *The Psychological Sense of Community: Prospects for a Community Psychology*. San Francisco: Jossey-Bass.

Scales, P. C., and Leffert, N. 1999. *Developmental Assets: A Synthesis of the Scientific Research on Adolescent Development*. Minneapolis, MN: Search Institute Press.

Scheer, S. D., Gavazzi, S. M., and Blumenkrantz, D. G. 2007. Rites of passage during adolescence. *Forum for Family and Consumer Issues* 12 (2).

Schiller, M., and Cooper, A. 2012. Learning together across generations: Because everyone matters. *AI Practitioner* 14 (3): 26–31.

Schlegel, A., and Barry, H., III. 1991. *Adolescence: An Anthropological Inquiry*. New York: Free Press.

Scholiast. 1925. *The Mystery Religions and Christianity*. Translated by S. Angus. London. John Murray.

Schorr, L. 1993. Keynote address. In *National Association of Social Workers, Effective Strategies for Increasing Social Program Replication/Adaptation* (7–18). Washington, DC: National Association of Social Workers.

Schumacher, E. F. 1973. *Small Is Beautiful: Economics as if People Mattered*. London: Blond & Briggs.

Search Institute. *Developmental Assets Profile 2005*. http://www.search-institute.org/surveys/DAP

Senese, G. B. 1991. *Self-Determination and the Social Education of Native Americans*. New York: Praeger.

Sharpe, K. 1984. *From Science to an Adequate Mythology*. Auckland, NZ: Interface Press.

Sheldrake, R. 1991. *The Rebirth of Nature: The Greening of Science and God*. New York: Bantam Books.

Shore, E. 1992. The soul of the community. *Parabola* 17 (1): 18–22.

Shujaa, M. J. 1995. *Too much schooling, too little education: A paradox of black life in white societies*. Trenton, NJ: Africa World Press.

Siegel, R. K. 1989. *Intoxication: Life in Pursuit of Artificial Paradise*. New York: Penguin.

Silko, L. 1977. *Ceremony*. New York: Penguin Press.

Skinner, B. F. 1953. *Science and Human Behavior*. Oxford: Macmillan.

Smale, G. 1993. The nature of innovation and community-based practice. In *Transferring Technology in the Personal Social Services*, edited by E. E. Martinez-Brawley with S. M. Delevan (pp. 6–12). Washington, DC: NASW Press.

Smith-Shank, D. 2002. Community celebrations as ritual signifiers. *Visual Arts Research* 28 (2): 57–63.

Somé, M. P. 1993. *Ritual: Power and Healing and Community*. Portland, OR: Swan/Raven.

Somé, M. P. 1994. *Of Water and Spirit: Ritual, Magic and Initiation in the Life of an African Shaman*. New York: Tarcher/Putnam.

Somé, M. P. 1995. Workshop at Rowe Conference Center. Rowe, MA.

Spock, B. 1946. *The Common Sense Book of Baby and Child Care*. New York: Duell, Sloan and Pearce.

Stanton, M. D., Todd, T., et al. 1982. *The Family Therapy of Drug Abuse and Addiction*. New York, NY: Guilford Press.

Steinberg L. 2008. A social neuroscience perspective on adolescent risk-taking. *Developmental Review* 28: 78–106.

Steinsaltz, A. 2005. I sleep, but my heart is awake. *Parabola* 30 (1): 24–31.

Stevens, A. 1990. *On Jung*. New York: Penguin Books.

Stuckey, C. 2001. Gauguin inside art. In *Gauguin's Nirvana: Painters at Le Pouldu 1889–90*, edited by E. M. Zafran (pp. 137–165). New Haven, CT: Yale University Press.

Sullwold, E. 1987. The ritual-maker within at adolescence. In *Betwixt and Between: Patterns of Masculine and Feminine Initiation*, edited by L. C. Mahdi, S. Foster, and M. Little (pp. 111–134). La Salle, IL: Open Court.

Sullivan, E. M., Annest, J. L., Simon, T. R., Luo, F., and Dahlberg, L. L. 2015. Suicide trends among persons aged 10–24 years—United States, 1994–2012. *MMWR* 64 (8): 201–205.

Sullivan R. J., and Hagen E. H. 2002. Psychotropic substance-seeking: Evolutionary pathology or adaptation? *Addiction* 97: 389–400.

Sydlo, S. J., Schensul, J. J., Owens, D. C., Brase, M. K., Wiley, K. N., Berg, M. J., Baez, E., and Schensul D. 2000. *Participatory Action Research Curriculum for Empowering Youth*. Hartford, CT: Institute for Community Research.

Szasz, T. 1970. *The Manufacture of Madness: A Comparative Study of the Inquisition and the Mental Health Movement*. New York: Harper & Row.

Talò, C., Mannarini, T., and Rochira, A. 2014. Sense of community and community participation: A meta-analytic review. *Social Indicators Research* 117: 1–28.

Taylor, A. C. 1993. Remembering to forget: Identity, mourning, and memory among the Jivaro. *Man* (n.s.) 28: 653–78.

Taylor, D. 1996. *The Healing Power of Stories: Creating Yourself through the Stories of Your Life*. New York: Doubleday.

Teilhard de Chardin, P. 1955. *The Phenomenon of Man*. New York: Harper.

Titiev, M. A. 1944. *Old Oraibi: A Study of the Hopi Indians of the Third Mesa*. Cambridge, MA: Peabody Museum of American Archaeology.

Toffler, A. 1971. *Future Shock*. New York: Bantam Books.

Trickett, E. 2015. *Ecological Community Psychology and Evidence Based Programs: An Uneasy Relationship*. Presentation at the Society for Community Research and Action, Division 27 American Psychological Association Biennial Conference, Bridging Past and Future, June 25–28, 2015. Lowell MA. Program Guide.

Tropman, J. E. 1969. Critical dimensions of community structure: A reexamination of the Hadden-Borgotta findings. *Urban Affairs Quarterly* 5 (2): 215–32.

Turner, V. W. 1952. *The Lozi Peoples of North-Western Rhodesia in Ethnographic Survey of Africa: Part III*. London: International African Institute.

Turner, V. W. 1967. *The Forest of Symbols: Aspects of Ndembu Ritual*. Ithaca, NY: Cornell University Press.

Turner, V. W. 1969. *The Ritual Process*. Chicago, IL: Aldine.

Union of International Associations. 1986. *The Encyclopedia of World Problems and Human Potential*. Munich: Author; New York: Saur.

van Gennep, A., 1908. *The Rites of Passage*. Chicago: University of Chicago Press.

van Gennep, A., 1960. *The Rites of Passage*. Translated by M. B. Vizedom and G. L. Caffee. Chicago, IL: University of Chicago Press.

Vogt, Y. 2012. *World's oldest ritual discovered: Worshipped the python 70,000 years ago*. Translated by Alan Louis Belardinelli. *Apollon Research Magazine*. University of Oslo. https://www.apollon.uio.no/english/articles/2006/python-english.html

Warner, W. L., & Associates. 1949. *Democracy in Jonesville: A study in quality and inequality*. New York: Harper & Row.

Watts, A. W. 1960. *Myth and Ritual in Christianity*. New York: Grove Press.

Weaver, L., and Kessler, R. 2011. Six passages of childhood. In *Educating from the Heart: Theoretical and Practical Approaches to Transforming Education*, edited by A. N. Johnson and M. Neagley, 49–67. Lanham, MD: Rowman & Littlefield Education.

Weaver, L., and Wilding, M. 2013. *The 5 Dimensions of Engaged Teaching: A Practical Guide for Educators*. Bloomington, IN: Solution Tree.

Weil, A., and Rosen, W. 1983. *From Chocolate to Morphine: Everything You Need to Know about Mind-Altering Drugs*. Boston: Haughton Mifflin.

Weissberg, R. P., Payton, J. W., O'Brien, M. U., and Munro, S. 2007. Social and emotional learning. In *Moral Education: A Handbook*, edited by F. Clark Power, Ronald J. Nuzzi, and Darcia Narvaez (417–18). Westport, CT.: Greenwood Press.

Wellman, B. 1979. The community question. *American Journal of Sociology* 84 (5): 1201–31.

Wellman, B. 1981. Applying network analysis to the study of support. In *Social Networks and Social Support*, edited by G. H. Gottlieb (pp. 171–200). Beverly Hills, CA: Sage.

Whyte, W., Greenwood, D., and Lazes, P. 1991. Participatory action research: Through practice to science in social research. In *Participatory Action Research*, edited by W. Whyte (pp. 19–55). Newbury Park, CA: Sage.

Wildcat, D. R. 2009. *Red Alert: Saving the Planet with Indigenous Knowledge*. Golden, CO: Fulcrum,

Wilson, B. R., ed., 1974. *Rationality*. Oxford: Basil Blackwell.

Wilson, D. S., and Wilson, E. O. 2007. Rethinking the theoretical foundation of sociobiology. *Quarterly Review of Biology* 82 (4): 328–48.

Wilson, E. O. 1978. *On Human Nature*. Cambridge, MA: Harvard University Press.

Wilson, E. O. 2013. *The Social Conquest of Earth*. New York: Norton.

Wittgenstein, L. 1965. *The Blue and Brown Books*. New York: Harper & Row.

Wolff, T. 2010. *The Power of Collaborative Solutions: Six Principles and Effective Tools for Building Healthy Communities*. San Francisco, CA: Jossey-Bass.

Woodard, A., Jr. 1996. *A HELPful PATH to the year 2000: Report on the Paths to the Year 2000*. Wethersfield, CT: Woodard & Associates.

Youth Passageways. 2015. Website. http://youthpassageways.org/

Zax, M., and Specter, G. A. 1974. *An Introduction to Community Psychology*. New York: Wiley.

Zollo, P., and Dylan, B. 1991. *The Song Talk Interview*. Transcribed from GBS #3 booklet. Retrieved from http://www.interferenza.com/bcs/interw/1991zollo.htm

INDEX

Page numbers followed by *f* indicate figures. Numbers followed by n indicate notes.

activities: guiding principles for, 212–213, 215
addiction, 4, 114–115
adolescent development, 6, 108; as call to
    adventure, 155–156; community rituals
    for, 74–75; as loss, 131; parent involvement
    in, 177. *see also* coming of age; youth
    development
adornments, 72
adventure: call to, 104, 155–156
affirmation, 215
African Americans, 2
African Proverb, 18, 22, 74, 187
alcohol use, 4–7
Alford, K. A., 53
alone time, 196, 214
American Red Cross, 228–229
ancestors: connections with, 151–153, 160, 214;
    stories from Takashima, 149–151
ancient Greeks, 9
anger, 74
anima archetypes, 103–105
anthropology, 52–54, 140–141
Apache, 48, 82, 167–168
appearance: change of, 215
Appreciative Inquiry, 218
appropriation, 94, 166, 168; cultural, 115–118
Arrien, Angeles, 112–113
art, public, 233–234
artists, 234
Astor, Nancy, 9
attraction at a distance, 117
authenticity, 168
awakening: opportunities for, 159

Bandura, A., 149
baptismo (baptism) ceremonies, 173–174
Bar or Bat Mitzvah, 116; Blumenkrantz's story,
    38–39, 86–88, 155; parent's blessings,
    177–178; separation in, 155
basketball, 114

bedtime rituals, 1
behavior: expectations for, 213; models for, 98;
    ritual behaviors, 90, 96; socially
    appropriate, 213
behavioral health problems, 2, 90
belief systems, 132
belonging, 64, 223
Ben-Nathan, Geoffrey, 241
bereavement counseling, 223–224
Berry, Wendell, 54
Bettelheim, Bruno, 85
Bible, 162–163
biology, 101–102
Blumenkrantz, David: Bar Mitzvah, 38–39,
    86–88, 155; creation myth (vision quest
    retreat), 29–47, 83–84, 87–88, 91–92;
    Dagara-based funeral experience (Somé
    retreat), 119–130; definition of rites of
    passage, 81; Order of the Arrow initiation
    (Boy Scouts), 164–168
Bly, Robert, 122
B'nai Mitzvah, 116
bonding, 146–147
Bonniwell, K., 54
Borhek, James, 132
Boy Scouts: Order of the Arrow initiation,
    164–168, 180
brain functions, 90
Buber, Martin, 11–12
buddy system, 228–229
bulletin boards, 70
bullying, 4–7
burial caves, 20–21
Bush Center for Child Development and Social
    Policy, 23

CADAC. *see* Connecticut Alcohol and Drug Abuse
    Commission
call of place, 84
call to adventure, 104

call to inquiry and action, 217–237

Cameron, David, 241

Campbell, Joseph, 3, 53–57, 79, 96, 102, 133, 234;
   The Hero with a Thousand Faces, 104

Camp Wamsutta, 242

capital, social, 7

Capital Area Substance Abuse Council (CASAC),
   187–188, 199–200

Carey, George, 168

caring climate, 2–3, 5, 226

caring neighborhood, 2–3

CASAC. *see* Capital Area Substance Abuse Council

Catalano, Richard, 192–193, 193*f*

Cea, Joanna Levitt, 182

celebrations, 196, 215; myths underlying, 151;
   stories from Takashima, 149–151

Center for American Progress, 4

Center for the Advancement of Youth, Family, and
   Community Services, 24

Center for Youth & Community, Inc., 24, 242

"Centers for the Study and Advancement of
   Initiation and Rites of Passage," 233

ceremony, 35, 63, 65, 72

Challenger 7, 109

challenges, planned, 195–196

Champion, Robert, 3

chanting, 122–125

chat rooms, 70

Chavis, D. M., 64, 67, 75

Chestnut, Chris, 3

child development, 6, 223. *see also* youth
   development

child industrial complex, 223

childrearing, 223–224; challenges of, 154;
   through rites of passage, 81; stories about,
   2; stories from the Masai, 153–155; village,
   18–20, 81, 172–173, 225

children, 206–207, 217–218; of color, 2; as fathers
   of men, 227–228; initiation/orientation
   events for, 195; stories for, 1–3; transition
   to adulthood, 54

Childs, 98

Chisholm, Shirley, 166

CHOICES (Simsbury), 200

Christmas, 9

"A Christmas Carol" (Dickens), 9

*The Circle of Life: Rituals from the Human Family
   Album* (Cohen), 54

circumcision, 132, 162–163; economic component,
   148; Masai rituals, 162–163; stories from
   the Kanuri people, 147–149; stories from the
   Teda people, 143. *see also specific rites*

civic organizations, 186

Clarke, Arthur C., 71

climate change, 56

climate of civility, 2–3, 5, 221, 226

CNN, 4

coffee, 76

cognitive development, 159

Cohen, R., 147–148

cohesion, 72

collaboration, 186

Collaborative for Social Emotional Learning, 226

college, 232–233

Collinson, Vivienne, 5–6

coming of age, 54, 69, 73, 108; *baptismo* (baptism)
   ceremonies, 173–174; Blumenkrantz's story,
   88; in Delaware Nation, 164; process of, 215;
   stories from Takashima, 149–151. *see also*
   rites of passage

Commission on Substance Abuse at Colleges and
   Universities, 4–5

communitas, 55

community, 11, 197; benefits of initiations
   for, 179–180; critical dimensions of, 71;
   home community, 213; interiorization
   of, 81; meaning of, 59–77; obligation to,
   146–147; place of, 62–63; predictors of, 71;
   psychological sense of, 20, 55–56, 64,
   68–69, 80, 187, 213, 222–223, 229, 232,
   234; quest for, 48–58; as relational, 64; role
   of, 131; as territorial, 64; as unit of solution,
   230; value of, 94; virtual, 70

community building or community development,
   73–77, 120, 198; new models for, 187–192;
   principles of, 189, 191–192; Project 2000
   (Paths to the Year 2000), 187–191; through
   rites of passage, 19, 137, 186–187

community celebrations, 97, 146–147; stories
   from Takashima, 149–151

community collaboratives, 198

community elders, 201–202

community empowerment, 198

community ethics, 204

community golf, 17–18

community institutions, 169–216

community involvement, 71

community membership, 64

community mobilization, 198

community myths, 220

community-oriented rites of passage, 228–229;
   authentic, 181–183; development of,
   192–194; elements of, 72

community psychology, 62, 68

community rituals, 48–58, 74–75, 221; funeral
   rituals, 131

community service, 196, 215

community values, 2–3, 212

competence, 67

confusion technique, 124

Connecticut Alcohol and Drug Abuse Commission
   (CADAC), 187

Connecticut Department of Mental Health and
   Addiction Services, 189

connection: consciousness of, 51

Conroy, Pat, 89, 92

consumerism, 17

conversations, 11–12, 236

Cooper, James Fenimore, 165
co-researchers, 194, 199
corruption, 8–9
counseling, peer, 195–196
Cranberry Wilderness Preserve, 27–28
creation myths, 25–47
The Creation of Settings and the Future Society
    (Sarason), 23–24
crowdsourcing, 183
crystals, 31
Cuchulainn, 106
cultural appropriation, 115–118
cultural belief systems, 132
cultural diversity, 196
cultural organizations, 186
cultural symbols, 141
cultural values, 204
culture(s): and myth, 102–107; sample
    ethnographies, 143–168
Curtis, Richard, 132
custodians, 225–226

Dagara traditions: funeral ritual for men based
    on (Somé retreat), 115, 119–133; lessons
    learned from, 130–133
daily rituals, 96
data-driven decision-making (DDDM), 3
death, symbolic, 196
de Chardin, Pierre Teilhard, 73
Deere, John, 223–224
Delaware Nation, 163–164, 166–167, 180
delinquency, juvenile, 17
Deloria, Vine, Jr., 167–168
Descartes, Rene, 81
design principles, 11, 14, 52, 77, 134, 142, 170,
    174, 183, 188–189, 191–192, 195, 198, 210,
    212, 216, 221, 226, 231, 235
determinism, reciprocal, 149
developmental assets, 2–3
Dickens, Charles, 9
Dinesen, Isak, 1
diversity, 196, 201
Dostoyevsky, Fyodor, 60
*D'où Venons Nous/ Que Sommes Nous/ Où Allons
    Nous?— Where Do We come From?/ What Are
    We?/ Where Are We Going?* (Gauguin), 10
dreams: sharing with fire (Blumenkrantz's
    creation myth), 36; stories to dreams,
    139–168
dress, 72
drinking, 4–7
drug use, 4–7, 17, 155–156
drumming, 122, 124, 127–130
Dylan, Bob, 168

East Africa, 51
economic contributions, 148, 150
Ecuador: stories from the Jivaroan people,
    156–160

Edelman, Marian Wright, 178
Edson, Carroll A., 165–167
education, 8–9, 223; college, 232–233; high
    school, 5–6; initiation as, 95; school(s), 10,
    74, 186, 227–228
educational challenges, 90, 195–196
educational programs, 90, 180–181
Einstein, Albert, 12, 112, 117
elders, 170–172, 201–202, 226–227; community
    elders, 201–202; youth elders, 204
Eliade, Mircea, 96–98, 109–110
emergence, 105, 111–112, 209–210
emergent design, 15, 111–112, 167, 169–170, 181,
    188, 194, 209
Emerging from the Chrysalis (Lincoln), 133
emersion, 53
emotional experiences or connections, shared, 64,
    69–70, 75, 131
enclosure, 53
engaged teaching, 226
environment: importance of, 168; lifeway
    relationships with place, 69
Erickson, Milton, 124–125
ethics, 8, 204, 212
ethnic sensitivity, 196
ethnography, 141; sample ethnographies,
    142–168
eusocial characteristics, 102
Everyman, 104–105
evidence-based myths, 221
evidence-based practice, 110, 181–183, 207–208;
    randomized control trials (RCTs), 181–183,
    207, 209
evidence-based programs, 82–83
evidence-based stories, 222
evolution, 207–208
exclusion, 64
Exodus, 25–26, 37, 117

Facebook, 70
families, 186
Family and Medical Leave Act, 229–230
female initiations, 160–163; *quinceañera*
    ceremonies, 173–174; structure of, 53, 105
fire: Grandfather Fire, 36; sharing dreams with
    (Blumenkrantz's creation myth), 36; *Tate
    Wari*, 27, 31–32, 35, 40–43, 46, 66, 86
First Nations, 65
Florida A&M University (FAMU), 3
Foster, S., 53
Frenaye, F., 138
From Science to an Adequate Mythology (Sharpe), 135
Fukushima Daiichi, 222
funding, 208–209, 231–232
funeral rites: community rituals, 131;
    Dagara-based, for men (Somé retreat), 115,
    119–133; history of, 20–21; Shiva, 39
future directions, 224–225, 229–231
Future Shock (Toffler), 112–113

gangs, 4–7, 17
Gauguin, Paul, 10
Gavazzi, S. M., 53
Geertz, C., 141
gender differences, 105
generation gaps, 103
Genesis, 117, 162–163
geography, 64, 70–71
Global Projects Center (Stanford
      University), 182
Godfathers (Padrinos), 173–174
Godmothers (Madrinas), 173–174
God's Eye, 43, 87
golf, 17–18, 113–114
Golf in the Kingdom (Murphy), 113–114
Goodman, E. Urner, 165–167
Gottschall, J., 9
government mandates, 186, 208–209
graffiti, 54
Grandfather Fire, 36
Great Society, 241
Greece, ancient, 9
Green, J., 183
greetings, ritual, 16
grief and grieving, 120, 123; funeral rituals,
      20–21, 115, 119–133; public grief, 120
grief technology, 223–224
Groissant, J., 94
group experiences, 201
Gruttman, Isodor, 38
Guber, Peter, 9

Hair, 17
Haley, Alex, 155
Halley, Jay, 80
Hanifan, E. J., 7
Hasidic Judaism, 58
Hawkins, David, 192–193, 193f
hazings, 3–7
health promotion, 183
Heckewelder, J., 164, 166
herbs, medicinal, 157–158
heritage, 204
hero archetypes, 98, 103
hero's journey, 79, 104, 106, 133
hero-type myths, 103–104
The Hero with a Thousand Faces (Campbell), 104
Hertzog, Julie, 4
high school, 5–6
Hillman, James, 81, 96–97, 122, 147, 151
Hinkel, Robert, 133
Hoffman, Lynn, 5–6
holidays, 72
home community, 213
honor society initiations, 164–168
Hopi, 151–153
Horton, R., 110
HRAF. see Human Relations Area Files (Yale
      University)

Huichol Indians, 27, 42, 75, 160; Virarica, the
      Healing People, 63, 65; vision
      quests, 83, 85–87
Human Relations Area Files (HRAF) Archive
      (Yale University), 139–140; "Puberty and
      Initiation" (Archive 881), 140; sample
      ethnographies, 143–168; selection of
      stories from, 142–143
hunting, 5
hypnosis, 124

I Ching, 139, 150, 172
identification, 91–92, 128–129, 215
identity, 74
illo tempore, 98
inclusion, 64
inclusiveness, 201
incorporation (ritual stage), 86–88, 215
indigenous peoples, 65, 69, 105. see also specific
      peoples
individualism, 57, 79, 94, 224
influence, 64
informal interactions, 71
initiation(s), 20, 121, 237; absence of, 6,
      114–115; aims of, 152–153; authentic, 168;
      benefits of, 179–180; central principles,
      symbols, and patterns of, 98; completion
      of, 88; of Cuchulainn, 106; as educational,
      95; emergence of, 164–168; female, 53,
      160–163, 173–174; forms of, 66; hallmark
      of, 98; indigenous, 105; interpretations
      of, 79; ongoing, 77; places of, 169–216,
      232–233; as process, 170; "Puberty and
      Initiation" (Archive 881), 140, 143–168;
      purpose of, 7, 66–73, 112, 171; and
      quest for community, 57; responsibility
      for, 88, 171; sacred in, 89–90; sample
      ethnographies, 143–168; of scholars,
      6; self-rendered, 3–7, 53–54, 143, 146;
      stories, 171–173; stories from the Delaware
      Nation, 163–164; stories from the Hopi,
      151–153; stories from the Jivaroan people,
      156–160; stories from the Kanuri people,
      147–149; stories from the Lozi tribe,
      161–162; stories from the Masai, 153–155;
      stories from Takashima, 149–151; stories
      from the Teda people, 143–147, 154;
      stories of, 219–221; symbols of, 59–77,
      78–88, 98, 106; as transformative, 88, 92;
      transformative potential of, 171; tribal,
      151–153; work of, 88; of youth, 94. see also
      specific rites
Initiation into Play, 194–195
Initiation of Scholars, 194–195
initiation/orientation events, 195
initiatory constellations, 50–51, 55, 145,
      160, 167–171, 174, 180–181, 209, 220,
      236–237
innovation transfer, 111–112, 183–184

inquiry: call to inquiry and action, 217–237; questions, 11–12, 134–137, 222; trinity of, 52, 210–211

Institute for Community Research, 230

integration, 64

intellectual development, 5–6

interiorization of community, 81

Internet, 70

interventions, 183

intoxication, ritual, 157–158

invocation, 91, 127–128

Iron John, 122

Irons, Shivas, 113–114

isolation, 105, 196

Israel of Rizhin, 58

Israel Shem Tov, 58

janitors, 226

Javanese circumcision ceremonies, 149

Jivaroan people, 156–160

Johnston, David C.-H., 188

Judaism, 63, 116, 137–138; Bar or Bat Mitzvah, 38–39, 86–88, 116, 155, 177–178; B'nai Mitzvah, 116; Hasidic, 58; initiatory practices, 166; lessons learned from ancestors, 177–178; Schema, 117; Shabbat or Sabbath, 117–118

Jung, Carl, 101, 103

Just Say No!, 17, 155

juvenile delinquency, 17

Kanuri people, 147–149

"Kasserian Ingera" ("And how are the children?"), 51, 211

Kauyumari, 29, 32, 42, 45

Keane, Richard, 178

Kelting, Thomas, 37, 59, 77

Kessler, Rachael, 226

Kimball, Solon, 79, 111–112

Kirk, G. S., 98

Kluckhorn, C., 102

Korten, David, 1

Kottler, J., 9, 61, 107

Kuhn, Thomas, 57

Lakota, 73, 116

language, 72, 77, 223

Latinos: *baptismo* (baptism) ceremonies, 173–174; *quinceañera* ceremonies, 173–174

laughter, 191

Lawson, Richard, 6

Leach, 98

leadership, 204

Leadership Project (West Hartford), 200

learning, 134

legends, 83

leisure time activities, 195

lessons learned, 130–133; from ancestors, 177–178; from swimming, 228–229; from Teda, 146

Lévi-Strauss, 98, 101

Life, 54

life-cycle transitions, 54. *see also* rites of passage

life stories, essential, 25

lifeways, 69, 167

liminality: as mother of invention, 48; as reflection, 86; as ritual stage, 90, 105, 213–214, 234–235

Lincoln, Bruce, 53, 105, 133

lip piercings, 143

living the myth, 99

localism, 71

loss, 121

Lozi tribe, 161–163

Lyons, Oren, 65

MacCormac, Earl, 108

Madrinas (Godmothers), 173–174

Magee, John Gillespie, Jr., 109

Maggid of Mezritch, 58

magic, 71, 101–102

Mahdi, Louise Carus, 179, 230

Maille, Leah Beth, 230

"Malidoma" ("friend of the enemy/stranger"), 119

Mandela, Nelson, 56

Mara Akame, 27, 43, 91

Maranda, 98

Masai, 51; circumcision rituals, 149, 162–163; "The Passing of the Fence" ritual, 104, 153–155, 175, 177

masochism, 85

Match.com, 70

Matsunagi, Japan: stories from, 160–161

Matsuwa, Don José, 63, 191

May, Rollo, 74

McKenry, P. C., 53

McMillan, D., 64

McMillan, D. W., 67, 75

Meade, Michael, 49–50, 122

meaningful roles, 215

medicinal herbs, 157–158

membership, 64

memory, 58

men's movement, 55

mental challenges, 195–196

mental illness, 2, 111–112

mentorships, 195–196, 201

metamorphosis, 53, 105

meta-myth, 131–132, 220; rites of passage as, 133–134; stories from the Kanuri people, 148

metaphors, 106

Mezritch, Maggid of, 58

Mi Casa, *Padrino & Madrina* (Hartford), 200

Middle East: stories from the Kanuri people, 147–149; stories from the Teda people, 143–147

midlife crises, 103, 174–177

Mitakuye Oyasin ("We are all related" or "All my relations"), 116

Moca Nova festival, 105
models: for behavior, 98; for community building, 187–192; myths as, 98; for rites of passage, 53; of science, 110; small, 187–192; social development model of youth development, 192–193, 193*f*
modern myths, 107–112
modern rites of passage, 107–108
Mohawk, John, 21
Moore, Robert, 122
morning rituals, 76
Moyers, Bill, 3, 53–54
multicultural sensitivities, 196
Murdock, George Peter, 139
myth(s), 72, 83, 96–98; in association with rituals, 100; authority of, 100; characters in, 98; community myths, 220; creation myths, 25–47; and culture, 102–107; evidence-based, 221; form or structure of, 133; functions of, 110; as ideal, 98; keeping alive, 234; as living, 99–100; meta-myth, 131–134, 148, 220; as models for behavior, 98; modern, 107–112; properties of, 98, 101, 107; prototypes, 102–103; reenactment of, 97–100; of rites of passage, 107–108; science as, 108, 112; *From Science to an Adequate Mythology* (Sharpe), 135; scientific, 109; as story, 98; ties to time and space, 98; traditional, 112; truth of, 100; underlying celebrations, 151; universal features of, 102–103

närings liv, 223
NASA, 109
National Citizen Service (NCS), 67–68, 241
national stories, 192
Native Americans, 2, 10. *see also specific tribes*
natural relationships, 65–66, 82–83
nature, 37, 65–66; connection with, 67–68, 74, 151–153, 214; encounters with, 196; lifeway relationships with, 69; retreat into the forest, 160
Navaho, 48, 82, 105
Neanderthals, 20–21
neighboring preferences, 71
Newberg, Andrew, 90
Newcomb, J. W., 166
news of the day, 3–7, 53, 56–57
Nierika, 32–33, 36–37, 45, 66, 85
9-11 (September 11, 2001), 75
nongovernmental organizations (NGOs), 186
nonlocality, 117
nonordinary states of reality, 214
Nyonca (Hartford First Baptist Church), 200

Obama, Barack, 107
Oedipus-type myths, 103
offerings, prayer arrow, 32
Ojo de Dios, 43, 87

Okayama, Matsunagi, Japan: stories from, 160–161
Okayama, Takashima, Japan: stories from, 148–151, 161, 163
older students, 227–228
Omaha Indians, 179
Onondaga Nations, 65
ontogeny, 50
Opler, Morris, 167–168
ordeals, 211, 213–214, 220
Order of the Arrow initiation (Boy Scouts), 164–168, 180
orientation events, 195

Padrinos (Godfathers), 173–174
paradigms, 79–80
paradigm shift, 52, 80, 82, 113, 180, 190–191, 212, 218
paradoxical intention, 124
paralysis by analysis, 3
parents, 172–173, 196–197, 204, 206–207; initiation/orientation events for, 195; Rite Of Passage Experience© (ROPE®) for Parents, 174–177
parent's blessings, 177–178
participatory action research (PAR), 230
"Participatory Action Research Curriculum for Empowering Youth," 230
Passage Club, 200
Passages (Windsor), 200
PassageWorks Institute, 226
"The Passing of the Fence" ritual (Masai), 104, 153–155, 175, 177
Patai, 98
Paths to the Year 2000 (Project 2000), 187–191, 209–210; design principles, 191–197; expansion, 205; funding, 198; general findings, 199–206; general principles, 189, 199; inclusiveness, 201; initial phase, 200; mobilization, 200; motivation to participate, 203; outcome, 197–199; participants, 200–205; projects, 200; rite of passage experiences, 199; survey responses, 200–205; theme, 188
Peck, Scot, 229
peer counseling, 195–196
person-environment fit, 67–68
perturbation, 158
Peru: stories from the Jivaroan people, 156–160
phylogeny, 50
physical challenges, 195–196
Piaget, Jean, 159
pilgrimage, 28, 35, 42, 63
place: of the heart, 86–88; lifeway relationships with, 69; vision quest, 29–35, 84
Plains Indians, 85
play, 191, 195, 214, 227–228
Plotkin, B., 53
policy, public, 208–209
Pollack, William, 76

positive leisure time activities, 195
positive play, 195
positive youth development, 70–71
positive youth development programs, 132
The Power of Myth (Campbell), 53–54
prayer arrows, 32
prayers for connection, 31–32
prevention, primal, 111–113
Price, Reynolds, 1
procreation, 160–163
professionals, 232
program development, 180–181; guiding
        principles for activities, 212–213, 215
Project 2000. *see* Paths to the Year 2000
pro-urbanism, 71
Proverbs, 25, 27
psychoactive plants, 156
psychology, community, 62, 68
psychotherapy, 80
puberty rites, 53–54; "Puberty and Initiation"
        (Archive 881) (HRAF), 140; stories from
        the Jivaroan people, 156–160; stories from
        the Kanuri people, 147–149; stories from
        Takashima, 149–151; stories from the Ute
        people, 161. *see also* initiation(s); rites of
        passage
public art, 233–234
public grief, 120
public policy, 208–209, 224–225
purification, 91, 126–127
Putnam, Robert, 7

quest for community, 48–58
questions, 11–12, 134–137, 222
quinceañera ceremonies, 173–174

randomized control trials (RCTs), 181–183,
        207, 209
Rappaport, Roy A., 102
REACH (E. Granby), 200
Reagan, Ronald, 109
Realm (Granby), 200
rebirth, 196
reciprocal determinism, 149
reciprocity, 43, 48, 50–51, 55, 59–77, 86–87, 94–96
recreational organizations, 186
reflection, 214; call to inquiry and action,
        217–237; liminality as, 86
reincorporation, 105
Reisman, David, 75
relationships, 64, 221, 234–236; importance of,
        212; lifeway, 69
religion, 108, 110
religious organizations, 186
remembering stories, 58
reproduction: preparation for, 160–163
retreats: Dagara-based funeral rite for men
        (Somé), 115, 119–133; into the forest, 160;
        vision quests. *see* vision quests

revelation, 85
Rimington, Jess, 182
Rite Of Passage Experience© (ROPE®), 24, 103,
        195, 241; evaluations of, 206–207; Paths
        to the Year 2000 (Project 2000), 187–206,
        209–210
Rite Of Passage Experience, ROPE (Avon), 200
Rite Of Passage Experience, ROPE (Newington),
        200
Rite Of Passage Experience, ROPE (Wethersfield),
        200
Rite Of Passage Experience© (ROPE®) for Parents,
        174–177
rites and rituals, 72, 94–118, 213; absence of, 6–7,
        114–115, 123; in association with myths,
        100; bedtime, 1; and biology, 101–102;
        community rituals, 48–58, 74–75, 221;
        contemporary programs, 90; creation of, 96,
        119–138; cultural appropriation of,
        115–118; daily, 96; as experienced,
        120–121; forms of, 90–92; generic structure
        of, 91–92; greetings, 16; guiding principles
        for, 210–216, 221; importance of, 136;
        individual rituals, 221; initiation rites. *see*
        initiation(s); during life cycle transitions.
        see rites of passage; morning, 76; potency
        of, 134, 136; preparation for, 31–32,
        113–114; preshot routines, 113–114; as
        primal prevention, 111–113; as reenactment
        of myth, 97–100; roots of, 95–97; sample
        ethnographies, 143–168; scientific, 108;
        Somé on, 126; stages of, 130; stories about,
        132; stories from the Kanuri people,
        147–149; stories from the Teda people,
        143–147; storytelling, 1; traditional,
        115–118; as transformative, 113;
        transporting, 115. *see also specific rites*
rites of confusion, 6–8
rites of passage, 11, 19, 78–88, 99–100, 237;
        absence of, 6–7, 114–115; case for, 56–57;
        community development through, 18,
        48–58, 137, 186–187; community
        institutions as places of, 169–216;
        community-oriented, 72, 104, 181–183,
        192–197, 228–229; contemporary,
        83–84; definition of, 81; development
        of, 170, 192–194; eight-stage model of,
        53; essential ingredients of, 104; female
        initiations, 53, 160–163, 173–174; forms
        of, 66, 92; function of, 64; funding,
        231–232; funeral rites, 20–21, 39, 115,
        119–133; guiding principles, 210–216, 221;
        historical importance of, 53; as individual
        experiences, 52–54; initiation rites. *see*
        initiation(s); liminal stage of, 90, 105,
        213–214, 234–235; as meta-myth,
        133–134; modern creation of, 107–108;
        myths of, 107–108; need for, 4; news of the
        day, 3–7, 53, 56–57; ownership of, 231–232;

for parents, 174–177; places of, 169–216; as powerful, 134; programmed, 84; programs featuring, 178–179; puberty rites, 53–54; public, 94; as public art, 233–234; purpose of, 64, 94, 155; raising children together through, 81; reciprocity of, 20, 55; rites of confusion, 6–8; Roy G. Biv design principles, 192–197; sample ethnographies, 143–168; self-rendered initiations, 3–7, 53–54, 143, 146; for social and intellectual development, 5–6; stories about, 67–68, 98, 132–134, 219, 222; stories from the Kanuri people, 147–149; stories from the Lozi tribe, 161–162; stories from the Teda people, 143–147; structure of, 53, 79–81, 105; study of, 52–54; symbols of initiation, 78–88; traditional, 132, 134, 172; village-oriented, 70–72; vision quests. *see* vision quests; as ways to convey truth, 134; youth development through, 18, 137, 186–187. *see also specific rites*

The Rites of Passage (van Gennep), 53, 207–208
Rizhin, Israel of, 58
Roots (Haley), 155
ROPE®. *see* Rite Of Passage Experience©
routines. *see* rites and rituals
Rowling, J. K., 57
Roy G. Biv design principles, 192–197

sacred, 110–111
sacred practices, 63; initiations, 89–90; revelation, 85
sacred space, 109
safety, 71, 74
Saitoti, Tepilit Ole, 233
Samoans, 149
Santayana, George, 53
Sarason, Seymour, 22–24, 48, 60, 220
scarification, 132
Schema, 117
scholar-practitioners, 22
scholars, 6
scholarship, 22
Scholiast, 132
school(s), 10, 74, 186, 227–228
Schumacher, E. F., 7–9
Schwartz, Harold, 2
Schweitzer, Albert, 240
science, 181; mingling with spirit, 137–138; models of, 110; modern, 107; as mythology, 108, 112; as religion, 108, 110; *From Science to an Adequate Mythology* (Sharpe), 135
Search Institute, 2–3
Secunda, Brant, 63
self, 81, 96–97
self-actualization, 228
self-discovery, 122–123
self-rendered initiations, 3–7, 53–54, 143, 146
self-torture, 85

separation (ritual stage), 91, 121, 210; challenge of, 83–86; in female rites of passage, 105; in funeral rites, 121–126; guiding principles for, 211–213; in initiation rites, 105, 155, 157
service, community, 215
service delivery, 224
service technology, 223–224
sex, 155–156
sex education, 160–161
Shabbat or Sabbath, 117–118
Shamans and Shamanism, 46, 63, 124; *Mara Akame*, 27, 43, 91
shared emotional experiences or connections, 64, 69–70, 75, 131
shared values, 72
sharing stories, 16–24, 60–61
Sharpe, Kevin, 98, 110, 135
Sheldrake, Rupert, 167
Shiva, 39
shrines, 130, 149–151
silence, 214
silo view, 69
sink estate, 6n2
skill building, 195
small models, 187–192
social capital, 7
social development: model of youth development, 192–193, 193*f*; rites of passage for, 5–6
social fabric, 70–71
socially appropriate behavior, 213
sociology, 52–54
solitude, 196, 214
Somé, Malidoma Patrice, 112–113, 235; Dagara-based funeral retreat for men, 115, 119–133; on ritual, 126
South Africa, 116–117
South America: stories from the Jivaroan people, 156–160
space flight, 109–111
spirit: mingling with science, 137–138
spirit guides, 123
spiritual development, 151–153, 160
spiritual shopping, 63
Spock, Dr., 10
sponsors, 143, 146, 172, 231
spooky attraction at a distance, 117
St. Patrick's Day celebrations, 151
Stanford University, 182
Stanton, M. Duncan, 114–115, 121
Steinbeck, John, 16
Steinsaltz, Adin, 159
Stevens, Anthony, 78, 103–105
storied thinking, 107
story(ies), 9–10, 48; Blumenkrantz's Bar Mitzvah, 38–39, 86–88, 155; Blumenkrantz's creation myth, 29–47, 83–84, 87–88, 91–92; Blumenkrantz's funeral retreat experience, 119–130; characteristics of, 98; about childrearing, 2, 153–155; for children, 1–3;

from the Delaware Nation, 163–164; from our DNA, 219–221; to dream by, 139–168; essential life stories, 25; evidence-based, 222; from the Hopi, 151–153; from the Jivaroan people, 156–160; from the Kanuri people, 147–149; from the Lozi tribe, 161–162; from the Masai, 153–155; of the mysteries of the visions, 46; in myths, 98, 107. *see also* myth(s); national, 192; remembering, 58; rites of passage stories, 67–68, 98, 132–134, 196, 222; sharing, 16–24, 60–61; Sufi, 236–237; from Takashima, 149–151; from the Teda people, 143–147, 154

storytelling, 9–10, 22, 174; bedtime rituals, 1; building stories, 234–236; changing the story, 221–222; importance of, 12, 57; invitation to, 212, 218–219

student comments, 206–207

students, older, 227–228

subincision, 132

subject matter experts (SMEs), 190

substance abuse, 4–5

Sufi, 236–237

suicide, 6–7

summer camp, 242

superheroes, 98

superstition, 164

swimming, 228

symbolic anthropology, 141

symbolic guessing, 141, 144

symbols, 101; change of appearance, 215; common, 72; cultural, 141; importance of, 141; of initiation, 59–77, 78–88, 106; interpretation of, 141

sympathetic magic, 101–102

Takashima, Japan: stories from, 149–151, 161

Talmud, 49–50

Tate Haramara, 31

Tate Wari, 27, 31–32, 35, 40–43, 46, 66, 86

Taylor, Daniel, 48, 61

teacher comments, 207

teachers, 225–226

teaching, engaged, 226

team building, 203

teamwork, 200–201

technology, 181

Teda people, 143–147, 154

Teen Action Research, 230

theories, 107

Thoreau, Henry David, 68

thought partners, 137

Tikkun Olam, 63, 70, 166

Time, 4

time management, 204–205

Tiyyar, 105–106

tobacco, 157–158

Toffler, Alvin, 112–113

Torah, 117

traditional myths, 112

traditions, 37; new, 89; rites of passage, 132, 134, 172; stories from Takashima, 149–151; in Western culture, 115–118

training, 202–203

transformation, 88, 92, 113, 171; at Somé funeral retreat for men, 129–130; stories from the Lozi tribe, 162; of young boys into men, 104–105; of young girls into women, 105

transitions: through adolescence, 131; to adulthood, 50; collisions of, 175, 197; coming-of-age. *see* coming of age; life cycle. *see* rites of passage; as losses, 114–115, 121; ways to order, 134

Treasure Island, Delaware River, 165

Trenfor, Alexandra K., 225

tribal initiations, 151–153

trinity of inquiry, 52, 210–211

Trojan horse, 9

trust, 74

truth: ways to convey, 134

Tukuna, 105

Turner, Victor, 53, 55, 96, 141

Twain, Mark, 27

"Ubuntu" ("universal bond"), 116–117

urbanism, 71

Ute people, 161

utilization technique, 124–125

values, 8; community, 2–3, 212; cultural, 204; shared, 72; transmission of, 73

van Gennep, Arnold, 53, 80–81, 105, 207–208

village(s), 11, 27n1, 130

village childrearing, 18–20, 81, 172–173, 225

village-oriented rites of passage, 70–72

Virarica, the Healing People, 63, 65

virtual community, 70

vision quests, 27–30, 59–60, 66, 82–83; benefits of, 179; Blumenkrantz's creation myth, 29–47, 83–84, 87–88, 91–92; challenge of separation in, 83–86; Delaware, 164; first, 86; Huichol, 83; preparation for, 29–35, 82, 84; traditional, 82, 84–87

visions, 46, 158

volunteerism, 67–68, 204

Watts, Alan, 98

Western culture, 115–118

West Side Story, 17

Whitman, Walt, 77

whole child to raise a village, 11, 18, 81, 145, 203, 216

Wiesel, Elie, 239

Wildcat, Daniel, 69

wild man motif, 122

Wilson, E. O., 95, 101–102

Wilson, Monica, 141

Wittgenstein, Ludwig, 98
Wofford, N.R., 242
wonderment, 159–160
Wordsworth, William, 227n2
World Café, 218

Yale University: Human Relations Area Files
    (HRAF) Archive, 139–140, 142–168
Yiddish, 49, 159
YMCA, 228–229
Yom Kippur, 166
youth, 2–3
youth development, 49–50, 73–77, 193–194;
    central question for, 113; empowerment
    activities, 195–196; engagement activities,
195–196; through initiations, 94; planned
    challenges for, 195–196; positive, 70–71,
    132; through rites of passage, 18, 99–100,
    137, 186–187; through rituals, 90; skill
    building for, 195; social development model
    of, 192–193, 193f
youth development programs, 132, 180–181,
    184–185
youth elders, 204
Youth Passageways, 178–179
Youth Service Bureau, 23
youth volunteerism, 67–68

"zakher" ("remember"), 117
Zigler, Edward, 23